the **social work** companion

Palgrave Student Companions are a one-stop reference resource that provide essential information for students about the subject – and the course – they've chosen to study.

Friendly and authoritative, *Palgrave Student Companions* support the student throughout their degree. They encourage the reader to think about study skills alongside the subject matter of their course, offer guidance on module and career choices, and act as an invaluable source book and reference that they can return to time and again.

Palgrave Student Companions – your course starts here …

Published
The MBA Companion
The Politics Companion
The Social Work Companion

Forthcoming
The Cultural Studies Companion
The English Language and Linguistics Companion
The Health Studies Companion
The Literary Studies Companion
The Media Studies Companion
The Nursing Companion
The Psychology Companion
The Theatre, Drama and Performance Companion

Further titles are planned

www.palgravestudentcompanions.com

the **social work** companion

neil thompson and sue thompson

your course starts here ...

palgrave
macmillan

First published 2008 by
PALGRAVE MACMILLAN

Palgrave Macmillan in the UK is an imprint of Macmillian Publishers Limited, registered in England, company number 785998, of Houndmills, Basingstoke, Hampshire RG21 6XS.

Palgrave Macmillan in the US is a division of St Martin's Press LLC, 175 Fifth Avenue, New York, NY 10010.

Palgrave Macmillan is the global academic imprint of the above companies and has companies and representatives throughout the world.

Palgrave® and Macmillan® are registered trademarks in the United States, the United Kingdom, Europe and other countries.

ISBN-13: 978–1–4039–3795–7
ISBN-10: 1–4039–3795–8

This book is printed on paper suitable for recycling and made from fully managed and sustained forest sources. Logging, pulping and manufacturing processes are expected to conform to the environmental regulations of the country of origin.

A catalogue record for this book is available from the British Library.

10   9   8   7   6   5   4   3   2
17 16 15 14 13 12 11 10 09

Printed in China

For Jo

contents

preface

We are pleased to say that, over the years, we have both come across a large number of examples of good practice, and indeed of excellent practice – the sort of work that makes us proud to be part of the social work world. However, we have both also had very disheartening and dispiriting experiences of coming across examples of very poor practice on the part of some social workers. In addition, we have known a number of good social workers who, when it has been necessary for them to draw on social work support in relation to their own personal or family issues, have been less than impressed with the practice they have then witnessed. We are convinced that much of the poor practice comes from the failure of some organizations to support their staff, to help them keep learning and to keep their workloads to manageable levels.

However, we are also convinced that some practitioners struggle to achieve good practice because they have not grasped the basics of what social work is all about, they have not got the 'big picture' (or, if they did once have it, they have now lost it), and thus their work becomes reduced to following procedures, ticking boxes and just getting through the day – rather than making a positive contribution to tackling the very real problems people encounter, rising to the major challenges and doing the best we can in difficult circumstances. As we shall argue in the Introduction below, it is important to be realistic and recognize that we cannot always expect major successes and that we will often have to settle for second – or even third – best. However, there is a world of difference between being realistic, which we see as a positive quality in social work, and being defeatist and cynical and settling for low standards and mechanistic responses to the challenges that we and our clientele face.

If we consider the negative experiences alongside the positive ones and add our own combined experience of over 40 years' worth of social work practice, management and education, we have a strong platform from which to offer our views of what is – or should be – good practice. This book, then, is part of our commitment to helping to develop good practice. We have taken the opportunity to put forward our views about what good practice is all about and how it forms part of the 'big picture'. Not everyone will agree with our views, of course, but we are confident that our approach will chime well with a wide range of other people's efforts to promote good practice.

We hope that you will find our contribution a positive and valuable one and that you will be able to draw on the materials provided here to develop your own understanding as a foundation for high-quality practice and continuous professional development.

Neil Thompson and Sue Thompson

acknowledgements

Producing a book of this size has been a major project, and so we have had to rely on a number of people for their assistance in translating the plan into the finished product. First, we would like to thank Catherine Gray at the publishers for her faith in us in inviting us to undertake this work. We hope she feels we have repaid that faith in terms of what we have delivered.

Catherine deserves our gratitude for her continuing support in developing our published work. In addition, Catherine's colleagues at the publishers have been very supportive. Sheree Keep has continued to be a pleasure to work with and we thank her very much for that. Sarah Lodge has also proved to be a very helpful colleague. In addition, we would like to thank Penny Simmons for her sterling copyediting work.

We are very grateful to our daughter, Anna Thompson, for the various ways in which she has provided practical support in bringing this project to fruition. Margaret Holloway also deserves a significant vote of thanks for the quality of her audiotyping and for being so friendly and helpful.

We also owe a debt of thanks to the various people who offered comment on drafts of part or all of the book or who have otherwise proved helpful in producing the finished work: John Bates of Liverpool Hope University, Bernard Moss of Staffordshire University and Nigel Parton of the University of Huddersfield, as well as our long-standing friend, Denise Bevan.

Finally, we reserve an immense vote of thanks for Jo Campling whose death in the summer of 2006 was a huge loss, to the two of us as authors, to the social work world and, more broadly, to the publishing world. Jo's support and advice over the years proved invaluable in general terms and, in relation to this publication in particular, she played a very significant role in shaping the plans for the book and how the first draft developed. She was a true friend and a much-appreciated guide and mentor. She leaves a hugely important legacy in social work education and we regard it as an immense privilege to be able to count this book as part of that legacy, as her influence is very much in evidence here. In dedicating this book to her we thank her and pay tribute to her.

introduction

Social work plays an important role in tackling social problems and promoting social well-being, rights and justice. It is a complex undertaking that operates at a number of different levels; is prone to competing perspectives on what it is and how it should be carried out; and changes over time. Social work, then, is not a simple or straightforward matter, and so the *Palgrave Social Work Companion* is not a simple 'how to do it' text. Indeed, it would be both pointless and dangerous to attempt that. It would be pointless because the complexity, subtlety and variability of social work are so great that no single book could hope to do justice to it. It would be dangerous because the situations we encounter in social work are far too intricate and multilayered for a 'cook book' recipe approach to do anything but distort and oversimplify some very important issues – and thus run the risk of doing more harm than good.

If this book is not a 'how to do it' book, then what is it? Primarily, we see this book as what we would call a 'gateway' text. It is designed to act as a foundation for your studies and future practice by:

- (i) giving you a flavour of the issues involved in contemporary social work;
- (ii) introducing some key concepts, themes, issues and challenges, alongside what we see as the principles of good practice;
- (iii) raising awareness of some of the main demands and rewards of social work; and
- (iv) providing guidance on future learning in the form of recommended reading and details of relevant organizations and websites.

It needs to be emphasized that the book is a *companion* to further learning and development, including wider reading, and is not a substitute for them.

The book builds on the ideas presented in Neil Thompson's *Understanding Social Work* (Thompson, 2005a). It is not necessary for you to have read that book before embarking on this one, but you will find it helpful if you have read it first. The two books can be seen as complementary, as both aim to contribute to providing a platform for more in-depth study of the broad range of factors that shape the social work world.

seven principles

In order to provide a coherent overview of a very wide-ranging and complex subject matter, we have identified seven principles or linking threads to help provide a picture of how the various elements of our thinking link together. Below we identify each of these seven principles, provide a brief explanation of them and explain why we feel they are important in developing our understanding of, and approach to, social work.

Principle 1: Social Context

Social work is precisely that – *social*. It is part of society's attempts to deal with social problems and promote social welfare. In the often unremitting pressure of the work, with demands for help coming from so many individuals, it is very easy to slip into a mentality that focuses exclusively on the individual and loses sight of the bigger picture that will have such an important bearing on the individual's experiences. This does not mean that individual issues are not important – on the contrary, they are vital, but they need to be understood in the context of the wider social picture, rather than in isolation. This means that our practice must take account of the need to challenge discrimination and oppression, the social roots of the problems clients encounter and the social implications of our practice. Our understanding must be a *holistic* one – that is, one that takes account of the wider picture: both individual *and* social issues.

why is this important?

If we neglect the social dimensions of our work we can adopt a highly distorted picture of the situations we are trying to deal with.

Principle 2: Empowerment and Partnership

Social work is about working *with* people to help them resolve their own difficulties as far as possible, and doing things *to* or *for* people should only happen when necessary. Empowerment involves helping people gain greater control of their lives and is therefore the opposite of creating or fostering dependency. It involves building on existing strengths and, where possible, trying to turn weaknesses into strengths. An important part of empowerment is *partnership*. This involves (i) working closely with clients and carers and not adopting a top-down approach in which it is assumed that the professional 'knows best' or should necessarily have the upper hand; and (ii) working as part of a multidisciplinary network – that is, recognizing that, while social workers have an important role to play, so too do other professionals that we work alongside.

why is this important?

If we do not focus on empowerment and partnership we risk creating dependency and adding to oppression rather than tackling it.

Principle 3: Critical Analysis

In social work we deal with complex issues. It is therefore important that we develop our analytical skills to enable us to make sense of these complexities. In particular, we need to develop *critical* analysis skills – that is, the ability to go beyond taking things at face value and to recognize the underlying social and political processes (for example: power relations, social exclusion or marginalization and scapegoating). As we shall see, an important part of this is the development of what is known as reflective practice (well-thought-out practice based on a professional knowledge base rather than simply on habit, routine or guesswork), an important part of which is research-minded practice (making sure our practice draws on insights from research studies relevant to social work). Critical analysis helps to avoid forms of practice that lack depth – superficial practice can be dangerous practice.

If we do not develop critical analysis skills we are unlikely to build up the in-depth understanding of situations that high-quality practice requires. We also risk making such situations worse by adopting a dangerously superficial approach.

Principle 4: Knowledge, Skills and Values

Being an effective social worker involves a combination of knowledge, skills and values. All three are important, and being very good at one or two of them will not compensate for being below standard on the third. Knowledge provides us with the depth of understanding we need to underpin our practice. Skills provide us with the ability to be able to put that knowledge to good use in practical situations. Values are linked to the ethical principles that enable us to make sure that we are practising *appropriately* – that is, that we are using our knowledge and skills in positive, constructive ways that are geared towards doing good rather than harm (for example, in ways that are not abusive or exploitative). The combination of knowledge, skills and values is an important foundation for social work education and thus for social work practice.

why is this important?

Without a clear foundation of knowledge, skills and values, we will find it impossible to become effective social work practitioners.

Principle 5: Loss and Grief

A common misunderstanding is that loss and grief issues apply only in relation to death. The reality is that loss and grief are never far away in social work, whatever the setting or client group. Grief arises in relation to any significant loss. This can refer to the loss of a person other than through death – for example, through divorce or other family breakdown; children being removed from their home and adults entering residential care. It can also refer to losing something other than a person or personal relationship – for example, losing security (perhaps through abuse or other such trauma); hopes and aspirations; markers of identity (possessions, status or position of respect); or abilities (perhaps through disablement). We therefore need to be quite sensitive to how these issues are significant in the situations we are dealing with.

why is this important?

Failing to recognize the prevalence of loss and grief in social work can mean that we fail to do justice to the painful circumstances of the people we are seeking to help.

Principle 6: Realism and Challenge

Social work is a demanding enterprise. It involves balancing negatives and positives. On the one hand, being negative and defeatist is not a helpful approach but, on the other hand, nor is a naïve optimism that fails to recognize the difficulties, problems and constraints involved. What is needed is a constructive balance between these two extremes, and this is what we would call *realism* – neither naïvely optimistic nor destructively pessimistic. Part of this realism is recognizing that social work is *challenging* – it is not easy, but it can be very rewarding, if not all the time, then certainly on certain occasions (and it is those very positive occasions that can make it worthwhile by making up for a lot of hassle and disappointment at other times). Being realistic therefore involves recognizing both the positives and the negatives and not taking a one-sided approach.

why is this important?

A naïve, rose-tinted approach to social work that does not recognize the significant challenges involved is doomed to failure. Likewise, seeing only the negatives and thus failing to draw on the positives is a recipe for very poor levels of practice.

Principle 7: Self-management

There are various sources of support for social workers and social work students, and all involved share a responsibility for promoting good practice. However, none of this alters the fact that each of us has to take responsibility for our own actions – our own 'self-management'. We therefore have to take responsibility for our own learning (others will help facilitate our learning but, of course, it remains our own responsibility primarily) and our professional decision making (others may guide us, but social work is more than simply following instructions). This links in with reflective practice and the importance of self-care. It is also part of the theme of professionalism – the idea that, as social workers, we are accountable for our actions. If we are to be held accountable, then it is, of course, wise to make sure that our actions are well informed and carefully considered.

why is this important?

The complex demands of social work mean that, if we are not able to practise 'self-management', we will struggle to be effective and we will not be able to reap the rewards of contributing to high levels of professional practice.

Of course, these are not the only themes or principles that could be drawn out from the pages that follow, but we wanted to keep the number to a manageable level, and have therefore decided to limit ourselves to what we see as the seven key principles.

We make reference to each of these seven principles from time to time in the main text. These 'Seven Principles' boxes are designed to remind you how important these themes are and to help you link together the disparate elements covered in the book.

defining social work

This book is intended partly as a guide to preparing for a career in social work and partly to act as a reference source throughout one's career. In view of this, it may be helpful to introduce a definition of social work that can act as a good starting point for our understanding of what is involved and can serve as a reminder when the complexities of social work may lead us into situations where we need to revisit our roots and refocus. The following definition is one that is now widely accepted:

> The social work profession promotes social change, problem solving in human relationships and the empowerment and liberation of people to enhance well-being. Utilising theories of human behaviour and social systems, social work intervenes

at the points where people interact with their environments. Principles of human rights and social justice are fundamental to social work.
(International Federation of Social Workers, http://www.ifsw.org/en/p38000208.html)

This introduces some important themes that will feature at various points in the book:

> *Promoting social change.* Social change is fundamentally a political matter and, on a large scale, beyond the scope of what social work can achieve. However, social work can make at least a small contribution towards positive social change in a variety of ways.

> *Problem solving.* Forms of social work that become reduced to rationing services have been heavily criticized over the years. It is therefore important to remember that social work practice is not simply a matter of providing services, but rather, more fundamentally, of tackling social problems as they manifest themselves in the lives of individuals, families, groups and communities.

> *Human relationships.* Strained relationships are often the source of the problems social workers encounter and positive professional relationships can be a major part of the potential solutions.

> *Empowerment and liberation.* A significant danger in social work is that of making people dependent and reinforcing oppressive systems and structures. It is therefore important that we have a clear and determined focus on developing empowering and emancipatory forms of practice.

> *Enhancing well-being.* Social work is about making a positive difference to people's lives, especially those people who are marginalized, disadvantaged and disempowered in various ways.

> *Utilizing theories.* Social work involves tackling some very complex and intricate issues. However, we have a significant and wide-ranging knowledge base and so it is important that we draw on this in order to be as well equipped as we can in rising to the challenges involved.

> *People interacting with their environments.* Early forms of social work were very individualistic in their focus, paying relatively little attention to the wider environment and social context – and even today pressures of work can lead some practitioners to adopt a narrow focus. However, as we shall see, good practice needs to adopt a more holistic focus.

> *Human rights and social justice.* Social work's clientele includes many people who may be denied their rights and/or discriminated against in some way. Safeguarding rights at an individual level and making a contribution to promoting social justice at a broader level are therefore important elements of social work.

For a fuller discussion of the thorny question of defining social work and the issues associated with it, see Thompson (2005a).

structure and content

The book is divided into seven parts. In Part 1, entitled *Studying social work*, we present a discussion of some of what we see as the foundations of future development. In particular, we examine the contextual underpinnings of social work by sketching out some of the key issues relating to the influence of law, policy and society in shaping social work. From this we move on to look at what you can expect in broad terms of a course of study leading to the status of being a qualified social worker – and what the course will expect of you. Finally in Part 1 we explore the important topic of 'maximizing your learning' – how to develop your study skills and make the most of the learning opportunities available to you.

In Part 2, entitled *Core topics*, our focus is on seven main areas of theory and practice that incorporate a range of core issues that will be of relevance to any social worker. These reflect what students can expect in terms of the likely curriculum of their course of study. They are:

> *Social work processes.* What processes are operating when we do social work? What is going on beneath the surface? What is happening and how can we make sure it is happening as we would want? These are some of the key questions relating to the topic of social work processes.

> *The social context.* We should never forget that the term 'social work' begins with the word, 'social'. The wide range of factors that make up the social context in which social work operates play a very important role in the development of the social problems we address in social work and also in shaping how we respond to them in practice.

> *Human development.* People are not static entities. We grow and develop over time. If we are to have an adequate understanding of the people we are trying to help and of the circumstances they find themselves in, then we need to have at least a basic understanding of the psychology (and sociology) of human development.

> *The organizational context.* The vast majority of social workers are employees of an organization – often a very large organization. The organizational context can be a major factor in determining what issues are addressed, how they are addressed and so on. Social workers need to have at least an understanding of how organizational life can be so significant, but preferably also the knowledge and skills needed to get the most out of their organization as well as to try and influence it in a positive direction.

> *Law and policy.* Part 1 includes a discussion of law and policy as important underpinnings of practice. Here we look at these very important issues in more depth, such is their importance in day-to-day practice – for example, in relation to decision making.

> *The value base.* Social work values are a central part of both learning how to be a social worker and actually operating in the social work world as a practitioner, a manager or educator. This chapter provides an overview of the major values issues in social work and shows why values are such an important feature of good practice.

> *Reflective practice.* Once we have learned the basics of social work, it is very easy to get bogged down in routines and habits and 'go onto automatic pilot'. However, it is also extremely dangerous to do this, as each situation, while it may have things in common with other situations encountered, will be unique and will need to be dealt with on its merits. Reflective practice offers a way of making sure we do not fall into this trap.

Part 3 is entitled *Key terms and concepts*. In it we present short summaries of over 100 important social work ideas. It was not easy choosing the ideas to focus on, as there are so many others that we could have chosen, and no doubt some people will feel that we have missed out one or more crucial ideas and have perhaps included some that they do not feel are particularly important. However, despite this, there is clearly much of value to be gained from developing an understanding of many of the ideas that feature so strongly in our understanding of social work.

If Part 3 is about some of the main building blocks of social work theory and practice, Part 4 is about the architecture. Entitled *Key theories and theorists*, it provides short introductions to a number of theoretical perspectives that seek to make sense of social work and the problems we encounter – frameworks that try to link together the various elements of our understanding in a coherent and helpful way.

Part 5, entitled *Drawing on research*, emphasizes the importance of research as a means of ensuring that our practice is *informed* practice. It explores what we mean by research, why it is important how it can be incorporated into practice.

Part 6 is concerned with *Career pathways*. It outlines an overview of the range of possible career directions and complements this with advice on maximizing your effectiveness when it comes to applying for jobs.

Part 7 is the *Guide to further learning*. It offers guidance on further reading and relevant organizations and websites. It complements the 'Suggestions for further reading' sections that appear at the end of each of Parts 1 to 6. As we emphasized above, this is a 'gateway' book, not a definitive or comprehensive text and so these signposts to further learning are therefore resources you should draw upon heavily.

how to use this book

If you wish, this book can be used in the conventional way of starting at the beginning and working your way through to the end. However, that is not the only option. You could, for example, read Part 1 to 'get your bearings' about your chosen subject and career and then read the other Parts in whatever order you wish as the need arises or as the fancy takes you. But, what we would wish to emphasize is that, whichever order you read the parts in, it is important to read them all, as each one has something important to say about the challenges of contemporary social work practice.

Parts 1 to 6 have guides to further learning at the end of them. These relate specifically to the materials covered in that particular part of the book. Part 7 is a further guide to taking your learning further, but this time it offers a broader overview of books, journals, organizations and websites that can be of value in establishing a solid basis of continuous professional development – that is, continuing to learn, grow and develop throughout your career. We strongly recommend that you make good use of these guides as it would be a serious mistake to assume that this book, although offering a great deal of information and insights about social work, is enough on its own. There is no substitute for the immense benefits of reading widely to develop our understanding and thus strengthen our practice.

Each chapter ends with a few 'Points to ponder'. These are intended to help you link the points raised in that chapter to your own circumstances and understanding. They are therefore an important bridge between theory and practice, and so we urge you not to simply skip over them. If you do, you will be missing out on some potentially useful opportunities to deepen your understanding and see how such understanding can be of use in practice.

We also provide 'National Occupational Standards' (NOS) boxes from time to time in order to help you make links with the key social work roles that these standards encapsulate. In the United Kingdom social workers are expected to be able to meet these standards in all their work. They are therefore important guides to practice.

Once you have read the book, it can then be drawn upon as a reference source as and when required – something you can refer to when preparing an essay, when dealing with a specific practice situation, or generally when you want to revisit important issues about your career and its development.

It was hard work putting this book together, but we feel it was worthwhile and we hope that you will too. We hope it can play an important part in your personal and professional development.

A note on terminology

In a recently published book, one of the present authors stated:

> People who receive assistance from human services professionals have traditionally been referred to as clients or patients. However, I agree with Juhila et al (2003, p. 16) when they argue that: 'it is hardly wrong to say that the notion of client is in a state of change'. In recent years the term 'service user' has become quite widely established, with other terms, such as user or consumer also being used. There is no ideal term, but my preference is for 'client' as it is a term I associate with professionalism and a commitment to treating people with respect, rather than 'service user' which has connotations of a service-led mentality.
>
> (Neil Thompson, 2006a, p. 7)

In addition, despite the common use of the term 'service user' in the UK, 'client' remains widely used in many other countries (as well as in the UK). We therefore agree with Malcolm Payne's comment to the effect that 'client' is a suitable term for an international readership (2005, p. xviii). We therefore use 'client' to refer to the users of social work services, although we sometimes use the term, 'service user' for the sake of stylistic variety.

studying social work   1

introduction

Social work is both an occupation and an academic discipline, in the sense that it is something that is both carried out in practice (across a variety of agencies) and studied at a higher education level. Studying social work usually begins when someone is commencing a programme of education and training leading to a social work qualification and is therefore associated with the early stages of becoming a qualified social worker. However, as we shall be arguing below, it is important that social workers carry on learning and developing their knowledge base throughout their career (the subject matter is far too vast and complex to rely simply on our initial period of training). We should therefore not make the mistake of seeing the topic of 'studying social work' as one that applies only until one becomes a qualified social worker and then becomes no longer relevant. Being awarded the degree means that you are considered competent to *begin* your social work career, but *remaining* competent will be something that will be your responsibility throughout your career, even though you may have that degree qualification under your belt.

NOS Key Role 5

Manage and be accountable, with supervision and support, for your own social work practice within your organization

In Part 1 we look at what is involved in studying social work, not simply to gain an academic qualification, but rather as a preparation for – and aid to developing – professional practice. We begin by setting the context for practice by explaining how such important factors as law, policy and society underpin the work of social workers. We cannot develop an adequate understanding of social work without a good appreciation of these important issues that have such an influence in shaping the nature of social work and how it is practised in various settings.

Next we move on to look at what is involved in becoming a qualified social worker in terms of the demands of the course you will need to complete satisfactorily to gain the qualification and thereby be in a position to register as a social worker. Also in Part 1 we explore the important topic of maximizing your learning. People engaged in professional education and training face the challenge of studying effectively in pressurized circumstances. Chapter 1.3 is intended to assist with this by providing guidance on what to expect and how best to respond to the demands involved.

1.1 law, politics and society

introduction

It is important to recognize that social work is shaped and constrained by a number of powerful forces. In this chapter, we shall explore three of these in particular, namely the law, politics and society. We shall examine how the law affects what we can and cannot do in certain circumstances, how it provides a legal framework and a fundamental basis for our work. Here we shall discuss the broad issues relating to the role of the law, but more specific discussion will be found in Chapter 2.5. We shall explore the political framework and the power of politicians and political actions to shape policy and practice. We shall also consider how social norms, values and expectations, public opinion and the role of the media can all have an impact on social work. Finally, we shall explore the key concept of professionalism – an increasingly significant topic in contemporary social work.

law

Social work is often loosely used as a term to refer to any caring or philanthropic work: 'I help out at the soup kitchen. I enjoy doing social work'. However, social work in its more formal sense – that is, as practised by actual social workers – is largely governed by law, although there is a complex relationship between the law and social work. It is not simply a matter of the law dictating exactly what social workers should or should not do (Braye and Preston-Shoot, 1997). If it were that simple, we would not need well-trained, well-informed professional social workers – we would simply need 'social technicians' to implement the law and its specific requirements. As we shall see in our discussion of professionalism below, being an unthinking 'social technician' who simply does what the law says is not what social work is all about.

One essential thing to recognize is that the important role of the law is not specific to the discipline of social work. If we look more broadly at how our society works, we can see that the law plays a role in regulating social practices in general. Social work is no exception to this. For example, the law governs how trade transactions take place, how health care is delivered, how the safety implications of transport systems are managed, and so on. However, social work goes beyond this general sense of law shaping social practices. This is because the law relating to social work:

> *Defines certain roles.* For example, in relation to mental health social work, there is a specific role, 'the approved social worker', which has certain legal connotations (that is, the ability in particular circumstances to apply for a person to be admitted to a psychiatric facility against their wishes). This is a very responsible role that

requires additional specialist training to ensure that approved social workers are well equipped to fulfil their legal duties.

> *The law regulates practice.* This can be seen to apply at two levels. First, there is a broad level in terms of policy – that is, as we shall see below, policies within social work organizations owe much to the law. Second, there is case law – that is, social work decisions can be challenged in the courts if necessary. For example, if a decision is made to withdraw a service from a client, an application can be made (in certain circumstances) to a court for the decision to be reviewed (this is known as a 'judicial review').   law and policy, see p. 115

> *Legal processes are involved in social work practice.* Many social work decisions (about removing a child from his or her parents because of abuse, for example) are made through legal processes. That is, in many circumstances, social workers do not have the direct power to make decisions and, instead, have to make application or recommendations to a court of law.

However, it is important to recognize that the law is not absolute. This is because:

1 The law leaves considerable scope for interpretation. Because the law applies potentially to so many different situations, it has to be phrased in quite broad terms, and this in turn leaves a great deal of room for interpretation. In many cases the interpretation is made within a court of law – for example, a judge making a decision about an elderly person with dementia who is no longer of sufficiently sound mind to manage his or her own affairs – but more often the interpretation comes at the level of professional practice (by the social worker and/or his or her team manager or through a case conference).

Principle 3 Critical Analysis

This is an important example of the need for critical analysis – to weigh up the situation and develop our own perspective on it, rather than simply look for direct instructions on how to proceed.

NOS Key Role 6

Demonstrate professional competence in social work practice

2 The law offers a broad brush understanding, not the fine detail of the circumstances that social workers deal with. It would be entirely unrealistic for an Act of Parliament to try to predefine how each situation should be dealt with. The situations encountered in social work are often very complex and the law would need to be extremely detailed and unwieldy even to begin to provide detailed guidance on professional practice.

3 The law can be challenged – for example, there can be an appeal against a legal decision. Appeals usually occur when there has been some breach of legal protocol (for example, the proper procedures were not followed) or when additional information has come to light that may challenge the validity of the earlier decision made.

This is parallel with the way the law works in other settings. For example, there are legal parameters in terms of how commercial companies do business. However, those companies still have to manage their businesses; the law does not tell them precisely what to do. It sets the broad framework or parameters and does not replace professional or managerial discretion. We shall return to this point below in considering professionalism. professionalism, see p. 11

It is not uncommon for those new to social work to express surprise about the extent to which the law features in their training programmes or to worry that they will be expected to become legal experts. If this is a concern, then be reassured that social workers are not expected to be legal experts – if they were legal experts, then they would probably be working in the legal field rather than in social work. However, we cannot escape the fact that there *is* a legal context to social work and so social workers need to know about relevant pieces of legislation, at least in broad outline. And, depending on the specific context in which you work, some pieces of legislation will need to be understood in more depth. For example, those involved in child protection work would need to have a good understanding of legislation such as The Children Act 1989 because it impacts on their day-to-day work in major ways. Understanding the legal context of one's work is part of the professional responsibility that goes with it – understanding the law in all its complexity is not. What *is* important is that you:

> understand what your obligations and powers under the law are;
> have the insight to recognize when you need further advice; and
> know where to get that advice should you need it.

> Alex was enjoying the teaching sessions on social work and the law. She liked to have structures to work to and felt that this would be where she would find them. But it soon became apparent to her that it was not going to be that straightforward. While discussing a hypothetical scenario in which Frank (a 50-year-old man with learning difficulties) and his parents were refusing to allow a social worker to assess his needs following concerns raised by a nurse attending his ailing father, Alex felt reassured that she would be able to turn to community care legislation for guidance should she have to face this type of situation in practice. However, when somebody raised the issue of human rights legislation, she began to realize that there could be a significant dilemma here in terms of protection from harm and the right to live the lifestyle of one's choosing. As they got deeper into the discussion about practice issues, Alex realized that, while having a legal framework would provide guidance to some extent, it certainly was not going to provide her with definitive answers to the dilemmas she would face.

practice focus

1.1

Principle 6 Realism and Challenge

The challenging nature of social work is illustrated in Practice Focus 1.1.

politics

Politics is often defined as the art of the possible. It can also be recognized as the exercise of power. Politics can be understood in a wide sense – for example, in relation to such matters as democracy and the state – or, more narrowly, in terms of, for example, office politics. In both cases, politics plays a significant role in shaping social work. Indeed, it would be fair to say that social work is shaped to a large extent by political processes. Within the UK, for example, this can be seen to apply at five levels:

1. *Transnational.* For example, EU directives can have a bearing on social work policy and practice.
2. *National.* The allocation of resources is in large part a political process. Within the UK, in particular, this is partly national in the sense of being UK-wide and partly national in the sense of relating to each of the four nations that comprise the UK. That is, since devolution, Scotland and Wales and, to a lesser extent, Northern Ireland, are in a position to influence policy and practice through political processes at this level.
3. *Local government.* The allocation of resources and the setting of policy are part of local democracy. Local councillors play a significant role in setting social services policy within their council area.
4. *Interagency.* There will be significant political processes involved in the collaborative arrangements between different agencies, for example, health, police and housing.
5. *Organizational.* As we shall explore in more detail in Chapter 2.4, there are significant political dimensions to organizational life.

One important point to note is that we should be wary of making the common error of assuming that it is only statutory services that are affected by the state and wider governmental processes. These issues, of course, apply to any form of social work, as all social work organizations relate in one way or another to the state. For example, if their funding is not being provided directly from state budgets, then there will none the less be a state role in regulating the services that are provided. The role of non-statutory services (that is, voluntary and private) is just as political as that of the statutory sector. Indeed, the relationship between the various sectors can in itself be of a very political nature.

We should also note that politics is not just a one-way process. Social work can also be a contributor to politics as well as something affected by politics. Social work at a collective level can make a contribution to positive social change. At one time in the late sixties and early seventies, for example, there was a school of thought known as radical social work which emphasized the importance of social work trying to seek to influence society at this broader level. In many ways this approach to practice helped to shape today's emphasis on anti-discriminatory practice and the need to avoid processes of unfair discrimination leading to oppressive outcomes. radical social work, see p. 258

Principle 1 **Social Context**

Anti-discriminatory practice helps us to appreciate the political significance of the social context.

A further important aspect of the political basis of social work is the notion of citizenship. Neil Thompson (2005a) presents citizenship as a social work value: 'A major implication of the status of being a citizen is having certain rights – and this is why citizenship is an important value, because it places emphasis on *rights* and *social inclusion*' (p. 124). Citizenship is also an important concept because it fits in well with the notion of partnership (to be discussed in more detail in Part 2). Working in partnership means working *with* people, rather than doing things *to* or *for* them. For this to be successful, it involves recognizing clients as *active* partners in the work we are doing together. Some traditional forms of social work have not always recognized this and have presented service users as relatively passive recipients of services – a far cry from the notion of citizenship.

Principle 2 **Empowerment and Partnership**

Citizenship illustrates well the theme of empowerment and partnership.

NOS Key Role 3

Support individuals to represent their needs, views and circumstances

Citizenship, then, is a useful idea, as it both helps us to understand the importance of working in partnership and acts as a bridge between actual practice and the political context of social work. Dwyer (2004, p. 4) sums this up well (by reference to the work of Lewis, 1998) when he identifies the following three salient characteristics of citizenship:

> the citizen is one way of imagining a link between the state and the individual;
> the concept of citizenship implies membership of some form of community, in turn the notion of community opens up questions of inclusion and exclusion;
> citizenship is a social status that allows people to make claims in relation to state-organised welfare services.

---

practice focus

1.2

While reading some social policy books Ed began to think more and more about the concept of citizenship. He had given a lot of thought to how he could become equipped to help 'the needy' but he realized that he hadn't given much thought to the people he conceptualized as being in need of help. After reading more about citizenship he realized that not everyone had the access to resources and status that citizenship of a society is claimed to endow. He wondered whether this might account for how certain groups of people are pushed to the margins of society and began to think about his role as a social worker in a wider context than he had done before. He knew he wouldn't be able to change things in a major way, but the realization that living on the margins is not necessarily down to personal choice or failing opened his eyes to the ways in which he might be able to make a difference in people's lives.

Principle 3 **Critical Analysis**

A critical approach helps us to appreciate underlying processes and relations that can be very significant.

society

Neil Thompson (2005a) argues that part of social work's task is to 'do society's dirty work'. That is, social work often involves carrying out the tasks that the wider public would prefer not to know about or deal with: problems of abuse, exploitation, poverty, deprivation and so on. Partly because of this, there is a lack of public awareness of what social work is. We have been subject in social work for quite some time to negative media coverage, and the question is often asked within social work circles: why do we not, as a profession, place much more emphasis on 'blowing our own trumpet', making the media more aware of the successes as well as the failures? However, there are two problems with this. First, there is the issue of confidentiality. It is difficult sometimes for us to talk of our successes without breaching confidentiality. Second, it would be naïve to think that the media would be interested in our successes. It has to be remembered that media organizations are primarily profit-making organizations. For example, a newspaper is not an educational body. It is a business designed to make profits from selling newspapers and, while so-called scandals may sell newspapers, tales of social work successes are far less likely to do so. This is not to say that we should not seek to promote a more positive public awareness of social work, but rather to recognize some of the difficulties involved.

Principle 1 `Social Context`

The idea of 'doing society's dirty work' reminds us of the public importance of social work, as well as its problematic image.

However, the situation is perhaps more complex than this. For example, the work of Aldridge (1994) has shown that there are two key issues in relation to media representations of social work. First of all, there are differences between how local and national media cover issues. Local media are far more likely to be interested in successes as well as failures. Second, there is a distinction to be drawn between children's and adult services. The media tend to take far more interest in issues relating to children than they do in issues relating to adults.

However, it is not only the media and their distortion of what happens in social work that can cause problems, there can often be a clash between social work and the wider community values. For example, there may be a so-called 'common sense' notion that 'young offenders should be locked up'. However, social work will be based on (a) a commitment to social work values that involves trying to prevent children and young people from being deprived of their liberty; and (b) research that shows that locking up young offenders is, for the most part, counterproductive, as it tends to 'teach them the ropes' rather than teach them a lesson (Muncie, 2002).

Principle 4 `Knowledge, Skills and Values`

Professional social work relies on more than 'common sense'.

Another important issue to consider is what Clarke (1993) refers to as being 'caught in the middle'. In other words, in certain circumstances we find ourselves trapped between social work's expectations of us and the wider society's. We can in certain circumstances be 'damned if we do and damned if we do not'. For example, in dealing with children at risk from abuse, we can find that, if we remove the child, we will be criticized for breaking up families. If we do not remove the child, and the child is subsequently harmed, we will be criticized for failing to protect that child. There is a very fine line between the two, but this in a sense is the nature of social work: dealing with the dilemmas, uncertainties and ambiguities of some of life's and society's challenges. Our understanding of these issues is generally not matched by wider society's understanding of these issues. We are, after all, specialists in this area and should not expect the general public to appreciate our role.

Principle 6 `Realism and Challenge`

Dealing with dilemmas, uncertainties and ambiguities is an inescapable part of the challenge of social work.

When Gita was asked the question 'and what do you do?', she often felt loath to tell people that she was a social worker. This wasn't because she didn't like her work – indeed she loved it and was proud of what she had achieved in her role – but she didn't enjoy having to justify her choice to enter the profession. The responses people tended to make when she told them she was a social worker suggested that they thought of her as either (a) a cold-hearted official whose sole aim was to split up families; (b) someone ineffectual in preventing children from being harmed; or (c) someone to blame when things are not working to their advantage. It didn't surprise her that her role was often misinterpreted, and she had become somewhat resigned to the fact that much of what she did went unnoticed and unrewarded in the public eye, but she longed for the day when someone would respond with a more informed or positive comment.

practice focus

1.3

professionalism

The notion of professionalism is a contested one. That is, there are different views of what the term means and what its role is – or should be – in social work. We have the traditional notion of professionalism which is based on elitism, the idea that professionals 'know best'. This traditional form of professionalism does not sit easily with social work values. This has led some people to reject the idea of professionalism and to develop what could even be regarded as a form of anti-professionalism:

The term, 'professionalism' is one that has a mixed history in social work. For many years, the notion of being a 'professional' was regarded with a great deal of suspicion, as if it were simply a way of seeking perks, privileges and status at the expense of the clientele we serve. Of course, it has to be acknowledged that professionalism can be abused in this way, used as an excuse for self-interest. However, we would see it as a significant mistake to reject the notion of professionalism for these reasons, as this amounts to throwing the baby out with the bathwater.   (Neil Thompson, 2002a, p. 4)

The tendency to reject professionalism (rather than reject the elitism with which it had become so closely associated) has proven to be a problem for social work, as it means that, without professional credibility, we have struggled to convince others of the value of what we are doing (as per the discussion of media and the general public above). What we are now moving towards is a new type of professionalism, an empowering form of professionalism – that is, one based on the idea of working *with* clients and carers, not being somehow above them and doing things to them (Neil Thompson, 2000a; 2007).

Principle 2 **Empowerment and Partnership**

Working with *people is a central part of empowerment and partnership.*

In our view, Davies (1994) captures well what professionalism is about when he argues that:

> the *true professional* is not someone who is cool, detached, career-minded and disinterested, but is the worker who can display friendliness ..., understanding and warmth of a manner which convinces the client of her active interest in and concern for the client's plight. And clients are remarkably sophisticated in being able to recognise that such professionalism is part and parcel of a social worker's formal occupation ... There is clearly an element of acting in this, but the performance emerges as crucial to good social work in the eyes of the client. Professionalism is the projection of a concerned interest in the client's welfare. (Davies, 1994, pp. 51–2, cited in Payne, 1995, p. 143)

Professionalism, in our view, is an important consideration in social work because, as Harris and Webb recognized as long ago as 1987: 'professionals do not create discretion; rather the inevitability of discretion creates the need for professionals' (cited in Jordan, 1990). The realities of practice are far too complex to rely safely on direct instructions, habits or formula responses. Approaches to practice that do not recognize the significance of discretion and thus of professionalism are therefore potentially dangerous forms of practice.

NOS Key Role 4

Manage risk to individuals, families, carers, groups, communities, self and colleagues

conclusion

Social work does not exist in a vacuum. It is part of a broader legal and political context. High-quality social work practice depends in part on having a good understanding of this broader picture, of appreciating where the actions of an individual social worker fit into this broader pattern. Without this broader understanding, there is a danger that we may act in ways which will cause us problems in terms of legal, political or social consequences that we had not envisaged. A wise social worker is one who is aware of this bigger picture and takes it into consideration in weighing up how to proceed in dealing with the day-to-day challenges of social work practice.

Principle 6 **Realism and Challenge**

Having a balanced approach to risk is part of realism.

In studying social work we need to keep coming back to this underpinning context of law, politics and society. Whether we are studying social work theories and methods, human development, community care, child protection or whatever, we must not forget to see them in the light of legal powers, duties and constraints; political processes, structures and policies; and social processes, institutions and divisions.

Principle 1 **Social Context**

The law, politics and society are all part of the social context of social work.

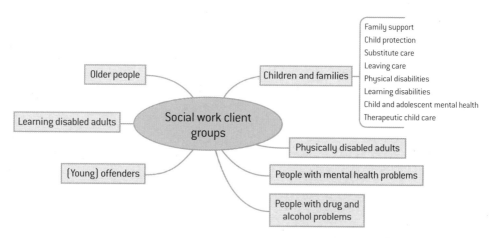

Figure 1.1 *Major social work client groups*

points to ponder

> Consider any major piece of social work law. Can you identify three ways in which that particular Act shapes social work practice?
> Can you identify three ways in which politics influences social work services?
> In what ways is citizenship significant for social work?
> What do you understand by the idea that social work 'does society's dirty work'?
> Why is 'professionalism' an important topic in social work?

1.2 your social work course

introduction

This chapter is entitled 'Your social work course' for a reason. While thousands of people will make their way through the same course or programme that you are undertaking, or very similar ones, the journey itself will be unique to you. Programme designers and presenters will take on the responsibility for teaching on social work courses and you will have support along the way from a variety of sources, as we shall discuss later. However, none of these people will carry the responsibility for the *learning* that will take place – that will be down to you and you alone. This may seem obvious to some, but it is a point that cannot be overstressed. Learning simply cannot be done for you.

Principle 7 Self-management

There will be people who can help you in your learning, but the responsibility lies with you.

As you will come to realize, however experienced or knowledgeable you are, a significant amount of learning (and sometimes 'unlearning') will be required of you in order for you to reach the level where you are deemed to have the knowledge, skills and values which will equip you for the role of qualified social worker. Of course, you will not learn everything there is to learn about social work on any initial qualifying course – this will just be the start of a learning curve which should last throughout your whole career. Indeed, if you wish to practise as a social worker after qualification, there will be an expectation on you that you demonstrate continuing learning, as it will be a precondition for keeping your registered status. As being a social worker will therefore also mean being a lifelong learner, space will be devoted to improving the learning skills you undoubtedly already have and to how you can adapt to new areas of learning and skills development. But before going on to discuss this in more detail in Chapter 1.3, let us first set the scene by exploring some important issues about:

> general expectations;
> how preparing for this qualification will differ from other forms of learning you may have undertaken; and
> what it takes to be successful in social work. registration, see p. 315

what should I expect?

Starting something new can be exciting, but also tiring. There is usually a lot of new information to absorb, and many students have ongoing family responsibilities or work commitments to maintain too. Support will be available from a variety of sources, but it is important to be clear about what tutors and practice learning colleagues can and cannot offer. They are not there to sort out your problems for you – would that we all had someone on hand to do that for us! Problem setting and problem solving are what social work is all about and so finding your way through the journey that is social work training will itself help to equip you with the understanding and skills needed for the work you will go on to do. Bear in mind that much of the learning and development that will take place in terms of your study skills will be transferable to your practice. For example, the strategies involved in researching and writing an assignment are also very necessary practice skills (as part of assessment, for example), and so it is important not to see the undergraduate and postgraduate phases as entirely separate. So, let us begin by being realistic. Over the next few years you can expect the following.

Principle 6 **Realism and Challenge**

Your course should be challenging but rewarding. Indeed, it should be rewarding because it is challenging.

Principle 7 **Self-management**

Your course will give you the opportunity to develop your self-management skills.

to have guidance, but not be spoonfed

As we will go on to discuss later, undertaking social work training may be different from other forms of learning that you have undertaken in the past – it is all about *guided* learning. That is, you will be given the parameters of what you need to know but not the detail. If you have not studied in this way before, you need to get your head round what it will entail. You will get some direct input from lectures and some presenters may be kind enough to supply handouts which you might find useful but, on the whole, you will be expected to search out and digest material for yourself and to learn from participating in seminars, workshops, simulations and real-life practice situations.

Programme tutors will usually guide you in wading through the huge amount of material that is available in a variety of formats, including books, journals, videos/ DVDs, CD-roms, internet sources and so on, by providing lists of suggested reading and details of useful resources. Staff from the agencies that work in partnership with your college or university base will provide you with the opportunity to learn from direct practice. However, their role necessarily stops at facilitating and assessing your learning. The learning itself is your job. Don't expect to have the same learning experience as anyone else, even colleagues in your own student group. Everyone's journey will be unique, and the quality of that journey will be in large part down to you.

to find the process challenging

Undertaking social work training will require you to think critically about the world around you and the processes that go on between people. It will require that you explore the professional value base of social work and consider many competing perspectives around a myriad of subjects and issues. You may not always agree with the perspectives of other people, nor will you be expected to. Indeed, the profession of social work is characterized by differences in the perception of situations, their consequences and the dilemmas that ensue. What you *will* be expected to do is to have an open mind and be willing to think through views and opinions you may have held for a long time and possibly re-evaluate them in the light of new learning. Of course, that is not to say that you will be expected to abandon your life views or conform to the dogma of others – far from it. But this journey will involve opening yourself up to self-examination – getting to know yourself and 'where you are coming from', and about developing a heightened awareness of how you, your views and your values impact on other people and vice versa.

Principle 3 Critical Analysis

Self-examination is part of critical analysis.

As a social worker you are training to be a 'people worker', but you are a person too. The people you will work with are going to be unique and multifaceted, in that they will have a personality, an identity, a history, a culture, a social location such as class and gender, a family context, a range of emotions, a sexual and spiritual dimension and so on – but then so do you, and keeping your own needs in mind is not always easy. Self-care is something we will look at in more detail in Part 3 but, for the present purpose of putting things in perspective, it is enough to keep at the forefront of your mind that these processes of awareness raising and self-reflection are very necessary and usually very rewarding, but not always comfortable.

Principle 1 Social Context

You are part of the social context too, of course.

Principle 7 Self-management

Self-reflection is an important part of self-management.

> Lynne was attending an induction event on the first day of her social work course. There were so many people there that it was difficult at first to work out who was who, but as the day wore on it became clear to her that the group included not only students and tutors, but also practice teachers, workplace supervisors and others who would play a part in her training. She was pleased to see that several service users were among those attending because it indicated to her that their role in social work training was valued. During one of the breaks Lynne chatted to Leo, a wheelchair user, and took the opportunity to ask his opinion about the support he had received from social workers. When he jokingly replied that he only liked those who offered placement opportunities for students, she realized that he was one of the tutors. She found this very embarrassing at the time, but it brought home to her that, without realizing it, she had been conceptualizing disabled people as necessarily dependent. She realized then that she would have to think carefully about the assumptions she made and be open to re-evaluating them in the light of new experiences.

practice focus 1.4

to work hard

As we have discussed above, it is likely that you will find your course quite demanding in emotional terms, but there will be other demands too. It is to be hoped that you will find it enjoyable and rewarding, but it needs to be borne in mind that the goal you are striving to reach will require a huge investment of your time and energy. The qualification you are working towards is one that confers professional status, and so it will be demanding at an intellectual level too.

Principle 3 Critical Analysis

Developing academic rigour is a sound foundation for critical analysis.

Principle 4 Knowledge, Skills and Values

All three of these are key parts of the foundations of your learning.

To some, social work might appear to be largely a matter of applying practical skills, but those practice skills need to be informed by, and in turn inform, their theoretical underpinnings. The integration of theory and practice is a fundamental premise on which social work operates and the reasons why will be revisited frequently throughout this book (see especially Chapter 2.7), but you will at least be aware that you will be expected to submit academic work for assessment and that such work will need to be analytical, focused, referenced and submitted to deadlines. As you work at managing competing priorities and try to cope with the unexpected situations that everyday life throws up, it may seem that such expectations are petty – enforced by people in ivory towers who have forgotten what it is like to operate in the 'real world'. At such times remind yourself that the profession of social work needs you to be a competent and analytical thinker with a sound knowledge base and skills in dealing with information management. The academic rigour which your course will expect of you will help equip you for that role. After all, isn't social work itself, in its efforts to support and empower people in difficult circumstances, a matter of being focused, analytical and working to deadlines?

Principle 7 Self-management

Both studying and practising social work involve self-management skills.

NOS Key Role 5

Manage and be accountable, with supervision and support, for your own social work practice within your organization

So, expect this course of study to be hard work, but expect it to be fun also. There is advice on time management available – see, for example, Chapter 2 of Neil Thompson (2002b) as a starting point, but each person's obligations will be different – you will need to give a lot of thought to how you can best manage *your* time to fit in *your* responsibilities. It will be good practice for your professional life to come!

to make mistakes

Nobody gets it right all of the time. Given that everybody gets it wrong some of the time, you will clearly be no exception. Nor will you be immune from making mistakes after you have qualified. As part of your social work course you will be given the opportunity to apply your knowledge and try out your skills in 'safe' environments, such as classrooms and supervised work placements. You may have the chance to work in specially designed skills laboratories, or simulations of environments, such as courtrooms. Put it this way, where would you like to make a mistake first, in a classroom or simulation situation, with the support of fellow students and a tutor or in an actual practice situation that is very much 'for real'! But, whatever opportunities exist for you, the advice is the same: get stuck in! Have a go and *expect* to make mistakes – learning from them is all part of the process.

Principle 6 Realism and Challenge

Learning from both our successes and our failures is part of realism.

Taking this first step will give you the opportunity to reflect on why something didn't work, how you might do it differently next time and so on. Evaluation is something which we will explore in greater depth in Part 2 when we look at social work processes and the principles of reflective practice. But as we have already discussed, adult learning is about taking responsibility for your own learning. Staying on the sidelines or not contributing to debates and discussions for fear of making mistakes is understandable, but not wise. Remember that your fellow students are in the same boat as you and, indeed, it is not at all uncommon for tutors and practice-based colleagues to make mistakes too, so do not feel unduly embarrassed. There is a lot to be said for getting as much practice as possible in before having to use your newly acquired or recently polished skills in a more public arena than the classroom setting or simulated environments.

> Rik was dreading the seminar. He had been asked to research and contribute to a short presentation on domestic violence, but was feeling very nervous about standing up in front of the rest of the student group. He had no shortage of material, but didn't feel confident about sharing it. He had been in this situation before, but had always taken a day off sick or left early to avoid having to face his fears. He knew this was not a good strategy, as he was only too aware that the exercise was designed not only to develop his study skills and knowledge base, but also to help develop practice skills – including planning and communication – and the confidence he would need if he were going to be an effective advocate, co-ordinator, problem solver, mediator and so on. And he realized that his tutor, in setting the task, was highlighting that good presentation skills are an essential part of a social worker's 'toolkit'. He decided to address the problem by being open about it. Once his two co-presenters realized how nervous he was, they negotiated with him that they would do the bulk of the presentation if he would agree to contribute something, however small. On the day, Rik kept to his word and his presentation, though short, was very competent. Although he had found the process very difficult, he realized that he now had a basis on which to build in terms of practice skills and regretted having avoided the issue for so long.

practice focus
1.5

to collaborate

Some people prefer to 'go it alone' and work their own way through problems and dilemmas. Some would much rather collaborate with other people in trying to address a task, using each other's skills to best effect in a given situation. Neither approach is better *per se* than the other, and individuals' preferred learning styles should be respected. However, it is very likely that you will have to work with representatives of other agencies, such as education, housing, police and health services. And, as you will discover, working collaboratively with service users is a core social work value. Those who might not have favoured collaborative working in the past might want to think seriously about the benefits of it at this stage. Social work training is not a competition to see who is the best at it, but rather a journey toward competence – a time for helping each other by sharing experiences, feelings, information and expertise, rather than being 'precious' about them.

Principle 2 **Empowerment and Partnership**

Skills in collaborative work are fundamental to partnership working.

By now you will no doubt have picked up that personal responsibility and 'self-management' are key themes of this book. This should extend to making sure that you keep a handle on what is going on and what is required of you, which can be difficult when moving from module to module, and between different learning environments. All too easily the rationale behind particular modules, and indeed the training as a whole, can be lost under a mass of detail. Introductions to particular modules or learning experiences should outline their purpose and help you to understand how they will equip you for the social work role, but, unfortunately, this is not always the case. But this is where personal responsibility comes in once again. If the rationale for any aspect of your course is not clear to you, then ask the questions: 'Why are we studying this?' or 'How will this impact on my role or equip me to carry out my obligations?' Competent social work practice requires you to keep a clear focus on what you are doing and *why* and so taking responsibility for making the learning experience work for you is something you need to take seriously from the outset.

systematic practice, see p. 261

Above all, it is important to realize that your social work training will not give you a formulaic solution for every situation you are ever likely to face. The fear that you will be sent out into the big wide world without knowing everything is not one that is specific to social work students. Most people who have undergone professional training of some sort will have experienced those feelings of anxiety to some degree. Realistically it is not possible to learn everything there is to know, but nor is there any need to even try. Each problem you will face as a social worker will be a unique one and will require a unique response. As we discuss elsewhere (see Chapter 2.7), that is what reflective practice is all about. So, in that sense, you will never feel totally prepared. But what will equip you to do your job is:

> having a basic knowledge base and the willingness to build on this and keep abreast of new developments over time;
> becoming competent in key social work skills and being prepared to build on and broaden your skills base; and
> understanding and respecting the value base of social work.

Principle 4 **Knowledge, Skills and Values**

Knowledge, skills and values are all important.

And, remember: there is a collective knowledge base and others out there working in the same field as you. Why not use and support each other?

learning in a different way

As you enter this field of study you and your fellow students will all be doing so with different educational backgrounds and with different experiences of study and learning. Some may be recent school leavers while, for others, formal education may be something you remember from your dim and distant past. For some, the experience may have been a pleasurable and empowering one but, if memories of schooling are associated with feelings of disappointment, unhappiness, demoralization or even fear, then beginning a course such as this may well bring anxieties to the fore. For example, students often worry about questions such as:

> Will I feel inferior in a group where some people are cleverer than I am?
> Will I be able to write well enough to pass formal essays?
> Am I going to make a fool of myself in front of others?

Principle 2 Empowerment and Partnership
Learning can be a very empowering experience and can form the basis for further empowerment.

Those who have little or no direct social work experience before coming into education and training often worry that they will appear uninformed and will perform inadequately in practice-based exercises, such as role plays. For others who may have been involved in the social work or social care practice field for some time, but have little or no academic background or expertise, the worry is often that they will not be able to keep up with the academic components of the course and may not be able to 'hold their own' in discussions and debates.

While these worries are understandable, they are often unfounded. As mentioned previously, the learning curve will be different for each individual, and each person will bring different skills, experience, expertise and insight to the situations you will encounter together. Training to be a social worker is not about competition. It is about you as an individual reaching a level of competence in your skills, knowledge and value bases, sufficient for you to be recommended for the award which will allow you to register as a qualified social worker. So it is a project that you can work on in a spirit of companionship and collaboration, rather than competition. As such, feel confident that you will have something to give, even if it is different from the contribution of your colleagues.

If your experience of learning has been based on the 'empty vessel' model, whereby the learner sits passively waiting to soak up information that is 'poured' into him or her by someone else with expertise or knowledge, then you need to move on from that mindset. The learning you need to undertake in your quest to become a qualified social worker will be based on methodologies appropriate to adult learning. That is, it will involve active learning (researching, debating, applying, reviewing, using case studies and so on) rather than passive learning (uncritical reading, waiting for information to be fed into you) and will require that you think about *how* you learn as well as *what* you learn.

Principle 7 Self-management
Developing active learning is an important part of self-management.

You will have the help of tutors and lecturers who take responsibility for particular aspects of the training and, as such, they will contribute to your knowledge base. Their role will be to flag up key issues or approaches which you will be expected to follow up for yourself. If you have always considered the key person in a learning situation to be the teacher, then you will need to revisit that assumption and put yourself in that key position instead. Many other people will guide and facilitate your learning, but you will always be at the controls. At the risk of overstating the point, this journey will be more about directed study than being taught, and about achieving competence and confidence rather than merely acquiring information. By all means look to lecturers and tutors for guidance – they will no doubt have knowledge and expertise to draw on – but to see them as 'guardians' of knowledge is to miss out on a whole range of other potential sources. It is not a one-way process – tutors learn from students and students learn from each other, from service users, from practice-based colleagues and from colleagues in other professions.

what does it take to be successful in social work?

There is no straightforward answer to this question:

> First of all, no two social workers will be the same. As with any profession there will, and indeed should be, diversity.
> Second, it depends on how you define success, as it too has a range of meanings.
> Third, social work itself is not a homogenous concept, in that its purpose and focus can differ from context to context.

So, given this diversity, it would be difficult to evaluate in detail what would constitute success in all of its applications. In broad outline, you will need to:

> Pass the various written assignments (although not necessarily at the first attempt, as you are likely to have the opportunity to resubmit at least some of the pieces of work if they do not reach a pass standard first time round – see the assessment regulations for the particular course concerned). You will be given some degree of support in tackling assignments, so there is no need to become unduly anxious about this. Social work courses have a long history of helping students develop their academic skills, including those who do not have a strong educational background. You will be given written feedback on assignments and it is important to take account of this, because your time on a course of study leading to a professional qualification needs to be seen as a developmental journey rather than simply a matter of whether you have passed or failed a particular assignment. We would urge you to treat feedback on assignments in the same way as you would feedback from practice teachers and employers in supervision sessions – that is, take it on board. Learn to accept constructive criticism and to engage in the debates which arise from what people have to say about your work, in whatever context.
> Pass the placements (or 'practice learning opportunities', to give them their formal title) – this will involve showing evidence that you are competent in relation to the National Occupational Standards (see Neil Thompson, 2005a). You will work with one or more representatives of the placement agency who will support you in your learning and assess your performance on an ongoing basis – they will share their views of your performance with you and be positive and encouraging in any criticisms they may have. Again, there is no need to become unduly anxious about this, as you will be helped to learn, and this involves building on any identified strengths and trying to rectify any gaps in your knowledge or skills. It is important not to see the learning you do on placement as separate from the learning you do when you are in the classroom – they are both part of the same learning process in

the sense that you will be drawing on the professional knowledge base that you are building up in the classroom and from private study to inform your practice and vice versa.

> On most courses you will also have to attend satisfactorily. This is because much of the learning is *shared, active learning* through group exercises, discussions and so on. Although private study is a vitally important part of your learning, it is no substitute for classroom-based activities.
> Fulfil other requirements, such as disciplinary ones. It perhaps goes without saying that a student whose behaviour is deemed unprofessional or otherwise inappropriate is putting their future as a social worker in jeopardy.

A major part of becoming a qualified social worker is meeting the recognized competences in fulfilling professional roles. It is therefore important to be clear about the core skills without which competent social work practice is not possible. What follows offers a brief discussion which you can supplement using the suggestions for further reading at the end of Part 1.

Even though you might feel unprepared or unconfident in some of these areas, there is the potential for you to become competent and confident if you engage with the learning opportunities that will be available to you. It is not the case that 'you've either got it or you haven't' – you have the potential to become that person.

It is likely that you are already skilled to at least some degree in those areas that figure prominently in social work. As we have already discussed, each person will have a unique starting point and a unique journey to make in terms of skill development. It might help to think in terms of *becoming* competent, rather than already *being* competent.

analytical and critical thinking

This is about not taking things for granted. For example, you might read a report in a newspaper that quotes facts and figures about the number of people seeking asylum in the UK, using these statistics and terminology such as 'swamping' to suggest that this is a major problem in terms of national security and identity. However, if one takes account of such factors as vested interest (for example, does this newspaper promote a particular political ideology?) and definition (do those statistics differentiate between those people seeking political asylum and those who are economic migrants seeking work?), it becomes apparent that situations are not always what they seem at face value, but rather are open to interpretation. In a newspaper of a different political persuasion, for example, one might get a very different portrayal of the situation, one in which statistical evidence is drawn on to suggest that asylum seekers are a minority group whose potential contribution to society's economic and spiritual well-being is overlooked and who are not getting a 'fair deal' while living in the UK. Being able to appreciate different perspectives is crucial if the process of assessment, to which we will refer in Part 2, is to be a fair one. A critical, analytical approach does not take anything for granted and asks questions such as:

> Who says so?
> Beneficial to whom?
> In whose best interests?
> At risk of what?

Analytical skills are an important part of high-quality social work practice. This is because we deal with very complex issues, with competing perspectives and vested interests to consider as well. The more skilled we are at looking carefully and critically at complex situations, the more well-equipped we will be for the demands of practice.

NOS Key Role 6

Demonstrate professional competence in social work practice

competence in problem solving

As we have seen, the concept of partnership is one that is likely to figure very prominently in your training, as it is a core social work value. Contrary to popular opinion, social work is not about sorting people's problems out. Rather, it is about working *with* people to help *them* to sort their problems out. Partnership working is a much wider concept than one-to-one collaborations, as we will discuss later in Chapter 2.6, but in terms of collaboration between individual social workers and clients, each party will have something to bring to the relationship in terms of expertise. The social worker will never fully understand what it is like to be experiencing the client's situation and the difficulties they are facing – only the client has expertise in that field. But what the social worker can bring to the partnership in terms of expertise is skills in problem solving – expertise and experience in being able to see ways forward, in being able to anticipate and deal with obstacles and to help develop strategies for progress (see Neil Thompson, 2006a). partnership working, see p. 199

NOS Key Role 3

Support individuals to represent their needs, views and circumstances

As we have already discussed, each situation you encounter will be different, and so it is unrealistic to expect that there will be a ready-made response that you can pluck out of thin air. As we shall see in Chapter 2.7 when we discuss reflective practice, a skilled social worker will have the skills required to 'tailor' their intervention to the specific circumstances encountered, and, in doing so, will draw on their knowledge, skills, values and experience. Over time you will build up a repertoire (often referred to as a 'toolbox') of techniques, and this is where much of your expertise will reside (see the 'Suggestions for further reading' at the end of Part 1 for guidance on finding out more about such 'tools' or practice methods). There is not sufficient space here to look at particular techniques, but no doubt you will focus on these during your time at your college or university base and while on placement. Our point here is that, in situations where people are distressed, they are often seeking calmness and direction – clear thinking when others may be running round like headless chickens or adopting the approach: 'If I ignore it for long enough, the problem will go away'. Such situations will call for someone who can act quickly and sensitively to get to the 'nub' of the problem – and that is where you will come in!

assertiveness

This is something which many students feel they do not have, or at least cannot put into practice until they feel confident about their role and their knowledge base. Students will start from different baselines in terms of assertiveness skills, but it is such an important core skill that no-one can afford to sit back and not work on this aspect of their self-management. In social work we spend a lot of time acting as advocates, negotiators and convenors, and we will be ineffective in these roles if we allow ourselves to be ignored or belittled. Nor are we likely to be effective if we try to get our own way by means of coercion or by disregarding or trivializing others people's feelings and perspectives. An assertive approach, then, is one that strikes a balance between submission and aggression, with the ultimate aim of reaching an outcome that works for everyone, rather than one in which one party 'wins' at the expense of any other. So much of social work is about managing change that any time spent on improving your assertiveness skills to the point where you can exert a positive influence will be time well spent.

Principle 7 Self-management

Assertiveness is fundamental to self-management.

As a social worker, you will be working at a number of different interfaces and will interact with colleagues from many different work sectors. Much of your work will involve negotiating the best possible outcomes for vulnerable individuals, client groups and communities and you may well have to negotiate with managers for a share of scarce resources or with service users who are resistant to change or are breaking the law in some way. Unfortunately, social work operates within a political and cultural climate which is not always supportive, and negative stereotypes of social workers abound, such as 'interfering do-gooder' or 'child snatcher'. Operating within this environment can be difficult, given that this negativity has to be overcome before the trust and confidence of the public can be won. This, however, makes it even more important that the right balance is achieved in terms of assertiveness. Facilitating change through respect for one's knowledge base and clear thinking is likely to be far more effective than change which is imposed by an abuse of power or role (see Coulshed et al., 2006, for a discussion of managing change).

observational skills

Being able to assess a situation involves taking information in from a whole variety of sources, and so you will need to become practised in being able to absorb information quickly. In our everyday lives we are constantly being bombarded by a whole host of stimuli and, if we stopped to analyse and process every one of those stimuli, we would never get through the day. In order to allow us to function, our brains work to filter out a lot of information which is not needed for what we are concentrating on at the time, pushing it to the background of our consciousness so that there is space in our heads to absorb what is most important in a given situation. For example, when we are carrying something heavy up a flight of stairs, we tend not to notice decorative details, such as the fine carving on picture frames, instead taking in the width of steps and the height of ceilings.

What we need to prioritize will vary from situation to situation and will be affected by what we need to take from a situation and why. For instance, take the example of entering a room in which a family is sitting talking. If you are a photographer intending to take a family photograph, you are likely to concentrate on those aspects which concern you most in your role – interesting focal points, the relative heights of the family members, whether any children present are old enough to take instruction and so on. On the other hand, an interior designer intending to decorate the room might concentrate more on the angles within the room, colour combinations and sources of natural light. As a social worker, you are more likely to pick up on the dynamics between family members, mood changes, whether people are welcoming or avoiding contact with you, whether anything in the environment reassures you or alerts you to possible danger or neglect, whether the family are living in poverty and so on. Some of what you pick up on will contribute towards an understanding of 'the bigger picture' or macro context of what you are experiencing. This will set a context for the detail you observe – the micro aspect – such as eye contact or its absence, body language indicating anxiety and so on.

Principle 3 Critical Analysis

Being able to observe critically (that is, being able to recognize what is going on beneath the surface) is an important social work skill.

NOS Key Role 1

Prepare for, and work with, individuals, families, carers, groups and communities to assess their needs and circumstances

an appreciation of the bigger picture

Much of social work operates on a one-to-one basis, but people do not exist in isolation – their lives have a social context, as discussed in Chapter 2.2. And so, when working with individuals, there needs to be an awareness of those factors which can have a significant impact on individual behaviour, life chances and so on, but which are beyond the power of individuals to change. For example, some would suggest that adopting a behavioural approach with a young offender who has a police record for stealing is likely to be ineffective when the context he or she lives in is one of extreme poverty and there is significant peer group pressure to engage in criminal activity.

There is another sense in which the 'bigger picture' needs to be appreciated. While some work independently, most social workers work as part of an organization, with all the constraints and opportunities that go along with that. Factors such as internal politics and dynamics, organizational culture, management styles and resource limitations will all impact on how you carry out your job at the individual level. Being an advocate for someone vulnerable, while also respecting the difficulties your employing agency might have in terms of its capacity to provide resources is likely to be an ongoing dilemma, and one which you will not be able to ignore.

realism and resilience

You will hopefully find social work to be enjoyable and stimulating on a number of levels but, by its very nature, you will be dealing with problematic situations and distressed or vulnerable people. It is often challenging, but it is in the overcoming of those challenges that the reward lies. Be in no doubt that there will be difficult times and there will be situations that you cannot resolve, however skilled and resourceful you might be. As Neil Thompson (2005a) argues, we need to have 'humility', which consists of:

> not having unrealistic expectations of what can be achieved;
> recognizing our limitations and therefore not having an inflated view of our capabilities;
> acknowledging the enormity of the social work task in seeking to address personal and social problems;
> understanding that new challenges can arise at any moment;
> recognizing that we regularly run the risk of making errors – we are not immune to mistakes.

Humility, then, is a sound basis for realism and for future learning, as an approach based on humility provides considerable opportunities for learning (humility is one of the key concepts discussed in Part 3).

Principle 6 `Realism and Challenge`

Humility goes hand in hand with realism and challenge.

In view of this, it is important that you recognize the need to keep things in perspective by being realistic about what you will be able to achieve – abolishing crime and feeding the world's hungry is beyond most of us but, even with less ambitious projects, you need to make sure that you are not setting yourself and your clients up to fail by setting the standards against which success will be judged too high. Unrealistic expectations (including unrealistic expectations we may have of ourselves) can be a significant source of stress (Thompson et al., 1994). It is therefore important that we do not adopt an unrealistic approach to our work (or allow others to pressurize us into this), and thereby leave ourselves open to the harmful effects of stress.

Principle 7 `Self-management`

Setting ourselves unrealistic expectations undermines our personal effectiveness.

Social work is about making a difference, but that difference does not necessarily need to be massive, nor does it need to be achieved in one step.

Given that successes rarely come thick and fast in this type of work, and that even positive change might seem insignificant or hard to identify, it is all too easy to become disheartened, frustrated, demoralized or demotivated (and sometimes all of these!). Being resilient in the face of negativity takes effort, but there will be opportunities to talk through those feelings with colleagues, managers and sometimes with service users themselves. Taking time out for reflection can highlight positive outcomes and put things into perspective when confidence is low.

NOS Key Role 5

Manage and be accountable, with supervision and support, for your own social work practice within your organisation

Several weeks into his practice experience with the Youth Offending Team, Kemal was feeling quite dejected. Despite the efforts he had made to help Emma build a better relationship with her family and to see the benefit of returning to school on a regular basis, this had not happened. And, while Jason had seemed to be enthusiastic about the programme that he and Kemal had jointly planned, this had been put in jeopardy when Jason had re-offended. Kemal confided to his supervisor that he probably wasn't cut out to be a social worker because he couldn't seem to 'get it right'. His supervisor helped him to put his negative feelings into context by getting him to think about what he regarded as success and failure. Through this process of analysis he realized that there had been elements of success even within projects and interventions that he considered to have failed. He also realized that he had perhaps been setting the benchmarks for success too high by anticipating early and major changes in behaviour and attitude, rather than the small, incremental changes that are more typical and achievable, but no less praiseworthy.

conclusion

This chapter has not covered everything you need to know about making the most of being a social work student, but that in itself reflects the reality of the situation: no-one can spell it all out for you. While various people may well be very helpful to you in taking your learning forward, ultimately it is down to each individual learner to take responsibility for their own learning – to draw on the support systems in place, to work collaboratively with fellow students to help one another, but also to make sure that you do your individual bit in terms of reading widely, thinking carefully about what you read, joining in discussions, trying out new skills, responding constructively to feedback given to you and so on.

In terms of making the most of your course in this way, much will depend on your level of confidence. This will depend, in turn, partly on how effective tutors, practice learning colleagues and fellow students are in boosting your confidence and partly on how much faith you have in yourself and your own ability to learn. We would therefore urge you to have faith in yourself, to have confidence that, through a combination of your own efforts and the support available to you, you should be able to go from strength to strength, building constantly on your experience and your developing knowledge and skills.

points to ponder

> Being an effective time manager is important for being both a student and a social worker. What strengths do you have in this area and what skills do you need to develop?
> How can you build up your skills in critical thinking?
> What skills do you feel you will need to become an effective problem solver?
> What part does observation play in assessment?
> How is humility relevant to social work?

1.3 **maximizing your learning**

introduction

There will always be more out there to learn than time available to learn it – not just as a student, but as a practitioner – being a professional worker means being a lifelong learner. It is not a case of having to do your job *and* learn as well – they should be part and parcel of the same thing. It is because the process of learning will figure so prominently from now on that we have called this section 'maximizing your learning'. What follows is a quick overview of some of the sources on which you will be able to draw, and some tips which you may find useful. reflective practice, see p. 137

use your time wisely

Studying effectively is not just about *what* you learn but also *how*, *where* and *when* you learn. It will therefore stand you in good stead to give some thought to how you learn best. Think about the following.

when am I at my best?

Some people have higher concentration levels and are more receptive to new ideas early in the day, while others feel sluggish on first waking up, but work more effectively as the day progresses. Analysing your preferences and habits allows you to individualize your study plan, so that you make best use of your energy and therefore your time. For example, if you are one of those people who work best early in the day, it might take considerably longer to read an article or plan an assignment if you try to work on it late in the evening. Conversely, what would take a 'late starter' an hour to get through once they have come up to full strength in the afternoon, might take two or three times that long if attempted in the morning when motivation and concentration are low.

reading for a purpose

It is easy to feel overwhelmed by the sheer amount of information that you will encounter, both during your training and afterwards when you are in practice. Reading lists in particular can appear daunting. One way of managing this is to bear in mind that not everything needs to be read or absorbed to the same degree. Tutors should be able to give some indication about which publications are core texts that need studying in detail, although it should not be too difficult to work this out for yourself. Information management is something you will have to address in the future, so you might as well start now!

Reading the Introductions, Forewords and lists of contents of books and the abstracts of articles should give you a clue to their content and focus and therefore their relevance. You will then have some basis for deciding whether that particular piece needs reading in depth, skimming through or abandoning altogether. For example, if your purpose is to just get an overview of a subject and to raise your awareness of the key debates within that field, then 'skim reading' selected sections will probably suffice. Burning the candle at both ends in an effort to read and understand every last detail may well be a waste of valuable time if that degree of detail is not called for. There will undoubtedly be occasions when skim reading will not be enough, and you may have to give more of your time to delving a little deeper into the texts, perhaps re-reading particular sections until you understand the points being made, or drawing on other texts to help you to understand a particular author's work. In terms of using your time effectively, the trick is to be a 'smart' reader – that is, one who uses their wits to pick out the key issues and reads selectively, rather than someone who presses on regardless and perhaps ends up reading a lot of material that is not very relevant or helpful.

keep track of your learning

Information has to be processed rather than merely taken in. It needs making sense of. For example, we are presented with theoretical accounts that conflict with each other, often witness behaviour that seems irrational and encounter dilemmas to which there seems no logical answer. Given the amount of new learning that you will be experiencing, there is the potential for confusion to reign and panic to set in. These feelings are emotionally draining and, as we have seen, trying to learn when tired is not good news. One very useful way of making sense of new information is to keep a learning diary or log. This is not just a matter of recording what you did on a particular day, but of *analysing* what you did – drawing out what you learned from it, what it threw up in terms of future learning, how you felt about it and so on. It need only take a few minutes to complete each day, but it can be an invaluable tool and an excellent example of spending time to save time. As documentary evidence of progress, it can also serve as a morale booster.

Principle 3 **Critical Analysis**

A learning diary can help to develop critical analysis skills.

When a tutor advised Oonagh to keep a learning diary she resisted the idea because she felt that she already had enough to do without having to take on board yet another task. Her view at that time was: 'If it isn't compulsory, then I won't do it.' However, she reconsidered this advice when she began to feel so overwhelmed by her new experiences and learning that ideas were spinning around inside her head and she was losing sight of the significance of what she was learning. She bought herself a notebook and, before leaving college each day, she spent just five minutes or so making a brief record of what she had done that day and why. She also made a note in the margin of the key words or concepts that had figured in her learning that particular day, or had given her food for thought. On the day in question she had realized that she would often be drawn into situations where she was not invited or welcome and so had highlighted self-care/staff care as something to remind her about those concerns. Spending those few minutes each day turned out to be an excellent use of time, rather than the waste she had envisaged. She felt more in control and found it so useful that she carried

practice focus

1.7

it over into her practice learning environment. As she became more used to drawing out the significance of what she was learning she began to better understand the course as a whole and her social work role in general. Recognizing that new learning was going to be an ongoing feature of her professional life, Oonagh decided to continue using her learning diary even when she was no longer a student. When people told her that she wouldn't have time 'in the real world', she replied that this would only be the case if she didn't make time.

Principle 7 Self-management

Managing one's time effectively is part of self-management

we're all in this together

Sharing the learning can save time and can also make it much more enjoyable. There will always be a range of ability and experience within any group, but each person in the group will have the same aim: to reach that level of competence necessary for being accepted for registration as a social worker and to maintain and build on that competence. Ultimately, how well or how badly you do will not impact too much on your fellow students and vice versa and so, as there is no need to be competitive, there is little point in shunning collaboration and joint working. You may have experiences or insights that will aid someone else's learning, but you could also find something in another's approach that can inform your own understanding. This reciprocity can help maximize your use of time in direct ways, such as sharing out research tasks and reporting back to group discussions, so that it is not necessary for every student to read every recommended text. Collaborative working can also have indirect benefits in terms of making good use of time, because of the effect it can have on morale and motivation. Some people choose to 'plough their own furrow', but it can become a very lonely process and one in which it is easy to become demoralized. Sharing the load with others can be fun, and does not necessarily dilute the learning experience, and so could perhaps be considered to be 'smart learning'.

Principle 2 Empowerment and Partnership

Thinking in terms of 'we're in this together' provides a good basis for empowerment and partnership.

be creative about learning resources

A very common complaint from students across all disciplines is a lack of books or journals available to be borrowed from the library. Where a particular book is recommended, or an assignment on a particular topic due, there is often a run on the library stocks. Books are relatively expensive, and buying everything you need to consult is not something that most students could afford or most educators recommend. However, apart from being first in the queue outside the library every morning, there are strategies for guarding against feeling under-resourced while studying.

For example, many programmes will give you an assignment schedule that covers at least a semester, if not an academic year. Being given the deadline dates early in the academic year puts you in the position of being able to plan your essay writing in advance, thereby creating the opportunity to work on an assignment other than the one which is due to be submitted imminently. Imagine that a class of 80 students is due to submit a law assignment by a particular date and you can see that there is a strong likelihood that every law book from the library stocks will be out on loan in the few weeks preceding that date. However, if you do some reading and note taking well in advance of that date, you will often find that you have the pick of the crop where useful books are concerned and are less likely to suffer the frustration of having a book recalled to the library just at the point where you really need it for your own purposes. The same is true of journals which are a prime resource given that they are often more topical and specialized than books. If you have recognized a particular edition or article as relevant, then the chances are that other students will also have done so and will be chasing those scarce library resources too. So the trick is to stay ahead of the game – remember that the submission date is when an assignment has to be submitted *by* rather than *on*. Early birds will not earn extra marks for that in itself, but are perhaps less likely to be disadvantaged by scarce resources than those who work in a chronological fashion through the schedule.

Of course, the Internet has opened up a whole new access point for viewing and downloading material drawn from books, journals, government reports and so on. This is reflected in some of the website addresses detailed in Part 7 and, no doubt, you will be able to add to that list if you have access to search facilities. And, in the spirit of collaboration that we recommend, why not share any 'treasure troves' you may find with your fellow students? (See also the discussion of the use of Internet resources in Part 5 in relation to the use of research as a primary underpinning of practice.)

While written material is a crucial resource in terms of learning, it is of course not the only one. Learning from observation and experience plays a major role, and so using each other as learning resources can be very enlightening. No two students will have the same pre-course work or life experience and, as we have discussed earlier, each will bring something unique to a group learning encounter – after all, if you had nothing to offer, you would not have been accepted onto a social work course. Hearing different perspectives, discussing experiences, debating differences, analysing mistakes and celebrating successes are all learning experiences. When we refer to the integration of theory and practice, we are not confining theory to formalized and named models or collections of ideas as written down in academic treatises, but would include any of those processes that contribute to practice being *informed* – that is, based on understanding rather than guesswork or habit. For example, observing members of the public interacting or listening to feedback from service users are both learning processes that have the potential to influence your practice.

Principle 4 **Knowledge, Skills and Values**

Knowledge, skills and values are the basis of an informed approach to practice.

taking notes

Recording what one has learned or needs to learn is something that requires an individualized approach. Given the amount of new learning you will experience, it is unwise to rely on memory alone and learning has to be processed if it is to be of use. There will be many occasions and contexts in which it is impractical or insensitive to take detailed notes and yet, without having something to read or digest after the event, there is the potential for learning opportunities to be lost because details have been forgotten since the event took place. Recording 'on the hoof' need not be a laborious or distracting task – jotting down a key word or reference is often all you need as a reminder for following up when you can or for reminding yourself of something that impressed or worried you but which could not be dealt with at the time.

It is difficult to advise on note taking because what suits one person may not suit another, but here are a few principles to bear in mind:

keep it short

Trying to transcribe everything that is said or every detail witnessed is difficult and rarely necessary. Trying to keep up with detail can lead to losing a sense of overview and context. It is generally better to record the information that will allow you to broaden out your learning after the event, such as key theorists and concepts. Otherwise, there is the potential for you to have a record of details and examples but little understanding of their overall significance.

don't rely on handouts

Students often request handouts from those delivering lectures and some speakers oblige. However, we would suggest that this is not always helpful, as it can shift the responsibility for learning away from the student and dilute the learning experience (and thus undermine self-management). Jotting down key words and phrases requires you to think about the *significance* of what is being presented, as well as the content, thereby making the session more of an interactive one than a one-way transfer of knowledge.

make use of summaries

Lecturers often finish a session with a summary of the key points. While it is counterproductive to try and write down everything a lecturer says, the point at which he or she summarizes can be a good one to take notes.

make the notes work for you

For example, some students find it helpful to keep notes in card index form, while others might find it more useful to store their thoughts and reminders in a specified folder on a personal computer. Others make notes directly onto reading material by underlining key passages and annotating sections that they find of particular interest, although we would not recommend the latter unless it is your own personal copy! Whatever method you choose, remember that, while verbatim recording is required of some people in some situations, your task as a student is to distil information to manageable proportions and in a format that will work for you when you revisit those notes at a later date. Otherwise you will end up with a mass of material that is daunting to revisit and time consuming to work through.

don't keep it to the classroom

Remember that note taking need not be confined to lectures and reading sessions. There will always be an expectation that you are critical about what you observe or hear – that you do not automatically take things at face value. Making notes while on observational visits, or wherever day-to-day interactions highlight something you want to debate or study further, will help to develop that critical 'edge' you will need in order to operate effectively as a social worker.

When making notes from books or other printed materials, you can make use of 'Post-it' notes or equivalent, placing one on any relevant pages, with a brief note about how or why that page is relevant (for example, to an assignment you are preparing for). This can save you a lot of time when you are looking for a particular quotation and can also help to make sure that you do not forget about important points.

mind mapping

Some people may find this technique useful when making notes. For those wishing to study it in more depth we would refer you to Buzan and Buzan (2003) for a detailed account or Neil Thompson (2006b) for a shorter, introductory overview. But, in a nutshell, it is about constructing a visual representation of the issues in question and how they interrelate. This visual overview can help us to think laterally and creatively and highlight themes, contradictions, omissions and so on that might not have been obvious from more conventional forms of note taking. It can therefore serve to move note taking on from being a purely descriptive process to an analytical one.

> practice focus
> 1.8
>
> Priya and Andy were thinking about an assignment they would have to submit before too long. They decided to collaborate by sharing the resources they had both found while working independently in the library. Priya had amassed files full of paper and it took her a long time to make sense of what she had collected over the past few months. She even abandoned some of it when she wasn't able to work out what her notes meant or why she had thought a particular reference or point had been worth recording. On the face of it, Andy's notes looked insignificant in relation to Priya's but, when he demonstrated how his system worked, she could see that being focused paid dividends. She noticed that he kept brief details of key concepts and approaches, with details of where to go for a more in-depth analysis should he need it. It became clear to her that she needed to re-evaluate the usefulness of copying long passages from books and articles, with no particular focus or rationale. She wasn't sure that Andy's system was the one for her, but she was already thinking about how she could adapt it to her own style of working.

why all these essays?

Although there will be some degree of variation, most courses will ask you to submit a fair number of written essays for assessment purposes. For some students this academic element of social work training is one that fills them with fear and dread, but it can help to think about the rationale behind setting these assignments. Social work is a profession, and so, as social workers, we need a knowledge base that we are capable of adapting and applying. We need to be able to absorb and process information and to reproduce it in a format fit for a particular purpose. We need to be able to influence by reasoned argument and to remain focused on a particular issue when there is much around to distract. And we need to work within a professional code of behaviour and to guidelines.

If you consider the requirements of good essay writing as detailed below, you should be able to see similarities:

> - sift out relevant material from a potentially vast range of information sources;
> - structure an argument so that the reader can easily follow your reasoning;
> - critically analyse – not just describe or reproduce material, but offer a critique of it;
> - integrate theory and practice – use your own examples to demonstrate that, in integrating, you are understanding;
> - effectively conclude pieces of work by highlighting key points covered and drawing out implications;
> - provide reference details so that others can check out for themselves what you are claiming and see that you are not engaging in plagiarism – claiming others' words or ideas as your own;
> - remain focused on the task in hand; and
> - present material in a format fit for purpose and to external deadlines.

Principle 3 Critical Analysis

Essay writing is good practice for developing critical analysis skills.

And so, rather than just being another hoop to jump through, essay writing is a useful assessment tool for testing out the skills you will use in carrying out your job. Approaching essays as an opportunity, rather than as a test, should help you to see them in a wider and more positive context of demonstrating competence and of lifelong learning. If you find essay writing difficult, we would urge you to seek advice (some programmes have specialist tutors or extra curricular classes) or turn to some of the books and guides that are available to students in general. Taking the task seriously, rather than thinking in terms of 'I don't care as long as I get a bare pass', will pay dividends in the long run because of the opportunities it offers in terms of skills development.

and why exams?

Much of what has been discussed above applies also to taking exams. There is some debate about the usefulness of exams and some courses rely more on continuous assessment than others, but for some modules you may find yourself having to sit an exam. Again, we would not want to play down the anxiety that they can provoke in some people but, as with essay writing, it can help if the purpose behind the process is understood. Generally speaking, exams are about testing out your ability to work under pressure and apply knowledge, rather than merely reproduce it and, as such, are just another means of assessing your capabilities alongside many others, such as observation of your practice. In terms of maximizing your learning, the exam process and the revision that precedes it will require that you review what has happened and what you have learned over the preceding months. It is in this synthesising process that the value of the exam process lies. If you do have to sit an exam, the following pieces of advice are worth considering:

know your task

Although you may feel the pressure to get writing as soon as possible, especially if other students have started their writing before you, spend as much time as you need to ensure that you understand the question or task set. There will be a reason why a question has been posed in a particular way, so do a bit of detective work by looking at the key words, phrasing and so on. These are clues to the specific focus of the question and you will run the risk of answering a different question if you do not pick up on them. An otherwise excellent piece of writing will nevertheless get a fail mark if it does not address the particular question set. If you think this sounds petty or harsh, then consider whether a tendency to miss the point will bode well for your effectiveness in a job that requires attention to detail and a considered response.

think ahead

Plan your answer before starting to write it. For example, if you have a number of concepts or issues that you *could* cover if you were not limited by space or time, then under exam constraints you need to decide which you will choose to highlight on this occasion and whether you will concentrate on a small number of points in some detail or cover more ground with less detail. Since part of your task will be to convince people that you are a clear thinker, taking a few minutes out to think about what form your answer will take should help ensure that the finished piece of work reads as a structured argument rather than a 'shopping list' of points that have occurred to you as you have gone along.

learning through revision

Try to think of exams as just another piece in the jigsaw of assessment of competence and as part of a process of learning rather than a one-off event. While your performance in the exam is of course important in that it contributes towards assessment, it is in the revision process that your learning will be maximized.

    If exam nerves do cause you problems, then you might find the above strategies helpful. We would suggest you also look to help from study guides and from tutors and colleagues. As a social worker you will often find yourself under pressure, and so you will need to find ways to overcome, or at least hide, any nervousness you feel.

seminars and presentations

Some people are used to speaking in front of a group or presenting material to an audience, and feel very comfortable with it. For others it can seem scary, and some will argue that it is an unnecessary pressure as they will not be called on to present such seminars in their future career, unless they have aspirations to become a trainer or senior manager. Taking this approach is to miss the point. As a social worker you need to appear confident and be able to deliver verbal reports in a competent and convincing manner if you are to command the respect of your peers and colleagues from other disciplines. For example, you may be required to:

> make court appearances;
> take part in multidisciplinary meetings;
> advocate on behalf of clients where there are competing agendas;

> be involved in projects, such as community development;
> contribute to team meetings; and/or
> explain your role to those outside of your agency or discipline.

Principle 2 **Empowerment and Partnership**

Gaining the respect of other professionals provides an important foundation for partnership.

No-one will expect you to give an Academy Award-winning performance but, on the other hand, a badly prepared and nervously presented one is unlikely to be effective in winning people over to your cause or influencing future decisions. Presenting seminars while still a student is therefore a great opportunity to practise getting your point across in a public arena while in the relatively unthreatening environment of a classroom. Not only that, but it also provides another opportunity to practise collating material into a useable format. So, while presenting a seminar might seem to be all about verbal skills, it will also serve to enhance key skills, such as report writing, planning and negotiating and, especially when the seminars are jointly presented, to highlight the benefits of collaboration and learning from each other. A useful tip is to try not to be too ambitious – think about getting your message across using appropriate material rather than focusing solely on the material itself. Your audience will need to get your message and so you need to be clear about it yourself. That should help you to keep the project focused and manageable and, in doing so, reduce any anxiety. If you are still anxious about leading seminars and presenting material, then remember that you are training to be a professional problem solver, so try out some techniques on yourself. For example, identify what it is that you are trying to achieve and what is getting in the way of that. It will be easier for someone to help you if you can define the problem and explain it to him or her, rather than just presenting with a generalized anxiety. While understanding the nervousness that some students feel about public speaking, we would nevertheless urge you to grab the opportunities you are presented with.

practice learning

You will often hear people saying things like: 'You don't really start learning about driving until after you pass your test', and it is fair to say that what you need to demonstrate in order to qualify as a social worker is a minimum requirement only. Indeed, as we will discuss below, postqualifying learning is a requirement for continuing registration, which puts paid to the idea that learning and practice are two separate worlds. Your time on placement as a student is a golden opportunity for making maximum use of the learning opportunities you will come across, such as:

> shadowing other workers
> managing your own caseload
> getting feedback from service users
> networking
> and so on.

While you will be 'going live' as it were, the learning environment will still be a relatively protected one in which you should only carry as much responsibility as is deemed appropriate for the stage you are at. Under close supervision you will have the opportunity to test out the effectiveness of approaches you may have read about, discuss dilemmas that arise from conflicting values, polish your skills and add to your knowledge base, as well as highlighting gaps in your learning or identifying skills you need to work on further. Learning situations and resources will abound, but these opportunities will be there only for as long as that particular placement lasts. That is not to say that you need to fill every last minute with new experiences, as to do that leaves no time for analysing how that learning is impacting on your practice.

As we have said previously, expect to make mistakes and do not shy away from the challenges you will be presented with. Whoever is facilitating your learning has the task of matching opportunity to need, and so you should not find yourself in the position of having to face something you are not experienced enough to deal with. While standing on the sidelines watching someone else has its place, your learning will not be maximized until you stretch yourself by trying something new.

Principle 6 Realism and Challenge

Practice learning can be challenging, but makes a major positive contribution to professional development.

Mags was excited about going to her practice placement at the advocacy project, but was also nervous. At their introductory meeting she had explained to Shamila that she didn't like to be put under pressure, as this made her nervous and prone to mistakes. Shamila reassured her that this was an understandable reaction, but that she would lose out on the opportunity to develop personally and professionally if she didn't take up opportunities to try out new skills and stretch herself beyond the 'comfort zone' in which she felt confident. When Shamila felt that Mags had been there long enough to settle in, she offered her the chance to become involved in drop-in sessions, interviewing people to find out about the problems they were facing. Because she hadn't done this type of thing before, Mags requested that she just observed others interviewing. On returning to her college for a study day a few weeks later, she realized that she had nothing to contribute when others were discussing what they had learned on their placements and how they felt they had moved on in terms of developing competence. The realization that only she could take those necessary steps forward made her resolve to get more involved when she returned to the project.

practice focus

1.9

Principle 7 Self-management

Practice focus 1.9 is a good illustration of the importance of self-management.

continuous professional development

Consider the following scenario. You board a plane for a long-haul flight and, as you are settling into your seat, you overhear the crew discussing how the pilot has not flown a plane for 20 years, but supposes that not much has changed. Would you feel safe putting your trust in someone who is unaware of the technological developments that have occurred in the fast-changing world of aviation and air traffic control?

What if you visited your child in school and found that he or she was being severely punished for writing with his or her left hand. Would you feel able to entrust his or her education to someone who was practising without taking on board developments in teaching methodologies, values and rights?

The field of social work is not a static one either, and so practising without reference to continuing professional development is potentially damaging to both your own reputation and the lives of the vulnerable people with whom you work. As a student, learning and development will be uppermost in your mind but you will run the risk of practising dangerously if you see qualification as a justification for an end to personal and professional development. In order to ensure that continuous professional development is taken seriously, social work has undergone a process of regulation which stipulates that we cannot continue to practise without producing evidence that we see learning as an ongoing process throughout our careers. Undertaking specially designed courses, such as that which culminates in a specialist postqualifying award would be one way in which you could prove that you were continuing to learn, but other forms of learning are also valid. Reading, researching, contributing to policy, attending or presenting at conferences and training courses would also be seen as valid experiences if you can demonstrate how these activities have impacted on the work that you do and prevented you from becoming complacent or 'burnt out'.

NOS Key Role 5

Manage and be accountable, with supervision and support, for your own social work practice within your organization

critical analysis and reflective practice

Reflective practice is discussed quite fully in Chapter 2.7, and so we shall not go into detail here. However, we do wish to make the point that you will come across a great deal of information and a wide range of views, methodologies and so on – if you accept them uncritically, you are likely to experience difficulties. Reflective practice includes, among other things, analysing your own and others' work – generally not taking matters for granted or at face value. This involves asking questions of approaches and opinions and assessing their usefulness for your particular purpose.

The use of critical analysis skills is also very relevant to making use of research findings, and so these issues will be revisited in Part 5 when we explore matters relating to the relevance of research as an underpinning of social work practice.

conclusion

As this is an introductory and broad-ranging text, we must limit ourselves to only a brief discussion of some very important complex issues – in effect, this is only skimming the surface (and this is partly why we earlier emphasized that this is a 'gateway' text and, as such, should be seen as a link to other, more in-depth reading, not as a substitute for it). It is therefore important, when it comes to maximizing your learning, that you take this important message on board and take every opportunity to develop your learning through reading, discussing, debating and trying ideas out in practice and so on.

We have already made the point on more than one occasion that the key is for you to take responsibility for making sure that you make the best use of the opportunities that become available to you, and that you take the necessary time to 'process' the learning that can come from these.

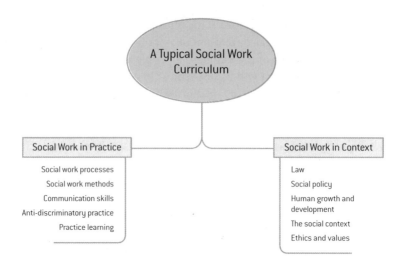

Figure 1.2 *A typical social work curriculum (based on the BA Social Work at Liverpool Hope University)*

1.4 conclusion

In Part 1 of the book we have tried to 'set the scene' by covering some of the key issues involved in 'Studying Social Work'. We have explored the important contextual underpinnings of social work by briefly examining the role of law, politics and society in shaping social work practice. We have also explored what you can expect from a course of professional training as part of seeking to become a qualified social worker and, linked to this, we have suggested ways in which you can usefully attempt to maximize your learning – both while you are studying formally and, indeed, throughout your career as part of a commitment to continuous professional development.

continuous professional development, see p. 315

In relation to all the issues covered in Part 1, we believe it is important for you to consider the important issue of 'self-care'. We have emphasized that the legal, political and social bases of social work raise many challenges. We have also stated that professional training in social work is demanding and challenging and that there are also many challenges involved in maximizing your own learning. This means that social work is not for the faint-hearted. It is a challenging but rewarding occupation. We hope that Part 1, by highlighting some of the challenges involved, will make you better equipped to deal with them. However, the challenges are significant, and so you have to make sure that you do not overdo things, that you make sure you look after yourself and draw on whatever sources of support you can, both while you are studying and throughout your career. This is a point to which we shall return in Part 3.

We hope that you have found our comments helpful and that this will spur you on to read more widely and deeply about the issues covered. The 'Suggestions for further reading' overleaf should be a useful 'springboard' here in pointing you in the right direction.

points to ponder

> What support possibilities can you draw upon to help maximize your learning?
> Do you have a well-ordered system for taking and storing notes?
> What approach to making a seminar presentation would you take?
> What are your priorities for learning when it comes to practice learning opportunities?
> How can you make sure that you continue to learn throughout your career?

suggestions for further reading

1.1 law, politics and society

Adams, R. (2002) *Social Policy for Social Work*, Basingstoke, Palgrave Macmillan.
A useful text that looks at the relationship between social policy and social work.

Alcock, P. (2003) *Social Policy in Britain*, 2nd edn, Basingstoke, Palgrave Macmillan.
A good general overview of social policy issues.

Baillie, D., Cameron, K., Cull, L., Roche, J. and West, J. (eds) (2003) *Social Work and the Law in Scotland*, Basingstoke, Palgrave Macmillan.
A broad-ranging anthology that looks at issues arising from working within the Scottish legal framework.

Cull, L. and Roche, J. (eds) (2001) *The Law and Social Work*, Basingstoke, Palgrave Macmillan.
This collection of work by both academics and practitioners is useful because it summarizes many of the legal issues relating to social work practice and also explores the tensions that implementation gives rise to.

See also:
Blakemore, K. (2003) *Social Policy: An Introduction*, 2nd edn, Buckingham, Open University Press.
Braye, S. and Preston-Shoot, M. (1997) *Practising Social Work Law*, 2nd edn, Basingstoke, Macmillan – now Palgrave Macmillan.
Ellison, N. and Pierson, C. (eds) (2003) *Developments in British Social Policy*, 2nd edn, Basingstoke, Palgrave Macmillan.
Jordan, B. (2006) *Social Policy for the Twenty-First Century: New Perspectives, Big Issues*, Cambridge, Polity Press.
Lewis, G. (ed.) (2004) *Citizenship: Personal Lives and Social Policy*, Bristol, The Policy Press.
Lister, R. (2003) *Citizenship: Feminist Perspectives*, 2nd edn, Basingstoke, Palgrave Macmillan.
Lister, R. (2004) *Poverty*, Cambridge, Polity Press.
May, M., Page, R. and Brunsdon, E. (2001) *Understanding Social Problems: Issues in Social Policy*, Oxford, Blackwell.

1.2 your social work course

Adams, R. (2003) *Social Work and Empowerment*, 3rd edn, Basingstoke, Palgrave Macmillan.
This is a classic introductory text which integrates theoretical models with practice in a variety of contexts.

Gilbert, P. (2003) *The Value of Everything: Social Work and its Importance in the Field of Mental Health*, Lyme Regis, Russell House Publishing.
Although the focus here is on mental health, there is a short section devoted to the role of the social worker in general, which sets the scene for further study.

Horwath J. and Shardlow, S. M. (2003) *Making Links Across Specialisms: Understanding Modern Social Work Practice*, Lyme Regis, Russell House Publishing.
Recognizing the trend towards specialist services, this collection highlights the need for

collaborative working between disciplines and looks at how this can be promoted at an organizational as well as individual level.

Thompson, N. (2005) *Understanding Social Work*, 2nd edn, Basingstoke, Palgrave Macmillan.
This is helpful for setting social work in its context, exploring what social work is and what it is not. It covers a wide range of topics, including the legal and policy context, social work values and integrating theory and practice.

See also:

Adams, R., Dominelli, L. and Payne, M. (eds) (2002a) *Social Work Themes, Issues and Critical Debates*, 2nd edn, Basingstoke, Palgrave Macmillan.
Coulshed, V. and Orme, J. (2006) *Social Work Practice*, 4th edn, Palgrave Macmillan.
Payne, M. (2005) *The Origins of Social Work*, Basingstoke, Palgrave Macmillan.
Payne, M. (2006) *What is Professional Social Work?*, 2nd edn, Bristol, The Policy Press.

1.3 maximizing your learning

Martyn, H. (ed.) (2000) *Developing Reflective Practice: Making Sense of Social Work in a World of Change*, Bristol, The Policy Press.
This is a collection of papers submitted by students on a postqualifying course which aimed to improve practice skills through promoting reflective practice. As well as the students' own evaluation of their interventions, it contains commentaries on the practice described, both from an academic and a practitioner perspective. Because of its emphasis on social work processes its usefulness goes beyond its children and families focus.

Redmond, B. (2004) *Reflection in Action: Developing Reflective Practice in Health and Social Services*, Aldershot, Aldgate.
This book describes the reflective teaching and learning model which emerged from the author's research into how professional workers perceive those who use their services. Its early chapters contain a useful overview of theorists such as Freire and Schön.

Thompson, N. (2006) *Promoting Workplace Learning*, Bristol, The Policy Press.
A helpful text that explores how the potential for learning in the workplace can be maximized.

See also:

Buzan, T. and Buzan, B. (2000) *The Mind Map Book*, London, BBC Worldwide.
Clarke, A. (2004) *e-Learning Skills*, Basingstoke, Palgrave Macmillan.
Cottrell, S. (2003) *The Study Skills Handbook*, 2nd edn, Basingstoke, Palgrave Macmillan.
Doel, M. and Shardlow, S. M. (2005) *Modern Social Work Practice: Teaching and Learning in Practice Settings*, Aldershot, Ashgate.
Gould, N. and Baldwin, M. (eds) (2004) *Social Work, Critical Reflection and the Learning Organisation*, Aldershot, Aldgate.
Taylor, C. and White, S. (2000) *Practising Reflexivity in Health and Social Welfare: Making Knowledge*, Buckingham, Open University Press.

core topics

2

introduction

Part 1 'set the scene' by exploring issues related to studying to become a qualified social worker. Part 2 now builds on that by examining a number of important topics that are central to our understanding, and practice, of social work. It will act as an introduction for those preparing for a career in social work and as a reminder or revision for those already established in their careers but keen to keep the ideas fresh in their minds.

This part of the book contains seven substantive chapters that broadly reflect subject areas that are likely to feature on the curriculum of social work courses. The first explores social work processes. In undertaking social work practice we become involved in a number of processes and, by being aware of what those processes are and how they tend to operate, we will be in a much better informed position to perform our duties. This chapter therefore highlights some of the key processes that tend to be at work in social work.

Following this we have a chapter on 'The social context' (one of the seven principles underlying this book, as outlined in the Introduction). In Part 1 we looked at how wider society is an important contextual feature of social work. In this chapter we examine in more details just how significant the social context is, how much of an influence it has on shaping the problems we encounter, what we do in response to them and how we do it.

Human development is the topic of the next chapter. Here we consider how matters of personal and social development are very relevant to the people we work with and the circumstances they find themselves in. To develop an adequate understanding of the people we are trying to help, we need to have at least a basic understanding of how people develop over time through the life course and what implications this has for each of the individuals we are working with.

All of the above also has to be understood in an organizational context, as the employment base of the worker will have a significant influence on what happens in practice, how policies are interpreted and implemented and so on. Chapter 2.4 therefore addresses the complex issues arising from the organizational context. An effective social worker needs to have a good understanding of how organizations work, how they can be influenced, and how they can do harm at times.

The law was introduced in Part 1 as an important underpinning of practice, a key factor in shaping social work. Chapter 2.5 revisits this topic and the associated topic of social policy and sets about explaining how so much of our work depends on law and policy issues at a macro level and how these are interpreted and implemented at a micro level. Practising social work without a satisfactory knowledge of the law and related policy is a very dangerous undertaking indeed.

But it is not only the law and policy that shape practice. Social work values also play an important part. The value base of social work is therefore a topic that is well worth examining, and this is what Chapter 2.6 does. Values are a very complex matter, and so we do not offer any simple approaches. What the chapter does is to emphasize the importance of being prepared to wrestle with the complexities and continue to learn over time.

Reflective practice forms the subject matter of Chapter 2.7. This is a very important topic as it is concerned with the basis of good practice. The chapter argues that high-quality practice needs to be based on clear thinking, self-awareness and a willingness to draw on the vast professional knowledge base available to us.

Each of the chapters is introductory in nature, as they cover very sizeable topics, each of which has a substantial literature base of its own. Part 2 should therefore be used in conjunction with each of the sets of 'Suggestions for further reading' at the end of each part as well as Part 7, the 'Guide to further learning', which will provide you with guidance on how to develop further your knowledge and understanding of each of the topics covered here.

2.1 social work processes

introduction

Social work operates at the point where people interact with other people. That 'space between people', as Hopkins (1986) refers to it, is therefore of crucial importance, and yet what goes on there is not always obvious, unless we are particularly concentrating, or there is something such as conflict which throws it to the forefront of our consciousness. If we were to be acutely aware of every process that occurs every time people come together, then it would become very difficult to function, and so we tend to take a lot of things for granted. The human brain is very adept at filtering out what is not considered important for present purposes as we go about our day-to-day business.

Of course, the processes are still happening, but we tend to ignore them – they become 'part of the wallpaper', as it were. For example, if you were to turn on the television at home, it is quite likely that you would not notice that other members of the family are reacting to that process, perhaps by choosing to leave the room, moving to a different chair, stopping a conversation and so on. Aspects of that group's dynamics will have changed without necessarily becoming obvious to those involved. But, imagine now that you are a social worker in that setting and that you are there because there is a problematic relationship between the father and the son in the family. The reaction to the television being turned on would take on more significance for you, perhaps highlighting a lack of respect for the other's feelings and privacy, or indicating an attempt to avoid discussion or confrontation. If the power relations within that family were of particular interest or concern, then such processes could be vital clues, rather than irrelevant detail. Part of being an effective social worker is being able to 'turn off the filters' and become more sensitive to the subtle interactions and complex processes that are going on.

Principle 4 **Knowledge, Skills and Values**

> *Knowledge in relation to the processes that go on around us is important, as are the skills and values that enable us to work with these processes appropriately.*

By their very definition social work processes have a social dimension. There are probably very few people in the world who live in total isolation, never coming into contact with other people. For the most part we are interacting with others on a regular basis. We live in a social context (as we shall discuss in more detail in Chapter 2.2 below), and so carrying out your job effectively will require that you develop a heightened sense of awareness of:

> the existence of social processes;

> the consequences of those processes; and
> how you yourself are impacting on that 'space between people'.

Principle 1 `The Social Context`

This shows how the social context underpins everything we do in social work.

As you progress, you will come to appreciate the complex and dynamic nature of what is occurring around you. You will notice how the processes you might once have taken for granted are operating within a number of interlinking contexts (such as partnerships, families, organizations, communities, societies) and are affected by a range of factors (such as location, values, emotion, intention).

NOS Key Role 1

Prepare for, and work with, individuals, families, carers, groups and communities to assess their needs and circumstances

So, if social work processes are so important, but also so complex, how can you begin to get your head around them? A useful starting point is to think in terms of two different sets of processes. To begin with we will pick just a few processes as examples of the many *interactive* processes from which we have a choice. We will then move on to a second set of processes, which Neil Thompson (2002b) refers to as 'the helping process'. These are more specific to social work intervention and provide a framework for reflective practice by alerting you to the need to plan and review your actions, so that they stay focused and relevant, and evaluating them so that you continue to learn throughout your career.

Principle 7 `Self-management`

This is another example of the importance of self-management: taking responsibility for our learning and our practice.

If you think about any interaction between people you should be able to see that there are myriad processes occurring at any given time, often working in conjunction with each other. For example, you could be interviewing someone while also engaging in the processes of observing and recording and, at the same time, challenging them gently about their aggressive attitude or perhaps helping them to relax and nurturing their confidence in being able to contribute to the discussion. And while all this is going on, you might also be negotiating with a third person that they leave the two of you to have this discussion without interruption.

While there is certainly a sense of interconnectedness, it might be helpful in this instance to make a broad distinction between those concerned with:

> interaction;
> intervention; and
> personal effectiveness.

We shall discuss each of these in turn.

We have chosen interviewing and observing as examples here because of their key significance to effective social work practice.

interviewing

The reasons for meeting with someone for a discussion are many and varied. For example, an interview can be an information-gathering exercise, a relationship-building process, the basis of an agreement for future action or indeed all three. Whatever the objective, it is one of the mediums through which social workers operate and, as such, needs to be planned and focused if it is not to turn into a general chat which fails to achieve anything specific or to take you forward in your work.

NOS Key Role 2

Plan, carry out, review and evaluate social work practice, with individuals, families, carers, groups, communities, and other professionals

Time is not a commodity that social workers have in abundance, and an unfocused discussion can waste both your time and that of your interviewee if it does not achieve anything. Nor will it do much to inspire confidence in your ability to promote change. Right from the start you should get plenty of chances to practise interviewing, and we would advise you to take those opportunities (or make them if they are not being offered). While it may look easy, it is in many ways a highly skilled process. For example, you will need to think about the following issues.

Can you be understood? The medium of communication needs to suit both parties if there is not to be an unhelpful power imbalance. For example, someone with a hearing impairment may miss some of what is being said if that impairment is not catered for, and may therefore be put at a disadvantage, as too would someone being expected to discuss personal and emotive matters in a language which is not the one they feel most comfortable with. And, while jargon can be a useful shorthand between colleagues, if you slip into the habit of using it with clients, it is likely to disempower them. If you have ever experienced someone talking to you in technical or medical terms, with the assumption that you are familiar with the terminology and concepts used, you may have felt overwhelmed or stupid and perhaps too embarrassed to ask for clarification. If that is the case, then you should be able to appreciate how being interviewed insensitively can feel from where the client is at.

Principle 2 **Empowerment and Partnership**

The inappropriate use of jargon can be a serious barrier to empowerment and partnership.

Are appropriate boundaries being maintained? This process of interviewing will happen in a context within which you will have a specific professional identity and role, and along with that will come 'rules' about appropriate behaviour. For example, you will be expected to maintain confidentiality and to respect personal privacy – being a social worker does not give you an automatic right to know everything there is to know about a person. This includes respect for personal space. There are social 'rules' about such things as physical proximity, touch and so on, and these rules can vary between cultures. Ensuring that the person being interviewed has a clear understanding of both the social worker's role and the reason for the interview is an important factor in getting the balance right between being perceived as, at one extreme, the person in this relationship who 'makes the rules' and, at the other extreme, someone there for just an inconsequential chat.

Are you creating an atmosphere in which people feel able to participate? While you can take the initiative in terms of keeping interviews focused, it is important to do so sensitively and not to be overly directive to the extent that people feel intimidated or that their contribution will not be seen as valid. For example, sometimes people need time to gather their thoughts, prepare themselves to say something or work through difficult emotions before being able to move on with the interview process. Tolerating silences can be uncomfortable but such 'time out' needs to be respected.

Have you chosen the right place and time? Within a busy and demanding schedule there will be optimal times when it would suit you to carry out an interview. It may be that you will be in a client's neighbourhood at a particular time, or that you have a preferred time which suits your own needs. Sometimes you may have to work to protocols which specify a time framework, so that the choice is more limited than it otherwise might be. But, imposing the timing and location of an interview on the other party gives the message that your time is more important than theirs and may well put them at a disadvantage. For example, a young parent taking part in an interview mid-afternoon may not be able to give their full attention, knowing that children will arrive home from school very soon or may need to be picked up. Interviewing someone with a debilitating illness late in the afternoon when they are at their most tired may make the process more difficult for them than it need be. And, ask yourself whether interviewing in a noisy sitting-room with television blaring and neighbours constantly popping in and out, or a school common-room on a rainy lunchtime, is likely to be conducive to an effective outcome?

Having considered, albeit briefly, some of the key issues relating to interviewing, we now also need to consider the importance of developing observational skills.

observing

This is one of those processes that are occurring all of the time, and you may be wondering why we are bothering to discuss a process which is so basic and familiar to us. The point is that you need to take the basic skill up a gear when you are in social work mode. It may be that you have come to social work from a background in which your observation skills are already good. For example, as a nurse you may have become adept at reading cues that indicate pain, or noticing where there is a limitation to someone's mobility. If you have been in the police service and become used to dealing with large crowds, you might be highly skilled in noticing changes of behaviour which indicate the likelihood of fighting breaking out. On the other hand, it may be that you have never been in a situation where you have regularly been required to think much beyond those factors which are relevant to you, your own needs and your own safety. Whatever your experience, the process of observing is one that will be a cornerstone of your practice. You need to be able to assess situations quickly and accurately, and so taking notice and making sense of what you see will be crucial.

As with other sources of information, much of what you see is 'filtered' by your brain as you scan the world around you. What you home in on will depend on the particular set of circumstances you are in at the time. For example, if you are in a burning building you will probably observe windows and doors, but not notice what the wallpaper looks like. If you are engrossed in watching an exciting football match you may recall information about the players on the pitch, but may not notice that many people in the crowd behind you left before the end of the game. Similarly, what you take on board in your capacity as a social worker will also be affected by external factors as well as your own priorities, and it may be, for example, that an unexpected turn of events may cause you to switch your focus of attention from a wide focus to a much narrower one, or from one issue to another. For example, we have come across many situations where a social worker was present in somebody's home dealing with matters unconnected with child protection, but have had to switch their focus when they begin to realize they are witnessing recognized indicators of abuse.

NOS Key Role 4

Manage risk to individuals, families, carers, groups, communities, self and colleagues

As part of the wider context or 'macro' picture and the more detailed or 'micro' one there will be many observational cues including, for example:

> interpersonal dynamics;
> body language;
> environmental issues, such as living conditions;
> what is happening that should not be;
> what should be happening, but is not; and/or
> sudden changes.

It may seem to someone who is inexperienced that you will have so much to concentrate on that your head will burst. If that is the case for you, then remember that social work is not a race or competition. It is rarely the case that you have only one opportunity to take things in – it is more usually a case of building up a picture from your observations over a period of time (although how much time you have will vary from setting to setting and case to case). That is often when the significance of what you have observed becomes apparent.

NOS Key Role 1

Prepare for, and work with, individuals, families, carers, groups and communities to assess their needs and circumstances

Interviewing and observation skills are not the only issues when it comes to interactive processes, but our comments on these two topics should be sufficient to give you a picture of what is involved in developing our competence in recognizing and dealing with interactive processes.

intervention processes

As with interactive skills, we shall limit ourselves to two examples of the types of process that can occur. These should be seen as illustrative of the broader field of study rather than directly representative of it in its totality. The two examples we have chosen are advocating and decision making.

advocating

Social workers can effect positive change in a number of ways. One of these is to help redress the power imbalance between relatively powerless and powerful parties by using their position and knowledge base either to:

> support a vulnerable person in having their perspective heard; or
> represent that person's interests on his or her behalf.

As you will see from the discussion in Part 3, there are many different forms of advocacy, some more formalized than others. Examples might include:

> a care manager pleading the case for a physically and mentally frail older couple to be allowed to live together in a nursing home, on the basis that to make them live out the last years of their lives in separate homes would be to fail to address their emotional needs;
> a social worker attending a planning meeting to represent the interest of a young man whose autism prevents him from being able to communicate easily or understand his own long-term needs;
> a worker using his or her influence in a community to support the cause of travellers who want their children to have access to educational facilities in the area, but are not being given the opportunity to make their case heard at planning meetings.

And so, while you may not have the formal title of advocate, the process is almost certainly one that will figure prominently in your work from time to time at least, whatever branch of social work you choose and whichever level you reach within the profession. As such, there will be dilemmas to consider and pitfalls to avoid. For example, if someone with whom you are working is not happy about a service provided or denied by a local authority, and you are an employee of that same authority, then you might find yourself being 'stuck in the middle' and your loyalty to either or both parties compromised. It is not always an uncomplicated role but, given social work's contribution to promoting social justice, it is a process which you, as a social worker, will be well placed to carry out and one which will utilize many of your skills, including assertiveness and planning.

advocacy, see p. 160

NOS Key Role 3

Support individuals to represent their needs, views and circumstances

decision making

As a professional worker, you will be judged to a certain extent on the decisions you make or fail to make. Even choosing not to take action on something is a form of decision. You have a professional responsibility to make them *informed* decisions, ones which you can account for if called upon to do so at any point, such as to your manager, to a client or carer, or even to a court or investigative body should that ever become necessary. Decision making will happen on a daily basis – you have to engage with it in order to be able to proceed in your work.

existentialism, see p. 250

Plan, carry out, review and evaluate social work practice, with individuals, families, carers, groups, communities, and other professionals

This might include making decisions about risk management (discussed in more detail in Part 3), workload management, as discussed below, or the appropriateness of particular theoretical approaches to problem management. But, for our purposes here, the actual focus of the decision making is secondary to the point that merely sitting around waiting for instructions is not an option for you. Colleagues will generally be supportive, but will have their own problems to be working on, and managers will expect that you work independently, calling on them for advice and reassurance rather than for direction. And so, as decision-making processes feature so prominently in your work, how can you make them as informed as possible and how can you feel confident that, if called to account, you would be able to justify them?

This is too vast a topic to cover here in detail, and much of what should inform practice will feature in your academic programme of learning and your practice learning experiences. The following are just a few pointers:

> Call on more experienced colleagues. They will have been in your position, and may be happy to advise and reassure you, although they will almost certainly not welcome a 'tell me what to do' approach from you.
> Explore the possibility that there might be a formalized decision-making tool in existence, which may provide a focus for the task you are facing.
> Remember that partnership working is a core social work value – operating in isolation of, and enforcing a decision upon social work clients when this is not necessary is hardly in the anti-oppressive spirit of modern social work. Think about whether a decision is yours to make.
> Think in terms of the consequences of decision making. They are made with a hoped-for result, but this does not always happen or, if it does, it may have unexpected or unwanted knock-on effects. It is important, therefore, to be very clear about what you want to achieve. systematic practice, see p. 261

The third of the three types of process we shall comment on is personal effectiveness, and so it is to this topic that we now turn.

personal effectiveness

As Principle 7 acknowledges, self-management is an important part of social work. It involves taking responsibility for our actions, as social work is too complex to rely on trying to follow orders or instructions from others. 'Personal effectiveness' is an important part of this, as it involves making sure that our efforts are harnessed and directed as effectively as possible. It includes the following important elements.

acting assertively

This is another of those key processes that you need to think about because how you present to others has implications for how effectively you can operate. It can be described as achieving the positive middle ground between two unhelpful extremes of behaviour: on the one hand, you are unlikely to wield much influence or inspire confidence if you act submissively when in an encounter with someone but, on the other hand, you will lose respect and trample over core social work values if you try to exert power over someone by acting aggressively in a bullying manner. While you may not always feel confident, especially in the early days, it is something to work hard on managing. This is because it is a process that can make a difference in many ways. For example, it:

> *counteracts the negative stereotypes that are often attached to social workers.* Coming across as someone who is confident in their abilities, knows their ground and is competent at keeping encounters focused will make those who think of social workers as ineffectual and indecisive think again.
> *gives people a sense of being 'grounded' when they are feeling anxious or uncertain.* That is, having someone who can help to see a way forward when they themselves cannot, can inspire confidence and promote good working relationships.
> *fits with the social work value base in terms of working in partnership with clients* and helping them to effect change for themselves, rather than using your own power to force it onto them through an 'I know best approach'.

Principle 4 **Knowledge, Skills and Values**

Social work values help us guard against misusing or abusing power.

Feeling underprepared or threatened can make that middle ground of assertiveness difficult to maintain at times, but one of the keys to being able to act assertively is to feel comfortable in your role. This is not just about having clear objectives in a given situation, but also about understanding your role in general – being clear about why a social worker is involved at all, what is expected of you, what powers and duties you have, what limitations there are to your role, and so on.

managing your workload

Social work is characterized by workloads that can be:

> heavy;
> unpredictable; and
> emotionally challenging.

There is a strong likelihood that crises will occur so that existing work needs to be re-prioritized. As a professional worker, you will carry the responsibility for managing your workload, and so you need to be aware of the processes operating, the effects they are having on you and what you can do about them As we shall emphasize in Chapter 2.4, workload management involves thinking about how you use your time and energy, your style of working, your working environment and so on. There are obviously differences between agencies in terms of referral rates and expectations of response time, but it is unlikely that you will be twiddling your thumbs looking for work. A more likely scenario is that there will be a constant stream of work waiting for you to make time in your schedule for it. Where there is more work to be done than people around to do it, there is the potential for social workers to feel pressure (be it from managers, colleagues or themselves) to take on more work than they can comfortably manage. This is where professionalism needs to come to the fore.

Making sure we do not become overloaded is an important self-management skill. An overloaded worker can do more harm than good.

NOS Key Role 5

Manage and be accountable, with supervision and support, for your own social work practice within your organization

If the responsibility for operating effectively and safely is yours, then so must the responsibility for keeping your workload under control. This means:

> Reviewing your workload regularly and recognizing when it becomes unmanageable.
> Declining requests to take on more work when you know you cannot do it without compromising its quality.
> Recognizing that you will never be able to address all the problems of the world, or even your own little patch of it – nor is it your responsibility to do so. More often than not, there will be unallocated referrals on waiting lists and people being turned away from social work agencies altogether. Feeling responsible for soaking up the pressure means that you may take on work for which you do not have the time or emotional resources and end up 'spreading yourself too thinly' – becoming ineffectual (perhaps dangerously so) because you do not have time to do anything more than skim the surface of each case.
> Keeping your manager in the loop. While managing an individual workload is indeed a personal responsibility for social work practitioners, managing a whole service is not. Strategic issues are the responsibility of strategic managers, but they will not necessarily know that an individual social worker or team is overloaded if excessive workloads are being absorbed at that level. Remember that your employers have responsibilities in terms of staff care, but you have responsibility to protect your own health and professional reputation by not taking on more work than you can cope with.

Principle 6 `Realism and Challenge`

Effective workload management, with support, is an important part of the challenge of social work. We have to be realistic about how much work an individual can carry.

NOS Key Role 4

Manage risk to individuals, families, carers, groups, communities, self and colleagues

It is clearly important to develop the skills of time and workload management, as being unprepared for managing a heavy workload can not only lead to poor practice, but also place your own health and safety at risk in terms of the potential for stress.

`the organizational context,` `see p. 101`

Winston had recently joined a busy social work team in a highly populated urban area. As part of the induction process he spent some time shadowing the duty social worker and taking some of the calls himself. Wanting to see the next step in the referral process he browsed through the collection of referrals that were waiting to be allocated. As the team manager worked

practice focus

2.1

hard at ensuring that individual workers were not overloaded, several referrals had been unallocated for quite some time. Winston found this difficult to accept, particularly after having taken calls himself. He could imagine worried individuals and families waiting for intervention in some form. He discussed this with the team manager who helped him to understand that the team, and indeed the whole service, could not respond instantly to every request, and that setting priorities would no doubt always be a feature of social work. Winston took this on board and, realizing that he would need to learn to manage these feelings, decided to raise it as a topic for discussion at the next study day.

the helping process

Neil Thompson (2002b) discusses a five-part process for helping people. Although this has much broader application than just social work, it is a very helpful approach to social work, as it gives a clear framework to work to – providing a structure and focus for practice.

The five elements of the process are:

> *Assessment* – gathering information and forming a picture of the situation in order to work out what problems there may be that need addressing, what strengths and resources may be available to draw upon, and deciding what steps need to be taken.
> *Intervention* – taking the steps to meet identified needs, address identified problems and so on. In effect, this means doing the work identified at the assessment stages as being needed.
> *Review* – taking account of changing circumstances and changing our plans accordingly.
> *Ending* – sooner or later bringing our intervention to a close and not allowing the situation to drift on unnecessarily or 'fizzle out' unsatisfactorily.
> *Evaluation* – looking at what can be learned from the work done. What might we do differently next time?

Each of these elements is an important part of the helping process, and so it is worth exploring each of these in more detail. However, before doing so, it is worth making the significant point that the helping process involves the important skills of planning and goal setting – these are discussed in Part 4 under the heading of 'Systematic practice', an approach that is highly consistent with the idea of the helping process.

assessment

You may well have thought about, or indeed have been asked the question: 'What is social work?' and have realized by now that it can be very diverse in terms of client group, workplace context, overall aims and so on. What is common to all forms of social work, however, is the concept of problem solving. That is, the core of your work will be addressing problems in partnership with service users and co-workers, to find acceptable solutions. In order to get to the point where you are able to intervene, it should go without saying that you first need to find out what the problem is. And yet, although this 'problem setting' seems like an obvious first step, it can be easily forgotten or the assessment process rushed, especially when there is pressure to act quickly. Without getting a clear picture of a situation, it becomes impossible to plan a way forward and, without establishing a strategy (that is, planning and goal setting), interventions are likely to be premised on chance or guesswork. Indeed, they may not even prove to be necessary. For example, social work agencies often receive referrals which go no further in terms of social work intervention when, on assessment, it becomes clear that this is not an issue for social workers to address, or that a concern raised by someone is misplaced. `systematic practice, see p. 261`

There is not enough space in this introductory text to do justice to exploring this key social work process. Learning more about the theory and practice of assessment is something that will develop as you work through your training programme and beyond, and your tutors and practice learning colleagues will guide you in this. What we can do at this point is to identify and briefly explain just a few of the key issues you will need to keep uppermost in your mind if the assessment process is to be fair and effective and to remind you that the assessment process underpins all of those that follow it.

Assessment is a process you undertake with other people, not something you do to them. We shall be emphasizing below, in the chapter on social work values, that it is important to work in partnership. As we have already seen, the assessment element is about defining the problem to be addressed, but it is not always the case that problems are perceived in the same way by all the parties concerned. For example, a son might define his elderly father's sleeping in an armchair at night as a problem, because he assumes that it indicates self-neglect, while his father merely finds it more comfortable than propping himself up in bed with pillows and does not perceive it as a problem at all. Similarly, the mother of a teenaged girl who stays out until midnight every night might perceive her behaviour as being 'out of control', whereas the young person herself may see this as a response to what she perceives as overstrict parenting, rather than as a problem in itself. Where there is a shared understanding of what needs to be done, then there is more likely to be a shared commitment to addressing issues. Where a social worker acts in a paternalistic way, assuming that *their* assessment and *their* proposals for action are necessarily the 'right' ones, the potential for resistance and resentment are high. It is therefore vitally important that assessment should be a *shared* endeavour. `partnership, see p. 199`

Try to view the situation through the client's eyes. If the purpose of the assessment process is to identify what it is, if anything, that needs to be addressed, then any assessment needs to take as its starting point, the client's 'social location' – that is, where they fit into society and how that affects how they live their lives. As we discuss below, we do not live our lives in a vacuum, but within a number of different contexts. So, for example, our class position will have an impact on the lifestyle choices we are able to make. Similarly, because of the prevalence of ageist stereotyping, our age will make a difference to how we are treated, as will our gender in a society where expectations about 'appropriate' gender roles continue to exert an influence, even from childhood (Connell, 2002; Stanworth, 1997). It will make a difference whether we are gay or straight, black or white, whether we have a physical or intellectual impairment and so on. If we begin the assessment process without taking into account that any or all of these aspects will have a bearing on the situation, then we cannot hope to get an accurate picture of what is going on. `human development, see p. 83`

Prepare for, and work with, individuals, families, carers, groups and communities to assess their needs and circumstances

An approach that assumes that life is a 'level playing field' and that resources and opportunities are open to all on an equal basis fails to take into account the discrimination that operates in many ways and on many levels. For any assessment process to begin without an appreciation of where an individual is located in terms of their social context is to run the risk of ignoring or minimizing some very crucial issues which are beyond their control, but which influence how they are able to live their lives and limit the choices they are able to make. social work values, see p. 127

Principle 1 Social Context

An understanding of the social context needs to be part of any assessment

Keep to what is relevant. People and situations are complex and can therefore generate a lot of information, but it does not follow that assessment involves gathering every bit of that information about everything that has ever occurred. If not carried out with sensitivity, then the assessment process can become intrusive and, without focus, it can become an exercise in gathering information for its own sake. Knowing what to concentrate on is something that will come with experience, and you will no doubt spend time in the next few years on becoming practised at picking up information from a variety of sources, such as non-verbal cues. It is useful to pay heed to the maxim of 'minimum necessary, not maximum available' (Neil Thompson, 2002b) when assessing a situation, if the process is to lead to a helpful next step.

Assessment is a process, rather than an event. It is often perceived as a procedural task which is performed because there is, in many cases, a legal obligation to carry out an assessment of need where vulnerability exists. While a one-off assessment may seem like a good shortcut when individual social workers are busy and services are stretched, they produce only a snapshot view of a situation at a particular point in time. Given that people and situations change, this is hardly adequate for getting as accurate a picture as possible of the complexities of people's lives.

It is also important to recognize that assessment should be concerned with *situations not people*. That is, it is not a social worker's role to assess an individual, as if making a judgement about him or her. Rather, it is a matter of assessing the overall situation to see what needs to be done.

intervention

Intervention can take many forms and there are many specific approaches which could be included under the banner heading of 'intervention processes'. However, again we do not have sufficient space to do full justice to this subject, but we can provide an overview of what is involved.

We would offer the following as key points to think about once you have entered the 'doing' element of the helping process:

Keep focused. There will be many distractions as you try to follow the action plans you will have constructed following the assessment element and so, without a clear focus on what you are trying to achieve, it can be easy to lose sight of your objectives. For example, where clients are confused, anxious or lacking in understanding, they will often be looking to you for direction and, where clients are resentful of your involvement, they may be uncooperative and try to deflect attention away from previously agreed plans. Keeping the process 'on track' is therefore is an important facet of the social work role. However, this is not to say that plans should be inflexible. As we have already seen, it is important to revisit the assessment process and, as a consequence of that, action plans may need to change too. But, while the focus itself may change, the need to stay focused does not.

NOS Key Role 2

Plan, carry out, review and evaluate social work practice, with individuals, families, carers, groups, communities, and other professionals

Know your limitations. This is not so much about recognizing your own strengths and weaknesses (although that is important in itself), but rather about remembering that your powers and resources are limited by external forces. Even the most experienced and knowledgeable social worker does not have a totally free hand or a bottomless pit of resources, and will be bound by legal and policy restrictions. Enthusiasm and lateral thinking are to be valued in social work, and we would not want to stifle either of those qualities, but it is important not to let your expectations of what is achievable run away with you.

Principle 6 Realism and Challenge

It is vitally important that we are realistic about what can be achieved.

humility, see p. 192

Don't be precious. As a social worker, you will have much that is unique to offer, but so too will colleagues from other disciplines. Trying to be all things to all people may result in their being denied help that someone other than you is better placed to offer. Some social workers operate in multidisciplinary teams alongside health, education or law professionals, which can make channels of communication between the helping professions easier (Harrison et al., 2003; Weinstein et al., 2003) but, even where multidisciplinary working is not so structured, it can still be facilitated.

Principle 2 Empowerment and Partnership

Being 'precious' will be a major obstacle to working in partnership at a multidisciplinary level.

Remember that you are a resource too. When involved at the intervention element of the helping process, it is easy to be drawn into a mindset which sees providing services as the only appropriate response to identified needs. In some cases it is indeed necessary to act as a facilitator, purchaser or broker of services, but it is important to remember that, as a social worker, you are a resource in your own right. That is, you will be able to intervene in ways that call on what you yourself can offer – empathy, counselling skills and so on. For example, imagine that you were asked to intervene in a situation where an elderly woman had been neglecting to eat or dress properly for many months and was causing concern to her neighbours by never leaving the house or allowing callers inside. Arranging for services such as meal delivery, home care support, befriending or transport to some sort of social activity would all be potential forms of intervention, but it is important not to forget 'use of self' in such situations. For example, using your communication skills sensitively to engage with her over a period of time might result in an understanding of *why* she is neglecting herself and becoming oblivious to her surroundings, thereby alerting you to consider approaches other than bringing in services. For example, if she had experienced a bereavement, then validating her feelings and helping her to work through them, might be more appropriate than, and indeed negate the need for, the provision of support services.

Principle 5 Loss and Grief

We need to be wary of the common mistake of neglecting the significance of loss and grief in the situations social workers encounter.

NOS Key Role 2

Plan, carry out, review and evaluate social work practice, with individuals, families, carers, groups, communities, and other professionals

practice focus

2.2

When Hilary called at Mr Greenwood's house she was totally unprepared for the reception she got. As soon as she was through the door Mr Greenwood wasted no time in telling her about everything that was causing him a problem in his life, while also making it clear that he didn't expect much in the way of competence from her. It soon became clear to Hilary that he had become very frustrated at the limitations his worsening heart condition had put on his physical and emotional energy and at the slow or non-existent response he had been experiencing from some of the agencies and organizations he had contacted for help. Hilary made it quite clear to him that she did not have a magic wand but would try to help by advocating on his behalf for a more sympathetic response. Although she had been offended by his initial comments, by putting herself in Mr Greenwood's shoes, she had appreciated how vulnerable and disempowered he must be feeling, and spent time with him validating those feelings. On returning to see him a week later she felt sure that he would be disappointed that many of his concerns were still outstanding. Instead, she got a very welcoming response. Mr Greenwood told her that the very fact that she had understood and validated his feelings had made him feel like a valued citizen, rather than a nuisance and a burden. When he told her that he didn't need her to call again, she realized that it was her understanding and empathy that had made the difference here, because it had helped to restore his self-esteem so that he felt able to fight his own battles again.

review

We shall emphasize below that the helping process is iterative – that is, the various elements need revisiting from time to time, rather than being one-off events. For example, to continue with a planned programme of intervention without reviewing it is to assume that nothing has changed since the situation was first assessed (and that your assessment was comprehensive and entirely accurate). As we are sure you will agree, this is unlikely to be the case, and yet it is all too easy to plough on without stopping to think whether your action plan is still appropriate. In some cases the review process is formalized within an agency, especially where service provision is involved. For example, it may be that your employers will expect you to follow a programme of reviewing within a certain number of weeks or months and to record achievements, unmet needs and so on in a prescribed format. Whether it is a formal requirement or not, it is a process that needs to be taken seriously if intervention is not to be:

> a waste of resources;
> counterproductive; and/or
> ineffective.

However, even where there is a formal system in place, you may need to review your work more frequently on an informal basis. For example, you may have a review meeting in which plans are confirmed and agree to have a further review in three or six months' time, but a significant change in the situation may occur the day after the meeting that necessitates changes to your plans.

Since every situation will be different, it is not possible to offer prescriptive advice on when to review. Indeed, this 'one regime fits all' approach would not fit with the ethos of reflective practice that we would wish to promote. However, there are certain triggers which can alert you to the idea that now is a good time to be reviewing the process. These include where there is:

> *A significant change in circumstances.* Your plans may still be appropriate, but this will need to be checked out.
> *A statutory requirement on you to undertake a review.* An example of this would be in relation to a child being looked after away from home.
> *A pre-agreed review point.* In commencing a piece of work, it can be useful to consider in advance when is likely to be a good point to review the situation.
> *A sense of not knowing what to do next.* Social work can be difficult and messy, and it is not uncommon for people to get stuck from time to time, to lose a sense of direction or begin to feel that progress is elusive. This can be a good time to review the situation and perhaps refocus.
> *A planned period of absence on the horizon.* If you are due to be away on holiday or absent for other reasons, other people may need to deal with one or more of your cases in your absence, this can be a good time to review where things are up to, so that anyone acting on your behalf has a clear picture of the current situation.
> *An intention to transfer the case to someone else or to cease involvement altogether.* When you are approaching the end of the line in terms of your own role, this too can be a good time to review and refocus.

(based on Neil Thompson, 2002b, pp. 215–16)

The following issues are all important when it comes to making sure that your practice is of a high standard in working your way through the helping process:

Making the time. When you are busy, and especially when you are immersed in the assessment and intervention elements of new pieces of work, reviewing existing work can easily slip down your list of priorities. But we would suggest that, to postpone or ignore this process is a false economy in terms of time management.

Manage and be accountable, with supervision and support, for your own social work practice within your organization

> For example, reviewing a particular case may lead you to the realization that it no longer needs to be on your caseload, thereby freeing up some of your time. It may also help you to identify where time is being wasted and alert you to how you might direct your energies to better effect. And, where the review process highlights success in achieving what you set out to achieve, it can have the knock-on effect of re-energizing you. Not least is the potential for clients to benefit from a fresh look at the circumstances.

> *Partnership.* As with all aspects of the helping process, reviewing is not something that should be done in isolation. Working with clients and carers in a spirit of partnership means that there will be more than one perspective on what has gone before – and these may differ. Even where objectives have been jointly agreed, what seems like progress or resolution to one party may not necessarily be a view shared by the other.

> *Accountability.* We have already talked in Part 1 about professionalism and the need to be accountable for our actions, our use of resources and the manner in which we represent the social work profession and promote its reputation. If you are an employee, as most social workers are, then you will be expected to use your employer's resources wisely, and that will include being value for money in your own right. While social work is not the highest-paid profession by any means, you are not a cheap resource, and so interventions that are not achieving their objectives are not a good use of scarce resources.

NOS Key Role 6

Demonstrate professional competence in social work practice

> *Avoidance of drift.* The pressures we face in social work can easily lead us to lose our focus and therefore to 'drift' away from our plans. Reviewing practice can help to make sure we do not fall into this trap. systematic practice, see p. 261

---

practice focus

2.3

85-year-old Mrs Kalish remained physically weak after an operation on her shoulder and was assessed by a hospital-based social worker as needing some assistance with household tasks and personal care to allow her to concentrate on recuperating. In collaboration with an agency in the private sector and the inter-agency 'home from hospital' team, a package of care was arranged following the assessment of need. While the assessment and planning processes had led to an outcome that was very useful at the time it was put into place, the review process did not take place for a further 12 weeks. During this time Mrs Kalish's needs changed significantly. Within four weeks her physical needs had lessened to the extent that she needed only minimal assistance. Having someone continue to call for a further two months left her feeling demoralized and worried that others saw her as someone who was vulnerable and not coping. Having perceived herself before the operation as a capable and independent woman, she now began to doubt her own judgement, and her confidence suffered as a result. When the review process finally took place, it became clear that the initial plan of action had long since become not only unnecessary, but actually counterproductive.

Beginnings are important in a working relationship, as they are a crucial time in establishing trust, agreeing aims and fostering a spirit of collaboration or, at the very least, a willingness to engage further. Endings too are important but this is a process which tends to be taken for granted, with little in the way of guidance or supportive literature. For example, Walker and Beckett (2003), in a detailed exposition of assessment and intervention, neglect issues to do with actually bringing intervention to a close – it is as if intervention is expected to be unending.

Social work interventions end for a variety of reasons, including the following;

> where aims have been met and the withdrawal of the social worker is mutually agreed;
> where clients have chosen to end the relationship or have moved away from the area;
> when the social worker leaves a post for whatever reason; and/or
> when organizational restraints or changes require a re-prioritization of resources.

Whatever the reason for ending the working relationship is, it needs to be as positive an experience as possible if your integrity and that of the social work profession itself is to be preserved. If the relationship between social worker and client ends with a sense of progress and feelings of respect and trust, then this is the image of social workers that is likely to stay with that person and will have positive implications for any future social work relationships, be they with you or any other social work colleague.

In a spirit of empowerment (and in keeping with Principle 2: Empowerment and Partnership) – that is, helping people gain greater control over their lives – your aim is to make yourself redundant, in the sense that we should be trying to help people help themselves and, where possible, no longer rely on professional assistance. Given the importance of empowerment in social work, we should, from the very beginning, be thinking about working towards (wherever possible) making our intervention no longer necessary – even if, in some cases, that may be a matter of years. An approach that neglects ending is therefore incompatible with an ethos of empowerment, as it runs the risk of creating dependency.

One significant obstacle to bringing intervention to a close is a situation arising where the needs of the social worker take precedence over those of the client. For example, a social worker may become quite attached to a particular family or individual and may therefore be reluctant to bring their work to a close, even though the client may no longer need their help, and so a risk of dependency creation is allowed to emerge.

NOS Key Role 5

Manage and be accountable, with supervision and support, for your own social work practice within your organization

Ending our involvement is not simply a matter of closing the case in an administrative sense. It is a skilled activity that requires a great deal of careful consideration to make sure that it is a positive step in the process. For example, it can be used as a means of boosting confidence by congratulating the client(s) on the progress made and the fact that they no longer need professional help.

Having closed a case, completed the necessary paperwork, ended the relationship with your client and put the case notes or records into storage, it may seem that this is the end of the story – that the helping process is at an end. However, there remains another process to engage with: evaluation. Although it might seem like the end of a set of processes, it is part of a cycle which, by its very nature, has no beginning or end. As part of a cyclical process it could just as well be described as a beginning as an end, because evaluation feeds into how we might approach a similar task or period of involvement in the future. What we learn will feed into another assessment process and inform how, or indeed whether, we intervene on another occasion. Like the review process, it is one that involves analysing what has been happening. So you might ask yourself questions such as these:

> Did I start from where the client is at? Did I seek and really understand their perspective and appreciate how their life circumstances might have had an impact on the situation we had been trying to address?

Principle 2 Empowerment and Partnership

Starting 'where the client is at' is a fundamental part of working in partnership.

> To what extent were my own values influencing the situation? Did I make the most effective use of the resources available to me?
> Did I record in such a way that the focus and rationale for any decisions, actions or inaction will be apparent to anyone who needs to question them, or to explore previous social work involvement at any time in the future?
> Was my practice anti-discriminatory or did I neglect, or even contribute to, the client's oppression? Did I take the opportunity to challenge discriminatory practices or attitudes where I came across them?
> Was I clear from the beginning what I was trying to achieve and was I able to maintain that focus?
> If our objectives were not achieved, do I understand why not?

Again, when you are busy, the time spent on evaluation might seem like a luxury you cannot afford. However, to dismiss evaluation in this way is to undermine the whole concept of learning and continuous professional development.

NOS Key Role 2

Plan, carry out, review and evaluate social work practice, with individuals, families, carers, groups, communities, and other professionals

We need to be aware of the things that do not work as well as congratulating ourselves on our successes and to take time out to think carefully about the wider implications of the courses of action we have taken. As Fleet comments:

> Evaluation provides the opportunity to review what has occurred and to note the outcomes. It is a unique vehicle for powerful intervention, in that it provides real evidence of the consequences, positive or disastrous, of what has been done and therefore offers fruitful ground for potent challenge, affirmation or learning. (Fleet, 2000, p. 90)

Choosing not to make time in our schedules for evaluation suggests that we do not see learning and development as important and are either happy to carry on regardless, in the hope that we have a positive rather than a negative impact on our clients' lives, or are arrogant enough to believe that our practice cannot be improved upon or that there is nothing left for us to learn. We would suggest, then, that, far from being a process that can be dispensed with in order to direct your energies to assessing and intervening, evaluation is a key part of the helping process, in that it will help to ensure that your practice is:

> *Informed by social work values.* Analysing your work to see what lessons can be learned from it will allow you to ensure that your actions have been consistent with social work values.
> *Focused.* As we noted earlier, the pressures of practice can mean that we are at risk of losing our focus and succumbing to 'drift'. Evaluation can help us check whether we did lose our focus at any time and perhaps identify any factors that led us to this.
> *Accountable.* As professionals, we are accountable for our actions, the decisions we base our actions upon and so on. The more we make use of the lessons to be learned form evaluation, the better equipped we will be for making sure our actions are appropriate and helpful.
> *Informed by research and debate.* As we shall argue in Part 5, research is an important underpinning of practice. We can usefully draw upon research-based knowledge and current debates as part of our evaluation – as part of our ongoing learning.

In Chapter 2.7 we shall explore the vitally important concept of 'reflective practice', and we shall see then that evaluation as a tool for learning from practice is an important part of this. We shall also consider evaluation in Part 5 when we examine issues relating to the role of research in relation to social work. critical evaluation skills, see p. 282

helping as an iterative process

It is important not to conceive of the five elements of the helping process as a rigid framework. This is because the process is 'iterative' – that is, it is not a simple, linear process. The situation is far more complex than this, in so far as:

1. The process can 'double back' on itself – for example, the review element may lead to a reassessment.
2. The elements will often overlap (for example, intervention may have to begin before assessment proper is complete).

We should therefore be careful not to equate the notion of 'the helping process', which is a helpful, flexible framework to assist us in understanding practice and in taking our actions forward, with a rigid set of 'stages' that oversimplify a very complex set of issues – which is far from helpful.

conclusion

In this chapter we have covered a wide range of issues that go under the broad heading of 'social work processes'. We have presented the material in two parts. First we looked at the 'space between people' – the various processes involved when we seek to help people. We further subdivided these into self-management processes, interactive processes and interventive processes. From this we moved on to examine what we described as 'the helping process', and we focused in turn on each of the five elements involved.

What our discussions have revealed is that social work is a highly complex set of activities, characterized by various processes. This confirms that we need to adopt a sophisticated approach to understanding what happens in a social work context, and indeed in putting that understanding into practice.

The various processes take place in a wider social context and are both influenced by that social context and play a part in shaping it. It is therefore to a consideration of the social context that we now turn.

points to ponder

> Why are boundaries important in communicating with clients and carers?
> Why are assertiveness skills important in social work?
> Why is assessment a key element of the helping process?
> What benefits are there to be gained from evaluating practice?
> What is meant by the idea that helping is an 'iterative process'?

2.2 **the social context**

introduction

In social work it is extremely important to recognize that we are dealing with individuals in a social context, as to fail to do so means that we are adopting too narrow a perspective that does not take account of very important issues, such as power, discrimination and so on. It is therefore important to incorporate an understanding of the significance of sociology as an academic discipline that provides insights into the work that we undertake. In particular, it is significant to remember the insights of Durkheim, one of the founders of sociology, who made the point that society precedes each individual (Giddens, 2006). In other words, each of us is born into a society that already exists and which is therefore bound to have an influence on us. We must never forget that the term 'social work' begins with the word 'social' – that is, it is not simply a matter of dealing with psychological issues. The tendency to reduce sociological matters to psychology is known as 'psychologism'. This can be a major problem, in so far as it can lead to what is known as 'blaming the victim' (Ryan, 1971). That is, individuals are blamed for matters that owe more to their social circumstances than to their own particular actions or characteristics. For example, someone who is living in poverty may be regarded as being poor because they are assumed to be 'lazy', even though the roots of their poverty are to be found in the economic and sociopolitical systems, rather than in the individual's character, temperament or level of motivation.

The sociologist, C. Wright Mills, was very critical of social work which he described as having a tendency to treat society as a series of unconnected individual cases (Mills, 1959). This is a significant criticism, and one that we must be careful to avoid.

One tendency that can lead us into psychologism is the fact that social work has strong roots in psychoanalysis. One of the major weaknesses of psychoanalytical thinking has been the failure to address social issues, to place far more emphasis on what happens within the mind of an individual, while neglecting such important social factors as the influence of poverty and deprivation, racism, sexism, exploitation, cultural pressures and so on.

We live and work in a highly complex social context. It is therefore dangerous to oversimplify this context and see it in narrow terms. For example, issues to do with race and racism have been treated in very simplistic ways by many people in the past, and this has led to a number of problems, not least of many people being very anxious about tackling issues to do with racism (see Neil Thompson, 2003a, ch. 5, for a discussion of this).

NOS Key Role 6

Demonstrate professional competence in social work practice

This chapter is therefore a very important one in setting the context. It will outline a number of important sociological issues that have a bearing on the work of social work practitioners and, indeed, managers. It will explore issues to do with social divisions, social institutions and processes, social problems and culture, identity and meaning.

social divisions

A central point to recognize is that society is not a level playing-field. The society in which we live and work is a hierarchical structure based on power. Where we are born into society will have a significant bearing on the power and life chances we have throughout our lives. For example, there will be major differences between someone born into a family of wealth, as compared with someone born into a family characterized by poverty and deprivation.

However, it is important to acknowledge that social hierarchy is not just a matter of class and income. It is in fact a multidimensional phenomenon, in so far as it includes a number of social divisions, such as gender, race and ethnicity, age, disability and sexual identity. These are referred to as 'social divisions' because they have the effect of dividing society up into sections and subsections, and where we fit into that interconnecting network of divisions will have significant implications in terms of how people perceive us, the opportunities we have, and so on. Let us look now in a little more detail at each of these in turn:

> *Class.* An official term for class is 'socioeconomic grouping'. This refers to where a particular individual fits into the social hierarchy in terms of income and wealth. While someone in a position of wealth will have obvious advantages over somebody with less wealth, it is not simply a matter of buying power. There are also significant issues to do with class in terms of, for example, health inequalities. There is a long tradition of research to show that the lower one's class position, the more vulnerable one is to ill-health (Whitehead, 1988).

> *Gender.* Despite the advances in terms of gender equality in recent decades, it is still clearly the case that we live in an unequal society as far as men and women are concerned. For example, it is very clear that there is a 'glass ceiling' operating in terms of career advancement for women (EOC, 2006).

> *Race and ethnicity.* Similarly, despite certain advances and the development of race equality legislation, there is still considerable evidence to show that Western societies are characterized by racial inequality. It is sadly the case that the colour of a person's skin can be a significant factor in terms of how that person is treated in society.

> *Age.* Although the significance of age has received less attention than other social divisions, it is none the less significant that a person's age can be a factor that can lead to discrimination. This can apply to people at either end of the age spectrum – that is, older people or children and young people (and indeed sometimes at other points in the life course too).

> *Disability.* The Disabled People's Movement has put disability equality firmly on the agenda and that is now supported in the UK by a growing body of anti-discrimination legislation. However, social workers none the less continue to encounter example after example of disability discrimination. Being disabled is still a major factor in leading to reduced levels of life chances.

> *Sexual identity.* A person's sexual preference is a further example of how being

classified in a certain group can lead to particular social disadvantages. Although we have made significant progress in terms of gay, lesbian and bisexual identities becoming more socially acceptable, the reality is still one of ingrained patterns of discrimination.

> *Language.* Although language issues are closely linked with race and ethnicity, there can also be significant issues relating to the language one speaks in itself. For example, someone who does not speak English can face major barriers and problems.

> *Religion or sect.* The history of 'the troubles' in Northern Ireland shows us how significant religion and sect can be in shaping people's social experiences and, of course, this is not the only example of how belonging to a particular religion or sect (or not doing so) can have significant social consequences.

> *Mental health status.* A person experiencing mental health problems can find him- or herself significantly socially disadvantaged because of stereotypes and stigma attached to people who undergo this type of difficulty.

It is important to recognize that this is not an exclusive list, and different theorists conceive of social structure in different ways. However, what has been provided should be sufficient to give an overview of the range of social divisions and some insight into how they can play a significant part in shaping the situations that we encounter in social work.

One of the major implications of social divisions and the social structure that they form is that they will have a significant influence on the distribution of power and life chances. By power we mean the ability to achieve one's aims, the ability to draw on particular resources that can be helpful in times of need. By life chances, we mean the opportunities that are presented to us in our lives. In some ways, being in a certain (privileged) part of the social structure will increase our life chances, but being in other, less privileged and even stigmatized parts of the social structure will reduce them. For example, being a white male in a white, predominantly male organization can be an advantage while being, for example, a black woman in that organization may lead to significant obstacles to overcome in order to make progress.

Of course, social work cannot be expected to change social structure in any major ways. It would certainly take more than what social work can offer to bring about such a radical change in the way society is organized. However, this is not a recipe for defeatism because what we can do is:

1 Take account of the social structure and the implications of social divisions in the work we undertake – for example, in our assessments.

2 We can seek to counter, minimize or avoid the negative effects of social divisions in the lives of people we are trying to help.

NOS Key Role 4

Manage risk to individuals, families, carers, groups, communities, self and colleagues

3 We can raise awareness (what is sometimes referred to as 'conscientization' – Freire, 1972) and help to empower people by aiding them in realizing that their problems have a social context to them, and that it is not simply a matter of individual failing.

4 We can make a small but perhaps in some ways significant contribution over time to society's development in the direction of a more egalitarian and humane society.

social institutions

In the sociological sense, an institution is not so much an organization, but rather one of the building blocks of society. By institution we therefore mean such things as the family, the state, the media, law and religion. It is worth exploring each of these in turn by way of example.

the family and marriage

The first point to recognize about the family is that the term means different things in different contexts. For example, when a person refers to his or her family, it may be a reference to either 'family of origin' – that is, the family he or she grew up in, or his or her current family, but, in addition, family can refer to one's partner and children or just to the children – for example, when someone says 'we have been married for two years now but we don't have any family yet'.

Despite these ambiguities, family is a widely used term and is a significant part of how our society works. This applies in a number of ways – for example, in terms of family values. Politicians of various political colours tend to emphasize the significance of family values, although it is not entirely clear at all times what they mean by this. In a positive sense, the family can be a place that provides a source of security, care, support and nurturance. But there is also a negative side to this, in so far as social work experience teaches us that the family can also be a site of abuse, exploitation, violence and oppression. The family can also be problematic in terms of its reliance on many occasions on 'patriarchy' – that is, traditional family values can reinforce gender stereotypes and lead to problems of sexual discrimination.

The family can also be problematic in other ways. For example, the emphasis on family housing has led to a preponderance of housing units designed for families. This has contributed to high levels of homelessness among some categories of single people (this is partly because a housing authority will understandably be reluctant to allocate a two- or three-bedroomed dwelling to a single person). Similarly, a major focus on the family can be problematic for those people who do not live in families. They may feel excluded and, in terms of some social policies, often are excluded because the prevailing ideology focuses primarily on families.

Our aim is not to paint too negative a picture of the family, but rather to counterbalance the overly positive position that is often put forward as part of political rhetoric and media representations.

Marriage is a concept closely associated with the family. At one time marriage was seen as central to the family, but this is a good example of how society changes over time. While marriage is undoubtedly still very important, it is clear that changes in society in recent years mean that it is not as important or central as it once was (Abercrombie, 2004).

state

'The state' is a shorthand term for the various 'arms' of government. This includes the following elements:

> *The legislature.* The legislature is the part of government that is responsible for developing and introducing laws.
> *The executive.* This is the part of government concerned with implementing and monitoring those laws. It is, in effect, a major part of day-to-day government of the country.
> *The judiciary.* This refers to the legal system, the courts and so on, which are an important part of government.
> *Central administration.* Central government is clearly a major part of the state.
> *Devolved administration.* In the UK, we now no longer simply have one overall national central government. With the introduction in the late 1990s of the Scottish Executive, the Welsh Assembly and the Northern Ireland Assembly, we have a tier of government in addition to the traditional central government.
> *Local administration.* Local government also has an important part to play as the local or regional part of the state.
> *The police and armed forces.* Government is based largely on democracy and consensus and is, to a large extent, geared towards maintaining peace and order. However, it has to be recognized that there are times when force needs to be used to maintain the rule of law.

In some ways, the state is the embodiment of social order. It is a means of ensuring that the collective good is promoted, and that some degree of protection is afforded to the state's citizens. However, we should not be naïve about this. While the state certainly does have a positive role to play, it is not entirely a positive situation. For example, inequalities in how the state is run are often in evidence. Newspaper reports over the years have also shown examples of corruption and the significance of vested interests in how the state is managed.

the media

The primary importance of the media is in terms of representation. How ideas are presented to the populace can be of major significance. The media are therefore very powerful in shaping people's sense of reality. Much of what we know about the world is brought to us through the media.

It is unfortunately the case that social work has, over the years, been poorly represented in the media. Representations of social work activities are often unduly negative and tend to focus on mistakes without presenting a balanced picture that sees relatively isolated mistakes as part of a much bigger context characterized by a great deal of success and high-quality practice. The treatment of social work in the media is differentiated between, first, children's and adult services (the press tend to be more negative about issues relating to children than they do about matters relating to adults) and national and local – that is, the national press tend to be more inclined to be negative towards social work than local press (Aldridge, 1994).

However, just as important, if not more so, is the issue of how social work's clientele is represented in the media. Here again it tends to be the case that they are poorly represented. Notions of scroungers, layabouts, undesirables, the undeserving poor and so on can often be perpetuated through the media. The media, then, play an important role in constructing what is regarded as a social problem, how such problems can best be tackled and who is responsible for them. Often the oversimplified representations of the media are at odds with social work's more in-depth understanding of the complexities. It is not surprising, then, that social work personnel are generally very wary of the media.

the law

The way the legal system operates is a significant part of society in general and social work in particular. In fact, it is such an important part of social work that it is addressed in some detail in both Chapters 1.1 and 2.5 of this book.

religion

It cannot be doubted that religion is a powerful influence on society, even in predominantly secular societies. For example, many people who would not regard themselves as Christians, none the less express a commitment to what they see as Christian values (that is, the values that they were brought up with), practise Christian rituals (in relation to weddings and funerals, for example) and celebrate Christian festivals (Christmas, Easter and so on).

Religion can shape our sense of reality, our social relationships, our values, aspirations and even our identity. Religions can bring people together in a shared endeavour but, of course, religions can also be the source of major conflicts. Religion is therefore highly significant sociologically in terms of how it affects wider macro issues of society as well as how it affects particular individuals – for example, in relation to their sense of identity. As Moss comments:

> Durkheim (1912) argued for the importance of religion as a cohesive influence upon a community, and stressed the significance of the 'sacred' as separate from the 'profane' of everyday life. Society needs the 'sacred' to be reminded of its core social values, and to provide a mechanism through its various rituals for social cohesion.   (Moss, 2005, p. 18)

In terms of social work practice, it is therefore vitally important to recognize that a failure to address religious issues can lead to very poor practice indeed. A neglect of religious issues can be the basis of considerable amounts of unwitting discrimination and, although such discrimination may be unintended, its negative effects can none the less be of major significance.

social processes

Society is made up of not only a set of social institutions, but also a number of processes that occur (and recur) over time. These processes make society a dynamic entity, constantly subject to change. This is because the social institutions described above (and indeed many other social institutions we do not have space to describe here) interweave with the various processes that operate. These complex interactions of processes and institutions are in many ways the life blood of society. When we add to this the dimension of social divisions – that is, a recognition that the institutions and processes do not operate on the basis of a level playing-field, but rather in a context of structured inequalities, then we begin to realize just how complex a set of issues we are dealing with when we are addressing the social context.

NOS Key Role 4

Manage risk to individuals, families, carers, groups, communities, self and colleagues

socialization

This is a notion closely associated with that of cultural transmission – that is, the idea that a culture is transmitted from one generation to the next through child-rearing practices. Socialization refers to the process through which each of us becomes a part of our society and our society becomes part of us. We learn how to become accepted within our society and, in doing so, we internalize the norms and values of that society. It is a means by which social order is established and maintained and, for the individual, it is an important source of security and identity.

Problems can arise in relation to socialization when the intended outcomes are not achieved – for example, where someone rejects their social upbringing in a way that is destructive, either towards that society or for the individual. An example of this would be someone who engages in anti-social behaviour because he or she feels alienated from the wider community and society and therefore has no qualms about behaving in a way that is contrary to the community's interests.

marginalization

This refers to the process of pushing certain groups or individuals to the margins of society, making them less a part of the mainstream. In effect, it is a form of social exclusion.

Marginalization can be overt as, for example, when people say such things as: 'people like that don't belong here' (perhaps referring to people who have previously been cared for in psychiatric institutions who are now being integrated into the community). However, marginalization can also be more implicit or subtle. For example, the term 'ethnic' is often used when it would be more appropriate to use the term ethnic minority (or minority ethnic). Someone may refer to members of an ethnic minority as 'ethnic' people but, of course, all people are ethnic, as the term 'ethnicity' refers to cultural background and identity. If we are not careful, the term ethnic becomes used as a shorthand term for 'not one of us'. Language can thus be used in a very subtle way to produce the effect of marginalization, of creating a situation where some people are made to feel that they do not belong in mainstream society.

Marginalization is often also accompanied by an element of stigmatization. That is, those people who are prone to marginalization are also likely to be stigmatized in some way. For example, they may be looked down upon as being 'lesser' people. There is also a parallel here with the process of 'alterity' which is discussed in more detail below.

medicalization

This refers to the tendency to regard psychological and social issues as if they were medical matters. It involves, for example, taking metaphors too literally. This could be where an individual who commits a crime is described as 'sick'. Similarly, dysfunctional organizations are often referred to as sick or unhealthy when, of course, it is not really a medical matter at all.

However, this is not simply a matter of splitting hairs about particular use of vocabulary. There is a very serious issue here in terms of how some matters become translated into medical concerns. This can apply in a number of ways, not least the following:

> *Mental distress.* Often problems relating to a person's mental state can be regarded as illnesses, even though this is a highly contentious area of social thought.
> *Alcohol and drug misuse.* Similarly, complex problems relating to matters of addiction are often oversimplified and reduced to medical matters (see Harris, 2005).
> *Trauma.* When an individual has experienced a traumatic psychological incident (being sexually assaulted, for example), the helping response is often couched in medical terms.
> *Behaviour problems.* Children who present behaviour problems are often diagnosed with a medical condition and prescribed medication.

Medicalization can be very problematic for various reasons, but not least because it tends to obscure more than it reveals – that is, in providing oversimplified explanations in medical terms of complex, psychosocial issues, it distracts attention from the psychological, social and political factors that are at work.

Medicalization is also 'pathologizing', in so far as it presents complex, multi-level problems as if they are something wrong within the individual – some sort of personal pathology. psychologism, see p. 69

---

practice focus

2.5

Gethin was visiting a project that had been set up as part of a wider initiative to address healthcare issues amongst young people. He knew that substance misuse was a widespread problem but had been taken aback by both the scale of the problem and the damage that individuals were inflicting upon themselves. Along with some of the young people, he had watched a film which highlighted the likely consequences of their habit and the potential for it to be fatal in some cases. Gethin was shocked by this film, but even more shocked to hear that it had not been particularly effective in dissuading people from substance misuse. He had a feeling that this could be accounted for by the existence of an 'addictive personality trait' which made some people more prone than others to engaging in risk-taking behaviour. He put his ideas to the project leader but, in doing so, he realized that he had given no thought to the social context in which these young people lived. On researching this further he found the same features cropping up time after time in individual case histories – poverty, exclusion from school, domestic tensions and so on. While he didn't discount his earlier thoughts altogether, he realized that to try to account for this behaviour at a purely psychological level was to ignore the social aspects which could be contributing to the situation in major ways.

discrimination

Discrimination involves treating people more or less positively according to perceived differences. It is a topic that will feature in Chapter 2.6 in our discussion of values and will also be discussed in Part 4. The workings of discrimination are particularly relevant to social work because a high proportion of social work's clientele is subject to being discriminated against.

values, see p. 127

alterity

This is a term associated with the work of the French existentialist writer, Simone de Beauvoir. It refers to the tendency to treat certain groups of people as 'other' and therefore as inferior. De Beauvoir uses the term to describe gender inequalities:

> The terms *masculine* and *feminine* are used symmetrically only as a matter of form. In actuality the relation of the two sexes is not quite like that of two electrical poles, for man represents both the positive and the neutral, as is indicated in the common use of *man* to designate human beings in general; whereas woman represents only the negative, defined by limiting criteria, without reciprocity.   (De Beauvoir, 1972, p. 15)

However, the term can also be applied to other groups who are defined in negative terms by reference to a more positively valued group. This includes people from ethnic minorities, disabled people, older people, people with mental health problems – interestingly, it encompasses most if not all of social work's clientele. In effect, alterity represents an 'us-them' mentality, with 'them' being seen as less worthy in one or more ways.

These are not the only social processes that can be seen to operate within society, but they should be sufficient to illustrate our central point that the social context of social work includes a number of such processes that can and do play an important part in shaping the problems we encounter and our response to them.

The theme that underpins the various processes described here is that of power. In effect, we could regard the various processes described here as examples of how power operates. This is a point that we shall return to below.

social problems

There is an important distinction to be drawn between social and personal problems, although the two often overlap. A social problem is something that has an effect on society overall, or at least on certain sectors of society and indeed the social order. Often what is defined as a social problem is a problem that may well have significant implications for particular individuals, but is seen as particularly significant because of its implications for society itself (where, for example, the persistence of that problem may present a threat to society). In this respect, a good example would be crime, where incidences of criminal behaviour can have major consequences for individual victims of crime. Crime goes beyond being a personal problem for those who experience it and becomes a potential threat to society and the social order. Excessive levels of crime could be seen to jeopardize the existence of society itself.

There is a close link between social problems and social policy (with social work being recognized as part of the broader discipline of social policy – see Chapter 2.5). This is because social policies can generally be linked with particular social problems – that is, the policies associated with the criminal justice system can be seen to have arisen in response to the problem of crime. If we did not have crime, we would not have a criminal justice system and the social policies associated with it.

Social problems bring into sharp relief the issue of care versus control. In order to care for people who experience problems, it is often necessary to engage in control issues in relation to people who are involved in social problems.

NOS Key Role 2

Plan, carry out, review and evaluate social work practice, with individuals, families, carers, groups, communities, and other professionals

For example, in order to care for people who have been or are being abused, issues of controlling the perpetrators of abuse arise. This is partly why issues of care and control are so central to social work, because social work is part of the overall process of a society trying to respond to what it perceives as social problems. This is another good example of why it is important for social workers to understand the social context in which they operate. Social work is not simply a matter of individual practitioners addressing individual problems with clients, but rather part of a much broader process of a society trying to deal with what it perceives as social problems.

Examples of the main social problems would include:

> *Poverty.* Being 'poor' is not simply a matter of a lack of money. The vast majority of people could claim to be poor if that were the case. Poverty involves having insufficient money to feel part of one's society and is therefore closely associated with the notion of social exclusion. A very important point to note about poverty is that it can underpin so many of the other social problems: crime, homelessness, alcohol abuse and so on. The relationship between poverty and other social problems is a very complex one, but it is none the less still a very strong interconnection.

> *Abuse.* Many people in our society are prone to abuse in some way. This may be child abuse, abuse of vulnerable adults (for example, people with learning disabilities) or domestic abuse (that is, violence in the home). It is sad to reflect that, in the twenty-first century, in a highly advanced industrialized society, we still have major problems with abuse.

> *Crime.* There is unfortunately a longstanding tendency to oversimplify crime and to see it basically as the result of people who are in some way evil or depraved committing immoral acts. The reality of crime is far more complex than this. For example, what counts as a crime varies from society to society and how crimes are dealt with varies not only across societies, but also through history. In dealing with crime, we are addressing a very complex set of issues that are closely interwoven with the nature of society itself.

> *Drug and alcohol misuse.* **Again**, these are very complex issues and not simply a matter of particular misguided individuals behaving inappropriately. The availability of drugs and alcohol, the way in which these are represented through the media, and so on, are all important factors in shaping the use and misuse of such substances.

> *Homelessness.* While there is a huge housing stock available to us, we continue to have problems with homelessness for a variety of reasons. Often the reasons are connected with other social problems, such as abuse or mental health difficulties.

> *Discrimination.* Forms of discrimination, such as racism, can be very significant problems for society.

It is important, in thinking of social problems, to recognize that social work is part of the wider social and governmental response to social problems. A well-informed social worker needs to have a good understanding of the nature of social problems and how these have an impact on the individual personal problems of the clients and carers that we encounter in our work.

NOS Key Role 6

Demonstrate professional competence in social work practice

culture, identity and meaning

We can see culture as being the basis of a shared perspective on the world and our place within it. Culture sensitizes us to some issues, but masks the significance of others. That is, being a member of a particular culture will throw some aspects of our lives into sharp relief, will highlight them and attach significance to them. For example, a culture steeped in a particular religious tradition is likely to place significant emphasis on aspects of religious rituals, and so on. However, in bringing attention to some issues, of course, a culture is distracting attention away from others. For example, patriarchal cultures may emphasize the importance of treating people fairly and with respect, but not draw attention to the fact that their treatment of women is inconsistent with this value.

Culture is also very relevant to identity, our sense of who we are. This can apply in a number of ways, not least the following:

> *Sense of roots and belonging or community.* Culture gives us a sense of who we belong to, who the people are that we are connected with in some way.

> *Shared values, morals and ways of seeing the world.* It is almost as if being a member of a culture is like being a member of a club and we are expected to follow the rules of that club to remain a member.

> *Rituals.* Every culture has a set of rites and ceremonies, some formal, some not so formal, which are part and parcel of the cultural heritage, the traditions that underpin that particular culture.

> *Interests.* Activities such as music, art and so on will be influenced to a large extent by our cultural upbringing and background.

Meaning making can be seen as a central part of human existence. By this we mean that, as we go about our business on a day-to-day basis, we are constantly trying to make sense of what befalls us. We are constantly trying to find a thread of meaning in our lives. Society does not make our meanings for us; it does not impose a particular way of making sense of the world. However, society in general and culture in particular play a part in shaping meanings by:

> *Providing the context.* Everything we do, everything we try to make sense of happens within a social context, and so it is not surprising that that social context will have a bearing on what happens to us and how we attach meaning to it.
> *Influencing our perceptions.* Society and culture reinforce certain aspects of the world and strengthen our perspective on certain things – for example, our sense of right and wrong, but they will also discourage or even punish other ways of perceiving the world. For example, in the days before we appreciated that the world is round, anyone who perceived the earth as being anything but flat would have encountered ridicule and other social means of discouraging such a perspective.
> *Opening some doors but closing others.* As we noted earlier, society plays a part in shaping our experiences of power and life chances.
> *Providing frameworks of meaning.* There are various ideologies or discourses that come as, in a sense, ready-made packages of meaning. Some of these are associated with particular cultures – for example, Muslim beliefs – but others are developed on a more localized basis.

The importance of meaning is reflected in a variety of theoretical perspectives on society – poststructuralist, postmodernist and existentialist, for example. While the traditional view of meaning and meaning making may be a predominantly individualistic one, a fuller understanding of the social context enables us to appreciate that meaning making is also a sociological phenomenon. This is extremely significant for social work practice, as we will often be helping people to make sense of very complex personal and social circumstances and trying to forge a positive way forward. We will struggle to do this without a good understanding of the social context and role of meaning making within it.

---

practice focus

2.6

Etta had been working with Ken for many months following his discharge from hospital. He had a long history of problems with balance and co-ordination and had been disappointed, but not surprised, finally to be diagnosed with a long-term condition that would put an end to his job as an engineer. The prospects of future employment seemed unlikely, and he was finding it difficult to adjust to staying at home all day. He became very demoralized and apathetic and his GP had begun treating him for depression. Etta was concerned that Ken's partner did not seem to appreciate his perspective and there was often tension between them. From his partners's point of view, the loss of Ken's job was not such a bad thing. He was able to spend more time with their children and this change of role allowed her to take on a full-time job in place of the few hours a day she had previously been restricted to. She tried to boost Ken's spirits by pointing out how good he was at being a full-time parent, but could not understand why he couldn't adapt to these changes. Etta explained to her that Ken had been brought up to see the world in a particular way – one in which it was his role as a man to provide for and protect his family. While some people might think that his worldview was old-fashioned and even oppressive, it was the one that held meaning for him, nevertheless. Now that this had been turned on its head, Ken was struggling to come to terms with what life means now that his reference points have been changed.

conclusion

For too long, social work was focused on individual issues and neglected the social context or, at least, did not appreciate the full significance of it. In recent years, we have learned to attach far more significance to the social context. This should not be interpreted as saying that the social context should be seen to replace an emphasis on the individual. Good practice needs to be premised on both. We need to develop an understanding of the specific circumstances as they affect each person we try to help, but we also need to recognize that the individual experiences of that person will owe much to the social context. Social work needs to be recognized as a psychosocial enterprise: not psychological *or* sociological, but rather *both*.

points to ponder

> How might the fact that society is 'not a level playing-field' affect your practice?
> How are 'social institutions' relevant to social work?
> What are the main differences between personal problems and social problems?
> How does culture influence a person's sense of identity?
> In what ways is meaning making a sociological concern?

2.3 human development

introduction

Human existence is, of course, not static. People are growing and changing all the time. It is very important for social workers to be aware of this and how it can be relevant to practice. We need to make sure that we do not fall into the trap of seeing people as fixed entities who 'are what they are', as this is far too simplistic an understanding of people. Because changes and developments take place slowly over time for the most part, it is very easy to make the mistake of assuming that change is not taking place. It is therefore important to understand the people we work with are growing, developing people, moving and changing over time. This takes us a long way from traditional notions of a person having a fixed personality or character.

In this chapter we will be concerned with the themes that underpin the developments that people go through in the course of their lives. We shall examine the life course – that is, the various stages that people go through from birth through childhood, adolescence, adulthood, and on to ultimate death. At each of these points in the life course there will be significant issues for us to consider. We shall also in this chapter examine what is known as 'existential challenges' – that is, the challenges that arise simply from the fact of existing, of being human beings. Linked to this is the important topic of life transitions and the loss and grief associated with them. Finally, we shall also consider important issues relating to the need for people to be protected from harm throughout their life course, but particularly at certain vulnerable moments.

Principle 5 Loss and Grief

Loss and grief are highly significant in relation to human development as loss is never far away at any stage of the life course.

the life course

Human development is a very complex subject. Part of the reason for its complexity is that it can be subdivided into various 'strands'. That is, development is not a simple linear process. It can be taking place at different levels at different times. These strands are primarily:

> *Biological.* As we grow and develop, there are significant biological changes that take place. While these are not solely responsible for changes in our life experience, they do play a significant part. We can subdivide biological development into two sections: first, there is what is known as normal development, and this relates to the range of changes that most, if not all, people will go through. In respect of this,

it is important to note what is generally referred to as 'the broad spectrum of the norm'. This is significant, because we wish to avoid having too narrow a perspective on what is considered normal. We shall return to this point below. The other aspect of biological development is where things do not go according to plan, as it were, where things go wrong. This can relate to illness and disability and other ways in which biological changes can lead to problems (for example, as a result of disfigurement).

> *Psychological.* As we grow and develop, we have to make sense of the world around us. This involves a number of psychological processes. These are partly cognitive, (that is, they relate to thinking processes and memory), partly emotional (that is, they relate to moods and feelings), and partly behavioural (that is, relating to our actual actions). All three dimensions of the psychological strand have important implications in terms of how we grow and develop and any problems we may encounter along the way.

> *Social.* Biological and psychological developments do not occur in a social vacuum. In keeping with Principle 1, we need to recognize that everything that happens to us happens in a social context. It is therefore important to understand human development as a social phenomenon, not simply a biological or psychological one. The influence of our culture and wider society can be of huge significance, as we noted in Chapter 2.2.

> *Moral.* The development of an understanding of right and wrong and other such moral or ethical issues is also a significant part of development. This is partly linked to social development in so far as our sense of morality owes much to our social upbringing, but there are also aspects of this development that are specific to the individual.

> *Ontological.* Ontology is the study of reality or being. It is concerned with questions relating to: What is the nature of reality? and What does it mean to exist? This is an aspect of human development that is often neglected and sometimes does not feature even in major textbooks. Ontological development, in some respects, pulls together other spans of development, in so far as it gives us a basis on which to develop our identity. Ontological development involves rising to the challenges of human existence, a point we shall explore in more detail below under the heading of 'Existential challenges'.

One matter that we must concern ourselves with is the importance of dealing with people according to their level of development. That is, if we recognize that people are indeed growing and developing all the time (note: *all the time*, not just in childhood), then this means that we have to be sensitive to the 'stage' of development a person is at. If we do not pay heed to this, then we can make one of two mistakes. We can either be patronizing and expect too little of somebody because we have not taken account of how advanced they are in their development, or conversely, we may be setting somebody up to fail by having too high a level of expectation in relation to that person's level of development. This is one of the main reasons why an understanding of human development is central to good practice in social work. We are not dealing with people who are simply fixed entities, we are dealing with people 'in transit' – that is, people who are moving from one part of their life to another, growing, developing and changing. Even though that movement may be very slow and gradual, it can still be highly significant.

This is something that can take a long time to develop in terms of the skills involved. None the less, it remains very important that social workers are able to have at least a basic understanding of where somebody is at in terms of their development. However, it also needs to be recognized that we have a good head start in this, in so far as relating to somebody according to their level of development is a basic social skill. For example, most people would be relatively skilled in terms of differentiating between how to communicate with, say, a 7-year-old compared with a 17-year-old, a 27-year old or a 77-year old. However, while we may have a good start in this direction, it is not enough on its own. This is partly because: first, not everyone develops such skills as part of their upbringing. It is not uncommon, for example, to encounter people who have great difficulty in communicating with people of a particular age group, whether this be young children or older adults. Second, an understanding of human development for professional social work practice needs to be at a more advanced level than that used in everyday social interactions. For example, in dealing with a case of neglect in relation to a child, it will be necessary to have a more detailed understanding of human development than simply that which is associated with the vast majority of adults in a society.

It is also important to recognize the significance of the strands of development in relation to what is known as 'uneven development'. What this refers to is the possibility that somebody can be (and indeed often is) at different levels of development in relation to the various strands. For example, there may be a child/young person who is biologically very well advanced, but who psychologically is at a much lower level of maturity. This can be significant in terms of such matters as sexual abuse where, for example, a 12- or 13-year-old girl may be physically mature enough for sexual intercourse, but where the law doubts that she will be of a sufficient psychological or even moral level of development to be able to engage in sexual activity without adverse consequences. Similarly, somebody may be well advanced in other areas of development but 'lag behind' biologically. It is both dangerous and discriminatory to assume that somebody whose biological development has been impaired in some way is therefore not mature in other ways.

Understanding human development in terms of the life course is not a new issue. It has a long history. However, that history is somewhat mixed. While there are clear benefits and advantages to understanding human development in terms of the 'stages' we go through from birth to death, there are also potential difficulties with this. The main difficulty is that it sets up a framework which, if we are not careful, can become rigid and stultifying. It can become oppressive if our expectations of people are too narrow and fixed.

Principle 5 Loss and Grief

We need to remember that death is part of life and therefore very important in relation to human development.

We need to understand the life course as being about broad parameters of development and not about specific developmental stages that can be defined in any great detail. (The term, 'stage' should not be interpreted as meaning a fixed, clearly defined period of time. Rather, we use it more loosely to refer to the flow of development over time.) To attach too much importance to the significance of life course development can lead to certain people being defined as abnormal or deviant, with all the stigma and marginalization that can go with this. It therefore has to be borne in mind that, when we are talking about the life course and so-called 'normal' development, we are dealing with, as we called it earlier, the broad spectrum of the norm. What counts as normal should be seen as primarily a statistical matter, rather than one of value. That is, the fact that somebody's development is outside of a statistical norm does not necessarily mean that it should be seen as a problem or a deficit of some kind. Such unhelpful assumptions have in the past been a major factor in the development of disability discrimination. We also have to be aware that what is defined as the norm is not entirely objective or value free. For example, traditional approaches to life course development can be criticized for having a class bias, being based primarily on what is seen as middle-class norms.

Principle 1 **Social Context**

For a discussion of the significance of class in relation to the life course, see Hunt (2005).

As part of his care management role, Wil had developed a good overview of the facilities that were available to support vulnerable adults in his locality. Knowing that it was difficult to find nursing homes in the area that could accommodate older couples, he took every opportunity to explore the issues with managers, in the hope that such provision could be promoted in the light of there being a demand for it. When he raised the issue of older people in same-sex relationships, he noticed that people often showed signs of being uncomfortable with the subject. At first, Wil thought this strange in a society in which gay rights are beginning to be taken more seriously than before and where strenuous efforts have been made to move away from a situation in which heterosexual relationships are seen as the only valid or acceptable ones. On giving this further thought he began to see that these responses fitted a pattern in which the many different aspects of an individual's identity tended to be hidden or denied once defined as 'old'. As Wil saw it, nearing the end of the life course often did involve changes, but much stayed the same, including a person's sexuality and the need for love and comfort.

practice focus

2.7

It is therefore very important that we are aware of the dangers of oversimplification that come with the notion of life course development. These can be seen to apply primarily, but not exclusively, in relation to the following areas:

> *Gender.* Traditional approaches to life course development have often adopted an uncritical approach to gender expectations. Feminist critiques of life course development have pointed out that the way in which boys and girls are socialized is very significant in terms of creating gender inequalities in later life. Issues of gender identity development are extremely complex and must be recognized as such if we are not to fall into the trap of unwittingly promoting gender stereotypes.

> *Race.* This is a subject surrounded in considerable controversy, not least because of the efforts of some people to argue that black people are of an inferior level of ability to white people – for example, in relation to intelligence and educational capability (Hernstein and Murray, 1994 – see also Fischer et al., 1996 for a critique of this view). As with gender, we need to recognize that issues of development relating to

race and ethnicity are very complex, and any tendency to oversimplify could result in unwitting racial discrimination.

> *Disability.* Traditional approaches to life course development have also been criticized for failing to recognize the significance of disability. If too much emphasis is placed on so-called 'able-bodied' norms, then there is a danger that disability is automatically defined as a problem. Although the term 'differently abled' has never really caught on, it can be seen as significant in this context. If we are too rigid in defining what is normality without taking account of different forms of normality, depending on whether one has a physical impairment or not, then we run the risk of reinforcing negative images of people with disabilities.

> *Sexual identity.* An overemphasis on biological aspects of development can lead us into the assumption that heterosexual relationships are the norm in more than a statistical sense – that is, that they are 'natural' and 'acceptable' and therefore, by implication, that same-sex relationships are unnatural or problematic. We therefore have to be very careful not to fall into the trap of discrimination by assuming that one form of sexual identity is inferior to another.

> *Determinism.* This refers to the tendency to assume that we have little or no control over our behaviour. Some people have interpreted traditional approaches to life course development as indicating how certain behaviour or attitudes are 'caused', as if the individual concerned has no control over these matters. This is a gross oversimplification of a very complex set of issues.

> *Family life course.* While it is fair to say that individuals can be seen to develop through stages of the life course, we also have to recognize that this applies to groups of people, particularly families. For example, when a family is first formed, there may be an adequate amount of disposable income. This may subsequently change on the birth of one or more children. Some years later, the position of having a certain amount of disposable income may return once those children have left home. This shows that it is not simply a matter of individual life courses, but also there is a need to consider how a life course perspective can apply at broader levels. Indeed, we can also look at how there is a social life course in the sense that society develops what is acceptable now, what in some respects may not have been acceptable 20 years ago and vice versa.

Principle 3 **Critical Analysis**

The life course, then, while an important concept, is not one to be used simplistically or uncritically.

Having introduced the important concept of the life course, we shall now move on to explore some of the key stages of that life course, beginning with child development.

child development

It has long been recognized that children are not just small adults, junior versions of full-grown adult members of society. Children are qualitatively different from adults in a number of ways. This is not just a matter of biological development but, as noted earlier, development according to a number of strands: psychological, social, moral and ontological. Children, then, are distinctly different from adults in a number of ways, although we have to recognize that this is at least, in part, due to societal expectations.

That is, it is not simply a matter of biology that makes children in our society stand out from adults. Much of the distinction that we can make between adult and child owes a lot to how our society and the various cultures within it have constructed notions of what is appropriate for a child, as opposed to what is appropriate for an adult.

Manage risk to individuals, families, carers, groups, communities, self and colleagues

One of the implications of recognizing that children are not just small adults is that, if we are to work effectively with children, we need to have some understanding of at least the basics of child development, of the key issues that influence children's understanding of the world, their reaction to it and their consequent behaviour.

One example of the importance of having an understanding of how a child understands or perceives the world is what is known as 'magical thinking'. This refers to the tendency of children to attribute certain things to magic. For example, if the parent of a child dies, that child may feel that the death occurred because he or she was 'naughty'. What would appear to be happening here is that the sense of guilt and regret associated with grieving is translated into a sense of direct guilt and responsibility, as if the child is trying to explain what has happened in terms of his or her own behaviour. A further example of magical thinking would be where a child assumes that, if he or she wants something sufficiently strongly, it will happen (a favoured birthday present, for example).

Principle 5 **Loss and Grief**

Grieving is a very complex matter and so ill-informed attempts to respond to someone's loss can be very harmful and counterproductive.

A very significant point to note in relation to child development is that children learn all the time, that they are at a stage in their life where they do not have the wealth of experience that adults have to draw upon. There is less scope for them to become complacent about their understanding of the world, because so much of it is new and unfamiliar. This has major implications for both parenting and social work because, if we take seriously the notion that children learn all the time, then we have to be very careful what we teach them – that is, we may unwittingly be teaching children to behave in ways that we would not want them to. For example, if we respond to attention-seeking behaviour, then we may well be teaching the child that attention-seeking behaviour is an effective means of achieving one's goals. This shows the implications of socialization, the process by which a child becomes part of their society by internalizing norms, values and expectations associated with that particular culture. In effect, what this means is that children are very susceptible to influence, and a significant part of social work practice with children and their families may involve trying to help children to unlearn problematic forms of behaviour or attitudes and to replace these with less problematic approaches – less problematic for themselves, for their parents, their wider family and, indeed, for society.

There have been many traditional influences on theory in this area. It is far beyond the scope of this book to address these in any detail, but it will be possible to give a brief overview:

> *Sigmund Freud.* Recognized as the founder of psychoanalysis, Freud's work has proven very influential in relation to child development, although his influence is increasingly on the wane.

> *Erik Erikson.* Often referred to as a neo-Freudian, Erikson developed some of Freud's basic ideas, but introduced his own concepts in order to take forward this thinking. He, too, has been a major influence on thinking in this field.

> *John Bowlby.* Also influenced by psychoanalysis, Bowlby's particular contribution was that of attachment theory – based on the idea that young children normally form emotional 'attachments' to their primary carer, but in some cases, this does not occur, resulting in significant problems for the child concerned as he or she grows up.

> *Jean Piaget.* Moving away from psychoanalytical ideas, Piaget's main interest was in cognitive development – that is, how children move through a set of stages which enable them to develop their thinking powers. His theories partly explain how children's perceptions of the world can be so significantly different from those of adults.

> *Symbolic interactionism.* A key part of this theory is the notion that we have what is referred to as a looking-glass self. What this means is that how we perceive ourselves is as if we were looking into the mirror of society – that is, we base our understanding of ourselves on how other people react to us, as if our sense of self is a mirror image of how other people treat us.

These are some of the main traditional theoretical bases of child development. However, we are increasingly seeing work develop from, for example, feminist and postmodernist perspectives that are highly critical of these traditional approaches.

One very important issue to emphasize in relation to child development is, as Principle 5 helps us realize, the significance of loss and grief. Indeed, this will be a theme of all stages of the life course because, as we grow and change, we experience loss, and so the potential for a grief reaction is always present. Unfortunately, this is an aspect of human development that has tended to be neglected. There are many cases on record of practitioners who have failed to recognize the significance of loss and grief in a child's life and have therefore provided a less than adequate service.

practice focus

2.8

In her role within the women's refuge, Pat was used to seeing women and children in a distressed state, and she often stepped in to help when mothers found it difficult to offer their children the attention they would normally give under less stressful circumstances. On the other hand, it was not uncommon for some mothers to cling more closely to their children in these situations of turmoil and change. However, on this particular occasion, Pat noticed that Emma, the young mother of a 4-year-old child, was constantly hugging him while crying inconsolably and telling him about her unhappy relationship with his father. Pat noticed that, when the child tried to move from her lap, she accused him of not loving her either and cried even more. Pat could see that the boy was upset by his mother's crying and guessed that he probably thought she was cross with him for some reason. She asked one of the other workers to console and distract him so that she could discuss matters with Emma. She hoped to make Emma understand that she was expecting too much of her son, given the typical emotional and intellectual maturity of a child of his age.

adolescence

Adolescence is basically the transition from childhood to adulthood. Literally the term 'adolescent' means 'becoming adult'. While we can see all stages in the life course as being transitional in some respect (that is, they bridge the gap between the previous and the forthcoming stages), adolescence is a particularly important transition because it entails developing a significantly different outlook on life, moving from the perspective of a child to that of an adult with all the responsibility that this entails. It can be a stressful and demanding time, but it does not have to be. Indeed, we should beware of the stereotype that all adolescents go through a period of 'storm and stress', as if adolescence is necessarily a time of strain. Similarly, we should not fall into the trap of adopting a stereotype of the adolescent as being rebellious. While there are indeed many examples of rebellious behaviour by adolescents, there are also a significant proportion of adolescents who do not engage in anything approaching rebellious behaviour (and many people who do engage in rebellious behaviour who are not adolescent). In fact, we can see that the majority of adolescents are highly conformist when we look at the situation without the distorting lens of a stereotype.

NOS Key Role 1

Prepare for, and work with, individuals, families, carers, groups and communities to assess their needs and circumstances

As mentioned earlier in relation to child development, loss and grief can be significant. Given that this is a period of such intense transition, it is not surprising that it will involve letting go of many treasured aspects of identity – the child's identity, that is – and so there can be significant grief reactions, although, again, these may not be recognized even by experienced practitioners, given the longstanding tendency to neglect the significance of loss and grief in the life course.

The question of uneven development also applies here. It is highly unlikely that individuals will proceed through adolescence at an even rate across the five different strands of development. Some strands will therefore progress more rapidly than others. It could be very misleading in a practice situation to assume, for example, that an adolescent who is socially well developed is equally well developed emotionally.

A key part of social work with adolescents is achieving the balance between addressing the adult while recognizing the child. To treat an adolescent simply as one would treat an adult could miss key issues, but similarly treating an adolescent as a child could lead to all sorts of barriers being erected that would stand in the way of progress and effective practice.

adulthood

This covers an extensive part of the human life course, and so it is necessary to break it up into smaller units. These can be described as early adulthood, mid-adulthood and late adulthood, although it has to be recognized that these are very broad categories.

early adulthood

This is a time when the challenges of adolescence continue up to a point. It is a period of life where the person concerned is trying to find a place in the adult world, trying to establish him- or herself in a position of relative independence. As in so many other aspects of social work, here the influence of the social context is significant. For example, consider how issues relating to young adults leaving home have changed in recent years: due in no small part to significant rises in house prices, young adults are now leaving the family home at a later age than was previously the case. Early adulthood can be a time of significant challenge in terms of meeting adult expectations. While parents may still play a significant supporting role for many young adults, their influence is not as direct in the majority of cases.

Principle 1 Social Context

Individual development needs to be understood in the context of the wider social sphere.

Another major challenge of this life period is avoiding the straightjacketing effect that social expectations can impose – for example, in relation to gender expectations or sexual identity. From a social work point of view, there may be significant matters arising here when young adults become parents after perhaps having experienced problems in terms of how they were parented. The demands of parenthood can be of major significance for everyone concerned, but for those people who do not have a history of receiving good parenting themselves, the pressures involved can be significantly higher and may lead to problems. This can be especially the case when such factors are exacerbated by wider social issues, such as poverty and deprivation or racism.

This is again a time of life associated with loss and grief. While for many people this may be a positive part of life, establishing themselves in relative independence, perhaps starting a family of their own and so on, it still involves letting go of earlier parts of life and this in itself can be a painful and difficult process with a grief reaction involved.

mid-adulthood

It is difficult, and not particularly helpful, to try and pin down a particular age at which a person moves from early adulthood to mid-adulthood, but these categorizations are, after all, only very broad.

Mid-adulthood is generally associated with a period of stability where, by this point, issues to do with family and career are, for many people, already well established and settled, although it would be an oversimplification to assume that this is the case for everybody. However, where a degree of settling has not occurred, this can be a source of problems for some people who feel under pressure from society to have established a particular way of life by this stage in their life.

A sense of loss can be associated with mid-adulthood, possibly in relation to family in so far as the leaving of home by grown-up children can bring about a sense of grief. But also, for many, they can feel that their career has not reached the level they would have wanted by now, and they therefore feel a sense of failure in terms of a loss of their earlier aspirations.

Principle 5 Loss and Grief

It is important to realize that a grief reaction can arise in relation to any significant loss and not simply when someone has died.

The point was made earlier that we have to be wary of allowing an oversimplified approach to the life course to influence our practice. This is particularly the case in relation to mid-adulthood. This is often seen as a stage of life where people settle into a stable family and career pattern. However, this can be problematic in a number of ways. First, there will be significant numbers of people for whom this is not the case, because they may have aspired to this degree of stability but have yet to achieve it. Second, there will be a significant proportion of people who do not wish to aspire to this sense of stability, because they do not identify with the ideological norm of the family and career. For example, a gay man or a lesbian may have deliberately chosen not to start a family, and other people, regardless of their gender or sexual orientation, may not have wished to engage with traditional notions of career. They may have other aspirations in their lives. Third, there may be people who, for example, due to disability, are not able and perhaps not interested in achieving the conventional aspiration of a settled family life and career.

For women, there can be major changes at this stage of life due to the menopause and the biological changes associated with it. However, once again we need to recognize the five strands of development and not reduce these simply to a matter of biology. Menopausal changes may, none the less, have implications for the person concerned and her family and other associates in terms of psychological, social, moral and ontological development.

The notion of a male menopause is one that has received a lot of media attention, although it is dangerous to assume, without the backing of an appropriate body of research, that such a transition actually occurs. None the less, it is important to recognize that men will also go through significant changes as they move from mid-adulthood to later adulthood, although how these changes are experienced will vary from individual to individual, according to a wide variety of factors.

later life

Growing old is, of course, part of life, but it is unfortunately the case that we live and work in a society that fails to accept this in many ways. This is evidenced by the very negative attitude that is commonly displayed towards older people, and a wide range of ageist stereotypes that are to be found. The challenges of later life can be very significant partly due to physical changes, but often, more significantly, due to the social changes associated with this as a result of (a) retirement and related matters; and (b) the entrenched ageism shown towards older people which can have a very detrimental effect on confidence and self-esteem.

Later adulthood is also a time of loss. Older people can lose friends, connections, abilities and other things that are important to them. However, it is unfortunately the case that the significance of loss and grief in old age is played down, dismissed by the ageist stereotype that older people are used to loss because, by this stage in life, they have experienced so much of it. The reality, however, ageist stereotypes aside, is that loss can be cumulative in old age, resulting in profoundly negative experiences for many older people whose grief is neither recognized nor addressed.

practice focus

2.9

death and dying

It cannot be denied that death is part of the life course. However, we are discussing death and dying in a separate section from that relating to later adulthood for two reasons. First, this is because we want to emphasize the point that later adulthood is a time of living, not dying. The notion that old age is a time of death is extremely misleading. For example, the assumption that a person who is 75 years of age is near to death, simply because of their age does not take account of the fact that that person may well live for a further 20 years or more. Second, it is misleading to associate death with old age too closely, because death can occur at any stage in the life course. Death, then, is not simply something that comes neatly at the end of the movement from childhood to adolescence to early adulthood to mid-adulthood to later adulthood. It is an aspect of all stages of the life course, in the sense that, at no point in the life course are we free from the threat of death.

Principle 5 **Loss and Grief**

> *It is important that we do not see death and dying as 'morbid' and therefore subjects to be avoided. They are important aspects of human development.*

For this reason, it is important to consider death and dying as overall themes of the life course, rather than simply a stage within it. What makes this difficult is the tendency inherent in society to avoid the notion of death. There has been much debate about whether Western societies are 'death denying', but what is clear is that the significance of death is often not addressed.

When someone dies, we often use the term 'bereavement'. Literally, bereavement refers to being 'robbed' which makes it a very apt term. While bereavement is the term used to refer to the loss brought about by death, grief is the term that refers to the psychological response to that loss. It can be subdivided into thoughts, feelings and actions. That is, when we are grieving, our patterns of thinking will be affected (for example, we may find it difficult to concentrate or to remember). Our feelings will clearly also be affected, and there is a wide range of emotional responses associated with grief (sadness, depression, anger, even elation at times). Our behaviour or actions will also be strongly influenced by grief, and it is for this reason that we may have to monitor somebody who is experiencing grief quite closely if there is any evidence to suggest that this is placing them at risk (for example, somebody who is becoming very forgetful as a result of the immense grief associated with cumulative losses).

Mourning is a term that is often used interchangeably with grief, but it can also be usefully seen as a term that refers to the social dimension of bereavement and grief. It is therefore used to refer to such matters as rituals associated with funerals and patterns of grieving. For example, the closing of curtains after a person's death is a ritual now becoming less common in practice, while other rituals are developing (for example, the placing of flowers at the roadside where a death has occurred as a result of a road traffic accident is a relatively new phenomenon in the UK).

understanding grief

Grief is commonly understood in terms of a set of stages. Indeed, this is the dominant view of how grief operates and is closely associated with the work of Kübler-Ross (1969). However, this approach has been heavily criticized in recent years, despite its dominance. There are theories now which strongly suggest that there is little or no evidence to support the notion that we grieve in stages. One alternative theory is that of dual process. This is associated with the work of Stroebe and Schut, two academics based in the Netherlands (Stroebe and Schut, 1999). They argue that we do not move from one stage to another, but rather, that what is happening when a person is grieving is that he or she is experiencing two orientations: a *loss* orientation (one in which the grieving person focuses on what has been lost and experiences a strong emotional reaction) and *restoration* orientation, where the person concerned is trying to rebuild their life after the drastic rupture that the loss has brought about. Stroebe and Schut argue that, as we grieve, we oscillate (that is, jump backwards and forwards) between these two orientations. Over time, they argue, the restoration orientation will come to predominate, but this will take time and we will never entirely get over the loss, as is evidenced by the fact that an anniversary of somebody's death or of their birthday, for example, may result in a swing back to the intense emotion of loss orientation, even many years after the person has died.

Another approach to understanding grief which challenges the traditional stages approach is that of meaning reconstruction theory associated with the work of American scholar, Robert Neimeyer and his colleagues (Neimeyer, 2001; Neimeyer and Anderson, 2002). The basic idea behind this approach is that, when we experience a major loss – for example, through the death of a loved one – we lose what that person meant to us. Grieving can then be understood as a process of reconstructing the meaning of our life without that person in the role they previously occupied.

What these theories tell us is that grief is a much more complex phenomenon than traditional approaches have led us to believe. In dealing with people who are dying or grieving, it is therefore very important that we develop a more sophisticated understanding of grief than the traditional theory provides for us (see the 'Suggestions for further reading' at the end of Part 2).

NOS Key Role 2

Plan, carry out, review and evaluate social work practice, with individuals, families, carers, groups, communities, and other professionals

understanding dying

The point was made earlier that old age is a time of living, not dying. The same argument can be put forward in relation to a dying person; that is, the dying person is a living person (Saunders, 2002). Dealing with people who are dying generally goes under the heading of 'palliative care'. Palliative refers to offering of comfort in so far as it is recognized that curative care cannot be offered. This is an approach that is strongly associated with the hospice movement, although it would be both naïve and inaccurate to assume that only hospice workers will encounter dying and the need for palliative care. However, the philosophy of hospice is one that offers us considerable benefits in terms of understanding the complexities of palliative care. Hospice literally means the provision of help offered to someone on a journey and is linked to the word 'hospitality'. Its aim is to make the final days, weeks or months of a dying person as comfortable and positive as possible. A major aspect of this philosophy is recognizing the importance of responding to the dying person's needs in relation to:

> *Physical needs.* For example the importance of pain relief, where appropriate.
> *Psychological needs.* Facing up to death is a mentally demanding matter, and people may need support in dealing with this.
> *Emotional needs.* It should not need emphasizing that a time of dying is a highly emotional time, with significant implications for the support that may be needed.
> *Social needs.* Dying people do not lose the need for social contact or to be connected to their wider world. It is a significant mistake to assume that a dying person needs to somehow 'disconnect'.
> *Spiritual needs.* This may refer to religious needs in particular, but may also be used more broadly to refer to systems of belief and meaning making, something that applies to all of us, whether we are religious or not.

A very important point to recognize in relation to working with dying people is the need to care for the caregivers. While clearly the primary focus is on the dying person, we should not neglect the needs of those who are closely associated with them and who may be providing care and support for them. We should also remember to include ourselves in this. Working with dying people is very demanding work and we should not underestimate the need for support in this.

Principle 7 Self-management

In dealing with the challenges of death and dying we should not be afraid to ask for support when we need it. This is an important part of self-care.

An existential challenge can be defined as a basic challenge of human existence. That is, a challenge that arises simply due to the fact that we are alive. Examples of existential challenges would include:

> *Maintaining identity.* Throughout our lives there may be challenges to our self-perception and our self-esteem. Other people may want to see us in ways that we do not want to see ourselves. Maintaining a coherent thread of identity is therefore something that we cannot take for granted. It is a task that needs to be achieved, rather than something that can be taken as given.

> *Realism.* As we have noted in relation to Principle 6, the term realism is used in different senses in different contexts, but here what we mean is the balance between optimism and pessimism (or between naïvety and defeatism). As we go through our lives, there will be positives and negatives, and we need to keep both in perspective. If we focus only on the positives, we leave ourselves open to all sorts of problems associated with the negative aspects of human existence. If, by contrast, we focus entirely or predominantly on the negatives then we do ourselves a disservice by failing to appreciate the positives and the strengths that are available to us.

> *Change, transition and loss.* As we have emphasized, the life course is a time that is characterized at each stage by change, transition and loss. How we deal with these, positively or negatively, will be a significant factor in how our life develops.

An important point to recognize in relation to existential challenges is that difficulties in handling earlier challenges can leave us less well equipped to deal with later ones. There can be a cumulative effect on confidence and self-esteem. For example, some people may learn to see themselves as 'losers' or ' no hopers', and may therefore give up before they have even tried when certain challenges arise.

A key factor in terms of social work practice here is the importance of empowerment, helping people to gain greater control over their lives. What we need to do is to avoid its opposite, that of disempowerment, which involves reinforcing somebody's sense that they are not good at coping because they have struggled with earlier existential challenges in their life. An example of disempowerment by professionals in this regard is the use of the term 'acopia'. This is a term that has been invented by mental health professionals to refer to people who, because of struggles with earlier existential challenges, find many of their current challenges very difficult to cope with. They have a low level of coping ability – hence the tongue-in-cheek term 'acopia', making it sound as though this is a Latinized diagnosis, when in fact it is just a judgemental term that fails to recognize the significance of earlier life experiences on how we feel in terms of current existential challenges.

In tackling existential challenges there can also be the potential problem of the return of magical thinking. This is a concept referred to earlier in relation to child development where children unrealistically associate events with their own thinking. Where people are struggling to cope with one or more existentialist challenges, magical thinking can be drawn upon to account for this, as is evidenced by comments such as 'I am being punished', 'I am jinxed' or 'Someone has got it in for me'.

This section of the book has placed great emphasis on the significance of loss and grief. It is important to emphasize that loss should not be seen as only death related. Any change, even a positive one, could involve loss and therefore a grief reaction. Every time we face a transition in life, major or minor, we face a potential loss.

This is closely related to the notion of crisis, a term that is often misused in social work. Crisis is not simply an emergency (although a crisis can be an emergency in some circumstances):

> A crisis is a turning point in someone's life, a situation where existing coping methods are no longer adequate and new ways of coping have to be found. This is often mistakenly equated with an emergency – that is, a situation that has to be dealt with urgently. The truth of the matter is that crisis and emergency often overlap but they often do not. Consider the following examples:
>
> 1. A 15-year-old girl finds that she is pregnant and her parents throw her out of the house, saying that they are disowning her.
> 2. A single mother with two young children arrives in a social services office late on a Friday afternoon because her benefits giro has not arrived and the Social Security Office is closed. The matter is easily resolved by a loan from an emergency fund that the duty social worker has access to. The mother copes quite calmly with the whole situation, confident that the Department would not let her children go without food over the weekend.
> 3. A 16-year-old boy who has spent the past three years in residential care moves into an outreach facility as part of a plan that had been agreed more than a year previously.
>
> In the first case we are encountering a situation that is both a crisis and an emergency. That is, it is a turning point in the young girl's life, but it is also a situation that has to be dealt with urgently. The second case scenario represents an 'emergency' in so far as it needs an urgent response – the situation cannot safely be left, but it is not actually a crisis in so far as it does not represent a turning point ... The third scenario, by contrast, describes a turning point and therefore a crisis situation, but it is not an emergency – it does not require an urgent response.
>
> (Neil Thompson, 2002a, p. 21)

The significance of loss and grief was discussed earlier in terms of different theories of grieving. It is therefore important to bear these issues in mind, not only in relation to when somebody is dying or has died, but more broadly in relation to any matter involving change and transition. An important concept here is that of 'cathexis'. This is a term used in psychoanalytical thinking to refer to an emotional investment. The idea behind it is that, when we form a relationship or an attachment (to a person or thing), we invest emotional energy in that relationship. When we experience the loss of that relationship, then we lose the emotional energy invested in it.

Grief can manifest itself in a number of ways, often hidden:

> *Destructive behaviour (including self-destructive behaviour).* This can appear as a 'Couldn't care less' attitude. Sometimes people get to the point where they are so punch drunk from grief that they feel that little else matters. A person's destructive behaviour may therefore be closely linked with considerable experience of grief.
> *Depression/withdrawal.* Although it is important not to confuse grief itself with depression (Schneider, 2000), it is important to note that depression can be

associated with grief. When we encounter somebody who is depressed, we should be asking ourselves as part of our assessment: are there any grief issues here that we need to take into account?

> *Physical symptoms.* Although grief is clearly not an illness, its powerful emotional impact can have a detrimental effect on our bodily systems and can lead to headaches, stomach pains and the exacerbation of existing illnesses – this is, in effect, a stress reaction.
> *Memory or thinking problems.* Grief can be very destructive to our cognitive processes, leaving us feeling much more confused than would otherwise be the case.
> *Confidence.* A person who is grieving may experience a significant drop in levels of confidence, and this can be very significant in many aspects of social work practice.

Clearly, it is very important for us to be sensitive to grief issues, and not just those that are death related. It is very ironic that many people can be very sensitive and supportive in relation to death-related losses, but actually quite callous and insensitive in relation to other forms of loss (which are much more common and can be just as devastating if not more so). This is not to suggest that people will be deliberately unfeeling towards non-death-related losses, but simply that they may not appreciate the significance of loss in matters that do not involve death.

One final point to note in relation to transitions, loss and grief is that grief, although very painful and sometimes very destructive, can also be a significant point of growth:

> Personal transformation can be the result of and the cause of joy and grief. Transformative potential is created when we can reassess what we have lost and discover an internal richness never appreciated before. (Schneider, 1994, p. 14)

protection from harm

Just as death and dying, transition, loss and grief are aspects of human existence that apply throughout the life course, protection from harm is also a major feature of human development in so far as social work practice often involves trying to ensure that people are safe from particular forms of harm. Of course, vulnerability is part of human existence. Everyone needs protection from harm at some point in their life, for example – that is why, among other reasons, we have a police force. However, while vulnerability is something that applies to everybody, it would be naïve not to recognize that some people are more vulnerable than others because of their circumstances. This includes:

> *Children.* For a variety of reasons associated with child development, children can be seen to be vulnerable to harm, partly because they are so impressionable and open to influence, and partly because they are relatively defenceless when it comes to the potential for abuse on the part of ruthless perpetrators of such abuse.
> *Physical disabilities and chronic illness.* There may be aspects of people's lives connected with illness or disability that may make them more vulnerable to harm. For example, it is sadly the case that many people with disabilities have been subjected to abuse and exploitation.

> *Learning disabilities.* Intellectual impairments can increase significantly the dangers of abuse and exploitation that people with learning disabilities face.
> *Mental health problems.* The nature of many mental health problems can leave people vulnerable to harm and exploitation at the hands of other people.
> *Old age.* For a variety of reasons, older people can find themselves subject to abuse. At one time, the idea of older people being abused (for example, by family members or other carers) was seen as an absurd notion, but sadly, we now know that such problems are far more widespread than was once thought.

There are formal protection procedures in relation to many groups of people (for example, child protection procedures or protection of vulnerable adult procedures), but such procedures present no guarantees. Somebody may be receiving very close monitoring and extensive support because of the risk of harm, but still experience abuse or some other form of harm. What is needed is a balance between complacency and overreaction.

NOS Key Role 4

Manage risk to individuals, families, carers, groups, communities, self and colleagues

What we mean by this is that it is important to recognize the potential for abuse and harm to take place (we should not allow ourselves to assume that this is a very rare occurrence when we now know that it is quite extensive). On the other hand, we have to be careful not to panic and overreact, as such an overreaction can cause as much harm as the actual abuse if not more so.

What makes such work difficult is that, while there may well be certain signs and indicators that can alert us to the possibility of abuse, these are not always present or visible. Responding to actual or potential abuse is as much an art as a science and we should not delude ourselves (whatever the media may think) into thinking that there are cast-iron guarantees in terms of protecting vulnerable people from harm. More realistically, we have to recognize that this is going to be an ongoing feature of our work.

conclusion

What we have tried to emphasize here is the importance of being aware of the significance of human development. It is not just an interesting background topic; it is something that is crucial for good practice – something that is central to undertaking professional social work at a high level of competence. We have also seen that there are significant dangers of oversimplifying and 'straightjacketing' – that is, playing a part in reinforcing the strong tendency in society to expect people to fit in with unfair and often oppressive expectations. An understanding of human development is not about trying to make people fit into some sort of stereotypical assumption of what is normal, but rather to recognize that there are significant patterns that underpin human growth and development and, indeed, the attitudes and behaviours associated with them. We need to understand the individual in the context of human development, but we need to focus on the person and social context. Human development is not just about the psychology of the individual. It includes much wider factors relating to social, political and, indeed, philosophical concerns.

> Why is it important to recognize that individuals are constantly developing and changing?
> What role do 'existential challenges' play in the lives of social work clients?
> In what ways are loss and grief significant in relation to human development?
> What is meant by the term 'transformational grief'?
> In what circumstances does social work involve protecting people from harm?

2.4 **the organizational context**

introduction

Social workers work in and through organizations – that is, while we have a degree of relative autonomy, we are, to a large extent, constrained by the organizations that employ us. It is important to have an understanding of how organizations can affect practice because:

1 organizations can undermine good practice, as we shall see below; and

2 organizations can harm staff, in the sense of causing stress or distress, undermining confidence, damaging career prospects, and so on.

It is therefore important to recognize that we need to understand at least the basics of organizational dynamics, how to survive them and how to influence them.

NOS Key Role 5

Manage and be accountable, with supervision and support, for your own social work practice within your organization

Working within organizations involves a set of skills. Neil Thompson (2003a) makes reference to the concept of 'organizational operator', by which he means someone who is skilled in influencing organizations in a positive direction, someone who has a good understanding of how organizations work and is able to draw on that knowledge in a positive way.

In this chapter, we shall examine the significance of organizational culture, structure, policies and procedures, communication, power and conflict, local management issues and supervision. Each of these has a significant bearing on organizational life, and so it is important that we begin to address these issues so that we are better equipped to work effectively in an organizational context.

organizational culture

The notion of culture is a very complex one, but a good basic starting point for us is to define a culture as 'shared ways of seeing, thinking and doing'. Culture involves 'shared meanings', commonalities in how we perceive and interpret events. Members of the same culture will tend to share a perspective on particular issues. They will have much in common in terms of how they make sense of that particular event or phenomenon. In this regard, a culture can be seen to comprise a set of what sociologists call scripts and rituals. A simple example of a script would be saying 'thank you' when receiving something from someone, although scripts can also be quite complex at times – for example, the standardized forms of language that are used in formal settings and processes, such as the courts. Rituals go beyond standardized patterns of language to incorporate standardized patterns of behaviour. Rituals can be formal or informal. A wedding ceremony would be a formal ritual, but we also have informal rituals, such as the tendency for people to buy somebody a drink on their birthday (or for him or her to buy others a drink – this varies from culture to culture). Scripts and rituals are important parts of societal cultures, but they can also be seen to apply within organizational cultures. Consider, for example, the organization you work in or an organization you have previously worked in. Can you identify particular scripts or rituals that are specific to that organization or that type of organization?

Organizational cultures also involve 'unwritten rules' – for example, a dress code. These involve institutionalized patterns of language, behaviour, thought and feeling. We can generally recognize such unwritten rules when somebody breaks one of them, when somebody does what is not 'the done thing around here'. These can be very powerful influences within an organizational setting.

Organizational cultures can be positive or negative, in the sense that they can help or hinder. They can help:

> *By playing a part in developing a sense of identity and belonging.* This is an important factor in developing teamwork.
> *By allowing useful shortcuts.* People who work within the same culture can take certain things for granted – for example, the use of jargon. Technical terms do not need to be explained if the people using them are part of the same culture and can use jargon as a shortcut.
> *In providing clarity about expectations.* Stress can arise where there is a lack of clarity about what is expected of us. An organizational culture helps us to get a picture of what is expected of us, of how we need to fit into that particular organization and its culture.

Cultures can hinder by:

> *Being of a negative nature.* Negative cultures can breed cynicism, defeatism and learned helplessness. The power of a negative culture to demotivate and demoralize should not be underemphasized.
> *By stifling creativity.* Some cultures can close off options by focusing too narrowly on favoured patterns, leaving little or no room for exploring alternatives.
> *By leading to conflict with other organizations.* Conflict can arise where there is a clash between the culture of one organization and another – for example, between a social services agency and a health authority.
> *By undermining social work values.* Cultures, as shared ways of seeing, thinking and doing, develop their own values. Often these will be consistent with social work values, but at times they may not.

Principle 4 Knowledge, Skills and Values

This is a further example of the importance of values in social work.

> *By reinforcing bad habits.* Cultures have a tendency to reproduce themselves. This means that alongside positive aspects of a culture, negative aspects (for example, such 'bad habits' as a tendency to avoid difficult issues rather than facing up to them) will also be reproduced.

> *By alienating newcomers.* Where there is a strong shared sense of identity, this can create barriers for new people joining a particular team, section or organization. New members of the staff group may find it hard to settle in and become accepted.

Cultures tend to have a range of characteristics. We can understand these characteristics in terms of a number of oppositions as follows:

> *Open versus closed communication.* To what extent does the culture of the organization encourage open communication and to what extent does a lot happen behind closed doors?
> *Inclusive versus exclusive.* Does the culture include all members or are there cliques or other such separate groupings that can lead to problems?
> *Supportive versus unsupportive.* Does the culture help people feel supported or is it a 'macho' culture based on the notion of 'if you can't stand the heat, get out of the kitchen'?
> *Written versus oral.* Is there consistency between written policies and what actually happens or is there a more powerful oral culture that contradicts and overrides the written policies?
> *Positive versus negative.* Is the culture energizing and positive or energy sapping, demoralizing and negative?
> *Participative versus authoritarian.* Does the culture encourage people to participate actively in how their organization is run, or is it simply a matter of people being expected to follow orders?

It is important to recognize that cultures are powerful, but they are not all powerful. That is, although they can be a strong influence on what happens within an organization:

(a) they can be countered – that is, people can work against cultures; people can ignore what their culture encourages them to do; nobody is obliged to follow the cultural patterns to which they are exposed in their day-to-day working lives;

(b) they can be influenced or changed, particularly over time on a collective level – that is, cultures are sets of habits, and so they are not written in tablets of stone.

In sum, when considering organizational culture, you should:

(1) *Be aware of your culture, its shared meanings and unwritten rules.* What tends to happen is that cultures become like the wallpaper. They may be there and in some respects quite visible, but we tend not to notice them because we are so used to them.

(2) *Evaluate the characteristics.* Look at what helps, what hinders, which aspects of the culture are worth reinforcing, which aspects are potentially problematic and therefore need to be addressed.

NOS Key Role 4

Manage risk to individuals, families, carers, groups, communities, self and colleagues

(3) *Identify strengths to build on and the obstacles to progress to be removed.* Consider the strong points of the current situation so that you can build on them and also identify any actual or potential barriers that may prevent you from taking this forward.

(4) *Be sensitive.* Cultures become part of us, part of our meaning systems and habits. It is therefore important to work together in trying to address cultural issues. If

people feel that their way of working is being undermined, they may react strongly to defend it.

organizational structure

Apart from small voluntary organizations, there will inevitably be some degree of structure in all social work organizations. An important notion here is that of bureaucracy, as discussed by the sociologist, Max Weber (1968). This is a term that, in day-to-day conversation, is often used to mean unnecessary form filling and red tape. However, in its more formal meaning, it refers to institutionalized patterns within an organization, standardized ways of working to create a degree of consistency and efficiency across diverse parts of an organization. In effect, the bigger the organization, the less likely it is that it will be able to handle inconsistencies and will therefore become relatively inflexible. However, bureaucracy in Weber's sense is not necessarily a bad thing as, in many circumstances, the alternative would be chaos (for an interesting discussion of the unhelpful rigidity that can accompany bureaucracy, see Payne, 2000).

Bureaucracy tends to involve a command and control hierarchy or what are often referred to as 'reporting structures'. That is, any particular individual will 'report' to his or her line manager who, in turn, will report to someone in the next layer of the hierarchy. Organizations vary enormously as to their degree of hierarchy. Some have very many levels, while others are relatively 'flatter'. Organizations also vary in terms of the scale of democracy within them. The fact that there is a hierarchy does not mean that the organization is necessarily an authoritarian one. Some forms of hierarchy are based on participation and consultation and thus a degree of democracy.

However, there is an extra dimension to reporting structures. A simple up and down hierarchy is not all that is involved. We also have what are known as 'matrix structures'. This means that somebody may be responsible to his or her line manager in general terms (for example, the team manager), but responsible to another manager for other issues (for example, to the service manager for a particular service that this particular practitioner uses or is involved with in some way).

It is also further complicated by the fact that, in addition to the formal structures that appear on an organization's hierarchical chart, we have informal structures. For example, while the team manager may be officially the power figure, there may be one or more experienced practitioners within the team who have an equally strong, if not stronger, influence on the team. power, see p. 202

What makes organizational structure even more complicated is that there is a very common tendency to reorganize from time to time. This involves starting from scratch in some respects, reassigning people to different parts of a newly devised structure. Such exercises can be very time consuming, very distressing, and often do not achieve what they set out to do (often because managers are attempting to change culture by changing the structure). Part of the problem is that there is no one correct structure. What is involved is looking at how best to arrange the resources (including human resources) available within a structure that makes sense.

A very important point to note is that organizational structures are very significant in terms of actual practice. Not just general points of background interest, they can be central to what happens in trying to help people deal with their problems. This is because organizational structures both constrain and enable. They constrain in the sense that they place limits on what can and cannot be done. It is therefore important for us to know our limitations in terms of these constraints. It is pointless trying to achieve something within our practice that will not work within our existing structures. Structures enable in the sense that they create opportunities. They create avenues that can be pursued for the good of the clients and carers that we are trying to support. It is therefore important to understand how such structures can be enabling, so that we can maximize the potential for giving positive help where we can.

Consequently, it is important to have some understanding of the structures of the organization in which you work (or will be working). If you are going to be part of a team, we would urge you to think carefully about what you would need or want from a teamwork environment and whether a particular team is likely to be able to meet those expectations. Teamwork is discussed further in Part 3.

It is surprising how many people fail to learn about the organizational structures in which they work and therefore:

(a) can create problems for themselves by not understanding the limitations;

(b) miss opportunities for taking matters forward due to their lack of understanding. It is important for practitioners, in order to maximize their effectiveness, to: (i) get to know who controls what within your organizational structure – for example, to understand the role of councillors, board members or trustees; (ii) to get to know the strengths of the organizational structure, so that these can be built upon, and the weaknesses, so that we can be wary of these and avoid the pitfalls that come with them; and lose sight of, or become confused about, issues of accountability. As professionals, individual social workers are accountable for their actions and decisions and so to fail to engage with the organizational context within which you operate is to put yourself in a very vulnerable position. Accountability is not something you can throw back to the organization should you be called to account – the *dynamic* between you and your organization is what will be at issue. See Part 3 for further discussion around this important concept.

policies and procedures

When you take up a post with a social work organization, you will be entering into a contract of employment. Implicit within such contracts (or even explicit in many) is the notion of adherence to policies and procedures – that is, in agreeing to work for an organization, you are thereby agreeing to follow its policies and procedures. It is therefore important for you to know what these policies and procedures are (in outline at least) and how to find out more about them when needed.

policies

These derive directly or indirectly from the law. This raises at least three key issues:

1. *There is the matter of legal compliance.* Policies can be seen as a way of making sure that managers are complying with the law as it applies to them directly and to their employing organization.

2. *They are designed to ensure a degree of 'singing from the same hymn sheet'.* That is, there is the matter of consistency to address. Although some degree of variability within a system is acceptable, if there is too much variability, this can create problems (for example, in terms of unfair allocation of resources).

3. *Quality is also an issue.* Policies help to establish clarity about what standards are expected and therefore give some indication of what is unacceptable.

Policies should not just be pieces of paper gathering dust on a shelf. If they are not helpful guides to practice, then this suggests that there may be something wrong with them, that they may not be fit for purpose. If this is in fact the case, then, as professionals, we have a shared responsibility for raising this as an issue. If policies are not useful guides to practice, then we are working in a less than satisfactory situation, and we should therefore consider in what way we can influence that situation positively. This is a key aspect of professionalism.

There is also the question of self-protection to consider. If a situation were to go seriously wrong in some way, resulting in some form of inquiry, investigation or even court case, then the fact that our practice was not consistent with the policy may be held against us. To argue that the policy is unhelpful and that no-one else followed it would, of course, not hold much water in some form of formal inquiry. Policies are not just an issue for managers. As professionals, we must be wary of the dangerous complacency that ignores policy issues.

These derive directly or indirectly from policies. Again, issues of consistency and quality are important, but they should not go so far as to promote uniformity. There is, of course, no substitute for professional judgement. Sometimes people misunderstand procedures and assume that they are rigid, step-by-step instructions that have to be followed. However, this is not the case. Procedures tend to provide a broad framework, but still leave extensive scope for professional decision making within them.

In order to work effectively within procedures, it is necessary to understand the distinction between 'may do' and 'have to do'. It is very dangerous to confuse these. In some respects, procedures tell us that there are certain options that are open to us (this is, the 'may do' option). In other respects, procedures tell us what we 'have to do' in certain circumstances. That is, they leave us no option.

The following two examples of types of procedures may be helpful in developing our understanding of the role of procedures. First we have protection procedures, whether child protection procedures in relation to children and young people or vulnerable adults procedures in relation to a range of adults, who may be abused (for example, elder abuse or the abuse of people with disabilities). Adhering to these procedures can be time consuming. However, this is worthwhile because such procedures are geared to ensuring that professionals work together and are therefore in a position to support one another by sharing responsibility for these difficult and demanding issues relating to abuse.

NOS Key Role 4

Manage risk to individuals, families, carers, groups, communities, self and colleagues

The second example would be complaints and compliments procedures (albeit referred to in different ways by different organizations). Having a complaint made against us is not something that we can really welcome, and unfortunately in social work, it is not unusual for this to happen. However, if the issue does arise, we should be careful not to panic. We should not see it as a sign of failure. This is because complaints often arise as a result of dissatisfaction on the part of a client that is beyond your control. Sometimes people make complaints whether they are justified or not. Sometimes complaints are justified, but are directed towards the wrong person (that is, towards the social worker, not the budget holder in the case of somebody who has been denied a resource or service). People often make complaints as well because of their distress and heightened emotions. They may fail to appreciate the subtleties and complexities of the social work role and simply regard the problem as one of your competence or your alleged unwillingness to help – they may not appreciate that you have done everything you reasonably could have done to help them. A complaint in such circumstances can actually be useful in clarifying the situation and enabling you and the client to move forward positively.

Although complaints and compliments procedures also include reference to positive comments (compliments), unfortunately these are less common. People will often express their gratitude and satisfaction for the help that they have received, but they may be less motivated to put this in writing through a formal procedure than is the case when they are dissatisfied.

*Having a complaint made against you can be quite challenging but it can
also give us excellent opportunities to learn and to improve our practice.*

In terms of policies and procedures, it is important that you should know the basics
of those procedures that relate to you and your work, and you should also know how
and where to find out more if you need to. If these issues are not covered in your
induction, then it is important that you seek out this knowledge. Ignorance is, of
course, no excuse.

> There were always groans in the office when new sets of guidelines or policy
> amendments were circulated. They appeared quite regularly, and many
> of Rose's colleagues took quite some time to get round to reading them, if
> they ever managed to at all. Rose's approach was different. It was precisely
> *because* of the frequency of change that she felt it necessary to give keeping
> up to date a high priority when planning her workload. She was well aware that, as a
> representative of her employer, she needed to be mindful of the organization's policies and
> values. That isn't to say that Rose followed instructions blindly – quite the opposite. There
> had been several occasions in the past when she had questioned policies that had caused
> her difficulties in her work, or where she had not understood the rationale behind them. As
> a practitioner enacting policy, she considered that she had much to contribute to the policy-
> making process. More than that, she felt it was her duty as a professional social worker to
> ensure that the process was a two-way one.

practice focus
2.11

communication

Good communication is, of course, essential to an effective organization. We can
understand communication in terms of the three S's: skills, systems and sensitivity. Let
us now look at each of these in more detail.

skills

Communication skills basically involve being able to put your message across clearly
and effectively both orally (for example, in meetings) and in writing (reports and
records). Unfortunately, both these areas have been undervalued in the past and
have not received the attention they deserve in terms of, for example, training and
development. There is therefore a need to make sure that we do not:

1. Come across as unprofessional in meetings through a lack of presentation skills; and
2. 'Skimp' on records and reports because we feel unconfident in writing them
   effectively or do not appreciate their significance – many disastrous mistakes have
   occurred because of poor or non-existent written communication.

systems

Different organizations will have different communication systems, although they
often have much in common. Communication systems should help to clarify:

> *Who?* Who do you need to communicate with?
> *What?* What needs to be communicated?

> *When?* What is the appropriate timing?
> *How?* What method or format of communication is appropriate?

There are many cases on record of communication breaking down because of the systems involved. However, systems depend on people. We therefore have to make sure we are not the reason for the system breaking down. Systems, then, are in large part dependent upon the communication skills discussed earlier.

sensitivity

Neil Thompson (2003b) introduces the notion of 'communicative sensitivity', which he defines as:

> the ability to identify the circumstances in which communication is required, the nature of that communication, the persons or organizations that should be communicated with, and so on.
> There is a great irony that it is so often the case that people who have excellent communication skills play a significant part in serious problems arising from communication breakdowns. This is because, in such situations, advanced-level communication skills are of little or no value if they are not put into practice. That is, if the person concerned fails to realize that communication is needed, problems will still arise, despite the high level of communication he or she is capable of. (Neil Thompson, 2003b, pp. 33–4)

Successful communication can therefore be seen to rely on not only well-developed skills and effective systems, but also a degree of communicative sensitivity.

Communication also involves listening. We need to be clear that we are 'tuned in' to what our organization (and the people in it) are trying to say. Without the effective use of listening skills, communication is likely to be very poor indeed.

NOS Key Role 2

Plan, carry out, review and evaluate social work practice, with individuals, families, carers, groups, communities, and other professionals

power and conflict

Power can be seen to operate in different ways in organizations, not least the following:

> *Structural.* An individual's position within the hierarchy will have a significant bearing on how much power he or she has and how this can be used. This is parallel with the discussion in Chapter 2.2 about the structure of society and how one's 'social location' influences the distribution of power and life chances. Our position in the hierarchy can be seen, then, as our 'organizational location'.

social divisions, see p. 70

> *Cultural.* As noted earlier, an organization's culture is a very strong force. Whether we swim with the tide of that culture or against it will be a matter of power. The existence of deeply ingrained patterns of behaviour and well-established taken-for-granted assumptions is a significant factor when it comes to the operation of power. Individuals will find it easier to 'go with the flow' of the dominant culture, rather than struggle against it.

> *Personal.* Individual skills, knowledge, experience, the respect an individual gains – these are all important in shaping the extent and use of power. Charisma – that is, force of personality – is also an important personal factor. Some individuals are highly skilled and experienced at using the opportunities to influence events that come their way, while others may be far less effective in making the most of the possibilities.

Power can be abused deliberately, as in cases of bullying, for example, or misused unintentionally – for example, unwittingly alienating somebody by behaving in a way that they find uncomfortable or disconcerting, but without your realizing that you are doing so.

Despite this potential for abuse or misuse, power is not necessarily a bad thing. Power keeps the wheels of an organization turning. The positive use of power in an organization where it is used legitimately is known as 'authority'. We must not be afraid of power and authority. We must treat them with respect. Power can do a lot of harm, but can also do a lot of good. For example, the appropriate use of power by a social worker can at times make a hugely positive contribution to clients' lives.

conflict

As with power, conflict can also do a lot of harm, but also has the potential to do good. Once we begin to explore issues of power, conflict is never very far away. This is because one person's exercise of power can get in the way of another person's exercise of power, thus leading to conflict. Sartre, the French existentialist thinker, was correct when he argued that 'hell is other people' (Sartre, 1955). For example, consider a traffic jam; the fact that you are trying to get from A to B, but so many other people are trying to get to B as well means that other people's intentions (they are exercising their power) mean that your attempts to get where you want to go are frustrated. These sorts of issues are particularly prevalent in social work because of the nature of the work itself. That is, we will often be trying to work with situations that involve power and conflict – situations where people are working against each other in some way. This can happen within families and communities, but also within and between organizations. It is therefore important that we should:

> *Not bury our heads in the sand and hope conflict will go away.* We need to develop the confidence and skills to be able to respond to conflicts, rather than pretend that they are not there.

Principle 6 **Realism and Challenge**

Managing conflict can be challenging but if we become skilful at it, it can become a very useful basis for high-quality practice.

> *Learn how to handle conflicts as constructively and effectively as we can.* There are considerable skills involved in effective conflict management, but these can be developed over time.

Principle 4 **Knowledge, Skills and Values**

Managing conflict is highly skilled work and we should not leave ourselves ill-equipped by failing to develop the skills involved.

> *We should support one another in managing conflict.* Conflict can be difficult and demanding, and so we should not feel that we have to tackle it on our own. Managing conflict is a shared responsibility.

workload management

When it comes to managing a heavy workload, we have two well-established problems:

① These issues have traditionally been neglected in social work education. It is as if it were being assumed that the knowledge and skills involved are somehow self-evident – perhaps just a matter of 'common sense'.

② Outside of social work education where these issues have been addressed, there has tended to be a simplistic emphasis on time management with little or no attention paid to the equally, if not more, important issue of managing motivation and morale – in effect, *self*-management as much as *time* management.

In addition to these problems, and partly because of them, we have a situation where there are a number of myths about workload management in existence. A high workload can be motivating, stimulating and rewarding – a source of great pride and satisfaction. However, an unrealistic workload is precisely that – it is *unrealistic*. It can be counterproductive when people have an unrealistic workload. They may actually achieve less than if they had been given a lower, but more realistic, workload. In this way, excessive workloads collude with a shortage of staffing resources. When people are overworked, managers who give them more and more to do are not addressing the underlying problem. The idea that the way to deal with work overload is to pile more and more pressure on social work staff is a dangerous fallacy (Neil Thompson, 2004). Failing to address work overload issues can have the following detrimental consequences:

> *A lowering of standards and an increase in the rate of errors made.* Quality is bound to suffer if people have more work than they can reasonably manage and, ironically, such work overload can lead to more mistakes being made which, in turn, can lead to greater levels of pressure in trying to pick up the pieces from those mistakes. It can become a vicious circle in which excessive work pressures lead to even more pressures.

> *Stress.* Excessive workload can lead to feelings of guilt and inadequacy which can undermine a practitioner's ability to fulfil their requirements. This can be very damaging for the individual concerned, for the people he or she is trying to help and for the wider organization.

Principle 7 **Self-management**
Self-management includes self-care. Allowing ourselves to be exposed to harmful levels of pressure does not do anyone any good.

> *There can be an undermining of arguments for additional resources.* This is the overload collusion referred to above.

Simply taking on more and more work when the workload becomes unrealistically high is dangerous. It is therefore important to:

> take whatever steps you can to manage your workload efficiently and effectively

as possible (the chapter on time and workload management in Neil Thompson, 2002b, is a good starting point); and

> recognize that, if/when we are experiencing excessive pressures, making it known that we are overloaded is good professional practice and not a sign of weakness.

NOS Key Role 6

Demonstrate professional competence in social work practice

As we noted in Chapter 2.1, there are skills involved in workload management, but we also need to recognize that maintaining workloads at a realistic level is also an organizational responsibility. As an employee you have rights and these include not being asked to do more than can be reasonably expected of one person, and being given the right tools (for example, information and skills training) for the job you are being asked to do. Employment rights can help to protect you by providing a benchmark and so, if you are unaware of your rights, you may be putting yourself at a disadvantage.

supervision

Employing organizations have a duty to ensure that social workers are fulfilling their professional roles. This involves as a minimum:

> *Standard setting.* This refers to accountability and involves advice and guidance to a large extent. In this regard the supervisor has a responsibility to ensure that staff are clear about what is expected of them and are performing to at least a minimum acceptable level.

> *Staff development.* This refers to continuous professional development, making sure that we are continuing to learn over time and are not getting into a rut. While the accountability element of supervision is concerned with meeting at least miminum standards, the staff development element is concerned with maximizing performance by focusing on maximizing learning and development. As we discussed earlier, while you have a duty to perform in a professional manner, you can also expect your employer to play a part in helping you do so.

> *Staff care.* This includes providing support in dealing with the pressures of the work (including the emotional pressures of what can be a very demanding job). This is partly about supporting staff through any difficulties they may encounter which may impair their ability to work effectively (for example, experiencing a bereavement in their private life) and partly about making sure that staff feel supported and appreciated at all times.

Principle 5 `Loss and Grief`

The fact that we encounter a great deal of grief in our work does not mean that we will not also experience it in our private lives.

Supervision can be enormously helpful for staff, although the quality and frequency can vary quite considerably between organizations and even within organizations.

your contribution

It is important to stress that supervision is a shared responsibility. While your supervisor will have a certain degree of responsibility for making sure it works, it is not his or her sole responsibility. It is a shared endeavour and so, in order to maximize its effectiveness, it is strongly advised that you should:

> *Prepare in advance.* In order to make the best use of the time available, it is important that you consider what issues you want to raise, to do anything else in advance of the supervision session to make sure that you are not wasting time during your time together.
> *Not play games.* It is unfortunately the case that some people become very defensive in supervision. They treat it as a game and try to prevent their line manager from finding out what they are doing. This is unhelpful for all concerned. Supervision should be approached as a positive, helpful experience. If it is not, then you need to consider what you can do about this as a professional, rather than shirk your professional responsibility by playing games in supervision.

Principle 7 **Self-management**

Being open to the benefits of supervision and maximizing the learning involved is a key element of self-management.

> *Try to tackle any problems.* It is important to be assertive. Supervision is an invaluable resource for promoting professional practice. Your clients will depend on your being able to do the best job you are able to do. Supervision can make a hugely positive contribution to making your practice effective. If you are therefore in a situation where supervision is not proving helpful, then you need to raise this as an issue in whatever reasonable way you can.

NOS Key Role 5

Manage and be accountable, with supervision and support, for your own social work practice within your organanization

Supervision is a key part of organizational effectiveness in terms of quality assurance, promoting learning, supporting staff, facilitating communication and problem solving. Its crucial role cannot therefore be emphasized enough.

---

practice focus 2.12

At her interview for her present post, Fiona had made a point of asking about supervision arrangements. She wanted to feel supported and to know that she would have time set aside for discussing her needs. Despite the reassurance she had been given at that point, she found that the rhetoric of supervision wasn't being put into practice. Time after time she was asked to postpone her supervision session as other issues were given priority. She was quite happy to be flexible, and knew only too well that the unexpected can, and often does, happen in her field of work. However, her feelings of frustration were beginning to turn to anger at being denied something she needed in order to be able to do her job safely and to develop within her role. When she thought about how to manage this situation she realized that she spent a good deal of her time encouraging service users to become more assertive, and yet she was not following her own advice. She had the power to do something about this, and yet she was not using it. Instead of continuing to act like a victim, Fiona knew that she had to take the initiative and make it clear that she regarded supervision as integral to her work, not as an added bonus if time permitted.

conclusion

It should be clear from our comments above that the organizational context plays a central role in shaping social work practice. To ignore it is dangerous because it:

(a) undermines our effectiveness if we are unaware of the subtleties of the context in which we are working; and

(b) can do a lot of harm. Organizations are dangerous places (Neil Thompson, 2003a), in the sense that the way organizations work can put excessive pressures on people and undermine their confidence and generally be detrimental to them.

It is certainly not the case that you are expected to be an expert in organizational analysis. However, we would strongly argue that it pays dividends to learn all the time as much as you reasonably can about the subtle and complex interweavings of organizational factors and how they affect you and your practice, and the practice of your colleagues.

points to ponder

> In what ways might an organization's culture influence working practices?
> Have you ever come across organizational rituals? What role(s) do they play?
> How can organizational structures both constrain and enable?
> Why is it important to understand organizational policies?
> How can complaints procedures be used positively and constructively rather than defensively?

2.5 law and policy

introduction

In the introduction to Part 2, the importance of the law as an underpinning factor for social work practice was discussed. We now return to this topic to examine it in more detail alongside the equally important subject of social policy. The law and policy are closely intertwined and both act as a bridge between the wider governmental and social framework and actual practice. This chapter also acts as a bridge; this time between the general introduction to this topic provided in Part 2 and a wider, more in-depth, specialist literature, details of which are to be found in the 'Suggestions for further reading' at the end of this part of the book.

Both the law and the social policy framework have significant implications for how social work is understood, conceived and practised. In many ways, the law and social policy provide the framework from which practice flows. They set the parameters, or boundaries, of what we can and cannot do within a social work context.

Brayne, Martin and Carr in their textbook on social work law, argue that 'the statutes tell you who you have responsibilities towards and how they shall be exercised' (2005, p. 1). While this is true to a large extent, it is slightly misleading. This comment clearly comes from the perspective of lawyers. Social workers have to take on board the significance of the law and its power, but are also bound by other matters, such as professional values. This is not to say that professional values will lead us to break the law, but rather that the law in itself is not a sufficient guide to action (a point well made in the work of Braye and Preston-Shoot, 1997). It is for this reason that this chapter contains a section on the law and professionalism. The law and, indeed, policy will help us to set the broad terms of reference to which we must work and, in some cases, will give us specific guidelines but, overall, this does not replace our professional duty to weigh up the situation that we are dealing with very carefully and decide on the most appropriate course of action. This is an important point to emphasize, as a misunderstanding of the role and nature of law and policy can lead to considerable difficulties. This can apply in two directions. On the one hand, if we are not clear on the power of law and policy we may find ourselves in trouble if we are behaving in a way that is not consistent with these. On the other hand, we may experience difficulties if we fail to adhere to legal or policy requirements. The implications of this should become clearer as this chapter progresses.

Principle 6 Realism and Challenge

Until you get used to it, the legal system can be quite anxiety provoking. However, if you act in good faith within the framework of law, policies and values, you should have nothing to fear.

The remainder of this chapter covers the following topics:

> *Law and the social worker.* Here we need to address the question of what is the relationship between the legal base and actual practice.
> *Legal processes.* What does the law actually do? What processes are involved?
> *Major areas of law.* Here we provide an overview of the law in relation to major areas of policy and practice.
> *Law and professionalism.* What do we mean by professionalism and how does this relate to the law?
> *The role of policy.* Here we present an overview of how social policy acts as a bridge between law and practice.
> *Linking law and policy to practice.* How do law and policy shape practice? This is the important question we need to consider here.
> *Pitfalls to avoid.* How can we avoid repeating other people's mistakes?

This chapter will not provide you with everything you need to know about law and policy (far from it), but it should give you a firm foundation on which to build – and, given the centrality of law and policy to social work practice, you will need to keep building throughout your career, developing your knowledge and skills as time goes on.

law and the social worker

An important point to emphasize is that social workers are not expected to be lawyers. Where such specialist knowledge of the law is required, we will generally have access to the necessary legal advisers to draw upon their advice and guidance as required. However, what social workers do need is a good knowledge of the law, as Levy comments:

> The practice of social work operates within the framework of the law and the legal system. Some knowledge of the law, an awareness of its implications, expertise in applying it and, when necessary, the ability to communicate with lawyers (not always an easy task!) are, in my view, essential requirements for those working in local authority social services departments or other social work organizations. In addition, in the context of court cases specifically, the social worker needs to know or have access to advice about the precise kind of evidence a court or tribunal will require. (Levy, 2001, p. ix)

The relationship between the law and social work is a complex one, and what the law demands of us will vary from situation to situation. However, in general terms, what social workers need in relation to the law is:

> An understanding of the law as a broad framework and set of parameters.
> Knowledge of specific pieces of legislation.
> An understanding of how to find out more as and when the need arises.
> The ability not to be overawed by the legal system.
> A willingness to draw on support when you need it.
> A commitment to keeping up to date with changes to the law and its implications.

Actual Acts of Parliament and guidance associated with them, together with other legal documents have to be written in a very precise form of language. This can come across as quite dry and difficult to follow. It can also appear to be unconnected with modern society. However, what we have to recognize is that such language should not be allowed to put us off understanding the specifics of the law. The emphasis on precision in drafting legal materials can act as a barrier to clarity and this can be very off-putting. However, there are two important things to recognize here. First, we only need to rely on legal materials as reference points. Given the complexity of the law and the written materials associated with it, we are not expected to know things by heart (even solicitors have to look things up much of the time). Second, we need to learn how to persevere with legal language, and it is likely that, over time, you will find that this perseverance pays off. What initially seems to be impenetrable technical jargon becomes much more intelligible after a while of becoming accustomed to the style of writing involved. Legal language need not, therefore, be a barrier to working effectively within the law.

> **practice focus**
>
> **2.13**
>
> Geri was on placement with a team who worked with older people. Amir, one of her colleagues, had been working with someone he knew was being physically and financially abused by a family member, but could do little to help because she insisted that it was not happening. When he mentioned the possibility of using the law relating to guardianship as a means of protecting her, Geri felt unprepared for practice, as she had never even heard of this, never mind understood its implications. However, Amir reassured her by explaining that it was a course of action that was not often taken and that, despite having been working as a qualified social worker in this field for some time, he himself would have to read up on guardianship in order to refresh his memory, discuss the implications with his team manager and take advice from the Department's legal section before deciding on any further action. As a result of this conversation, Geri moved on in her understanding of the legal context and expectations of her in this regard. She realized that even qualified and experienced social workers were not expected to be experts in the law, but she could appreciate how crucial it would be for her to develop an awareness of key pieces of legislation, what they required of her in the carrying out of her duties, and the impact that they could have on people's lives, if she were to become a competent social worker.

As social workers within a legal framework, we need to recognize that the law is:

> *A roadmap.* As indicated earlier, the law will not tell us precisely what to do (except in a very limited set of circumstances), but it will provide broad guidance on what direction we need to go in, and so on.
> *A source of authority.* As far as possible, we should be working in partnership with clients and carers. However, it is often the case that we need to use formal authority in order to make progress (in relation to child protection issues, for example). In this regard, recourse to the law can be a very useful tool in the social worker's toolkit.
> *A means of making progress.* Sometimes social work situations enter a stalemate phase and it requires some sort of legal process in order to enable progress to be made – for example, a dispute to be resolved or a decision to be made.
> *A set of limitations for protection.* We have already used the term 'parameters' a number of times. Parameters or boundaries are important because they set limits on what can and cannot be done. These parameters provide for protection for ourselves as professional workers, our clients and the organizations that we represent.

In this part of the chapter, we examine how the law actually operates and what processes are taking place when the law is being used. We begin by looking at the important terms of powers, duties and constraints.

Plan, carry out, review and evaluate social work practice, with individuals, families, carers, groups, communities, and other professionals

A power is something that the law gives us permission to do. Some of these powers relate to what individual social workers may do in carrying out our duties. Others, however, relate to what departments or organizations may do at a broader organizational level. What specific powers are bestowed upon us will vary from law to law and situation to situation.

Duties are what we have to do, not so much what we may do (power) but what we must do. For example, if it comes to our attention that a child appears to be subject to abuse, there is a legal responsibility on the local authority to enquire into the circumstances relating to that child and his or her well-being.

Constraints are the things that the law forbids us from doing. For example, contrary to popular belief, social workers do not have the legal right to enter someone's home without permission, except in very limited circumstances as defined by the law.

It is important to be clear about these terms so that we do not 'overstep the mark', so that we are clear about what we may do (power), what we must do (duty), and what we must not do (constraint).

The law comprises a number of significant processes. The following list includes the major ones, but it is by no means an exhaustive account of what is involved in the world of legal process.

> *The law acts as a vehicle for democratic processes.* It is no coincidence that laws are referred to as Acts of Parliament. It is through such laws that the government is able to act on behalf of the electorate.

> *The law seeks to protect vulnerable people from abuse and exploitation.* The protective element of the law is particularly significant for social work, as protecting people from harm (especially in terms of abuse and exploitation) is a significant part of social work duties.

> *The law promotes and safeguards rights.* A good example of this is in relation to human rights, a topic we shall explore below.

> *The law makes decisions about the welfare of individuals and groups.* Much of the case law that social workers will be involved with involves this aspect of the law.

> *The law reviews decisions made by other bodies.* For example, a decision made by a local authority may be subject to 'judicial review' in certain circumstances, which means that the decision made may be overturned by a court of law.

> *The law seeks to resolve disputes and grievances.* The use of mediation as an alternative to court has been increasing in recent years. However, the courts still play a major role in dealing with disputes and grievances (in civil cases, for example).

> *The law administers criminal justice.* This can be very relevant for those social workers working specifically within community or youth justice fields. However,

it can be of relevance to any social worker in any setting at times, as they may be working with someone who is involved within the criminal justice system, even though this may not be the primary reason for their involvement with this person or family.

> *The law contributes to the maintenance of the social order.* The law acts as a vehicle as noted above for democratic processes and a key part of this is in maintaining a degree of social order.

Principle 1 `Social Context`

The law is part of the broader social context.

major areas of law

Here we provide an overview of the major aspects of legal provision across various settings. We try to avoid making reference to specific laws because: (1) these vary from country to country within the UK and beyond; (2) they change over time, sometimes quite rapidly; and (3) this book is no substitute for detailed study of the relevant legal materials – what we are offering here is a gateway to a basic understanding of the law, rather than a study of the law in itself.

child care

This can be subdivided into three main sections. The law relates first to general child welfare and family support. Here the emphasis is on prevention of problems. Second, there is a considerable body of law relating to 'looked after' children – that is, children who are looked after away from their home in children's homes, residential schools or in the care of foster carers. Third, there is the law relating to child protection. Safeguarding children from harm is a key part of child care law and, indeed, child care social work.

community care

There is a significant body of law relating to supporting people in vulnerable circumstances in the community, with a major overall aim of trying to provide sufficient support where possible to maintain people in the community and thus avoid the need for residential or hospital care.

residential care

Where community care has not managed to prevent the need for residential care, the law provides safeguards in relation to care standards. The law provides for the inspection of institutions providing residential or nursing care. This relates to both adults and children. The care of children in residential settings has been particularly significant in recent years, in no small part due to the Waterhouse Report which reported on major investigations into abuse in children's homes and residential schools (Waterhouse, 2000).

mental health

There are two main aspects of mental health law. First we have the supportive aspect which is geared towards helping people with mental health problems to live as normal a life as possible within the community. In this respect, it is closely linked to community care law. However, the other side of the coin is the protective element of mental health legislation. This refers to protection of both the client and the broader public. The law allows, in certain narrowly defined circumstances, for individuals suffering from mental health problems to be admitted to a psychiatric facility against their will. This compulsory admission procedure is closely monitored and involves a high level of professional skill in balancing the rights of the individual and the safety of the public and, indeed, of the individual him- or herself. Before somebody can be compulsorily admitted to a psychiatric facility of some kind, there has to be clear evidence that the person's mental condition is making him or her a risk to him- or herself, or to others.

human rights

This is a major area of law that cuts across all areas of practice. Whatever client group we are working with and in whatever circumstances, we need to take account of human rights. However, we should note that human rights are not unlimited. The law relates to specific human rights. The fact that someone claims something to be their human right does not automatically make it so. Social workers therefore need to have a good understanding of the human rights legislation and how it applies to the particular circumstances they are dealing with.

NOS Key Role 3

Support individuals to represent their needs, views and circumstances

discrimination

There is a huge and growing body of law relating to the prevention of discrimination and the seeking of remedies and compensation where discrimination can be seen to have taken place. Given the importance of anti-discriminatory practice as part of the social work value base, this body of law is particularly important as an underpinning element of social work practice.

---

practice focus
2.14

During their first supervision session of Carolyn's placement with the Children and Families Team, her practice teacher was dismayed to hear her say that she had made a decision not to attend any of the university lectures or seminars on mental health issues because she was planning to work exclusively in the field of child care. At first, she could not make Carolyn see what a blinkered approach this was, and how she was failing to appreciate the complexities of people's lives. And so she set Carolyn a task, which was to choose any ten case files from the team's filing system and identify whether mental health issues and legislation had been a feature in any way. This exercise opened Carolyn's eyes to the extent to which mental health problems being experienced by parents and siblings impacted on the lives of many, many children. It also brought home to her how many children and young people experienced mental health problems themselves. One of her learning objectives for the placement had been to learn more about legislation relating to child care, but she had come to realize that her legal knowledge base would have to be considerably wider than that if it were to reflect the reality of people's individual and family lives. While studying different aspects of social work in separate and discrete packages at university, she had forgotten to take on board that these are not so easily separated off in people's lived experience. She renegotiated her learning objectives so that they incorporated how legal issues in general impact on the lives of children and families.

law and professionalism

The point was made earlier that the law does not give detailed prescription for practice. This introduces a need for discretion which, in turn, introduces a need for professionalism. This is because, if the law does not give us detailed instructions, then we have to decide for ourselves within certain boundaries how to proceed.

NOS Key Role 6

Demonstrate professional competence in social work practice This places a professional responsibility upon us. We have to be accountable for our actions.

However, the history of professionalism in social work is not an entirely positive one:

> The term, 'professionalism' is one that has a mixed history in social work. For many years, the notion of being a 'professional' was regarded with a great deal of suspicion, as if it were simply a way of seeking perks, privileges and status at the expense of the clientele that we serve. Of course, it has to be acknowledged that professionalism can be abused in this way, used as an excuse for self-interest. However, we would see it as a significant mistake to reject the notion of professionalism for these reasons, as it amounts to throwing the baby out with the bath water. (Neil Thompson, 2002a, p. 4)

Professionalism can be seen to include the following elements:

> *A professional knowledge base.* This includes a knowledge of the law but goes beyond this to include a wide range of other factors that are relevant to decision making and other aspects of practice.

> *A set of values.* One of the defining features of professionalism is a commitment to professional values and, while social work values are largely consistent with the law, this is not always the case. There may, for example, be some aspects of the law which do not sit comfortably with social work values.

> *A degree of autonomy.* While no professional is entirely autonomous, in the sense that they can do what they like without any limits to this, professionals do enjoy a degree of autonomy (in the sense that the situations they deal with are so complex that it would be unrealistic to expect any success if the actions of social workers were simply based on following instructions). The complexity of the work brings about the need for autonomy, itself a key part of professionalism – and, of course, self-management (Principle 7).

> *Accountability.* If we are not simply following instructions, then this means that we are accountable for our actions. We have to be able to justify what we did (or did not do) and why. This can be done partly by reference to the law but, as noted above, the reasons for our actions include the law but are not confined to legal requirements. There will be other factors that influence our decision making, not least our values and wider professional knowledge base.

As far as professionalism is concerned, we can be seen to be in a transitional period in social work. We have moved from a situation of elitist professionalism with its emphasis on 'we know best' through a period of largely rejecting professionalism, but we are now beginning to establish the firm foundations of an empowering professionalism based on partnership (Neil Thompson, 2007).

the role of policy

Social policy can be seen as society's response to social problems. That is, the term is used to refer to the variety of policies developed through the state and related institutions in response to what are perceived to be social problems. Social policy, as such, is enacted through:

> *The law.* There are specific Acts of Parliament that form the basis of social policy – for example, the government's policy on mental health will be enacted through legislation relating to mental health.
> *The policies of government agencies (national and local).* The law will be interpreted by the various bodies involved in its implementation, such as central and local government departments and related bodies, such as 'quangos' (quasi-autonomous non-governmental organizations).
> *The practices of professionals.* Social workers and others involved in human services will carry out their day-to-day practice based on the prevailing law and policy.

The state plays a central role in this, but it is not exclusively a state matter. The voluntary sector, the private sector and the various community contributions – for example, through informal care – also play a major role. However, what puts the state at centre stage is the fact that the activities of others are, to a large extent, overseen by the state. While it is now debatable as to whether we have a welfare state in the UK, historically we can see an important development from the 1940s onwards where various Acts of Parliament were put on the statute book in order to tackle the problems that were identified following the end of the Second World War. Strenuous efforts were made to respond to what were recognized as the five giants – disease, want, ignorance, squalor and idleness.

While much has changed since the 1940s, there is still much of that work apparent today in shaping how society is run and how we respond to what is identified as a social problem. To what extent the term 'welfare state' applies is an interesting question, but the state (and its policies) is none the less a central plank of society's efforts to address social problems and social needs, and to support and protect vulnerable members of society. Social policies act as a bridge between the law and wider government apparatus and social order, on the one hand, and natural professional practices on the other.

We therefore need more than just a technical understanding of law. We need to be able to see the broader picture of law and policy as the context in which we work. The relationship between law and policy, on the one hand, and between policy and practice on the other, is complex and multidimensional. However, we need not concern ourselves with the details of this, but we do need to recognize that at least a basic understanding of the role of policy in shaping social work practice is needed if we are to appreciate the foundations on which our work is built.

linking law and policy to practice

Chapter 2.7 explores the important issue of reflective practice. A major part of reflective practice is the relationship between day-to-day actions as a practitioner and the wider theoretical, political, legal and policy context. The question of linking law and policy to practice is therefore very much a question of developing reflective practice. This is therefore a point to which we shall return in Chapter 2.7. However, there are other points that are worthy of emphasis at this stage:

> We need to make sure that our actions and decisions are within the law and consistent with policy. Although there is considerable scope for interpretation and, as we have noted, the law and policy are not the only influences on our actions, we none the less have to make sure that we are not breaking the law or acting in ways that are inconsistent with the policy basis of our work.

> Being consistent with the 'spirit' of the law. While at times there may be a need for detailed discussions about the specifics of particular legal provisions, we should at all times bear in mind the broader spirit of the law. Why was it introduced? What is it trying to achieve? and so on. We should be wary of the mistake of getting bogged down in detail and losing sight of the bigger picture that we are working to.

> Similarly, we need to ensure that our work is consistent with the purpose of social policy. We need to make sure that we do not lose sight of why social work services exist and what we are trying to achieve.

pitfalls to avoid

It is inevitable that in social work we will make mistakes from time to time, that we will fall foul of particular pitfalls. Given the complexity and breadth of social work, this is not surprising. However, it can be disconcerting. What can add to this sense of being disconcerting is the recognition of just how complex and wide ranging the law and social policy are. It is therefore important to bear in mind one key piece of advice: don't panic. It is vitally important that we do not allow the complexity of the situation to overawe us. This is particularly significant when we first approach these issues because they can seem so large and daunting. However, once we start to get used to them, once we start to feel comfortable in addressing the issues in partnership with others involved in our work (managers, legal advisers and so on), we can start to feel more confident and comfortable in addressing the issues and rising to the challenges involved. Social workers have been doing this successfully for decades, and there is no reason why you cannot manage to do it as well, provided you do not allow yourself to panic.

Principle 7 **Self-management**

Keeping cool under pressure is an important social work skill.

In order to help you avoid some of the many pitfalls that are around in relation to law and policy, we present some guidelines that we trust you will find of assistance. To begin with, we wish to challenge six myths that relate to the use of law:

> *Social workers have to be legal experts.* This is a basic misunderstanding of the relationship between law and practice. While we do need to have a good understanding of the law, this is a far cry from being an 'expert'.

> *I don't need to worry about the law because my work does not involve court work* It is clearly a mistake to equate the significance of the law with court work. Many social workers will go through their entire career without ever being involved in a court case, but this does not alter the fact that every day of their working life will be affected by the law (for example, in terms of powers, duties and constraints).

> *I just do as I'm asked. It's my manager's job to worry about the law.* While it is certainly true that the law is a concern for managers, it is also, of course, a concern for practitioners. To ignore the significance of law and place everything in the

hands of one's line manager is a very dangerous strategy. Social work involves making professional decisions, and so the idea that we just 'do as we're told' is both inaccurate and dangerous.

> *The law dictates what we do. There is no room for discretion.* This is another misunderstanding of the law that fails to appreciate that the situations we encounter in social work are far too complex for the law to be able to predefine exactly what happens. The law provides the broad parameters; professional discretion has to do the rest.

> *The law is so vague that you can more or less do what you like anyway.* This is the converse of the previous example and is equally mistaken. While it is clearly the case that there is scope for discretion and autonomy, to argue that we can 'more or less do what we like' is certainly a major exaggeration. The reality of the situation is somewhere between the two mistaken extremes of no discretion and complete discretion.

> *I'm a childcare worker, so as long as I'm up on the Children Act 1989, I don't have to worry.* This very narrow perspective on the law is very worrying, although we have encountered a number of people who do in fact adopt this perspective. In addition to child care law, there will be issues relating to discrimination law, human rights law and so on for child care social workers and, of course, the law applies equally to workers in adult services and, indeed, any aspect of social work. It would be a mistake to equate social work law with child care.

As far as social policy is concerned, one of the major pitfalls to avoid is the tendency to see social policies as largely irrelevant to practice, as broad contextual issues unconnected with the real job, as it were. Such an attitude fails to recognize the close interweavings between the broad context and actual practice. If someone's practice is disconnected from the broader policy context, then this indicates that there is something seriously wrong.

---

practice focus

2.15

His tutors had often commented on how social work was characterized by dilemmas and Lee's first case as a qualified social worker highlighted how true this was. The parents of a 25-year-old man with learning disabilities were refusing to let him attend a day centre because they were in dispute with the local authority about a new charging policy, which significantly increased the contribution they were expected to pay for the service their son was receiving. As a representative of the local authority Lee felt duty bound to explain and enforce the charging policy, but he could understand the family's point of view, and also felt it unfair that the young man's personal and social development was being compromised by a dispute over financial matters. He felt pulled in three different directions and wasn't sure of his next step. In order to clarify his thoughts he tried to see the situation from the different viewpoints. He could see that the family had a micro perspective on this situation, which was understandable, because they were experiencing first hand the hardship that the charging policy was causing. But Lee could also see how the local authority had to adopt a macro perspective in order to offer as equitable a service as possible to all of the people in the population it served. He remembered once sitting in at a meeting of senior managers while he was on a student placement and being alerted to how their policy decisions were informed and constrained by legal and policy directives. Before looking at the 'big picture' Lee had felt that the local authority was being unfair but, after this exercise, he could appreciate that senior managers had to work within the law and to government policy on welfare provision too, and could no more act as 'sole operators' in this matter than he could. He still wanted to champion the family's cause, but now wouldn't do so from a standpoint of naïvety about policy constraints.

conclusion

This chapter should, by now, have given a clear picture that what we are dealing with in terms of law and social policy is a very complex area, but one that is bread-and-butter stuff when it comes to social work. It may seem daunting at first, but it is a subject matter that you will get used to over time and will come to rely on it as a sound foundation to guide your practice. What may seem initially a hindrance will, once you feel more comfortable with it, be seen as a very helpful body of knowledge and guidelines to signpost you in the right direction.

One final point to emphasize is that in all our dealings with the law and policy, we need to remember the issue of professionalism and therefore adopt a critical approach. Social workers are not social technicians. We are not there simply to follow orders in an unthinking way. We need to use our critical faculties to weigh up the situations we encounter – yes, to make sure that our actions are consistent with law and policy, but not simply to do so in a mechanistic way without a more critical understanding of the complex issues involved (for example, in relation to social work values, such as anti-discriminatory practice).

NOS Key Role 6

Demonstrate professional competence in social work practice

In our experience, the best practitioners are those who have a good understanding of law and policy but who are also able to adopt a critical perspective on this so that, when it comes to linking law and policy issues with actual practice, they are very well equipped to do so. They are able to use their analytical skills to make sense of the complexities rather than fall into the trap of trying simply to implement the law as if it were such a straightforward matter.

points to ponder

> In what sense can the legal framework be seen as a 'roadmap'?
> What is the difference between a power and a duty?
> Why are human rights important?
> What pitfalls can you identify in relation to using law and policy?
> What do you understand by the idea of seeing the 'big picture' of policy?

2.6 the value base

introduction

We have already likened social work training and, indeed, your social work career, to a journey. On this journey you will constantly be discovering things about yourself and about the way the world around you operates. Values will have already played a big part in your life, although you may not always been aware of it. If you have not thought much about the value base which underpins your thoughts and actions, then you are probably in the majority. It is not something which tends to crop up in conversation, and it is in the nature of values that they operate beneath the surface, rarely becoming explicit or obvious.

However, values are a core concept within social work, for reasons we will discuss below and so, in the same way that Chapter 2.1 showed that our awareness of processes needs to be enhanced, this chapter shows that we need to raise our level of awareness of values. Part of this consciousness raising will involve looking at your own value base – thinking about where you are coming from as a person and what the principles are that affect your thoughts, feelings and actions. This process of self-reflection is not always easy, and it is not uncommon for your own values to be challenged by what you read, see or hear on social work courses and in practice. Moss refers to this process as identifying 'where the shoe might rub' (1999, p. 8). This is a useful metaphor, in that it highlights the need to identify and deal with difficulties or dilemmas if the outcome is to be one we feel comfortable with. Many students report finding the study of values difficult because:

> the process can be emotionally challenging at times; and
> values are not tangible concepts that can be easily understood or described.

Nevertheless, it is something that cannot be shied away from. Values are not optional extras, something that can be downplayed or missed out because other aspects of the course seem more interesting, less complicated or more relevant. Rather, the value base is fundamental – a core concept which underpins every other aspect of social work. Skills and knowledge are essential, but values affect how you use those skills and that knowledge, and so are integral to the way the profession operates.

NOS Key Role 2

Plan, carry out, review and evaluate social work practice, with individuals, families, carers, groups, communities, and other professionals

We will need to spend a little more time on the matter of definition before going on to look in more detail at why values are important; how we can recognize them; and how they influence practice.

what are values?

At a very basic level, values are what we hold dear – literally those things that we value. Our value base is that set of principles which underpins what we think, what we do, what we refuse to do and so on. To a large extent, it will be unique to each person and, while self-reflection might not come easily to some, your personal perspective on life is something you need to make explicit to yourself at least if you are to be able to appreciate that not everyone will share your views or the values that underpin them.

Doel and Shardlow discuss this in terms of 'worldviews':

> Everybody has a world-view, even if it is not very clear or consistent. A world-view is just another way of saying how we make sense of the world, including personal theories we use to explain what is going on around us. Problems can arise if we have views which exclude other interpretations to such an extent that we are unaware of other people's world-views, whether they are colleagues or service-users. Problems can also occur if we are not aware of the personal beliefs which lead us to act as we do. (2005, p. 30)

While our personal values will certainly have an impact on how we operate as social workers, it is important to appreciate the wider context in which values operate. For example, organizations, communities, professions and whole societies are informed by the values that underpin them. Consider the case of political parties or regimes. For example, welfare policy which emerged during Margaret Thatcher's leadership was underpinned by 'New Right' values which espoused personal responsibility, to the extent that even the need for social work itself was put under some challenge. Similarly, the activities of organizations such as Greenpeace are influenced by the values that underpin it, such as the right to live in a safe environment, the importance of preserving the balance of nature and so on. Religious communities have their foundation in a value base which has an impact on how adherents to those religions live out their lives. For example, religious values can affect power relations between men and women, dictate career choices, affect social mobility and so on (Moss, 2005).

So what of social work's values? Most of those people who enter the profession are drawn to it because they share similar values to those they see operating in what social workers do – the protection of vulnerable people, the fostering of respect and dignity, non-judgementalism, promoting equality, the challenging of injustice and so on. However, it is not something that the social care field can risk leaving to chance, and so values have been incorporated into codes of practice, such as that published by the General Social Care Council in 2002, and against which employers are expected to judge competence.

NOS Key Role 6

Demonstrate professional competence in social work practice

This document makes clear that social care workers must:

> protect the rights and promote the interests of service users and carers;

> strive to establish and maintain the trust and confidence of service users and carers;
> promote the independence of service users while protecting them as far as possible from danger or harm;
> respect the rights of service users whilst seeking to ensure that their behaviour does not harm themselves or other people;
> uphold public trust and confidence in social care services; and
> be accountable for the quality of their work and take responsibility for maintaining and improving their knowledge and skills.

And, as we can see below, the Code of Ethics produced by the British Association of Social Workers is an attempt to make explicit the particular values of the social work profession itself – to try and express in a tangible way what the point of social work is.

Code of Ethics, see p. 185

It has been acknowledged (see, for example, Shardlow, 2002) that values are hard to define or pin down and this introduction may not have reduced any anxieties you have about understanding the concept. If that is the case, then you are not alone. Indeed, it is this very complexity which makes it all the more important that you continue to engage with the many debates which will present during your career. As Neil Thompson argues:

> values are one of those things that we will need to wrestle with for as long as we practise. Values arise from different people dealing with life's complexities and 'existential challenges' in different ways, from different perspectives, and with different objectives in mind. The values picture is therefore one that is constantly changing, a kaleidoscope of a wide range of issues, each with a bearing on the situations we encounter, and each with its own intricacies and nuances ... I would see the need to wrestle with these complexities as a basic component of professionalism. If values were a simple matter that could be resolved by a rulebook or manual of procedures to be followed slavishly, we would not need to have professional practitioners schooled in the arts of dealing with complex, messy and changeable situations. (Neil Thompson, 2005a, pp. 128–9)

Values, then, are a complex matter, so why do we place so much importance on them if they are so difficult to grasp? It is to this topic that we now turn.

why are values important?

You will be aware by this point that, in order to qualify as a social worker, you will need to have reached a level of competence in a wide range of skills and to have acquired a knowledge base of relevant information, such as an understanding of key pieces of legislation, expected 'norms' in terms of human growth and behaviour, the social context within which individual lives are played out and so on. This knowledge base and skills training will help equip you to do the job, but your values and those of the social work profession will not only guide you in terms of *how* to do what you do, but will also serve to remind you of *why* you do what you do.

Values are a central part of social work for various reasons, not least the following.

they guide us

Social work is characterized by change and uncertainty, and we are often working with people who may have become unsettled, disorientated or traumatized. When working with people we are working to some extent with emotions and, when these become highly charged, situations can become even more uncertain and may get out of hand if we are not careful. When we also bring group dynamics into the equation, we have yet another factor which can 'muddy the waters' in terms of coping with the present and planning for the future. There are often competing perspectives as each party in a situation brings his or her own values and objectives to a situation. Amid all this it is all too easy to lose sight of what is important in such situations, and having a value base can help us to feel 'grounded' – to remember what is most important to us and to those we are working with.

> Liam was a single father trying to raise his four young children alone after the unexpected death of his wife. At first he felt convinced that he did not have the skills to look after them and began to suffer from anxiety attacks. Petra, a social worker, began her working relationship with Liam by coming to an agreement that they both shared the same aim – to rebuild his confidence to the extent that he felt able to care properly for the children. It was agreed that Petra would support Liam in any decisions he needed to make, but would not take over, as this would be counterproductive to the aim of rebuilding confidence. After a few months of working in partnership to this end, Liam's confidence was growing steadily, but then his youngest child was admitted to hospital following an accident. Petra abandoned her supporting role and took over the situation completely, as she felt that it was the quickest and easiest option for him at that time. But, while the immediate crisis was managed more quickly and efficiently by her than it might have been had it been left to Liam to organize, Petra lost sight of what had underpinned their agreement. This had the effect of undermining Liam's fragile confidence to the extent that he now became even more convinced that he 'just hadn't got it in him to cope'.

practice focus
2.16

This is a good example of how a skilled and knowledgeable social worker did more harm than good by losing sight of an important value commitment – that of empowering people and promoting independence.

they help to maintain a sense of identity

As individuals, what we do, or indeed do not do, is underpinned by what is important to us. For example, if you value the right to free speech, then you are likely to oppose political regimes where this right is denied. Some people choose to live a vegetarian lifestyle because they value animal rights. What we hold dear in our lives contributes to who we are in the world, and so the way in which we live out our lives will be influenced by what we see as important in terms of religious values, family values, political values and so on. As social workers we remain individuals, but we also take on board another identity: a professional one. What helps to define a profession is a shared set of values – that is to say, a set of assumptions about what is good practice within a profession, and a sense of agreement and commitment to shared aims and ethical principles. In many cases, it is those individuals whose personal values 'mesh' with social work's professional values (social justice, individual rights and so on) who are drawn into the profession, but it would be naïve not to recognize that there can be conflicting values at times. For example, someone who has been brought up to regard disabled people as being unfortunate individuals who need to be protected from life's pressures and taken care of may find it difficult (initially at least) to accept the importance of supporting disabled people to be as independent as possible.

they highlight dilemmas

As we will discuss below, one of the reasons why values are so difficult to conceptualize is that they are not always explicit, and it is often only when values contradict each other that we become aware of their importance for the work we do. There is rarely a definitive answer, but one of the reasons why values are important is that they bring these issues to the surface and allow them to be explored and debated. Consider the following examples:

> People have a right to make their own choices, but does this extend to having the choice to end one's own life?
> People also have a right to live in conditions of their own choosing, but what if this endangers that person's health or the health of others – for example, if someone chooses to have more than 20 cats in a small house or flat?
> It is important to show respect for cultural and religious variations in terms of child-rearing practices, but what if that extends to forms of corporal punishment that some might consider to be child abuse?
> Attitudes to gender roles can also raise dilemmas. For example, you do not want to impose the 'rules' of your own culture on others, but what if women were expected to be subservient to men, denied access to education, employment and so on?

---

practice focus

2.17

Nils hoped that the study session on values would help him to better understand the concept itself and why it was given such a high profile in social work training. He had read a lot around the subject but still couldn't quite get his head around things and hoped that working through case examples in the seminar would make it all clearer. However, what each case study highlighted was that social work tends to be characterized by dilemmas. In the first scenario, in which an elderly man was refusing treatment for his cancer because he thought someone younger should benefit, Nils defended the man's right to choice and autonomy. But when someone else pointed out that anti-ageist values should alert social workers to challenge attitudes and practices which discriminate on the grounds of age, he could see that this value stance was valid too. As they worked through each case scenario Nils could see that there was never going to be a 'right' answer and that he would have to think long and hard about what was important in each individual case, rather than having a prescriptive list of dos and don'ts. He had hoped for more clarity and in one respect he had got it. What had become very clear was that he needed to question what underpins the choices people make, the actions they take, why organizations exist, the way they operate, and so on. He had begun to appreciate why the social work profession makes its value base explicit and why social workers need to delve beneath the surface of taken-for-granted assumptions.

---

they highlight the danger of being judgemental

An important part of the social work value base is not being 'judgemental'. This does not mean that we should not make judgements, in the sense of forming views or making professional decisions, but rather that we should not make unfair assumptions about people by categorizing them as 'deserving' or 'undeserving' – that is, judging them to be worthy or unworthy. This is not as easy to do as it sounds, as our attitudes can show through in subtle ways, even though we might be trying hard not to make them explicit. The following passage from Banks helps to highlight the part that our value base plays when we interpret situations:

> It is often assumed that knowing that, or 'factual knowledge', is value-free. To say we know that there is a user in the waiting room surely does not entail commitments to any particular value position? In one sense this is true. In another sense, if we consider more carefully, we realise that just seeing the person in the waiting room as a 'user' is already constituting the situation in a particular way. We are already categorizing the person in terms of our relationship to her, which may have connotations of the user as needing to be helped, or as part of the bureaucratic social work system which involves people sitting in rooms in a subservient fashion. We have already evaluated the situation according to our own perspective. This is not the same as making a straight-forward value statement like 'this user ought to be helped', but it does have value connotations. (Banks, 2001, pp. 63–4)

they help us to see the wider context in which social workers operate

Social work does not operate in a moral or political vacuum. There are different approaches to political and theoretical approaches to social work, and these different approaches are likely to reflect different value positions. For example, a New Right approach to welfare (the political philosophy associated with the Thatcher government) is premised on a different set of values from, say, a radical social work approach. Both approaches may question the role of social workers – but from very different perspectives, the former based on the idea that social work can prevent individuals from taking responsibility for their own welfare, while the latter would have concerns about social work being used to quell political discontent (by preventing people living in poverty and disadvantaged circumstances from challenging the status quo).

There are numerous other value perspectives in between these two extremes, but what this example shows is that values are not just an issue for individual practitioners, but are also part of the wider political framework of which social work forms a part.

law, politics and society, see p. 5

how do we recognize values?

Values are not tangible entities. We can not see them, touch them or smell them – they are abstract rather than concrete. However, we should not allow this to mislead us into thinking that they do not have concrete consequences, as they clearly do. What it does mean, though, is that we cannot witness values directly; we can only see the results of values, their imprint, as it were. Indeed, a useful way of understanding this is to think of values as being visible only in terms of the 'footprints' they leave, just as H. G. Wells's fictional *Invisible Man* (when not wearing his bandages) is visible only by the footstep trace he leaves. To recognize values, then, we need to see how they appear in people's actions, attitudes and language use.

As part of its professional base social work has a professional code wherein the values it upholds are made explicit, and there is an expectation that all those in the profession will commit to promoting those values. As defined by the British Association of Social Workers' Code of Ethics, these are:

> human dignity and worth;
> social justice;
> service to humanity;
> integrity; and
> competence.

It is one thing to see them written down, but it is another thing entirely to be able to recognize them in practice – to 'surface' them, as it were, and bring them to the forefront of our thoughts.

It will be expected of you that you can identify the values issues – whether that be through case studies or in actual practice situations as part of supervision on placement – your practice assessor will need to be convinced that your practice is value driven and that you are aware of *how* those values are operating.

Examples of how values issues can be identified in practice would include:

> *Where there is a conflict between one value and another or between one set of values and another.* Where we encounter someone who does not value treating people with respect and dignity, we may become angry – the emotional response of anger is the more tangible and obvious consequence of a conflict of values.
> *Where someone's values are offended.* This can arise as a result of cultural differences. For example, when a particular set of beliefs or a lifestyle is seen as 'deviant' because it is outside of the mainstream.
> *Recognized professional standards.* Such matters as confidentiality, dignity and respect for the uniqueness of the individual are bread-and-butter issues that arise very frequently.
> *Policy requirements.* Particular policies are generally the concrete outcome of a particular set of values. We can therefore identify values issues by exploring the basis and implications of one or more policies (for example, by asking: what are the values underpinning child protection or the protection of vulnerable adults?)

how do values influence practice?

Values influence practice in a number of ways. The following are some of the most significant:

> *Empathy.* If we are not aware of someone else's values (that is, if we are not taking account of what is important to them), then we cannot claim to know enough about them to be able to work in partnership with them. If we do not have even a basic grasp of what makes them tick or which rules they live or want to live their lives by, then we are going to struggle to make progress in helping them. Having at least a basic appreciation of other people's values is therefore an essential part of good practice.
> *Standards.* Having professional values made explicit gives us a framework against which standards can be judged. To become a qualified social worker it is necessary to prove competence in relation to being able to understand and work with values, in addition to the skills and knowledge requirements. Values are important, then, in helping us to reach a qualifying standard and to maintain our registration by fulfilling the professional values requirements.
> *Professionalism.* Values are also important because they underpin the notion of professionalism and professional identity. To a large extent, the value base defines

the profession of social work and thereby protects service users – they can expect those using the title to show respect for persons, to challenge oppression, to help them to make positive choices and so on. In this sense, values are part of offering a guarantee of a degree of professional integrity

When the time came for Shelley to evaluate the work she had done to help Alec move out of the care system and into the world of independent living, she asked him for feedback on the role she had played in the transition. Although the relationship had not always been an easy one, and they had disagreed on a number of occasions, Shelley had always tried to respect his individuality and his right to make his own choices. And it was clear from his comments that Alec had recognized that. He told her that she had allowed him to be himself and had been the only person in his life who had not criticized him for the choices he had made. For instance, she had been unhappy about his decision not to stay in full-time education but realized that getting a job was more important in terms of his self-esteem at that point in his life. She wondered what she would have done had Alec made lifestyle choices which involved criminal activity or something of which she disapproved. Would she still have felt comfortable with championing self-determination? At this point she was reminded of the comment made by one of her social work tutors: 'no-one said it was going to be easy!'

practice focus **2.18**

Principle 6 **Realism and Challenge**

'Nobody said it was going to be easy' sums up well an important element of this principle.

conclusion

Some people have made the mistake of assuming that, because values are abstract entities and difficult to pin down in a practical, concrete sense, they are not important. This is a huge mistake to make. As we have seen, although values are abstract, they none the less have very significant practical consequences, in so far as they can play a major part in shaping:

> *Law, theory and policy* – all major influences on practice.
> *Motivation* – what makes people determined to achieve a particular goal is, in part, value driven.
> *Relationships* – how we relate to one another owes much to our respective values.
> *Integrity* – professional integrity is very much a matter of values.

What makes values particularly important is that they have been so much a part of our upbringing that we tend to take them for granted and be relatively unaware of how they are influencing our thoughts, feelings and actions. This 'taken-for-grantedness' can be quite significant, as it can lead us to adopt an uncritical approach to some very important issues (power relationships, for example). Challenging this taken-for-grantedness can, by contrast, help us to build up a more critical, self-aware approach to the important work we undertake in social work.

Principle 3 **Critical Analysis**

A good understanding of values provides a sound foundation for critical analysis.

points to ponder

> Consider one of the key social work values. How does this value shape practice?
> How do values contribute to a person's sense of identity?
> How can we recognize the influence of values?
> Can you identify three values that you personally subscribe to? How do these relate to social work practice?
> What dangers are involved in failing to consider the values dimension of social work?

2.7 reflective practice

introduction

Reflective practice has become a very influential subject in social work education in recent years. However, it is not a new idea. One of the recognized founders of reflective practice, Donald Schön, wrote a key text on the subject that was published as long ago as 1983. What is new, though, is the importance that has been attached to this concept. Educators and practitioners alike are increasingly becoming aware of how significant an idea it is; how helpful it can be in promoting good practice and continuous learning. While some writers (for example, Ixer, 1999) are sceptical of the value of reflective practice, there is much to commend it as a way forward.

In this chapter, we shall address the important questions of: What is reflection? and What is reflective practice? We shall also examine the importance of theory, the importance of linking theory to practice and the vital role of lifelong learning. The chapter will also explore issues relating to the barriers to reflective practice and the steps we can take to promote a culture of reflection and reflective practice throughout social work.

what is reflection?

At its simplest level, reflection means thinking. Social work is an intellectual activity, in the sense that good practice depends (as we noted in Chapter 1.2) on the ability to use analytical skills and to make sense of complex situations. It involves gathering information, sifting it, weighing it up and making sense of often confusing and contradictory elements of knowledge. The ability to think clearly and effectively is therefore an important part of the successful social worker's repertoire. Reflection in this sense, therefore, means making sure that we find the time and space to use our mental capacities. It involves avoiding the danger of 'routinized' practice (Neil Thompson, 2005a) – that is, the danger of falling into habits and routines and thus getting stuck in tramlines. It is a very easy but costly mistake to get into sets of habits and therefore deal with the situations we encounter in routine, unthinking ways. There is a very real and significant danger of adopting routine responses to a non-routine situation. This can lead to potentially disastrous mistakes.

NOS Key Role 4

Manage risk to individuals, families, carers, groups, communities, self, and colleagues

It can also give the client the message that they are not important, that we are not prepared to put in the effort of dealing with the situation in a way that does justice to it, but rather are content simply to adopt a routine approach. Also, such a routine approach is likely to remove any sense of job satisfaction we may gain and may ultimately become a source of stress, as it is important to recognize that job satisfaction is in some respects a good way of insulating against the experience of stress.

Reflection, however, is not simply about thinking. It can also be used in the sense of reflection as in a mirror. In this regard, reflection can be seen as a way of looking back at oneself, looking at what we have done, what we are doing now and what we plan to do in the future. Reflection is therefore a way of promoting self-awareness, recognizing what part we are playing in the situations that we are trying to deal with, reviewing whether what we are doing is effective and whether there are better ways of doing it.

what is reflective practice?

Basically, reflective practice is professional social work practice based on reflection (in both senses of the word: thinking in general and looking back on our own work in particular), rather than the uncritical use of routines or guesswork. In a sense, it is mind*ful*, rather than mind*less*, practice. This involves recognizing that our work should be much more than:

> *Routine or habit.* There are some tasks that can be carried out in a routine way, but it is dangerous to overgeneralize and place too much emphasis on mindless habit based on routine, rather than mindful practice based on understanding.
> *Guesswork.* Even though that guesswork may be educated guesswork.
> *Following orders or instructions.* Social work is not entirely free of 'orders from above', but professional practice is far too complex to rely on being told what to do by others.
> *Copying what others do and hoping for the best.* There is much that can be learned from others, but this has to be done in a critical, reflective way, rather than just copying others unthinkingly.

It has long been recognized that social work is characterized by shortage of resources – that is, by scarcity. Even if budgets were to be doubled, there would still be people who remain in need, people for whom we cannot provide services, and yet in this scenario of scarcity one of our most powerful resources – our thinking capacity – often goes untapped. The pressure of work can mean that our greatest asset in dealing with such pressures is not used. Our thinking capacity is switched off and we rely on habit, routine or guesswork. This is a great pity when we consider the importance of thinking as a practice tool. The renowned writer on thinking skills and the inventor of the notion of 'lateral thinking', Edward de Bono, makes apt comment when he argues that:

Thinking is the ultimate human resource. Yet we can never be satisfied with our most important skill. No matter how good we become, we should always want to be better. Usually, the only people who are very satisfied with their thinking skills are those poor thinkers who think that the purpose of thinking is to prove yourself right – to your own satisfaction. If we have only a limited view of what thinking can do, we may be smug about our excellence in this area, but not otherwise. (de Bono, 2000, p. xi)

Schön, one of the most influential thinkers in the development of reflective practice, was critical of what he called 'technical rationality'. What he meant by this was the tendency to assume that we can simply apply theory or technical knowledge to practice in a direct and simple way; as if it were a matter of practice providing the questions, while theory provides the answers in a direct or straightforward way. The reality, of course, is much more complex than this, and so one of the implications of Schön's thinking is that we need to *integrate* theory and practice, rather than simply apply one to the other in a direct or simple way. Redmond captures this point well when she argues that:

> Instead of practice being a lower-order manifestation of cleaner and tidier theory, it becomes, in Schön's hands, *a combination of knowledge and action* 'producing a sense of professional freedom and a connection with rather than a distance from clients'.
> (2004, p. 36, emphasis added)

We shall return to this point later.

Schön was aware that professionals draw on a professional knowledge base. Indeed, it is a characteristic of being a professional that there is a knowledge base to draw upon (for example, in medicine, law, architecture and so on). To a large extent, a profession is defined in part by its professional knowledge base. Clearly, then, professionals engaged in their day-to-day activities are somehow drawing on that knowledge base, even if it is not done in a simplistic, technical rationality way. Schön was therefore interested in answering the question: How do professionals draw on their professional knowledge base in their day-to-day practice?

Schön drew a distinction between what he called the 'high ground' and the 'swampy lowlands'. He used the term 'high ground' to refer to the professional knowledge base of theory and research, and he used 'swampy lowlands' to refer to the complex realities of actual practice. This is very rich and useful terminology. High ground implies that the knowledge base of a profession gives its practitioners an overview of the terrain in which in operates. It provides a picture of how different elements interconnect. The swampy lowlands, by contrast, are characterized by uncertainty, 'stickiness' and difficulty in negotiating the complexities of the terrain. Schön's argument basically is that using professional knowledge is not simply a case of using the insights gained from the high ground to navigate a way through the swampy lowlands.

This can perhaps best be understood by means of a tailoring analogy. If we think of the professional knowledge base, the high ground, as the cloth, then the task of the reflective practitioner is to cut that cloth to suit the requirements of the practice situation being dealt with (the swampy lowlands). The cloth is not enough on its own and cannot simply be applied in a blanket fashion. It requires considerable skill on the part of the reflective practitioner to be able to draw out the relevant aspects of their knowledge base and apply them to this situation – to tailor the cloth, to create the garment that fits. The knowledge base will not provide off-the-peg, ready-made garments (although many students and new practitioners fall into the trap of trying to look for 'the answer' in the professional knowledge base, rather than recognizing that it is their task to *construct* that answer).

Another important distinction in Schön's work is that between 'reflection-in-action' and 'reflection-on-action'. The former refers to the type of thinking that is done while we are practising; the thinking on our feet, as it were, as we go about our professional duties. This again emphasizes the importance of thinking as a social work resource. Reflection-on-action refers to what happens after the event when we have finished a particular piece of practice. For example, following the conclusion of an interview with a family, we may wish to draw out from it the lessons to be learned, the conclusions to be drawn and so on. Reflective practice involves not only reflection-in-action and reflection-on-action, but also the ability to connect the two – that is, to make sure that our thinking on our feet is informed by our professional knowledge base, rather than by just guesswork or habit, and that our reflection-on-action draws on the actual events that we have been involved with in order to connect the high ground to the swampy lowlands.

One aspect of reflective practice that Schön did not address was what we shall call reflection-for-action. This refers to the importance of planning. Planning involves:

> *Anticipating problems.* Many of the problems we encounter in social work will be unpredictable. They will arise out of the blue. But, equally, many can be anticipated if we think ahead. For example, there are many cases on record of people experiencing violence which, with hindsight, could have been avoided if they had taken an alternative approach.

> *Avoiding mistakes.* Sometimes we can find that we are repeating a mistake that we have made before. However, if we had planned ahead, we might have been able to spot the potential for repeating the mistake and, therefore, in doing so, put ourselves in a position where we were better equipped to avoid repeating that mistake.

> *Greater sense of control.* As we have noted in relation to Principle 6, social work is difficult and demanding work, and so having at least some idea of what we are likely to face can give us a greater sense of security, greater control over what happens, rather than leaving ourselves open to whatever may come our way without having taken the opportunity to plan ahead.

> *Better time and workload management.* If we are clearer about what is likely to happen, we are in a better position to make sure that we do not end up in a situation of work overload. In this respect, reflection for action can be a very good way of preventing stress from arising.

> *Greater credibility.* If we fail to plan ahead and make the most of our ability to anticipate developments, then we can come across as quite amateurish and, frankly, unimpressive. While it is not our aim to try and impress others, there is the important question of professional credibility. If we lose that credibility, we lose the power to influence people and the events that we are trying to deal with.

practice focus
2.19

After reading about reflective practice, Alan looked back over his own recent work. Mr Hughes had been in hospital for several months and was going back to his house with an occupational therapist to assess whether any changes needed to be made to his home environment. It had been suggested that this take the form of a multidisciplinary assessment and, because Mr Hughes had been diagnosed as having Alzheimer's disease, Alan agreed that both he and Mr Hughes' son and daughter should also be present when the visit took place, so that the assessment would be as informed as possible. He had seen the benefits of multidisciplinary working for all concerned and was keen to promote this as good working practice in every case. However, what he had not anticipated was the potential for Mr Hughes to feel under so much pressure with so many people in his house that he couldn't concentrate on the job in hand, and the so the visit was a waste of time. In retrospect, Alan realized that he could have anticipated this, especially as he had read widely about the effects of dementia. While looking back ('reflecting-on-action') he could see how he should have thought more about the consequences of having a large number of participants and so have planned the event differently ('reflection-for-action'). He could also see how recognizing on the day that this procedure was becoming counterproductive was an example of 'reflection-in-action'. By drawing on what he had read about reflective practice, Alan began to see that it was not appropriate always to conduct such assessments in the same way as a matter of course, and that he needed to be careful about working in a routinized way himself or colluding with routinized practices.

One important part of reflective practice is what is known as 'surfacing'. What this means is making the implicit explicit. Instead of dealing with things 'under the table', as it were, it is better to put them 'on the table', to be clear about what we are dealing with.

NOS Key Role 2

Plan, carry out, review and evaluate social work practice, with individuals, families, carers, groups, communities, and other professionals

This involves having a greater foundation for learning and development. If we are clear about what we are dealing with and how we are dealing with it, we are in a much better position to learn from that experience or, to put it another way: How can we get better at something if we do not know what it is? If we are achieving results, but we are not sure what exactly we did to achieve them, then we are in a weaker position in order to achieve such positive results in future.

the importance of theory

The term theory is one that can cause confusion. For example, some people use theory to mean 'as opposed to reality' when, for example, they say things like: 'Oh, that's the case in theory, but in reality ... '. It is important to move away from that confusion and recognize that theory, in the sense we are using it here, is a shorthand term for the professional knowledge base, the conceptual frameworks we use for understanding and making sense of the reality of practice.

We can distinguish *formal* theory which involves the crystallization of knowledge. This, in effect, amounts to drawing on other people's studying, practising and researching. In the past, people have recorded their views and understandings based on practice, research and study, and we can draw on the benefits of that by reading their work in books, journal papers, research reports and so on. However, there is also *informal* theory, in the sense that we take the formal theory (the textbook theory, as it were) and we make it *our* theory, not by taking it at face value, but by using it critically and integrating it with out own knowledge and experience, our own perspective. This is a very important part of reflective practice: being able to draw on the formal theory base, while also combining it with our own understandings, based on our own perspective, our own experience and our own thinking.

Neil Thompson (2000b) refers to 'the adventure of theory'. By this he means the importance of engaging with knowledge and making it into a useful tool – and the pleasure and even excitement that can be gained from doing so. It involves going beyond seeing formal knowledge as something separate from the reality of practice or as something to be feared and avoided. He advocates engaging fully with the professional knowledge base and, in effect, reclaiming it – so that it becomes an important tool for helping to understand the complexities of the problems we encounter in social work.

integrating theory and practice

It is also in the work of Neil Thompson (2000b) that we find the concept of 'the fallacy of theoryless practice'. What he means by this is that it is commonly assumed by many practitioners that their work does not draw on a theory base; that they are simply practising on the basis of their own personal understanding of the situation. Neil Thompson refers to this as a fallacy because, he argues, our actions inevitably draw on a theory base – a knowledge base and a conceptual framework for making sense of both the previously acquired knowledge and the experience we are having.

Those people who advocate 'sticking to practice' are therefore falling into the 'fallacy of theoryless practice'. Sticking to practice, if by this we mean not concerning ourselves with theory, is not an option. This is because we do draw on theory, whether we know it or not and whether we like it or not. For example, in dealing with somebody with an alcohol problem, we will be drawing on our own understanding of alcohol based on what has been found out about alcohol through decades of research. While we may not be experts on this research, it is likely that our everyday understanding of alcohol will be influenced by broader social understandings of alcohol, its effects, its problems and the potential solutions. The question, then, is not: Should we draw on theory? but, rather: Are we clear about what theory we are drawing on and its appropriateness, validity and so on? It is also important to ask: How well do we understand that theory? Is it safe to practise on very limited understanding? Should we be developing our knowledge and understanding over time?

It is therefore important to *integrate* theory and practice, to look at how our knowledge base and our actions interrelate, look at how our thinking and our doing are connected. We need to ask ourselves: are we aware what ideas we are basing our practice on, what assumptions we are making, or what perspective we are adopting? If not, how can we make sure that we are:

1 *Maximizing our effectiveness.* Developing a more sophisticated level of understanding can open doors to a wider range of avenues to pursue, as opposed to relying on a very basic understanding which may not take us very far.

2 *Being consistent with anti-discriminatory practice.* Forms of social work practice based on unexamined assumptions or uncritically accepted ideas swallowed whole may be discriminatory (for example, by relying on stereotypes).

3 *Finding stimulation and job satisfaction.* As mentioned earlier, social work is demanding and challenging work. We need stimulation and job satisfaction to keep us going. How much job satisfaction is there in routine, uncritical practice, based on very limited understanding?

The challenge of integrating theory and practice is therefore an important one. It means first of all being aware of what theory base we are drawing on. Instead of undertaking a course of study and then simply allowing what we have learned to fade away over time, we need to make sure that we are refreshing that knowledge base by keeping up to date with developments, by reminding ourselves of the key issues that we have learned. Second, we also need to make sure that we are giving ourselves the space and time to draw on that knowledge base to be able to use our thinking skills, to be able to make sure that our practice is of the highest standard we can manage. Sometimes pressures at work can make that difficult. This is a point to which we shall return below under the heading of 'Barriers to reflective practice'.

Erin was running a workshop with a group of support workers. She wanted to help them to understand that relying on nothing more than 'it seemed like the right thing to do' to guide their actions can result in ineffective, or even dangerous, practice. She wanted them to take on board that practice needs to be informed by drawing on what has gone before, but met a lot of resistance when she talked about the relationship between theory and practice. There were several comments like: 'But you're the trained social worker here – we haven't been to college or university and read all about theories'. She realized then that she needed to talk a bit more about the concept of theory. When she explained that it didn't just refer to formal or named theories, but also to such things as knowledge gained from previous experience, general reading, insights gained on training courses and so on, they began to highlight examples of where they had integrated new learning into the way they carried out their work. They began to realize that theory, broadly defined, is very relevant to practice.

practice focus
2.20

lifelong learning

One of the major benefits of reflective practice is that it provides a foundation for continuing to learn and develop over time. If our practice is based on the uncritical use of habits, routines and guesswork, then our opportunities for learning are very restricted. We could go for years simply repeating experiences without being able to draw out from them lessons to be learned. It is often said that 'experience is the best teacher'. However, this is not quite the case. In reality, it is what we *do with* our experience that is the best teacher. Simply having an experience will not necessarily teach us anything. Reflective practice involves drawing out the learning from our experience, being open to further development in our thinking and our practice.

We will all have met people who have had a lot of experience in a particular job, but have learned little or nothing from it. It is not safe to assume that, the longer a person is in a particular job, the better they are at doing it. For many people, they may achieve an element of basic competence and then 'coast in neutral' thereafter. This can be not only a recipe for poor practice, it can also be a source of considerable problems, but perhaps most significantly of all, it acts as a barrier to learning and is a huge waste of important learning resources. It is therefore important to recognize lifelong learning as a sound foundation for professional practice.

The importance of lifelong learning has been recognized in the requirements for professional registration. When a social worker first becomes registered, they will begin a period of three years during which time they will need to maintain a record of their 'continuous professional development' (or CPD for short) if they wish to re-register at the end of that three-year period. It is no longer acceptable for someone to qualify as a social worker following an extensive period of study and then just 'switch off' from learning and 'get on with practice'. The dangers of such an approach have long been recognized, but it is only relatively recently that registration requirements have challenged that unhelpful mindset.

barriers to reflective practice

While it is certainly our intention in this chapter to emphasize the importance of reflective practice, we do not want to leave you with the misleading impression that we are trying to say that it is necessarily easy to do. Being important to achieve and being easy to achieve are two different things. It has to be recognized that there will be a number of obstacles to reflective practice, and so, in this section of the chapter, we highlight a number of common barriers and offer some potential ways of tackling these. However, the list is not comprehensive, and you may well come across other barriers in your own attempts to develop reflective practice. We hope, though, that the guidance we give here will give you some insights into how you might want to tackle other actual or potential barriers:

> *Organizational culture.* Organizations develop a set of habits, routines, unquestioned assumptions and taken-for-granted, unwritten rules. Sometimes an organization's culture can be very helpful and supportive. At other times, however, it can lead to problems and blockages. For example, it is unfortunately the case that many organizations have what is known as an 'anti-learning culture'. This is where there is a strong set of working habits, and any attempt to change or develop patterns of work is strongly resisted by some people at least (often influential people). A very important point to recognize here is that while organizational cultures are powerful, they are not all-powerful. That is, while an organizational culture may put individual members of that organization under considerable pressure to conform with the norms of that culture, it is possible and often desirable to do what we think is appropriate despite that culture. That is, cultures may seek to *influence* our behaviour, but they do not *determine* our behaviour. It is perfectly possible to work in a reflective way, even if the culture in which you work does not support that. Being in an unsupportive culture will tend to make the task harder, but it does not make it impossible. One possible strategy to help you in the challenge of being reflective in a non-reflective culture is to seek out like-minded people. Are you alone in wanting to promote reflective practice? If not, can you form a supportive alliance with others, even if they are in a minority, in taking forward ideas around reflective practice?

NOS Key Role 5

Manage and be accountable, with supervision and support, for your own social work practice within your organization

> *Time and workload management.* A commonly heard comment is: 'I haven't got time to think', as if to say reflective practice is a luxury that we cannot afford in today's busy work environments. However, this approach is a mistaken one, and a very seriously mistaken one at that. This is because the busier we are and the more pressured we are, the more important it is that we should be reflective, the more we need to be 'on the ball' and not allowing ourselves to drift away from a focus on the key issues we are dealing with. Being able to manage reflective practice in a highly pressurized work situation is a highly skilled task, but it is one that can be achieved over time by working at it. Giving up and assuming that 'there isn't time for reflection' will not improve the situation – in fact, it may make it worse and can leave us prone to poor practice and all the potential negative consequences of that.

By taking (or making) the time to think, we can then get greater control over our workload, establish clear priorities, avoid time-consuming mistakes, and make sure that we are focused on achieving clearly identified goals.

> *Stress.* Where stress is involved, there is always the danger of the vicious circle. That is, excessive work pressures can lead people's performance to drop because they feel stressed. That drop in performance can mean that they are then less well equipped to deal with the pressures, which means that they then feel even more pressurized, which can then lead to their feeling even more stressed and therefore less able to cope, and so it goes on, deeper and deeper into a spiral of negativity. Where this happens, reflective practice becomes extremely difficult if not impossible. It is therefore vitally important that we use reflective practice as a means of preventing stress. It involves making sure that we are clear about our priorities and that we do not allow ourselves to be put in a position where there are unrealistic expectations on us, as unrealistic expectations can be a major source of stress (as we acknowledged in Chapter 1.2). A high workload can be stimulating and rewarding. A workload that is too high – that is, unrealistic – is not stimulating and rewarding. It can lead to significant problems, not least those associated with stress. Reflective practice can help us to make sure that we are dealing with realistic expectations and, where people have unrealistic expectations of us (clients, carers or managers, for example), then we are able to use our negotiation skills to re-establish clear and realistic expectations.

> *Pressure from others.* In social work we can often be put under immense pressure from others to do what they want us to do, to do it now if not sooner, and to tackle issues from a particular point of view. This can arise because other people may have different agendas from our own or it may be as a result of 'de-professionalization' – that is, the tendency of some people to want to use social work in a way that is not consistent with its professional principles. For example, some people may wish that a social worker should simply follow procedures in a mechanistic sort of way without digging more deeply into the presenting situation. This can mean that reflective practice is being strongly discouraged by others. The 'antidote' to this is assertiveness. This refers to the ability to make sure that we do not allow others to bully us into getting their way at our expense (while also making sure we do not bully them into getting our way). It involves trying to establish a 'win-win' situation where both parties are reasonably happy with the outcome. This is quite a skilled approach, but it is a set of skills that can be developed over time, and indeed *should* be developed over time, as they are very important social work skills.

> *Lack of confidence.* This can arise in at least two main ways. First, there can be the assumption that 'I'm not very bright', associated with a discomfort or even fear when it comes to using formal theory and knowledge. However, it should be remembered that drawing on a professional knowledge base is not the same as being asked to be an expert on that knowledge base, or even to write an essay on it, but rather to be able to understand its significance and how it relates to practice situations. If somebody has reached the level of qualified social worker, they should be well able to undertake this, and it may be their own sense of low confidence that is holding them back. Lack of confidence can also apply in terms of not so much using the theory base, but in terms of being able to link it to practice. Many people, for example, say that they do not feel able to do this unassisted, that they need somebody else to 'bounce

ideas off' in order to be able to formulate their own thinking and come to their own conclusions. They feel unable to do this on their own. This is not really a problem, as even the best, most experienced social workers may find it helpful to share ideas with others, to get feedback and to draw on the knowledge, experience and views of others. There is no shame in sharing ideas with other people in order to take your own thinking and practice forward. If you are able to do this through supervision, that can be a very helpful means of achieving your ends but if, for some reason, that is not possible, then the other alternatives would include discussing issues with colleagues on an informal basis, or even looking for a more formal basis for helping one another (for example, some teams have a 'buddying' system in which social workers pair up to support one another in their practice).

There are, then, clearly a number of barriers to reflective practice, but none of these is insurmountable. The value of reflective practice is such that it is well worth the effort of taking the necessary steps to try and overcome these barriers and, of course, it should be remembered that promoting good practice in general and reflective practice in particular is a collective responsibility as well as an individual one, so do use whatever support mechanisms you can have access to in order to take this forward.

> *practice focus* **2.21**
>
> Kash enjoyed being busy. He worked in the mental health field and it was not unusual for him to have to deal with unforeseen crises on a fairly regular basis. Even when he was very busy, he never felt that his workload was out of control, because he knew what he was doing and why in each particular case. However, because of staff shortages, Kash found himself dealing with a much higher caseload than usual. He was well used to carrying extra work when colleagues were taking annual leave, but this went on for months. It began to seem like everything that could go wrong was going wrong, and Kash had no time to get over one difficult situation before he was called on to deal with another. It was during a supervision session that he began to see the effect that this was having on him. Talking about his casework highlighted that he was taking shortcuts and not practising in his usual systematic way. In many cases he wasn't able to explain the purpose, method or focus of what he was doing and realized that he might indeed have been causing, or at least contributing to, the mistakes that were being made and the tensions that were arising. He tried to 'go back up a gear' but knowing that he had lowered his usual standards led to his feeling demoralized and drained of energy and commitment. Kash's manager could see the effect that this was having on his self-confidence and allocated no new cases until he felt confident that Kash was once again using his considerable knowledge and experience to inform his work. Once the stress caused by an unmanageable workload had been addressed, and Kash had re-focused, he realized that this had been a salutary lesson about dangers of working on 'automatic pilot'.

conclusion

This chapter has shown that reflective practice is an important approach to professional social work. We have argued that a good social worker is a thinking social worker, someone who draws on a professional knowledge base, who is aware of what is going on around him or her and does not fall into the trap of uncritical routines, knee-jerk reactions or simply following what is perceived to be an order or instruction. Social work is far too complex to rely on such simplistic approaches, and those people who make the mistake of trying to practise in this way are skating on thin ice, and may well find that they encounter major difficulties at some point in their career.

Manage risk to individuals, families, carers, groups, communities, self and colleagues.

A much wiser and more effective approach is clearly that of reflective practice. We will not get it right all of the time. We will miss certain issues, we will find that we have not been as reflective as we could have been at times, but if we make every reasonable endeavour to promote reflective practice, then there is no reason why we should not have a significant level of success compared with the alternative of 'mindless practice'.

points to ponder

> How can we avoid getting into 'tramlines', uncritical routinized practices that can be quite dangerous?
> How can the 'high ground' be helpful in the 'swampy lowlands' of practice?
> How can practitioners benefit from the 'adventure of theory'?
> How can we deal with barriers to reflective practice?
> How can we make sure that we continue to learn and develop throughout our careers?

2.8 **conclusion**

Part 2 of the book has been concerned with 'Core topics'. Our choice of what we consider to be core topics is, of course, a reflection of our own approach to social work – and no doubt, other authors, with different approaches, may have chosen different topics to be regarded as 'core'. But, even within our own frame of reference, we would not wish to claim that the topics discussed here are the only important ones. We do, however, have to be realistic about space restrictions. This is a lengthy book, but it could easily have been twice as long, and so we have had to make difficult decisions about what to leave out.

However, having made our choice of core topics, in Part 2 we have tried to put across clearly and helpfully what we see as the foundation stones of your future learning and practice in social work. And, of course, we would argue that they are precisely that: foundation stones, rather than the edifice itself. What we present here will point you in the right direction and give you a positive start, but it would be naïve in the extreme to see Part 2 as being in any way complete or definitive. Anyone who is tempted to see it that way should revisit Chapter 1.3.

In all, we have addressed seven major topics in Part 2. We began by exploring the fundamental topic of social work processes. In that chapter we looked at two broad types of process. First, we looked at the processes that are concerned with the 'space between people'. Social work is, after all, carried out largely through interactions with other people – clients, carers, colleagues within our own agency and colleagues in other agencies too (health, housing, police and so on). Understanding how such interactions work as a basis for effective practice is clearly an important part of what we need to do in developing our knowledge and skills.

The other type of process we examined was that of 'the helping process'. This is not intended to be a rigid prescription for practice, but rather a helpful structure and framework for trying to make sure that we keep a clear focus on what we are doing, why we are doing it, where we are up to, what we need to do next, and so on.

systematic practice, see p. 261

In the following chapter, the social context was our topic. We were keen to emphasize that good practice depends very much on taking into consideration the wider social context. This is because:

> The circumstances of the people we are trying to help will owe a great deal to aspects of the social context – for example, poverty and deprivation, racism, socially exclusive attitudes towards disabled people and many other such issues.

> The problems we are trying to tackle will also often owe much to aspects of the social context – for example, mental health problems caused in large part by social

stresses or ageist attitudes towards older people contributing to social isolation and associated problems.

> The social welfare system we work in is part of the wider social context and so, law, policy and, to a certain extent, theory will also be shaped in part by that social context.
> Our own social background will influence how we perceive the world, our values, our priorities and so on, and so the social context is also very significant in this regard.
> Our actions in social work, collectively at least, can contribute to the social context. For example, if we fail to take account of sexist stereotypes in our work, we are likely to be reinforcing those stereotypes, but if we challenge them and work in an anti-sexist way, then we are playing at least a small part in social change by being part of a movement geared towards promoting greater gender equality.

Human development was the topic receiving our attention in Chapter 2.4. The key issue here is that, as human beings, we share certain developmental tendencies (that is, patterns of growth and development over time) that can be very significant in terms of the problems we encounter and how we deal with them. However, it is not simply a case of human development being a set of fixed processes – the reality is much more complex than this. The broad strands of development, while very important as broad principles and patterns of behaviour, have to be considered in the context of cultural differences, gender differences and – not least – individual differences (each individual will react in subtly different ways to the influences of human development factors. Such factors provide a framework or set of parameters for human behaviour; they do not *determine* our behaviour).

We were keen to argue in Chapter 2.2 that our actions in social work need to be understood in the light of a broader social context. To this we must also add that such behaviour is shaped in part by an *organizational* context – that is, the organization we work for (and other organizations we work with) will have a significant bearing on our practice. This will apply in terms of its power relations, its established habits, patterns of behaviour, 'unwritten rules' and taken-for-granted assumptions (in other words, its culture), its resources, its policies and procedures and its relationship with other organizations. We argued that a skilled social worker should be seeking to influence in a positive direction the organization for which he or she works (and indeed other organizations in the multidisciplinary network) in order to maximize the likelihood of positive outcomes for the people we are seeking to help. It is not necessarily an easy thing to do, but it is an important one none the less.

Another set of contextual factors formed the subject matter of Chapter 2.5, namely the law and social policy. The law affects some forms of social work more than it affects others, but *all* branches of social work are significantly influenced by the law in various ways. It would be both naïve and dangerous to neglect to take account of the legal context. Similarly, the influence of social policy is enormous, and so an approach to social work that does not incorporate an understanding of the social policy issues that impinge on practice is a woefully inadequate one – and one that could lead to considerable difficulties.

The final set of contextual issues that we have presented in Part 2 are those connected with the social work value base. Chapter 2.6 explored the nature and significance of values and argued strongly that these are at the heart of practice. Although values can be difficult to pin down, their consequences are often very clear. It is very much our contention that a social work practice that is not rooted in an appropriate set of professional values is a dangerous practice, one that can do a lot of harm.

We began Part 2 with a discussion about important practice issues – namely social work processes. This was because, in planning the book, we felt it was important for an analysis of core issues to begin with a focus on actual practice. However, it is difficult if not impossible to gain an adequate understanding of (and therefore basis for) practice without at least a basic grasp of various contextual factors. We therefore moved on from our discussion of social work processes to explore contextual issues relating to the social context, human development, the organizational context and the significance of law and policy in largely setting the terms of reference for social work.

To conclude Part 2, we then returned to our theme of actual practice by examining what is involved in the notion of 'reflective practice'. We argued that good practice must be thinking practice, in the sense that effectiveness as a practitioner depends to a large extent on our ability to use our analytical skills to make sense of complex situations. Practice also needs to be reflective in the sense of 'reflexive' – that is, looking back on itself. In this way we can learn from our experience and build on our knowledge, skills and values bases over time. This is an important alternative to forms of practice based on the uncritical use of routine, habit and guesswork.

Part 2 has provided a great deal of food for thought, and we hope that you have found it useful in terms of both the knowledge it has provided and the foundation it provides for further learning.

In Part 3 we build on the work done in Part 2 by presenting short introductory accounts of over 100 key concepts that should help to flesh out much of what we have covered so far. It is to these that we now turn.

suggestions for further reading

2.1 social work processes

Everitt, A. and Hardiker, P. (1996) *Evaluating for Good Practice*, Basingstoke, Macmillan – now Palgrave Macmillan.
Provides a basic understanding of assessment, planning and evaluation on which to build further.

Kemshall, H. and Pritchard, J. (eds) (1996) *Good Practice in Risk Assessment and Risk Management*, London, Jessica Kingsley.
While there is an emphasis here on practice issues, they are presented in a context of making sure that practice is underpinned by a knowledge base.

Parsloe, P. (ed.) (1999) *Risk Assessment in Social Care and Social Work*, London, Jessica Kingsley.
This collection has contributions which focus on work in specific areas, such as mental health, but also includes discussion on broader issues, such as ethics and accountability.

See also:
Milner, J. and O'Byrne, P. (2002) *Assessment in Social Work*, 2nd edn, Basingstoke, Palgrave Macmillan.
Nelson-Jones, R. (2005) *Introduction to Counselling Skills: Texts and Activities*, 2nd edn, London, Sage.
Parton, N. and O'Byrne, P. (2000) *Constructive Social Work*, Basingstoke, Macmillan – now Palgrave Macmillan.
Thompson, N. (2002) *People Skills*, 2nd edn, Basingstoke, Palgrave Macmillan.
Thompson, N. (2006) *People Problems*, Basingstoke, Palgrave Macmillan.
Thompson, N. and Thompson, S. (2007) *Understanding Social Care*, 2nd edn, Lyme Regis, Russell House Publishing.
Trevithick, P. (2005) *Social Work Skills: A Practice Handbook*, 2nd edn, Maidenhead, Open University Press.

2.2 the social context

Abercrombie, N. (2004) *Sociology*, Cambridge, Polity Press.
This will be of use to those who have not had an introduction to key sociological themes and concepts. It is a very accessible text which will help with an understanding of social context and the need to challenge 'taken-for-granted' assumptions.

Barry, M. and Hallett, C. (eds) (1998) *Social Exclusion and Social Work: Issues of Theory, Policy and Practice*, Lyme Regis, Russell House Publishing.
Poverty, user marginalization and citizenship are among the key concepts explored in this edited collection.

Graham, M. (2002) *Social Work and African-Centred Worldviews*, Birmingham, Venture Press.
This book challenges the dominance of a Eurocentric viewpoint in social work.

See also:
Back, L. and Solomos, J. (2000) *Theories of Race and Racism: A Reader*, London, Routledge.
Brown, H.C. (1998) *Social Work and Sexuality: Working with Lesbians and Gay Men*, Basingstoke, Macmillan – now Palgrave Macmillan.
Carabine, J. (ed.) (2004) *Sexualities: Personal Lives and Social Policy*, Bristol, The Policy Press.
Christie, A. (ed.) (2001) *Men and Social Work: Theories and Practice*, Basingstoke, Palgrave Macmillan.

Dwivedi, K. N. and Varma, V. P. (eds) (2002) *Meeting the Needs of Ethnic Minority Children, Including Refugee, Black and Mixed Parentage Children: A Handbook for Professionals*, London, Jessica Kingsley.

Swain, J., French, S., Barnes, C. and Thomas, C. (eds) (2004) *Disabling Barriers – Enabling Environments*, 2nd edn, London, Sage.

Williams, C., Soydan, H. and Johnson, M. R. D. (eds) (1998) *Social Work and Minorities: European Perspectives*, London, Routledge.

2.3 human development

Arber, S. and Ginn, J. (eds) (1995) *Connecting Gender and Ageing: A Sociological Approach*, Buckingham, Open University Press.

Biggs, S. (1999) *The Mature Imagination: Dynamics of Identity in Midlife and Beyond*, Buckingham, Open University Press.

Burr, V. (2003) *Social Constructionism*, 2nd edn, London, Routledge.

Crawford, K. and Walker, J. (2003) *Social Work and Human Development*, Exeter, Learning Matters.

Dickenson, D., Johnson, M. and Katz, J. S. (eds) (2000) *Death, Dying and Bereavement*, 2nd edn, London, Sage.

Gubrium, J. and Holstein, J. (eds) (2003) *Ways of Ageing*, Oxford, Blackwell.

Hockey, J. and James, A. (2003) *Social Identities Across the Life Course*, Basingstoke, Palgrave Macmillan.

Hunt, S. (2005) *The Life Course: A Sociological Introduction*, Basingstoke, Palgrave Macmillan.

Neimeyer, R. A. (ed.) (2001) *Meaning Reconstruction and the Experience of Loss*, London, American Psychological Association.

Thompson, N. (ed.) (2002) *Loss and Grief: A Guide for Human Services Practitioners*, Basingstoke, Palgrave Macmillan.

Thompson, N. (2002) *Building the Future*, Lyme Regis, Russell House Publishing.

Thompson, N. (2004) *Group Care with Children and Young People*, 2nd edn, Lyme Regis, Russell House Publishing.

Thompson, S. (2005) *Age Discrimination*, Lyme Regis, Russell House Publishing.

2.4 the organizational context

Coulshed, V. and Mullender, A. with Jones, D. and Thompson, N. (2006) *Management in Social Work*, 3rd edn, Basingstoke, Palgrave Macmillan.

Henderson, J. and Atkinson, D. (eds) (2003) *Managing Care in Context*, London, Routledge.

Linstead, S., Fulop, L. and Lilley, S. (eds) (2004) *Management and Organization: A Critical Text*, Basingstoke, Palgrave Macmillan.

Mullender, A. and Perrott, S. (2002) 'Social Work in Organisations', in Adams, Dominelli and Payne (2002a).

Reynolds, J. et al., (eds) (2003) *The Managing Care Reader*, London, Routledge.

Seden, J. and Reynolds, J. (eds) (2003) *Managing Care in Practice*, London , Routledge.

Thompson, N. (2003) *Promoting Equality: Tackling Discrimination and Oppression*, 2nd edn, Basingstoke, Palgrave Macmillan, ch. 6.

2.5 law and policy

Bateman, N. (2003) *Welfare Rights*, London, Care and Health.
  Useful for its overview of the welfare benefits system, this book also has a section on tactics in welfare rights work.

Brayne, H. and Broadbent, G. (2002) *Legal Matters for Social Workers*, Oxford, Oxford University Press.
  Amongst the many areas discussed are anti-discrimination and human rights legislation.

See also:

Brayne, H., Martin, G. and Carr, H (2005) *Law for Social Workers*, 9th edn, Oxford, Oxford University Press.

Clements, L. (2004) *Community Care and the Law*, 3rd edn, London, Legal Action Group.

Cooper, J. and Vernon, S. (1996) *Disability and the Law*, London, Jessica Kingsley.

Lyon, C. (2003) *Child Abuse*, 3rd edn, Bristol, Family Law.

Pearl, D. and Hershman, D. (2002) *Care Standards Legislation Handbook*, Bristol, Jordan Publishing.

Puri, B. K., Brown, R. A., McKee, H. J. and Treasaden, I. H. (2005) *Mental Health Law: A Practical Guide*, London, Hodder Arnold.

Ridout, P. (ed.) (2003) *Care Standards: A Practical Guide*, Bristol, Jordan Publishing.

Roberts, J. (2003) *Using the Law in Social Work*, Exeter, Learning Matters.

2.6 the value base

Moss, B. (2007) *Values*, Lyme Regis, Russell House Publishing.
>	An excellent introduction to the importance of values.

Thompson, N. (2005) *Understanding Social Work: Preparing for Practice*, 2nd edn, Basingstoke, Palgrave Macmillan.
>	Chapter 5 provides an overview of social work values.

Also of importance:

Adams, R., Dominelli, L. and Payne, M. (eds) (2002b) *Critical Practice in Social Work*, Basingstoke, Palgrave Macmillan.

Allison, A. (2005) 'The Ethical Issues of Working in Partnership', in Carnwell and Buchanan (2005), Maidenhead, Open University Press.

Banks, S. (2006) *Ethics and Values in Social Work*, 3rd edn, Basingstoke, Palgrave Macmillan.

Baxter, C. (ed.) (2001) *Managing Diversity and Inequality in Health Care*, London, Bailliere/Tindall.

Dean. H. (2004) *The Ethics of Welfare: Human Rights, Dependency and Responsibility*, Bristol, The Policy Press.

Dwyer, P. (2004) *Understanding Social Citizenship: Themes and Perspectives for Policy and Practice*, Bristol, The Policy Press.

Griseri, P. (1998) *Managing Values: Ethical Change in Organisations*, Basingstoke, Macmillan – now Palgrave Macmillan.

Hugman, R. (1998) *Social Welfare and Social Value*, Basingstoke, Macmillan – now Palgrave Macmillan.

Hugman, R., (2003) 'Professional Values and Ethics in Social Work: Reconsidering Postmodernism?', *British Journal of Social Work*, **33**(8).

Lister, R. (2003) *Citizenship: Feminist Perspectives*, 2nd edn, Basingstoke, Palgrave Macmillan.

Thompson, N. (2003) *Promoting Equality: Tackling Discrimination and Oppression*, 2nd edn, Basingstoke, Palgrave Macmillan.

Thompson, N. (2006) *Anti-Discriminatory Practice*, 4th edn, Basingstoke, Palgrave Macmillan.

2.7 reflective practice

Schön, D. A. (1983) *The Reflective Practitioner: How Professionals Think in Action*, New York, Basic Books.
>	This ground-breaking text has informed much of what has followed in this field.

Thompson, N. (2000) *Theory and Practice in Human Services*, 2nd edn, Buckingham, Open University Press.

Thompson, S. and Thompson, N. (2008) *The Critically Reflective Practitioner*, Basingstoke, Palgrave Macmillan.

See also:

Fook, J. (1999) 'Critical Reflexivity in Education and Practice', in Pease and Fook (1999).

Gould, N. and Baldwin, M. (eds) (2004) *Social Work, Critical Reflection and the Learning Organization*, Aldershot, Ashgate.

Jasper, M. (2003) *Foundations in Nursing and Healthcare: Beginning Reflective Practice*, Cheltenham, Nelson Thornes.

Martyn, H. (ed.) (2000) *Developing Reflective Practice: Making Sense of Social Work in a World of Change*, Bristol, The Policy Press.

Taylor, C. and White, S. (2000) *Practising Reflexivity in Health and Welfare: Making Knowledge*, Buckingham, Open University Press.

Redmond, B. (2004) *Reflection in Action: Developing Reflective Practice in Health and Social Services*, Aldershot, Ashgate.

Thompson, N. (2006) *Promoting Workplace Learning*, Bristol, The Policy Press.

key terms and concepts

3

3.1 introduction

In this part of the book we provide short explanations of over 100 key terms and concepts commonly used in social work. If you wish to know more about a particular item featured here, please note that many, but not all, of the terms and concepts discussed feature in the 'Suggestions for further reading' section at the end of this part of the book, where you will be able to find recommendations for further reading. Some entries make reference to other items in Part 3: these are highlighted in bold.

In selecting the 100 or so terms and concepts to be covered here, we have borne in mind the fact that a number of key social work issues are discussed elsewhere in this book. There is little point repeating here what is said elsewhere in the book, and so we do not include the following in Part 3 because of their appearance in other sections: assessment; intervention; review; ending; evaluation; bereavement, grief and loss; empowerment; identity; reflective practice; systematic practice; professionalism and; of course, many others. The absence of a term or concept from Part 3 should therefore not be interpreted as meaning that it is not important.

Please note that the explanations given here are brief, introductory ones and should be used as a means of developing your knowledge and awareness and preparing you for more in-depth study of the issues involved. The explanations will not be sufficient in themselves to give you a working understanding of the ideas involved, and it can be dangerous to assume that you have a good or sufficient understanding of a concept based on one short, introductory account. For example, reading the entry on mediation will not make you into a mediator and reading the section on discrimination will not equip you for anti-discriminatory practice. However, they will both begin to take you in the right direction. Please, then, use this part of the book as a gateway to further learning, rather than as a substitute for further study, debate and learning.

3.2 **terms and concepts**

introduction

We present the ideas in alphabetical order to prevent anyone assuming that the order in which they are presented represents any sort of hierarchy or set of priorities. We have tried to present the ideas clearly and helpfully, but of course, given the short space available for each one, that is a very difficult task. We have sought to do the best we can in the circumstances.

We would suggest that you can use Part 3 in one of two ways. First, you could use it simply as a reference source, looking up particular terms as and when required. Second, you could read the whole of Part 3 from start to finish, methodically working your way through it. Our advice would be for you to adopt the second of the two strategies to begin with, and then use Part 3 as a reference source in future to remind yourself of some of the key issues covered. In this way you can get the best of both worlds.

`accountability` Accountability is largely about taking responsibility on board. In terms of social work practice it is an important issue at a number of levels which do not always fit together in a neat way. Social workers have:

> *Legal accountability.* We are answerable in law for our actions (and inactions) and decisions. Legal and policy guidelines can offer some degree of guidance when trying to deal with the many dilemmas we face as social workers, but the law is not prescriptive in all cases, and often it is a matter of interpretation.

`interpreting law, see p. 115 and p. 122`

> *Professional accountability.* We also have a responsibility to work in accordance with a professional code of ethics and values and not to bring the profession into disrepute. This involves being able to account for our actions, to demonstrate what underpins our decision making. This means that our decision making needs to be carried out on an informed basis. At any point we can be called to account for our actions (hence the term accountability).

> *Moral accountability.* Social work is committed to **social justice** and other such values geared towards treating people fairly, humanely and positively. We therefore have a moral responsibility as part of our role – in effect, we have accountability to the people we work with and the society we are part of.

Principle 7 `Self-management`
Accountability is part of the reason why self-management is so important in social work.

Principle 4 `Knowledge, Skills and Values`
Accountability is also part of the reason why knowledge, skills and values are so important – particularly the values that make sure our work is ethically acceptable.

Accountability does not mean that we should be held responsible for matters over which we have no control – that would be unfair, but it does mean that, when we are carrying out our duties, we have to remember that we have certain obligations and must therefore act responsibly at all times.

Accountabilty is something that each individual worker needs to be aware of and take seriously, but it is also a part of the management system, particularly in terms of supervision. That is, supervisors share a degree of accountability for the staff they supervise. It is part of their managerial responsibility to have at least a basic awareness of the work of their supervisees so that they are in a position to try and ensure that good practice is being maintained. We should therefore not allow the issue of accountability to be a source of unnecessary anxiety. We should remember that social work duties are a shared responsibility and we should be able to draw on support in managing the pressures involved.

NOS Key Role 5

Manage and be accountable, with supervision and support, for your own social work practice within your organization

adoption A major feature of the law relating to children is an emphasis on keeping them with their parents wherever it is safe and in their interests to do so. Where it becomes necessary for them to be removed from home (in cases of severe abuse, for example), efforts are to be made to return them home as soon as is reasonably possible. However, in some cases, it is not possible for children to remain with their natural parents. This may be because intensive efforts over an extended period of time to return the child home have failed; the parent(s) may have rejected the child; the parent(s) may be unable to care for the child (due to serious illness or **disability**, for example); or the parent(s) may have died. In such cases alternative long-term carers will be required.

Adoption is the legal process by which the rights and responsibilities of parenthood are transferred, on a permanent basis, from a child's birth parents to another individual or family. In effect, adoption means that, in legal terms, the biological parents are no longer regarded as parents. For many years adoptions were 'closed' – that is, contact with the birth parents was not maintained. However, changes in the law (Adoption and Children Act, 2002) have made adoptions more 'open'.

Social work involvement in relation to adoption can include work around:

> Assessing the suitability of potential adoptive parents and preparing them for the role (for example, through training). This is a very lengthy and thorough process, as it is vitally important that the people accepted as adoptive parents are entirely suitable. Some prospective adopters may become impatient with the process, but it is better to risk annoying applicants than to risk rushing the process and possibly putting children in unsafe or unsuitable hands or in a situation that breaks down very quickly. Making such a mistake can be disastrous for the adopters too, as the strain of a failed placement can be immense.

> Assessment of the adoptee's needs and history and of the ability of the adopter(s) to meet those needs. Careful 'matching' of adoptive parents to adoptive child is a very important process and one that involves a lot of skill and expertise. It includes a careful consideration of the ethnic background of the child and the proposed carers – a subject that has generated a huge amount of debate over the years.

NOS Key Role 1

Prepare for, and work with, individuals, families, carers, groups and communities to assess their needs and circumstances

> Supporting one or more of the parties, including siblings, through the transition and losses involved. The process of adoption can be a very emotionally charged one for all concerned (child, siblings and other relatives, birth parents, adoptive parents and their relatives – including any other children they may have – and, possibly to a certain extent at least, the social worker), and this generates a wide range of support needs.

> Ongoing recruitment and training. In addition to the process of assessing the suitability of prospective adopters, there is also much work to be done around publicizing the need for adopters, recruiting, training and supporting future adoptive parents.

advocacy In essence, advocacy is part and parcel of what social workers do all of the time. That is, we speak up for and represent those who are unable to do so for themselves, be it through:

- low self-esteem;
- lack of opportunity;
- communication difficulties;
- learning difficulties;
- paternalistic attitudes; or
- any other issues that prevent people from having their say or getting their interests recognized and addressed.

However, there are differences of focus within the broader definition which have implications for the role we can play as social workers.

NOS Key Role 3

Support individuals to represent their needs, views and circumstances

The key theme which appears to run through all of its forms is the recognition that some people are unable to have their voice heard in situations where there is a power imbalance and that advocacy can either represent a person's voice or facilitate the hearing of that person's voice. How this is put into practice can differ enormously, and there is a lot of debate within the advocacy movement about the extent to which advocates can act purely as mouthpieces for other people's words, especially when there is a mismatch between the personal values of both parties.

Principle 2 **Empowerment and Partnership**

Advocacy is very relevant to both empowerment and partnership

Walmsley and colleagues link this with the degree of independence from agencies:

> Whether independence is best secured by people who are trained, paid and formally accountable, or whether that is best left to volunteers, is a continuing dilemma. Furthermore, some argue strongly that advocates need to represent the wishes of the people they advocate for (substituted judgement), rather than put forward views which the advocate believes are in the best interests of the client.
>
> (Walmsley et al., 2005, p. 73)

It could be argued that advocacy is a core social work task, such as when a care manager speaks up on someone's behalf for the allocation of a share in scarce resources or a social worker represents the interests of a child or family at a child protection case conference. However, there are also initiatives that operate in more specific circumstances and often independently of social work. For example, 'citizen advocacy' is defined by the facilitation of a one-to-one ongoing relationship between a person disadvantaged in some way and a volunteer who can be called on as and when that person needs help to have their voice heard, or their perspective recognized. 'Peer advocacy' offers support based on a similar model but the advocate is someone who has subjective experience of what is contributing to the person's **vulnerability**. Sometimes people are able to manage their own affairs under normal circumstances, but may become especially vulnerable in particular situations when their coping skills are severely challenged or channels of communication are disrupted for some reason. Calling on someone to help make one's voice heard in such one-off situations is often referred to as 'crisis advocacy'.

Given the dilemmas about impartiality and competing allegiances, social workers need to consider whether they are best placed to act as advocates. We can use our influence and power to further a disadvantaged client's cause as far as we are able, but we need to be realistic about organizational constraints and call on more independent advocacy bodies to mediate where impartiality is compromised by allegiance to employing authorities.

ageism This is a form of **oppression** whereby individuals are discriminated against on the basis of age alone as an indicator of competence. It is most often used to refer to the unfair treatment of older people but applies equally to **discrimination** against children and adolescents. Ageism as an ideology portrays both groups as undeserving of respect and representation because of an underlying assumption that people at both extremes of the age continuum are unworthy of the citizenship rights that adulthood supposedly brings. Ageism can manifest itself at a number of levels:

- *The personal level.* This is where the comments and actions of individuals reflect a view that 'different' means 'inferior'. As social workers, we can operate at this level to challenge such views and to help those on the receiving end to feel confident enough to do so also and not to 'internalize' the idea that they are no longer worthy of full citizenship and all it entails.

NOS Key Role 3

Support individuals to represent their needs, views and circumstances

> *The cultural level.* This is the level of shared attitudes, and accounts for how these ideas are spread. As we can see from popular humour and the media in a variety of forms, there are shared expectations within a society about how people at either end of the age spectrum (older adults and children and young people) should behave and be treated. For example, it is not generally accepted that older people have the same need for physical intimacy as do younger adults (Bevan and Thompson, 2003) or that children experience grief reactions in situations such as family breakdown (Kroll, 2002). Stereotypes abound which equate old age with frailty and incompetence and youth with laziness and irresponsibility, promoting the view that this is how things are and ought to be. We need to be sure that our own practice, and the policies and procedures to which we work, are not reinforcing the assumption that competence is age related.

Principle 5 Loss and Grief

An easy mistake to make is to assume that children do not experience grief because they are 'too young to understand'.

> *The structural level.* How society is structured will have an impact on how much power people can wield, what opportunities they are likely to encounter, how much credibility they are given and so on. Age, like gender, ethnicity and class, is a social division and changing the social order is beyond the power of individuals, although that is not to say that we cannot play a part collectively over time (based on Neil Thompson, 1995).

Principle 1 Social Context

Social structures are an important part of the social context and therefore very relevant to social work.

Ageist processes include:

> welfarization – where old age is portrayed as a problem to be dealt with, rather than merely a stage in the life course;
> medicalization – where old age is equated with the sick role, even though not all older people are in poor health;
> infantilization – referring to older people by pet or first names without their permission, as if they were children, and denying them the right to dignity and respect that adults can expect.

While most of the literature relating to ageism focuses on older people, children and young people can also be discriminated against on the basis of age. This includes not involving them in decision making even when they are old enough and competent enough to do so (see the discussion of **partnership** below).

An important part of challenging ageism is to promote a model premised on empowerment, rather than on simply providing care in ways that encourage passivity and **dependency**.

alcohol abuse Consuming alcohol can be a very pleasurable experience that can 'lubricate' social interactions and ease an individual's tensions and pressures. However, it can also cause considerable problems, especially when consumption reaches levels of excess. Prolonged misuse of alcohol can have serious detrimental consequences for both physical and mental health. However, there are also wider social issues to consider, as excessive consumption of alcohol can lead to considerable strain on relationships and have a negative impact on other aspects of family and social life.

The consumption of alcohol causes a chemical reaction that has mind-altering effects and can thus distort thoughts, feelings and actions. The result of this can be very unwise actions that have very detrimental effects, not least the following:

> taking unnecessary or reckless risks that can lead to accidents, conflicts or even violence;
> attempting to drive or using machinery when incapable of doing so;
> putting a strain on relationships by acting in ways that create tensions; and/or
> attempting to become intimate with someone who does not welcome such an approach.

Alcohol misuse is likely to instigate a vicious circle. People often use alcohol to counteract or escape from problems and worries they have. However, it does not help to tackle these problems and is likely to make them significantly worse. This can then lead to an increased reliance on alcohol which, in turn, makes the problems worse or at least fails to address them. Such a vicious circle can have catastrophic effects.

The detrimental consequences of alcohol misuse are very significant for social work, as they have far-reaching implications for the range of problems that are regularly encountered in the social work world: for example, family breakdowns and related child welfare concerns (including child abuse); mental health problems; crime; abuse of vulnerable adults; and so on.

NOS Key Role 4

Manage risk to individuals, families, carers, groups, communities, self and colleagues

It is therefore vitally important that social workers have a good understanding of the significance alcohol misuse and its implications for practice in a wide variety of fields.

Traditionally alcohol misuse problems have been addressed in a reductionist medicalized way, with alcoholism being conceptualized as a disease in need of treatment. However, there is now an increasing use of psychological models to explain and respond to alcohol misuse – for example, the use of cognitive-behavioural therapy. Efforts to go beyond the individual level to consider the wider social context none the less remain relatively neglected. The scope for developing broader, more sociologically informed understandings of, and approaches to, alcohol misuse is therefore immense.

asylum seekers and refugees There tends to be a lot of confusion about these terms and this can contribute to myths that can make already traumatized individuals and families feel threatened and unwelcome. The Refugee Council defines asylum seekers as those who have fled persecution in their homeland, made their presence in the country explicit and taken up the legal right to apply for asylum under the rules established by the 1951 Refugee Convention. The term 'refugee' refers to those whose application to stay has been accepted, Sometimes misrepresented as coming to the UK in order to get state benefits or help they would not be entitled to in their countries of origin, many do not even want to be here and would return home if they did not feel that their lives, or those of their families, would be put in jeopardy if they did. With more people coming into the UK to seek work (economic migrants) and some visitors attempting to stay in the country when they have no legal right to (illegal immigrants), there is the potential for asylum seekers and refugees to be resented if their histories and intentions are misunderstood. There seems to be a popular myth that asylum seekers and refugees are 'flooding' the country and putting a strain on health, housing, education and social care resources, but figures released by the Refugee Council claim that, for example, of all foreign nationals entering the UK in 2004, only 0.035 per cent were seeking asylum.

www.refugeecouncil.org.uk

However, while a relatively small group, they are likely to be a disadvantaged one. Currently, government policy places restrictions on working within the first year, even though many asylum seekers are well-qualified and only too willing to support themselves and their families. Nor do they receive full state benefits. Immigration officers have the right to detain asylum seekers and their families, which can have significant implications in terms of access to education, health care, housing and other aspects of social care. It is not unusual, then, for asylum seekers and refugees to experience both poverty and hostility during a time when they are already facing fear and uncertainty about their futures. The social work role can potentially involve:

> promoting **welfare rights**, especially those of the children and vulnerable dependants of asylum seekers and refugees;

NOS Key Role 3

Support individuals to represent their needs, views and circumstances

> recognizing and challenging **discrimination**: and
> validating the significant **losses** experienced in such circumstances.

attachment This is a term that arose from the work of psychoanalyst, John Bowlby. It is based on the idea that young children normally form a strong emotional bond or 'attachment' to their primary caregiver(s) (the original theory stated 'mother', but this has since been shown to be an unwarranted sexist assumption). Such attachments are held to be major features of the child's sense of security and identity. It is therefore argued that children who do not form such attachments will lack that security and will experience emotional and behavioural difficulties as a consequence. At one time this was a widely used theory to explain offending behaviour in young people, based on the notion that they had become 'affectionless thieves' (Bowlby, 1944) whose anti-social behaviour owed much to the absence of proper attachments in their early childhood. It is now recognized that offending behaviour cannot be explained in such a simplistic way and that a wide range of factors are likely to be operating (sociological as well as psychological). However, this does not mean that attachment issues are not part of the explanation – rather, that they are not the only or even main part of it.

Attachment issues are also very relevant where they were initially formed, but later broken (as a result of divorce or bereavement, for example), as they can be a significant source of distress. Grief reactions can be partly explained as a response to one or more attachments being broken (temporarily or permanently). Similarly, the quality of attachments can be significant for a child's development. Attachments can vary in strength and can also have a degree of ambivalence or inconsistency, the latter being very confusing (and thus potentially distressing and problematic) for the child.

Principle 5 **Loss and Grief**

Attachment is a significant issue in relation to experiences of loss and grief.

Attachments can be seen to be very significant in relation to the development of **self-esteem**. A child with clear, strong attachments is likely to have a good sense of self-worth, whereas a child with weak and/or ambivalent attachments is likely to feel less valued by others and therefore value him- or herself less.

Early versions of the theory concentrated on the significance of early years attachments. However, it is now recognized that attachments are made and broken throughout the life course and do not relate solely to early childhood. This further emphasizes the significance of loss and grief in social work, hence the importance of Principle 5: Loss and Grief.

autistic spectrum This is an overarching term, used to describe a range of disorders which have common features, usually referred to as the 'triad of impairments'. Autism is a lifelong developmental **disability** and is characterized by difficulties in the following areas:

> *Social interaction.* People with autism are often described as 'being in their own little world'. This is true to an extent, but only reflects one extreme of the whole spectrum. However, difficulties with making friendships and initiating social contact are characteristic of this disorder and associated with difficulty in understanding social cues and conventions about 'appropriate' behaviour when people meet. Not understanding and therefore not being able to respect those conventions can lead to situations where a lack of social interaction is thought to be deliberate and described as aloofness or disdain.

> *Communication.* This can include difficulty with verbal communication but also with reading non-verbal cues such as facial expression or gesturing. Being unable to recognize or interpret such cues can contribute to difficulties with social interaction as described above.

> *Imagination.* It is often difficult for people with autism to engage in imaginative play, or to understand subtleties, such as double or hidden meanings, irony and sarcasm, because of a tendency to take things very literally.

There is a wide range of intellectual ability within the spectrum and, although there is often an associated **learning disability**, this is not necessarily the case. Indeed, many people with forms of autism such as Asperger's Syndrome lead independent lives and can be academically gifted. Those who have been able to describe autism subjectively, portray life as a chaotic experience and one hard to make sense of in the face of a hypersensitivity to external stimuli (Williams, 1996). This might help to explain the tendency toward the repetitive and routinized behaviour that is often a feature of autism, perhaps helping people with this disorder to impose some degree of order on the world as they experience it.

Because there are usually no visible features which indicate the difficulties people with autism experience, it can perhaps be described as a 'hidden disability' where emotions, behaviour and intentions are often misunderstood and misinterpreted. As social workers we can play an important role in promoting understanding and inclusion, challenging discrimination and promoting collaborative working with health and education colleagues.

NOS Key Role 2

Plan, carry out, review and evaluate social work practice, with individuals, families, carers, groups, communities, and other professionals

avoidance behaviour This is a term that derives from the psychology of animal behaviour. It refers to how animals learn how to avoid painful or harmful stimuli. In this sense it is a positive, helpful type of behaviour. However, it has been extended to apply to humans in a less than positive way. As the term implies, 'avoidance behaviour' is behaviour, such as withdrawal or denial, which serves to shield that person from having to face the reality of the situation they are in. While it can be seen to have some positive benefits, in the short term at least, it is generally recognized as unhelpful. This is because it involves avoiding a problem, rather than facing up to it and dealing with it. This means that the problem concerned can fester and do more harm than it needs to.

Examples of situations where avoidance behaviour might occur include:

> avoiding someone that we are in conflict with and thereby perpetuating the conflict rather than seeking to resolve it as constructively as possible (managing conflict is an important part of social work);
> having an anxiety-provoking task to do, but constantly delaying it (procrastination) and thereby running the risk that the anxiety

grows over time: the more we delay, the more anxious we may become;
> trying to deny to ourselves that a particular painful event has occurred or is about to occur, as if this will protect us from it (see **catharsis**) – for example, not facing up to the fact that a relationship is over.

Avoidance behaviour can be very significant in social work in the following ways:

> Clients and/or carers can display this type of behaviour and it will sometimes be part of our task to help them move beyond this and the problems it causes. For example, we may need to help one or more people face up to aspects of their situation that they find unpalatable, but which need to be tackled if progress is to be made.
> Colleagues may display this type of behaviour. For example, someone working with a child displaying signs or indicators of abuse may find it difficult to accept that abuse may be taking place (especially in a family that does not fit the stereotype of an abusive family). We may need to handle such situations very carefully and sensitively to make sure that the child is protected.

NOS Key Role 4

Manage risk to individuals, families, carers, groups, communities, self and colleagues

> We may display this behaviour ourselves at times – no-one is immune from the type of problems involved. Self-awareness can be very useful in becoming aware of this issue and supervision also has an important role to play.

Principle 7 **Self-management**
Self-awareness is a key part of self-management.

bipolar disorder This condition, also known as manic depression or manic depressive disorder, is characterized by mood swings between great happiness or elation and feelings of low mood or despair. As with most conditions, the severity of experience can vary, as too can the length of time between experiencing the extremes of mood. In what is known as a 'mixed state', both can be experienced at the same time.

At one end of the continuum is **depression**.

Typical features include sleep disturbances, lack of motivation, and sometimes thoughts of self-harm. At the opposite end is mania, or hypomania (a less severe form). In this state there is often a decrease in self-control, a rise in risk taking and the possibility of psychosis. It is more common for people to seek help when they are feeling low, and so this condition can sometimes be masked because the manic phase is not observed or reported.

It is generally recognized as a long-term condition, and one that can be controlled by forms of medication that seek to balance out the extremes of mood and behaviour. It can be a very distressing condition, not only for the person who experiences it directly, but also for friends, relatives, work colleagues and so on who may find it difficult to cope with either or both ends of the spectrum.

It is possible for people with this condition to enter into a vicious circle whereby their extremes can make it difficult to hold down a job, maintain relationships or remain in housing tenure. If, as a result of such difficulties, employment opportunities, relationships and housing become more problematic (perhaps leading to financial problems, social isolation and even homelessness) which, in turn, can place the person concerned under great **stress** and thereby amplify the problem. Social workers can sometime play an important part in trying to break that vicious circle.

brokerage A broker is someone who acts as an agent between parties involved in transactions, such as buying or selling, and who manages the contractual arrangements that come out of such negotiations – as, for example, in the case of an insurance broker who will not provide their own insurance services, but will have access to a wide range of insurance providers. The broker seeks to get the 'best deal' for their client from the range of existing providers.

One of the main strands underpinning the implementation of the NHS and Community Care Act 1990 was the establishing of the 'purchaser/provider split' – that is, a move away from a system in which local authorities provided services via an in-house workforce to one where, for the most part, they contract those services from external providers, including the voluntary and private sectors. This made a big impact on welfare provision because it promoted a market economy.

One outcome of this change has been the creation of an added responsibility for many social workers, that of brokerage. The organizing of individualized packages of care in response to complex and unique needs requires someone to act as a broker, since a number of different providers are likely to be involved and it is likely that there will be fees and charges to be negotiated in each case. Given the scarcity of financial resources that applies in most social work agencies, the broker usually also has to work within the confines of an allocated budget. Of course, therein lies a tension in the brokerage role – having more than one interest to consider. Social workers find themselves having to deal with competing obligations: on the one hand, acting as advocates on behalf of disadvantaged people who find themselves in vulnerable circumstances, but also, on the other hand, as gatekeepers of limited resources. As you will see below, brokerage in the form of **care management** has become a key feature of the social work role in many settings in recent years.

burnout Burnout is a situation which can result from being exposed to long periods of **stress**. In a profession in which the demands on one's time and emotional reserves are often high and unremitting, the potential for experiencing stress is high and, if it is not addressed, it can lead to 'burnout'. A common mistake is to regard burnout as a form of stress. However, it would be more accurate to see it as a *response* to **stress**. That is, if someone faces a situation where the pressures they face are excessive, they can attempt to cope with them by switching off from them, becoming insensitive to them, as if they have grown an extra skin that protects them from the harm that stress can inflict. Burnout, then, is an attempt to cope with high levels of pressures, but not a helpful approach, as it is counterproductive, causing as many problems as it solves. In fact, to be more accurate, it does not solve any problems, it merely masks them.

Burnout is not conducive to creativity and commitment because it is characterized by:

> emotional exhaustion – where the reserves

needed for dealing with difficult situations have been used up and creativity stifled so that practice becomes routinized and unthinking, almost as if we are operating on 'automatic pilot';

> lack of motivation and a sense of purpose – the sense of individual achievement and pride in our work and the difference we can make is lost or buried;

> an inability to connect with clients as people – a tendency to depersonalize them and see them as problems to be dealt with, rather than as people with problems.

It is almost as if burnout is infectious, in so far as a team with one or more burnt out people in it can create a culture characterized by the above three sets of problems, thus making it more difficult for other team members to avoid experiencing burnout themselves.

As burnout is a response to stress, the main way to deal with it is to tackle the underlying stress-related issues – that is, to try and rectify the problems that lead people to feel the need to enter the emotionally numb state that burnout is.

NOS Key Role 4

Manage risk to individuals, families, carers, groups, communities, self, and colleagues

care management With the NHS and Community Care Act 1990 came a change in the way that health and social care services were delivered. One of its key features was the move away from institutionalized care and towards enabling vulnerable people to live in their own homes and to be supported and involved in their own communities. The post of care manager developed in response to the need to facilitate this and the role of many social workers employed in the adult services field began to incorporate the brokerage role described above. Seven core functions of care management have been identified:

> *Providing information.* Many people are unaware of their legal entitlement to an assessment of need or the support that is available to them. Care managers are well placed to highlight these.

> *Determining the level of assessment.* Where needs are complex, it is often the case that

several different service providers need to be involved. Care management is about recognizing when needs are such that a co-ordinating role is required so that clients receive as near as possible to the ideal of a 'seamless service'.

> *The assessing of need.* A core feature of community care policy is an emphasis on holistic and 'needs-led' assessment, one which starts with what people need and then looks creatively at how that can be addressed, rather than one which merely fits people into pre-existing services.

> *Producing care plans.* This involves making the process of care provision explicit by keeping records of who will provide a service and when, and sharing this with clients.

> *Securing resources.* This is about working in a cost-effective way to supplement family and voluntary resources with services bought in from the private sector.

> *Monitoring the arrangements.* This is a task for the key worker in terms of keeping an overview of the package of care and notifying others of concerns or changes.

> *Reviewing need.* Needs change over time, and so a care package based on an assessment of need at a particular time may not remain an appropriate response.

(based on the work of Phillips, 1996)

There has been some debate about whether social work skills are best utilized in such a role (Lloyd, 2002; Thompson and Thompson, 2005) – indeed, many local authorities do not require their care managers to be social workers. Nevertheless, many social workers feel that there has been a redefinition and bureaucratization of their role, at the expense of its more therapeutic aspects, although Lloyd makes the following point:

Recent studies focusing on the carrying out of care management, rather than the overall implementation of the community care reforms, claim evidence of social work practice surviving and proving its value. For example, Hardiker and Barker (1999: 421) claim that social workers demonstrated 'skilled methods and pro-active decision-making, adopting advocacy roles and identifying "empowerment"' as a method to enable service users to negotiate around limited choices. The case studies showed utilization of 'a wider range of individualized, imaginative solutions' (p. 425). Accepting that this study was concerned with people who were getting a service, and does not address the wider question of unmet need or those falling through the net, it nevertheless provides some counter to the picture of a deskilled, mechanistic response.   (Lloyd, 2002, p. 163)

Given that social work has always been about responding to need in the context of scarce resources, this fits with the conceptualization of care management as a branch of social work rather than an abandonment of it, as we have suggested elsewhere (Thompson and Thompson, 2005). Care management, as with any aspect of welfare provision, has the *potential* to be carried out in a bureaucratic and 'service-led' way. Social workers have the skills and value base to ensure that this is not the case.

Principle 4 Knowledge, Skills and Values

Making sure that care management does not become bureaucratic and mechanistic can be a real challenge for our knowledge, skills and values.

NOS Key Role 2

Plan, carry out, review and evaluate social work practice, with individuals, families, carers, groups, communities, and other professionals

carers This is an extremely broad term, which can be used in a variety of senses. For example, the term can apply to those who undertake care provision on a paid basis, often referred to as 'formal' carers. But there are also those who provide care for vulnerable relatives or friends on an informal and unpaid basis. Included in this category are:

› partners, relatives and friends – although, because of their relationships, they may not recognize themselves as 'carers';
› parent carers – those parents who provide care for their disabled children at a level over and above that which would normally be expected of parents;
› young carers – there are 175,000 young

carers in the UK providing care for dependent parents and siblings (2001 census figures).

As social work involvement brings us into contact with both types of carer, formal and informal, it is important that we differentiate between the two so that there is no confusion. For example, you may conceptualize the spouse of someone who has had a stroke as his or her carer, because this is what you see that person doing, but that spouse may see him- or herself as a husband or wife who provides care out of love or duty, but not as a carer. There has been much campaigning over recent decades to have the work undertaken by informal carers recognized and recompensed and carers' rights have now been recognized to some extent in law. However, the mismatch of perceptions can lead to many of those who could benefit from carer support not accessing it because they do not recognize themselves as possible beneficiaries. While recognizing and responding to the needs of carers has always been part of good social work practice, the right to an assessment of need in their own right, and independently of the person they are caring for, is now enshrined in law in the form of the Carers (Recognition and Services) Act 1995.

It is an easy mistake to make to become so concerned with addressing the needs of the primary client(s) that we fail to pay adequate attention to the needs of carers who are, of course, an important part of the network of people involved in maintaining people in the community. It is therefore important that we adopt a broader perspective and take account of: (i) the needs of carers and the potential breakdown in the situation that can occur if these are not taken seriously; (ii) the potential for abuse if (some) carers are not adequately supported and become overstressed – see **protection of vulnerable adults**; and (iii) the complex dynamics (including power relations) between carers and the people they care for that can have a significant bearing on the situation.

NOS Key Role 4

Manage risk to individuals, families, carers, groups, communities, self and colleagues

case conference Broadly speaking, a case conference is any meeting convened to discuss a particular case, to pool information, to review progress and to make plans and decisions. It can involve professionals from various backgrounds – social services, health, education, the police and so on – depending on the nature of the case and the problems or issues being discussed. In many cases it will also involve the client(s) and carer(s) or parent(s).

However, the term is often used in a narrower sense to refer to a child protection case conference, convened under the child protection procedures (the formal, multidisciplinary procedures that govern matters relating to the safeguarding of children). Such conferences are called when there has been sufficient concern about a child or young person's need for protection from harm to warrant such a level of attention.

Senior officers from the key agencies with responsibility for children (social services, education, police, health, NSPCC and so on) will be invited, along with the staff from those agencies who are, or have been, working with the children or young people concerned (social worker, teacher, health visitor, school nurse, GP and so on). The parent(s) involved will also be invited unless the police object to this (if their presence might prejudice a prosecution, for example). In addition, the child(ren) or young person(s) involved will be invited unless they are not able to contribute meaningfully because of their age or a learning disability.

The case conference will determine whether there is sufficient concern to enter the names of the child(ren) or young person(s) concerned on the child protection register (see **child protection**). If registration does occur, then a date will be set for a review conference (usually after three or six months) to decide whether registration should continue (if sufficient concerns persist) or should come to an end (if sufficient progress has been made in removing or minimizing the risk of harm).

Case conferences are not trials. Rather, they are a professional decision-making tool involving the pooling and comparison of information, sharing of concerns and identification of possible ways forward.

NOS Key Role 2

Plan, carry out, review and evaluate social work practice, with individuals, families, carers, groups, communities, and other professionals

catharsis Deriving from the Greek word for 'purging' or 'purification', catharsis refers to the freeing up of strong feelings that have been repressed for one reason or another. It arises in situations where an emotional blockage has occurred which prevents the person from functioning as they would like and which affects their ability to cope with everyday activities. Circumstances in which a person might repress emotions because the feelings involved are too painful to handle would include:

> as a result of experiencing abuse;
> following a bereavement or other significant loss (redundancy, divorce or other relationship breakdown and so on); and/or
> in response to a traumatic incident, such as a serious accident or being the victim of a crime.

Principle 5 **Loss and Grief**
Catharsis can be very significant as a part of a grief reaction.

It is as if the human mind has the capacity to put painful feelings 'in a box', as if to deny that they exist. This can be a useful mechanism if used on a temporary basis until the individual is ready to handle those feelings, when they are less 'raw' and when he or she has achieved enough distance from the original incident and begun to come to terms with it. However, it can be problematic if it adversely affects the individual in terms of his or her ability to deal with emotional issues.

Catharsis can be likened to the opening of a dam, in so far as the water that has built up behind it is able to pour through the blockage and a feeling of relief is eventually reached. Although it can be a very positive and helpful process, it can be painful and distressing while it is happening, leaving the person concerned feeling disorientated.

Catharsis can arise in a variety of situations, but these can be subdivided into two types: incidental and planned. The former refers to situations that involve unexpectedly being faced with the issues they have been avoiding – for example, witnessing an attack on someone else might stir up repressed feelings in someone who has been a victim him- or herself, or witnessing a funeral when one has had difficulty coming to terms with the loss of an important person.

The latter refers to situations that involve a deliberate strategy, as when a skilled worker guides the process and helps someone to 'face their demons' in order to help them to move through the pain towards resolution.

> Sometimes people's lives can be highly problematic because they have reached an emotional impasse. This can be very disabling, leaving people very ill-equipped for the day-to-day demands that they face.
>
> There can therefore be a very significant role for the worker in unpicking the lock of this impasse in order to allow people to regain control of their lives and come to terms with the emotional pain and difficulties they have encountered. Helping someone to achieve catharsis can therefore be a task of major importance, a significant form of empowerment. (Neil Thompson, 2002b, p. 143)

This is a highly skilled job that involves significant risks, and so this approach is not recommended for inexperienced practitioners who may unleash strong feelings that they do not have the knowledge, skills or experience to handle safely and effectively.

child protection An important part of a social worker's role is to contribute to making sure that children and young people are protected from abuse. While there are many social workers who specialize in child protection work, it should be noted that *all* social workers have some degree of responsibility for protecting children from harm, even if they are working outside of children's services – for example, in mental health services.

Child protection basically involves safeguarding children and young people from abuse (**physical**, **sexual** and **emotional abuse**, **neglect** and so on). This can be preventative (providing family support to prevent family tensions overspilling into abuse, for example); investigative (making inquiries when abuse is alleged or suspected); interventive (working with families where abuse has occurred to prevent it from reoccurring); therapeutic (helping children and young people who have been abused to deal with the potentially **traumatic** aftermath); or a mixture of these.

A child or young person who is felt to be at significant risk of abuse (or further abuse if it has already happened) will be the subject of a specially convened meeting (see **case conference**) at which a decision will be made as to whether to place his or her name on the 'child protection register' (an official register of children deemed to be at serious risk of abuse). When registration takes place, steps are taken to develop a child protection plan. Such a plan will identify what needs to be done to remove or significantly reduce the risk of harm. For example, if the abuse is connected with a parent who has a drink problem, then arrangements may be made for him or her to receive help in tackling the problem. In extreme cases, the child or young person may be removed from home for their own safety. However, this is generally seen as a last resort, because: (i) removal from home may do more psychological harm than the actual abuse; and (ii) there is no guarantee that where the child is placed will be entirely free of abuse (there are, unfortunately, many cases on record of children and young people being abused in residential or foster care).

Child protection (or 'safeguarding children and young people' as it is often called) is a very complex and sensitive subject with a large literature and research base. Such matters need to be handled very carefully and in conjunction with other professionals – safeguarding children from harm is a responsibility we share with other professionals, and so we should never be working in an isolated way, as that may lead to significant problems in terms of potential harm to: (i) children, young people and their families; (ii) ourselves by risking undue anxiety and stress; and (iii) the efficient and effective working of the multidisciplinary child protection system.

Principle 2 **Empowerment and Partnership**
Multidisciplinary collaboration is vital in responding effectively to the challenge of child abuse.

The emotional demands of child protection work make effective self-management a necessity if we are not to be harmed by such work.

children's guardian (guardian *ad litem*)

This is the term used to describe an independent social worker who is appointed to safeguard the interests of a child involved in public law proceedings. He or she is appointed from a panel of suitably qualified and experienced people to act independently to ensure that the court hears and understands the child's wishes, and that the best interests of the child are promoted.

A guardian can be appointed in such cases as adoption or where application is being made for a care order, an emergency protection order or a supervision order. He or she will interview the child (or children), family members and any other significant carers, as well as the professionals involved. The guardian's role involved forming an assessment of the situation, advising the court on his or her views of the child's needs and, in so doing, making sure the child's needs and interests are at the forefront of the proceedings. The guardian may appoint a solicitor on behalf of the child if this is felt appropriate.

NOS Key Role 3

Support individuals to represent their needs, views and circumstances

Some social workers feel threatened and uncomfortable when a guardian is appointed in a case they are dealing with. However, there is no need to become anxious about this, as the guardian and the social worker should be 'on the same side' in so far as they are both primarily concerned with the child's welfare. In fact, having an experienced guardian involved in a case can be very helpful, as it is likely that he or she will have a lot of expertise and experience to draw on in working towards the best outcome for the child or children concerned.

For many years the Latin term 'guardian *ad litem*' was used, but this has now largely been replaced by the more user-friendly term 'children's guardian', although the older term has not died out altogether.

community care

As a form of social welfare policy, community care highlights the following as key issues:

> the promotion of a mixed economy of care in which health and social care for adults are delivered by a combination of public, private and voluntary sector agencies;

> assessment as the starting point of intervention, so that the delivery of welfare services operates on a needs-led, rather than a service-led, basis (that is, it focuses on the person's needs as the starting point with a view to tailoring services to suit them as far as possible, rather than simply trying to fit people into existing services);

NOS Key Role 1

Prepare for, and work with, individuals, families, carers, groups and communities to assess their needs and circumstances

> the need to contain social welfare costs to the state to manageable proportions;

> an emphasis on care being provided in people's own homes or in small, family-based residential units within the community, rather than in large institutions.

Current policy in this area has its roots in earlier initiatives to move from the old regime of large-scale institutions towards a community and family focus.

For a very long time the dominant way of dealing with certain groups of people was to remove them from society and place them in an institution. For example, people with mental health problems or learning disabilities were placed in hospitals away from mainstream society – 'out of sight, out of mind', as it were. The philosophy underpinning this approach was based on the idea that it was safest for both those institutionalized and for society at large if they were kept separate.

In recent decades we have adopted a different approach, one in which the detrimental effects of institutionalization have been recognised. Over time policy makers have come to realize that integrating people into the community is a more humane way of dealing with issues relating to mental health and disability. Thus the era of community care was

born, an era in which great efforts have been made to replace large-scale institutions with a range of services geared towards maintaining people in the community as far as possible.
(Thompson and Thompson, 2005, p. 5)

Community care is closely associated with the idea of **care management**, the development of care packages based on assessment of needs and circumstances. However, the overall policy is much broader than this and includes responsibility for housing providers, the social security system and the health service to promote community-based care – that is, to provide help in ways that facilitate people remaining in their own homes as far as possible. Community care, then, is a broad social policy area, rather than simply a social work method or branch of social work practice.

community social work Community work in general operates in a number of different ways, but its core feature is intervention at the level of communities, rather than with specific individuals or families. To this end it has its focus in: (i) addressing community problems at a community level; and (ii) promoting change at a policy level through community action. Community work, although far less in evidence than was once the case, involves developing schemes and projects in areas of deprivation and high levels of social problems, to involve members of the community in accessing resources and seeking to address local problems.

Community social work is closely linked to community work, but is also significantly different. It arose in large part from the publication of the Barclay Report in 1982, a report that emerged from a review of social work and its direction at that time. Stepney and Evans explain the relationship between community work and community *social work* in the following terms:

Comparisons are sometimes made with community work, as both seem to share common theoretical assumptions and core skills. Here it is worth acknowledging a fundamental difference in orientation. Whilst community work is concerned with tackling injustice and inequality by organizing people

and promoting policy change at the local level, all of which finds expression in collective action (Jones and Mayo, 1974; Twelvetrees, 2001), community social work is concerned with developing more accessible and effective local services (Smale, 1988). It is also about finding alternative means of meeting the needs of individual service users.
(Stepney and Evans, 2000, pp. 108–9)

Community social work, then, is located somewhere between the collective approach of community work and the bureaucratic basis of traditional social work. It is concerned with moving away from the obstacles that arise from traditional structures and systems to develop closer working relationships with the communities we serve.

NOS Key Role 2

Plan, carry out, review and evaluate social work practice, with individuals, families, carers, groups, communities, and other professionals

As it is concerned with wider structures of delivery, it is not a matter that individual social workers can take forward in major ways without the backing of an organizational commitment to this style of working. Individual social workers can, however, explore ways of making their own practice more in tune with local communities (see **networking**).

confidentiality Although respect for confidentiality is one of social work's key values, it is one which can present ethical dilemmas, and so must be considered within a wider context of legal, policy and moral guidelines. As a social worker, you will be party to highly personal information, and there is the potential for a service user's **rights** to be breached, their dignity hurt and your relationship with them compromised if information imparted is not dealt with sensitively. Unless there are valid reasons not to, it is good practice to honour a bond of confidentiality between social worker and service user, in the interests of building up a relationship of trust. However, it must be recognized that the confidentiality relates to you as a representative of your employing organization and not to you as an individual. If that is not made clear to a service user, then any transfer of information within that agency is likely to be seen as a breach of confidentiality, which can then have devastating consequences in terms of future relationships of trust – not just with the individual concerned, but potentially for the whole organization or even profession.

While being something to strive for as far as possible in order to fit in with the social work ethos of respect for **rights**, maintaining confidentiality can become problematic if it is taken to the extreme and without due regard for the complexities involved.

NOS Key Role 6

Demonstrate professional competence in social work practice

For example, if someone told you something in confidence and you knew it would result in harm to someone, or be detrimental to a particular community, would you consider the greater good when deciding what to do with that information, even though given to you in confidence? What if someone told you they were going to take their own life and asked you to keep it a secret? And what about the transfer of information between colleagues working in a **multidisciplinary** team context where there are shared aims? Of course, there are also instances where the law will require you to pass on information which may have been given to you in confidence, such as where **child abuse**, or a threat to public safety is suspected. By now you might be feeling a sense of being 'pulled in all directions' or of 'not being able to do right for doing wrong'. If you do, then this is only to be expected – these are not easy dilemmas to resolve and you may have to take advice from colleagues and managers if there are no clear policy guidelines in a particular situation.

It would be impossible, even given more space than is available here, to be prescriptive about what to do in any given circumstances. Indeed, being a professional worker is all about drawing on values, knowledge and skills to inform a plan of action appropriate to a particular situation, rather than sticking rigidly to a set of predetermined 'rules'. But what can help in such circumstances is to try always to work within a framework which values the right to

confidentiality and strives to maintain it unless other considerations are considered important enough to overrule it. The 'fallout' which accompanies the breaking of a confidence often results from a misunderstanding of motive, or a lack of awareness of another person's perspective or obligations. If you work in a spirit of partnership with a service user, being open and honest about what you can and cannot promise in terms of maintaining confidentiality, and explaining *why* that is the case, then the trust between social worker and service user is less likely to be broken because a carefully considered breach of confidentiality has been seen as a 'simple' matter of betrayal and an abuse of **power**.

conflict This is a term used to refer to the tensions that arise between two or more people (or sets of people). It is a very important concept in social work because our practice commonly involves dealing with conflict. Indeed, in social work we are never far away from conflict. It can arise in a wide variety of ways, including the following:

> Between clients – for example, members of a family.
> Between clients and carers – relationships between carers and the people they care for can be very harmonious, but can also be characterized by conflict – sometimes quite severe and intense.
> Between clients and/or carers and the social worker – for example, where a client is behaving in a self-destructive way and we are trying to prevent this from continuing.
> Between social worker and manager(s) – perhaps where a bid for a particular service to be offered is declined by a manager who sees the case as low priority;
> Between social worker and other professional(s) – multidisciplinary working does not always run smoothly.

Clearly, then, an important part of the effective social worker's repertoire is the ability to manage conflict. Simply trying to avoid conflict is not really a helpful approach, as conflict is so prevalent that this is not a realistic option. This is not to say that it is not wise to seek to avoid conflict, but rather that this is not enough on its own. Learning how to manage conflict constructively and helpfully is therefore a key part of becoming a competent social worker. Some people will say: 'I don't like conflict'. Of course, you do not have to like conflict, but you do have to be prepared to tackle it constructively rather than seek to brush it under the carpet.

There are various conflict management techniques that can be used, including a formal **mediation**. A central feature of any attempt to manage conflict is the importance of listening. Not being listened to (or feeling that one is not being listened to) can be a significant source of conflict, and failing to listen in a conflict situation can perpetuate or even exacerbate the problems. Effective listening is therefore an essential requirement for developing skilled and successful conflict management.

counselling This is commonly used in a broad sense to describe a range of situations which involve support or advice giving, but the sense in which it is most often used in social work is that of helping someone to explore and understand their feelings and circumstances and to empower them to take control of their own lives. The need for counselling often arises out of some form of crisis, where usual coping mechanisms are overwhelmed but the need can also arise without the occurrence of a precipitating crisis.

Counselling is recognized as a profession in its own right, but it could be argued that the process itself is not one which is distinct from therapeutic social work intervention. Its philosophy and methods are compatible with what social workers strive to achieve – empowerment, development of self-awareness and self-understanding and decision making (particularly about emotional issues).

Nelson-Jones provides helpful comment when he argues that:

> In a nutshell, the main purpose or goal of using counselling skills is that of assisting clients to develop personal skills and inner strength so that they can create happiness in their own and others' lives. Counsellors ... assist clients to help themselves. As such, they use counselling skills to develop clients' capacity to use their human potential both now and in future.   (Nelson-Jones, 2005, p. 10)

A full, in-depth programme of counselling is often not feasible in terms of a social worker's workload and time constraints, and it will often be necessary to refer on to a specialist counselling service where such facilities are available. However, even where in-depth counselling is not possible, social workers can still make very good use of counselling skills in helping people deal with their problems.

NOS Key Role 2

Plan, carry out, review and evaluate social work practice, with individuals, families, carers, groups, communities, and other professionals

We should beware of making the mistake of seeing counselling as only a long-term, in-depth process. Counselling skills can be very helpful and effective as part of short-term work. task-centred practice/solution-focused work, see p. 263

cultural competence At its simplest level, this refers to the recognition that we grow up within a particular culture and take on board its social rules and values. In essence, we become competent in what it means to belong to that culture. However, the term is increasingly being used to indicate what other authors have extensively referred to as 'ethnically sensitive practice'. Operating within a culturally diverse society we will be called on to support (and work with as colleagues) people whose life experience, worldviews, customs, beliefs and values may be very different from our own. Culturally competent practice is a form of practice that recognizes the need to:

> work towards an understanding of what it means to be part of another culture; and
> accept that *ethnocentric* practice (that is, practice that assumes that one's own perspective is the 'correct' or only one) is not consistent with an anti-discriminatory stance.

As such, it is not only a personal responsibility, but an organizational one too, as part of a broader commitment to promoting equality and valuing diversity.

Burford reviews a number of cultural competence models and identifies the following shared characteristics:

What cultural competence does not involve is: (i) a reliance on stereotypes; and (ii) an assumption that cultures are monolithic entities, with no subdivisions within them (sub-cultures). In relation to: (i), it is important to recognize that stereotypes are oversimplified distortions of reality that can be very dangerous, but it is unfortunately the case that discussion of cultures other than one's own often become reduced to the level of stereotypical assumptions. In relation to (ii), it is important to note that 'culture' is a complex concept. It is not only possible for sub-cultures to exist and for individuals to interpret their cultural context differently from one another, it is actually quite normal for this to happen. It is therefore important that we adopt a sophisticated approach to culture that recognizes its complexity, rather than a simplistic one that does not.

day services The provision of day services is a central part of **community care**. Such services are available to pre-school children (for example, in crèches, nurseries and family centres) and to vulnerable adults. Adult day services include day centres for older people and/or people with physical disabilities and centres for adults with learning disabilities (often with a focus on work-related skills). In the case of older or disabled people, the service may be provided in a dedicated day centre, as an additional facility as part of a residential home, or in the homes of individuals and families where such schemes exist.

Day services can be very helpful in:

> reducing social isolation and the associated problems (loss of confidence, for example);
> monitoring someone who is at serious risk or who has complex needs;
> developing skills (social and life skills, work-related skills and so on);
> providing respite for carers;
> assisting in rehabilitation.

Day services are often used where the needs of the person concerned are greater than can be provided for in their own homes, but where residential care is not needed or wanted. It is important to think in terms of a service (or set of services) rather than simply a building. Establishments differ significantly in terms of the specific services they offer and also in terms of their degree of integration into the local communities.

In considering referring someone for day services it is important to be quite clear about what need(s) such a referral would be intended to serve. Places are generally limited, and so it is important to see day services as part of an overall plan for meeting someone's needs and addressing their problems and to be quite specific about what you feel the client concerned would gain from attendance. It is important that day services should not be seen as simply a social or leisure activity. If this is what someone needs, we should be helping them to explore other opportunities, such as luncheon clubs and facilities provided by voluntary bodies and the education and leisure departments of the local council.

debt The importance of poverty in social work has long been recognized. However, what has received less attention is the significance of debt. Poverty is characterized by the stresses and strains involved in trying to 'make ends meet' on a very low income. Issues of debt go a step further than this in so far as being in debt brings additional pressures and problems:

> Interest payable can mean that people on low incomes who are in debt are fighting a losing battle and often find that, over time, they are getting into more and more debt. This can particularly be the case where money had been borrowed from unscrupulous sources that charge significantly higher rates of interest than high street banks. The irony here is that it is generally people who have a poor credit rating because of debt who are refused a loan from a bank and therefore feel the need to draw on the services of

organizations that capitalize on this fact – thus incurring higher interest charges and potentially more debt.

> Debt can leave people feeling trapped in a vicious circle of debt and this, in turn, can lead to depression, anxiety and other such problems. Being in debt can undermine **self-esteem**. At times this can further contribute to the cycle by placing the individual concerned where he or she is less able to generate income (for example, through missing work as a result of depression). In terms of the psychological response to debt, there is a further irony, in so far as people who are in debt can at times treat themselves to luxury items to help them cope with the pressures of debt – to 'cheer themselves up', as it were. While it is perfectly understandable that people may want to do this, it is clearly a problem in terms of adding to the debt mountain to be climbed.

> The pressures of debt can lead some people into criminal behaviour as they may see no other way out of their predicament. A further irony is that, in many cases, the response of the courts to such matters is to impose fines, thus adding to the problem.

As social workers, we need to make sure that we are aware of the significance of debt in some people's lives and do not underestimate its detrimental effects and its impact on other problems (for example, family tensions may be exacerbated by debt – especially if one or more members of the family are trying to be prudent, while one or more are adopting a different approach, such as comfort spending or criminal behaviour). There are ways and means in which debt problems can be tackled. Citizens' Advice Bureaux can be very helpful in providing debt management services, as can some other voluntary bodies. Putting people in touch with such an agency can be a useful first step, but the negative impact of debt may mean that there are other social work tasks that arise – it is therefore not simply a matter of referring people on when debt issues become apparent.

`dementia` While dementia is by no means an inevitable part of ageing, a significant number of people will experience its effects or become the carer of someone who does. It is a condition (or set of conditions) which can have quite devastating physical, intellectual, psychological and social consequences and these can vary significantly between different forms of dementia. All too often, dementia is equated with one particular form, such as Alzheimer's Disease and the specific features of that illness are assumed to be typical of all dementias. We have chosen to describe just three of its many forms as an indication of how different the range of symptoms and implications can be:

> *Alzheimer's disease.* With this condition there is damage to the nerve cells and their connections in the part of the brain that controls memory, behaviour and other 'higher' functions. Symptoms can include disorientation, language and perception difficulties, depression and aggression. The process of deterioration is irreversible and, in time, suffers become more and more physically incapacitated and die.

> *Lewy-body dementia.* In this form of dementia, thought to be caused by bodies of protein present in nerve cells, confusion is episodic, rather than constant, and there are particular difficulties with keeping one's train of thought or finding the right word for a context. As such, then, someone might appear competent in some contexts but not others, and the dementia can be masked or misinterpreted.

> *Vascular forms of dementia.* This is where damage is caused by an insufficient blood supply to cells in the brain. This can cause a decline in the brain's capacity to function and, if severe or repeated, can lead to confusion and specific symptoms associated with whichever part of the brain has been damaged.

There is a tendency for people exhibiting confusion to be described as having dementia, even though these symptoms are very commonly associated with chest or urine infections and can quickly disappear once the infection clears. Knowledge about our clients' routines and networks can put social workers in the position of being able to highlight changes to usual patterns, and thereby contribute towards the diagnosis and misdiagnosis of dementia. The field of dementia studies is a complex and fast-changing one and social workers are not expected to be experts in this area. However, we must not lose sight of the fact that dementia is a range of conditions, rather than a single condition per se and that we need to strive to ensure that:

a) those who *do* have dementia are treated with dignity and respect and that they and their families receive understanding, support services and therapeutic interventions in response to their needs; and

b) those who *do not* have dementia are not assumed to have it because of an ageist tendency to associate old age with inevitable confusion and mental decline.

dependency To a certain extent, everyone is dependent on other people or systems. For example, we depend on the local refuse service to empty our bins, on the police force to protect us from crime and so on. Some degree of dependency is therefore perfectly normal and not at all problematic. However, it is important to make sure that, in providing social services, we are not making people unnecessarily dependent on us. We should be promoting independence rather than encouraging dependency. For example, we should not be doing things for people that they are capable of doing themselves. This may involve:

> Helping to boost someone's confidence to be able to complete a particular task.
> Teaching someone how to do something they have not done before; and/or giving someone moral or practical support in tackling something they can do but find challenging.

If, by contrast, we act in ways that encourage dependency, then we will be perhaps causing more problems than we solve, not least the following:

> Reducing someone's motivation to undertake task themselves.
> Reinforcing low levels of confidence and low **self-esteem**.
> Giving ourselves unnecessary additional tasks and thereby creating additional workload demands.
> Possibly giving other people (other family members, for example) the false impression that the social work role is to do things *for* people.

Encouraging dependency is not only unhelpful in practical terms, it is also contrary to the social work values of partnership and empowerment.

In many cases, however, we will be working with people who are dependent on others even for basic tasks such as feeding and toileting. Where this is the case, we need to make sure that: (i) the support offered is given with as much dignity and respect as possible; and (ii) that it is not overextended (for example, the fact that someone cannot do certain things for him- or herself does not mean that he or she cannot do *anything* independently.

Given that some degree of dependency is inevitable for everyone and quite a lot of dependency for some people, some writers (for example, Lustbader, 1991) prefer to use the concept of 'interdependency'. This refers to a recognition that people do rely on other people, but this should be done in a way that does not leave them feeling that they have lost any dignity or self-respect. Where we work with people who do rely on services because they are not able to do things unaided or at all, we have to make sure that we handle such situations very sensitively and do not forget that a person who needs basic tasks doing for them is still a person none the less.

depression Depression is a contested concept – that is, there are different conceptions of what it is and how it should be dealt with. The most dominant conception is based on a medical model – that is, depression is seen as an illness, and the logical response to it is therefore some form of medical treatment (for example, prescribing anti-depressant medication or, in extreme cases, electro-convulsive therapy). Alternative conceptions see it as a response to problems and pressure in one's psychosocial environment, as if it is a way of 'shutting off' from exceedingly difficult circumstances. For example, feminist writers have pointed out that incidences of depression are significantly higher in women than in men and seek to explain this by reference to patriarchy and the oppression of women (Chesler, 2000, Ussher, 1991). Indeed, the tendency to conceptualize depression as an 'illness' can be seen, from this perspective, as part of the oppressive apparatus in so far as a medical approach individualizes the issue and distracts attention from the wider sociopolitical causes or contributory factors.

Whichever explanatory model we adopt, depression is recognized as being characterized by the following:

> low mood, dejection, pessimism and a sense of hopelessness
> tiredness, irritability and poor concentration
> sleep disturbances
> loss of appetite
> in many, but not all, cases: suicidal thoughts.

It can last days, months or even years. Some people affected by the condition are in a perpetually depressed state, while others have depressive episodes from time to time (frequency can vary quite significantly), but manage to evade depression the remainder of the time. It can be seriously disabling and debilitating in terms of daily life. Eating, socializing, studying, working and parenting can all be very adversely affected.

Depression can occur across the life course, including in children and young people and older people. However, due to the workings of ageist assumptions, it is often overlooked at either end of the age spectrum – that is, in children and young people and in older people (Sue Thompson, 2005).

It is important to note that the term 'depression' is often used very loosely in general conversation to refer to any experience of feeling low or disappointed, as in: 'I thought I was due to go on holiday in two weeks' time, but I've just realized it's three weeks actually. I feel really depressed now.' We have to be careful to distinguish between this very loose use of the term and its professional usage. Depression is a very serious problem, and so we should be careful not to underestimate it by confusing it with ordinary low feelings and assume that 'everyone gets depressed from time to time'.

disability There is considerable debate about how disability can best be defined, but the term literally means 'difficulty with ability' – having some form of intellectual or physical impairment which causes problems in understanding or functioning. For a very long time the 'individual'

model (sometimes referred to as the 'tragedy' model) has been the dominant one in terms of explaining disability. It locates the problem in the individual and his or her impairment, so that it is the impairment that marginalizes them by preventing them from being able to travel, study, work, socialize and so on. Locating the cause of the disability in the individual defines him or her as different or 'deviant', and for this reason it is sometimes referred to as the 'pathology' model. From this perspective, the appropriate response is seen as helping disabled people to adapt to societal arrangements as they currently exist or, if that is not deemed possible, to compensate through charitable efforts and welfare benefits.

However, in recent years we have seen the development of the 'social model' of disability, as discussed in the writings of Michael Oliver and other key writers in this field. The social model has been challenging the traditional perception of disability. This new approach locates the problem in the way that society is structured and organized around the needs of non-disabled people, so that people with impairments are prevented from participating because of the obstacles that are put in their way, such as:

> physical barriers – for example, poor or non-existent access to buildings and public transport; entry systems that rely on being able to announce one's presence and hear the reply; a reliance on visual media for directions and information;
> patronizing and prejudicial attitudes; and/or
> inflexible working practices.

Principle 1 Social Context

The social model of disability reminds us how important the social context is.

If the causes of disability are seen as being located in the structural and cultural spheres (that is, it is society that disables), then there would seem to be a role for social workers that goes beyond ensuring that their own practice is not discriminatory. Oliver (2004) describes the social model as a tool for producing social and political change, rather than a theory, and suggests that social work with disabled people has relied too heavily on the individual model to make its input meaningful. Sapey (2002) poses questions about whether social work with disabled people, as part of a system of welfare, perpetuates the idea that disabled people need welfare. If we are to make a difference as social workers, we therefore need to engage with developments in the disability movement and find ways of working which focus on justice, rights and inclusion.

NOS Key Role 3

Support individuals to represent their needs, views and circumstances

discrimination Literally, to discriminate means to identify a difference and, as such is not necessarily a problem. In fact, being able to identify differences is an important skill in many aspects of our work and in our lives more broadly. However, in its legal or moral sense, discrimination refers to the process whereby we not only identify a difference (between two people or two groups of people, for example), but also treat people unfairly as a result of that difference. For example, we can clearly identify many differences between men and women in social life. However, sexism involves treating one group (mainly, but not exclusively, women – see **sexism**) unfairly as a result of that difference (in terms of rates of pay, for example). In legal terms, one group 'suffers a detriment' – that is, experiences a disadvantage.

patterns of socialization, see p. 75

Discrimination, then, is a two-stage process. First, it involved identifying a difference between two groups or categories of people and attaching a social significance to it (in terms of skin colour or national origin, for example); and, second, it then involves treating one group less fairly than the other – in effect, placing one group in a superior position to another, creating or sustaining power relations in the process and contributing to a situation of considerable unfairness.

Discrimination can take many forms, including the well-known and well-documented ones of sexism and racism, as well as not so closely studied ones, such as **ageism**, disablism or **heterosexism**. However, the list is even longer (and potentially infinite), in so far as discrimination can arise in relation to any differences identified (religion or sect, accent, regional culture, class, political outlook – to name just a few).

The outcome of unfair discrimination is generally **oppression**. This means that discrimination is not a trivial matter, in so far as its negative consequences can be of major proportions for the people affected by it. And, when we bear in mind that social work's clientele comprises groups who are largely very strongly subject to discrimination, then we can see that discrimination, and the oppression it leads to, is a significant problem to be tackled in social work. This is why anti-discriminatory practice is such a central part of good practice – because: (i) discrimination is so widespread among social work client groups (think of any client group and the chances are that you will be able to identify strong elements of actual or potential discrimination); (ii) many of the problems we are trying to deal with in social work are in part caused or exacerbated by discrimination (**depression** in old age as a result of **ageism** or the **social exclusion** of disabled people as a result of disablist assumptions or structures, for example); and (iii) we have a moral duty to promote **social justice** and clearly discrimination and social justice are not compatible.

social work values, see p. 133

disenfranchised grief This is an important concept introduced by the American scholar, Kenneth Doka (2001). It refers to grief that is not socially sanctioned, not accepted as legitimate, and is thus stigmatized in some way. Doka explains that it can apply in three main ways:

❭ *The relationship is disenfranchised.* Where someone loses a lover, for example, people around us will tend to be supportive and recognize the significance of the loss. However, where the relationship is a secret one (a long-term extramarital lover, for example), the grief cannot be openly acknowledged and so less support is likely to be offered. In many circumstances this can also apply to gay relationships. While the relationship may not be secret, it may be socially disapproved of (in some quarters at least), with any grief reaction possibly being at least partly disenfranchised.

❭ *The loss is disenfranchised.* This can be seen to apply in situations where the nature of the loss is stigmatized in some way. Examples would include suicide, death from AIDS and drug-related deaths. Such losses can be made more difficult to deal with by these social reactions to them. It is as if there is a pretence that the 'problem' did not exist and therefore the grief associated with the loss does not exist.

> *The griever is disenfranchised.* Discriminatory assumptions can lead to some people's experiences of grief not being recognized. For example, there is a common assumption that older people 'get used to grief' (whereas the reality is more a case of the compound effects of cumulative grief – Sue Thompson, 2002a). Similarly, it is commonly assumed that people with learning disabilities do not grieve because they 'cannot understand loss', and that children are 'too young' to grieve. These are dangerous assumptions to make, as they fail to recognize the significance of grief and can be an obstacle to people receiving the support they may need.

This is a very important concept for social work as we will frequently encounter situations of disenfranchised grief, even though we may not recognize them as such. We should also remember that grief is a response to any significant loss, not just to death-related losses. The same can be said of disenfranchised grief – it applies to a wide range of losses.

Principle 5 Loss and Grief

The concept of disenfranchised grief helps us to understand that loss and grief are social as well as psychological phenomena.

domestic violence While violence within families has long been a social problem, it has only in the past 50 years or so that it has been conceptualized as a crime (The Domestic Violence Act 1961). It is generally, but not exclusively, used to refer to violence against women, although it is recognized that women can at times be the perpetrators in abusive relationships. The term covers a range of forms of violence, including:

> physical harm
> financial abuse
> psychological intimidation
> sexual attack, including rape.

Research commissioned by the National Group to Address Violence Against Women (Greenan, 2004) suggests that a significant number of women experience more than one type of violence and, across the whole range of types of violence, are more at risk from men that they know. Because of the recurring themes of humiliation and degradation, many women experiencing violence have self-esteem issues to deal with as well as risk management, especially where children and young people are witnessing or directly experiencing violence or living with the potential for this to occur at any time. As a social worker, you may well become involved in domestic violence situations, perhaps because of child protection issues, but it is important to remember that domestic violence can occur across the life course. For example, long-standing abusive relationships can continue into old age and new ones may develop, especially in situations where relationships become strained because of extra demands on physical, financial and emotional resources in times of illness, incapacity and so on.

NOS Key Role 4

Manage risk to individuals, families, carers, groups, communities, self and colleagues

Women's Aid is an important voluntary organization that offers refuges and advice, although many people who are exposed to domestic violence are reluctant to accept help from any source.

It is important to recognize that, while safeguarding children from harm is a very important concern, domestic violence is a significant issue in its own right, not just as a potential source of child abuse. Women in abusive relationships can feel trapped – damned if they stay in the relationship, damned if they leave it. Domestic violence can have a very detrimental effect on mental health, relationships, work and studying, as well as the obvious harm in terms of health and physical well-being.

drug misuse The use of drugs for non-medical purposes is not a new issue. For example, the use of alcohol and tobacco for social and recreational purposes has become an established part of modern western societies. The fact that both alcohol and tobacco make a major contribution to rates of illness and death does not stop their use from being socially acceptable (although not without dissenting voices). Alcohol, in particular, is a significant factor underpinning other social problems that social workers encounter: crime, child abuse, domestic violence and so on. While there are some social workers who specialize in alcohol-related problems, all social workers need to have at least a basic understanding of alcohol and its implications for practice, such is its prevalence as a practice issue in a wide variety of settings and cases.

In addition to alcohol-related problems, the misuse of drugs is a very relevant issue for social workers in connection with the use of illegal substances (marijuana, cocaine, heroin and so on). This is because the use of such substances can cause problems in terms of criminal behaviour, family tensions, child care (although it should not be assumed that someone who uses illegal drugs is necessarily a 'bad' parent) and, of course, the physical, psychological, social and economic problems arising from apparent dependency. This is a field of practice that has traditionally been heavily medicalized, but there is a growing voice for alternative approaches that are more consistent with social work values (see, for example, Harris, 2005). It is also a field characterized by a great deal of media sensationalism and 'moral panics'. It is therefore important that, in tackling these issues, we base our practice on a good understanding of the actual issues, rather than a distorted view based on stereotypes and oversimplifications.

A third strand of drug misuse is the inappropriate use of prescribed medications, such as tranquillizers. While this topic does not get as much attention as the use of illegal drugs, it is unfortunately not uncommon for social workers to come across situations where someone is experiencing major problems because they have come to rely on drugs that are not intended for long-term use and can be harmful. Such people may rely on a lack of proper supervision by medical staff or, where medical staff are vigilant enough to prevent prescriptions being made available, they may rely on manipulating others to obtain the drugs on their behalf or may have to purchase drugs from criminal sources who are seeking to profit from this problem.

duty/intake When people first approach a social work organization for help (for themselves or to make a referral in relation to someone else), how they are treated can be a crucial factor in terms of how they subsequently relate to staff of that agency. The duty or intake function is therefore vitally important. However, historically our record on this is quite mixed. There are many examples on record of organizations that have done excellent work in this area, while there are also far too many examples of this aspect of practice being neglected, leaving people who approach us feeling less than happy at the response they have received (often because it came across as bureaucratic, unresponsive or tokenistic). It is perhaps significant that large proportions of people involved in duty or intake work have never had any training in the knowledge, skills and values involved.

Principle 4 **Knowledge, Skills and Values**
A great deal of time, effort and resources can be wasted if people involved in duty/intake work do not take seriously the significance of the knowledge, skills and values involved.

High-quality intake work should be based on:

> *Basic courtesies.* (Both of the present authors have had experiences of visiting social work agencies and being less than impressed with the welcome we received in terms of the quality of the reception process.)
> *Assessment.* The duty or intake process is not a matter of 'taking messages' or filling in a form. There is much more to it than this, as it is part of an assessment process (often the first step in that process and therefore very important).
> *Being focused on resolution where possible.* It is often the case that matters brought to our attention at this point can be swiftly dealt with, rather than passed through for allocation to a social worker. Referring someone on to a more appropriate agency, giving advice and information and so on can often deal with a matter to the satisfaction of the

referrer without the need for allocation (thus being both a positive step for the referrer and a positive contribution to workload management for the agency).

> *Skills in setting priorities.* Hurtling out to deal with something as an 'emergency' when that is neither necessary nor helpful can be a terrible waste of time and resources, while not responding promptly to something that is urgent can be disastrous. Being able to engage with people and ask the right questions to obtain a picture of the urgency or otherwise of the situation are therefore important skills.

> *Effective communication.* Work done at this early stage in the process can go sadly (and dangerously) wrong if we are not communicating effectively in terms of *what* needs to be communicated to *whom* and *when*. Time pressures in a duty/intake setting can mean that people cut corners and may thereby fail to communicate appropriately.

It is very important indeed that we take the duty/intake function seriously and do not skimp on it or treat it as just a bureaucratic task – it is a vital first step in promoting high-quality social work.

NOS Key Role 6

Demonstrate professional competence in social work practice

education social work Social workers in this field are employed within the education sector of local authorities. There are many issues that can get in the way of making the school experience a productive and enjoyable one, including a lack of appropriate resources to meet specific educational needs, truancy, bullying, teenage pregnancy, social exclusion and disruptive behaviour in the classroom. Issues outside of the school situation will also impact on school attendance and progress. These might include, for example, the effects of poverty, family tension, loss experiences, discrimination, misuse of drugs and so on. As such, then, it is often difficult to separate out education issues from the wider context of family and social issues. Work in this field can therefore be very varied, but will usually include at least some of the following tasks and many others:

> promoting school attendance and addressing problems of poor attendance;
> liaison between school and parents in terms of rights and responsibilities;
> working with children exhibiting disruptive behaviour to help prevent it, or to find suitable alternative education;
> helping travelling families to secure access to education for their children;
> helping to ensure that children with disabilities or special educational needs are not disadvantaged within the education system.

Much of education social work, therefore, is carried out in a multidisciplinary context, including collaborative work with teachers, police officers, youth justice workers, healthcare workers and drug and alcohol agencies, as well as with colleagues in statutory social work agencies.

NOS Key Role 2

Plan, carry out, review and evaluate social work practice, with individuals, families, carers, groups, communities, and other professionals

elder abuse The abuse of older people is a complex issue that goes far beyond the deliberate intent of one individual to harm another. It occurs at a number of levels and is not always intentional or even recognized as abuse. Being abusive can be about being misinformed or wrong, as well as being malicious. Nevertheless, the outcome is that older people are harmed in one way or another by an act, a policy or a regime. As Sue Thompson comments:

> Whole organizations too can be guilty of abusing the power they have over the lives of vulnerable people, so that challenging abuse is not just a matter of sacking 'the bad apple', but also looking at practices and policies within organizations to see whether they lay the foundations for abuse, or contribute towards hiding it from view.
> (Sue Thompson, 2002b, p. 192)

So, we can see that, while the perpetrator can be an individual, regimes can be abusive too. For example, the misuse of medication to keep confused or agitated people sedated and 'manageable' in a residential setting would also constitute abuse. While it may be the action of one individual or one regime, condoning it through lack of action to regulate such practices could be seen as an indication of it being sanctioned at a much higher level.

Manage risk to individuals, families, carers, groups, communities, self and colleagues

As well as operating at different levels, elder abuse can take different forms. As with many such issues, it is not always easy to make clear-cut distinctions. For example, treating someone negligently to the extent that they develop pressure sores could be categorized as physical abuse as well as neglect, and the lack of respect for dignity and rights as an emotional or psychological issue. Broadly speaking, though, the following categories are generally recognized:

> neglect – where the basic needs of a vulnerable person are ignored or inadequately met;
> physical – the non-accidental causing of injury or pain;
> psychological or emotional – terrorizing, demeaning, belittling, invasion of privacy, and so on;
> sexual – any intimate touching or sexual intercourse that is not consented to, or where the ability to understand consent is impaired;
> financial – stealing from an older person or deliberately mismanaging their financial affairs to the perpetrator's benefit.

Responses to elder abuse are in part determined by PoVA procedures – see **protection of vulnerable adults**. The existence and prevalence of elder abuse can be seen to be due in no small part to the significance of ageism which reinforces a low status and social value for older people.

eligibility criteria Social work operates in a context of scarcity, in so far as the need for help is infinite, but resources for meeting such needs will always be finite. Even if the social work budget were to be doubled or trebled, we would still be in a position where we need to make hard decisions about who receives a service and who does not (although this is not to say that we should not be pressing for a greater allocation of resources to social welfare budgets). This is a process known as 'gatekeeping'. Some people

object to this and argue that it is unethical or even oppressive to 'ration resources'. However, such a view fails to take account of the reality of scarcity as an inherent feature of social welfare. What can be unethical or oppressive is a situation where decisions made are based on criteria other than need (for example, when someone is judgemental) or where approaches to decision making are too rigid, not allowing for the flexibility needed to take account of specific circumstances.

Working within budgetary constraints can be frustrating, but dealing with the challenges involved is an important part of what social work is all about.

Demonstrate professional competence in social work practice

In such a context of scarce resources, we need to have clear criteria for deciding who is entitled to receive what level of service, so that such decisions are not made arbitrarily. This is where the notion of eligibility criteria comes in. Commonly, they establish categories of need in terms of level of priority. If someone's needs are not felt to be of a sufficient severity, they may be refused a service or offered a lower level of service. Of necessity the criteria specified are very broad, as they would be far too cumbersome if they tried to incorporate the wide range and significant diversity of situations we encounter.

Eligibility criteria are usually set at a local level, although they tend to be quite similar from one area to another. They are more widely used in adult services than in children's services, although they do feature in child care too in many areas. They can be a useful tool to help make the difficult decisions that are necessary in a situation of resource shortfall, but they are a fairly blunt instrument and are no substitute for proper assessment.

emotional abuse This is a term that has its roots in child protection, but is also increasingly being used in the context of the protection of vulnerable adults. It refers to the ways in which a person's treatment of another can do emotional harm – for example, in undermining **self-esteem** and confidence. It can occur in its own right as a form of abuse or can be a dimension of other forms of abuse – that is, it can arise as a consequence of such processes as **physical abuse**, sexual abuse or neglect, thus exacerbating the harmful effects of such abuse.

Emotional abuse can occur as a result of various actions, not least the following:

> persistent criticism and/or ridicule;
> intimidating behaviours; and/or
> outright rejection or vacillating between rejection and acceptance.

Emotional abuse is closely linked with **neglect**, in so far as it can be seen as a neglect of emotional needs. While such abuse can be very **traumatic** and damaging at any point in the life course, it is particularly significant in childhood as it can have a very adverse effect on the child's development and thus store up considerable problems for the future.

Where it is suspected that emotional abuse is taking place, the appropriate procedures should be invoked (child protection procedures in the case of children and young people, protection of vulnerable adults procedures in the case of adults). Such situations have to be handled very carefully and sensitively in order to ensure that the intervention of officialdom does not make matters worse.

`empathy` It is important to distinguish between empathy and sympathy. The latter refers to sharing feelings – that is, if we sympathize with someone who is sad, then we too feel sad. Empathy, by contrast, is where we recognize that another person is sad (or angry or disappointed or frightened and so on) and respond accordingly, but we do not experience the same feelings ourselves.

Sympathy can be very draining and can lead to stress and burnout. Working with a wide range of people and taking on board the various feelings we encounter would soon lead us into a situation in which we are overwhelmed by the weight, range and intensity of emotions to which we have been exposed. Developing empathy rather than sympathy is therefore an important self-care skill. Without it we could quickly find ourselves in a situation in which

our effectiveness is significantly reduced if not eliminated altogether.

NOS Key Role 5

Manage and be accountable, with supervision and support, for your own social work practice within your organization

Empathy involves being able to listen attentively, genuinely taking an interest in what is being said, the concerns being expressed and the feelings underpinning these. An important word here is *genuinely*. Simply going through the motions of pretending to be interested is clearly not enough, although some people who are struggling to cope with the emotional demands of social work may well be tempted to distance themselves from people's feelings in this way (see the discussion above of **burnout**). Where this occurs it can do a great deal of harm as it ruins any real basis of trust and professional rapport.

It is important to recognize that *pure* empathy is an 'ideal' that we are unlikely to meet at all times and is not necessarily desirable. For example, if we are dealing with someone who is grieving following a major loss, it would be very surprising (and perhaps a little worrying) if their immense pain did not touch us at all. What we need to aim for, then, is more of an emphasis on empathy than sympathy, but with a recognition that some degree of sympathy is not only inevitable at times, but also helpful in keeping us in touch with the depth and range of human feelings that are part and parcel of the social work world.

`essentialism` This refers to the tendency to assume that we have 'essences' or qualities that we are supposedly born with and cannot change. So, for example, we might claim that we cannot be assertive because 'I'm not that type of person' or 'It's not in my nature'. This can be linked to the idea of 'bad faith', as used in existentialist philosophy (Neil Thompson, 2000c) – a process by which we, in effect, lie to ourselves in not facing up to the responsibility we have for making decisions about our lives.

A major problem with essentialism is that it focuses on individual personality and distracts attention from wider social, cultural and political issues. It also presents the individual as the 'finished product' rather than a 'work in progress', dynamic and changing over time. It can also be very counterproductive in terms of developing empowering forms of practice. For example, if we use the term 'vulnerable' in an essentialist sense, we can see vulnerability as a characteristic of the individual (and to do so can be quite disempowering and even demeaning) – it presents the individual as 'weak' and perhaps failing in some way. Instead, we need to recognize vulnerability as a dynamic feature of the overall circumstances (psychological and sociological), rather than a personality trait of the individual (see **vulnerability**).

Some approaches to anti-discriminatory practice, particularly in the early stages of its development in the 1980s, fell foul of essentialism and presented discrimination of various forms (racism and sexism, for example) as if they were inevitable characteristics of individuals, rather than manifestations of complex, multidimensional phenomena – see also **reductionism**.

An anti-essentialist approach highlights that personal and social change are possible and seeks to help people build on their strengths. It seeks to move away from the simplistic notion that particular behaviours or attitudes are inherent in the individual concerned, rather than arising from a complex range of factors and not just individual characteristics.

ethics Bullock and Trombley define ethics as:

> The branch of philosophy that investigates morality and, in particular, the varieties of thinking by which human conduct is guided and may be appraised. Its special concern is with the meaning and justification of utterances about the rightness and wrongness of actions, the virtue or vice of the motives which prompt them, the praiseworthiness or blameworthiness of the agents who perform them, and the goodness or badness of the consequences to which they give rise.   (2000, p. 284)

As might be imagined, it is a field that promotes a great deal of debate. Social work offers no definitive answers to the questions raised by ethics (nor would it be appropriate to do so).

However, there is a Code of Ethics available, produced by the British Association of Social Workers, which offers broad guidelines.

www.basw.org.uk

Social work is a professional practice and therefore involves accountable decision making (see **accountability**). However, decision making is not simply a technical enterprise, as it involves a number of dilemmas – indeed, it would be fair to say that social work is characterized by dilemmas, and these are mainly ethical dilemmas. Banks gives a good example of a social work dilemma:

> For example, in a child protection case, if the child is removed from the family both the child and the mother will be unhappy and the child may have to spend some time in institutional care, which may be damaging. Yet if the child remains with the family, there is a chance that the child will suffer physical abuse from the father and may be injured or even die. The way to resolve the dilemma is to try to work out whether one of the alternatives is more unwelcome than the other and then act on that. Of course, we also need to try to work out how likely it is that each of the unwelcome outcomes will occur. (Banks, 2001, pp. 20–1)

Professional practice needs to be ethical practice, in the sense that we need to be able to satisfy ourselves (and others who have an interest in our work) that our actions and inactions are morally justifiable. This introduces the notion of values, as it is by reference to a set of values that we make judgements about what is and what is not morally acceptable. The discussion of values in Chapter 2.6 is therefore very relevant to the topic of ethics.

ethnocentricity Ethnicity refers to a person's cultural background and the sense of identity that stems from it. People from a common background, with shared experiences, will therefore be seen as being from the same ethnic group. Ethnocentricity can be defined as the tendency to see the world through the lenses of one's own ethnicity without taking into consideration the fact and importance of ethnic diversity. It therefore refers to the danger of seeing situations narrowly from the standpoint of one's own culture and its moral values and norms, and assuming that the same rules apply (or should apply) to all cultures. This can easily lead into assumptions that one's own ethnicity is superior to others (what is often referred to as the 'deficit' model of culture), which in turn feeds into racism. This occurs when someone disapproves of a particular cultural practice, simply because it is different from his or her cultural practices. For example, a white, non-Moslem person may be very suspicious of cultural practices associated with Islam and therefore look down on them.

Of course, there is nothing wrong in feeling proud of one's ethnicity and cultural background, but taking pride in your own ethnicity and assuming that other people's backgrounds or approaches are inferior are two different things. Ethnocentricity is therefore antithetical to notions of valuing diversity.

Ethnocentricity needs to be guarded against at three levels in social work:

> Clients or carers may demonstrate ethnocentric attitudes – for example, an elderly user of home care services who refuses to have a black home carer because 'she's not like us'.

> Colleagues within our own agency or within the multidisciplinary network are, of course, not immune from making ethnocentric assumptions from time to time.

> We also need to have a sufficient degree of self-awareness to recognize that each of us will have been brought up in a relatively ethnocentric cultural context and will therefore have a certain amount of 'unlearning' to do. We cannot be complacent about our own vulnerability to ethnocentricity.

Principle 7 Self-management

This is a further example of the importance of self-awareness in relation to self-management.

NOS Key Role 5

Manage and be accountable, with supervision and support, for your own social work practice within your organization

failure to thrive There are projected milestones of physical and psychological development in infancy and early childhood. 'Failure to thrive' is the term used to describe situations in which there is a mismatch between expected development (in terms of weight, height and so on) in relation to chronological age and actual development. Such a disparity between expected development and actual development can trigger a concerned reaction, as such 'developmental delays' as they are known may indicate either a physical problem (an undiagnosed medical condition, for example) or a social problem, such as abuse.

The reasons for 'failure to thrive' can vary, and may include failure to absorb food as well as a lack of adequate nutritional intake, for reasons such as inadequate parenting, poverty or abuse. While it is not necessarily an indicator of **neglect** or abuse, it can alert professionals involved with a family that there may be a cause for concern – physical or otherwise. When the alarm is raised about a child, extensive medical checks can be carried out to establish whether there are any physical causes. If physical causes are identified, steps can be taken to remedy them where possible or to minimize their impact if a remedy cannot be brought to bear. If no physical causes are identified, then a referral will normally be made for a social worker to undertake an assessment to see whether the problem is associated with abuse or other such family problems.

'Failure to thrive' situations need to be addressed on a collaborative basis, involving good partnership working with health visitors and other health professionals. This is because: (i) it is important to have clear channels of communication so that the professionals involved are not getting in each other's way or not 'singing from the same hymn sheet' (as this can not only be very ineffective, it can also be very inconvenient for the family concerned); and (ii) it is often the case that the problems are not simply *either* physical *or* social, but rather a complex mix of the two – thus calling for a joint approach.

NOS Key Role 4

Manage risk to individuals, families, carers, groups, communities, self and colleagues

family support Child care social work is commonly divided into three main groupings: child protection, substitute care and family support. One danger is that this traditional division places family support in the position of a 'catch-all' – that is, anything that is not concerned with substitute care or child protection goes into the 'family support' category. This is misleading, as it casts family support in a secondary role and fails to show what an important part it has to play in high-quality child care social work.

A more positive view of family support sees it as a crucial set of services geared towards keeping families together, promoting resilience and family and individual strengths and helping to promote positive parenting. It encapsulates the following areas:

> Work with individual families to address identified difficulties and develop strengths.
> Work with groups of families (for example via a family centre).
> Schemes and projects geared towards giving children a better start in life in terms of education, health and social well-being.
> Supporting young people leaving care.
  (Canavan, Dolan and Pinkerton, 2000).

A significant feature of family support is an emphasis on prevention. This can be achieved by preventative interventions in the early stages of problems developing or by intervening in crises with a view to helping the family learn how to deal with the difficulties experienced (so that they will be better equipped to deal with such issues if or when they arise in future).

NOS Key Role 2

Plan, carry out, review and evaluate social work practice, with individuals, families, carers, groups, communities, and other professionals

Family support is a highly skilled form of work that can make a significant difference to families and the children within them. In so doing it supports other forms of child care social work, in so far as it reduces the likelihood of child abuse taking place and it also reduces the likelihood of substitute care (foster or residential care) being needed. It is therefore unfortunate that scandals in the residential care of children and young people (Waterhouse, 2000) and tragedies relating to child abuse deaths have pushed family support down the political list of priorities.

financial abuse Responding to the abuse of vulnerable adults has developed partly in parallel with earlier developments in child protection, but financial abuse is one area where this has not occurred. This is because children have not normally reached a state of financial independence, and so are not as vulnerable to financial exploitation. Many adults, however, are indeed vulnerable to being abused in this way. This can apply to people in two main sets of circumstances:

1. Straightforward theft or fraud where unscrupulous persons remove cash or valuables or transfer funds to their own account by deception.
2. Situations where others can access their finances on their behalf. This would apply in circumstances where someone (a relative, for example) has obtained 'power of attorney' or equivalent (that is, a legal provision that allows one person to manage the financial affairs of another) in relation to someone who is not able to take responsibility for their finances due to dementia, mental health problems or severe learning disability.

Financial abuse is certainly not a new phenomenon, but we have certainly been more aware of its prevalence in recent years. Perhaps one factor that has made us less aware in the past is the fact that it can be difficult to accept that relatives or other people entrusted with the financial affairs of someone who relies on their honesty and integrity can actually abuse that trust. Sometimes financial abuse can be cold and cynical – sheer exploitation – but, at others it can be out of desperation (for example, where a carer has major debts and feels the need to exploit someone else in order to get themselves out of trouble). It can also vary in scale, from a few pounds here and there to depriving someone of their life savings and even, in some cases, deceiving them into signing their house over to them.

Financial abuse is likely to be covered by local **protection of vulnerable adults** procedures, and so it is important to make sure that, if you encounter or suspect financial abuse, your response is consistent with these procedures and their requirements.

forensic social work 'Forensic' means relating to evidence, and so the term 'forensic social work' is used to refer to those aspects of social work that involve working in the legal or court system. Roberts and Rock describe the main tasks involved in this type of work:

1. Risk assessments of mentally ill and substance-abusing offenders, with special attention to their risk of future violence and repeat criminality.
2. Assessment and treatment of mentally ill offenders in the criminal justice system and forensic mental health units.
3. Assessment of dangerousness among convicted sex offenders.
4. Mental health assessments to determine whether or not an alleged offender is competent to stand trial; and assessment of a defendant's *mens rea* against responsibility standards in criminal cases.
5. Presentence reports for juvenile court and criminal court judges.
6. Child custody evaluations and assessments to determine whether parental rights of mentally ill, convicted felons, and/or abusive parents should be terminated.
7. Assessment and treatment of involuntary offenders in the criminal justice and forensic mental health systems.

(2002, p. 661)

These authors clearly conceive of forensic social work in medical terms (mental illness rather than mental health problems; treatment rather than intervention). However, this is their specific preference, as there is nothing inherent in this type of work that necessitates a medicalized approach, rather than one based on empowerment (Principle 2: Empowerment and Partnership) and premised on a sociological understanding (Principle 1: The Social Context).

Given that forensic social work operates in tandem with the legal and psychiatric systems, the relationship between care and control can clearly be seen as a significant issue. A major challenge for forensic social work practitioners is to maintain a focus on caring and social work values in a context heavily influenced by social control considerations.

fostering It is not always possible or desirable for children and young people to remain in the care of their parents. It is therefore necessary to have a back-up system so that children and young people can be looked after elsewhere whenever needed. Foster carers are an important part of that system. They provide substitute care in their own homes for one or more children or young people on a short-, medium- or long-term basis.

Child care social work is geared towards returning children and young people to their own family as soon as is reasonably possible, although it is not always possible (for example, where parents are not able to offer acceptable levels of care due to such problems as illness or mental health problems or are not able to offer care at all, for instance, where parents have died or a single parent is serving a life sentence in prison). Residential care is an option for some children and young people, but the overall philosophy is one that regards a family placement as being a better option than an institutional one.

Applicants to become foster carers are very closely scrutinized and assessed before they are able to register formally as foster carers.

NOS Key Role 1

Prepare for, and work with, individuals, families, carers, groups and communities to assess their needs and circumstances

Once accepted they are given training and have the support of a social worker to help deal with any problems or concerns that may arise. It is a very demanding type of work, but it can also be very rewarding and satisfying.

goal setting Very often the situations we deal with in social work are very complex and 'messy'. It can sometimes be difficult, especially in the early stages, to have clarity about what our role is or what is expected of us. It can be the case that the situation is so problematic in so many different ways that we do not know where to start. If we are not careful, this can lead us into some very unfocused (and thus potentially unhelpful) forms of practice. It is therefore important that we establish some clarity as soon as we reasonably can about what problems are to be solved, what needs are to be met and so on. In effect, we need to clarify what our goals are.

Goal setting is something that needs to be done in partnership, partly because partnership is an important social work value and partly because the chances of success are much lower if the people we are trying to help have not played a part in agreeing the goals to be aimed for. Goal setting that does not involve partnership would therefore be both unethical and ineffective.

An important part of goal setting is 'setting out your stall'. This involves making it clear to clients and carers what you can and cannot do, what is your role and what is not. It is important to do this in the early stages, as people often do not have a clear picture of what to expect from a social worker and may therefore have unrealistic or inappropriate expectations. Also, some people may deliberately attempt to manipulate you into doing things to their benefit, but which are not part of your role (for example, doing things for them, rather than helping them to do them for themselves). Setting out your stall can be very helpful in preventing confusion or ill feeling at a later stage.

NOS Key Role 2

Plan, carry out, review and evaluate social work practice, with individuals, families, carers, groups, communities, and other professionals

Goals need to be realistic, as setting unachievable goals will undermine confidence and trust and make progress less likely rather than more. Goals also need to be specific. If you are too vague in clarifying what you are trying to achieve, you will have difficulty in knowing whether you have achieved it or not. Goal setting is an important part of systematic practice, to be discussed in Part 4.

good enough parenting Child care social work often involves supporting parents in the demands of parenting (see **family support**) and, where necessary, making alternative arrangements for children to be cared for.

In undertaking such work it is important to have an idea of the boundary between what is an acceptable level of parenting and what is potentially harmful to a child.

Winnicott (1965) was a strong influence on child care theory and practice in the 1960s and he introduced a term that is still with us today, namely 'good enough parenting'. There can be no absolute notion of correct parenting, as what counts as appropriate parenting will vary from situation to situation and will, of course, depend on the needs of the child in question, which will also vary. We can also bring the concept up to date by adding that parenting will vary from culture to culture.

However, this does not mean that 'anything goes' and any form of parenting will do. Where an approach to parenting is harmful in some way (for example, see **neglect**), then social workers have a duty to intervene to safeguard the welfare of the child or children involved. This is a complex topic and needs to be managed very carefully if we are to avoid the potentially oppressive approach of 'parenting the parents' (Neil Thompson, 2002a).

What social workers should not be doing is expecting people to be ideal parents, hence the notion of 'good enough parenting'. Once we are satisfied that parenting is of an acceptable standard (that is, is not harmful to children), then we should not be pressing for further changes, as this risks overstepping our role and becomes a civil rights issue. That is, we have a mandate to intervene when parenting is harmful to children, but we have no mandate to improve on what is already at an acceptable level (although we may do this on a voluntary basis as part of **family support** in some circumstances).

heterosexism and homophobia
'Homophobia' is a term that refers literally to a fear of homosexuality (that is, of same-sex relationships), but is generally used in a less literal sense to refer to a dislike of, negativity or even hostility towards those who do not fit the heterosexual 'norm' (see **sexuality**). It is closely linked with the concept of 'heterosexism', which is defined as unfair discrimination on the grounds of sexuality. It involves assuming that heterosexuality is the valued norm to be

aimed for and that alternative lifestyles are deviant and, in some way, substandard. This has the effect of stigmatizing gay men, lesbians and bisexual people by presenting them as 'unnatural' and thus as second-class citizens.

Heterosexism is not simply a matter of personal prejudice. Parallel with other forms of discrimination, such as **racism**, **sexism**, **ageism** or disablism, heterosexism is also institutionalized, in the sense that it can be part of the wider institutional context of cultural or structural formations. As Carabine comments:

One effect of the institutionalizing of heterosexuality, and with it marriage and family as the preferred social arrangement for partnering and parenting, is to privilege it over and above other arrangements such as same-sex and cohabiting heterosexual relationships. ... The institutionalizing of heterosexuality as acceptable sexuality and as the norm has meant that those not conforming are marginalized or discriminated against. Through its institutionalization in a range of legal and social policies – but particularly through marriage – married heterosexual couples and parents are assigned sets of rights in relation to inheritance, tax and pensions.   (Carabine, 2004a , p. 13)

Homophobia and heterosexism are very relevant to social work, in so far as issues of sexuality arise in a wide variety of social work situations. This is, of course, not surprising, given that sexuality is a fundamental part of both an individual's identity and of social relations more broadly. It is important that we should recognize the influences of our upbringing which are likely to have been supportive of heterosexism to some degree and to be prepared to 'unlearn' these (as indeed we do in relation to other discriminatory aspects of the influence of the cultural context).

For many years, homosexuality was regarded as a medical condition, a psychiatric disorder, and it is only relatively recently that this legacy has diminished significantly to make way for a non-oppressive approach to sexual identity issues. It is therefore important, of course, not to regard someone's sexuality as necessarily a problem or social work issue in itself, as that would itself be an example of heterosexism and a return to the days of seeing same-sex relationships as a form of pathology.

home care This is part of the philosophy of community care in that it is a service which aims to support people in vulnerable circumstances to live as independently as possible in their own homes and communities. It has its origins in services provided to nursing mothers and infants in the early twentieth century when mortality rates for both were high. Subsequent legislation, such as the National Health Service Act 1946 and the Chronically Sick and Disabled Persons Act 1977, led to a widening out of the scope of the service, although the emphasis remained on the provision of domestic support.

However, in recent decades, there has been a move away from tasks such as housework and shopping, and towards an emphasis on providing assistance with personal care, such as keeping clean, getting dressed and undressed, eating nutritional meals and so on. The term 'home carer' is now more common than 'home help' and reflects this difference in role. As local authorities move away from being providers of services to become commissioners of those services (see **care management**), a large proportion of home carers tend to be employees of private sector agencies, and their services are bought in by care managers on behalf of the people who need help because of disability, chronic illness, dementia and so on.

Home care also has an important role to play in terms of monitoring. Home carers can provide invaluable feedback to a social worker about how a particular client is coping – for example, to report on any deterioration in a medical condition or other such problem.

It is unfortunately the case that home care services are often very scarce compared with the high number of people who need such support. The available home care resources therefore have to be used very carefully to make sure that they achieve maximum positive impact in maintaining people in the community.

hospice This approach to palliative care (that is, the care of people who are terminally ill) is premised on the right of individuals to die with dignity and without pain and, to this end, it offers holistically based care and support to people with life-limiting and life-threatening conditions. Hospices are generally perceived of as buildings, but it can be useful to think of hospice as a philosophy and a service, rather than a place. It can be described as a philosophy of care, and therefore hospice care can be carried out in people's own homes too and, increasingly, some hospitals are trying to incorporate the principles of hospice care into the care they offer to terminally ill people. Dame Cicely Saunders (2002), often referred to as the founder of the hospice movement in the UK, highlights the following aims of the palliative care that hospice offers:

> The affirmation of life and the recognition of death as a part of life.
> To respect the worth of individuals.
> The relief of pain and distressing symptoms.
> To help people deal with difficult and unfamiliar feelings and to feel at ease with themselves and their relationships with others.
> To offer a support system to those experiencing the death of a loved one.

Some social workers are employed within hospice services and deal with palliative care as a central part of their role, but a much larger number of social workers will engage with hospice services from time to time in relation to specific individuals they are working with. An understanding of hospice is therefore important for all, and not simply restricted to palliative care specialists.

A clear strength of the hospice movement is that it places great emphasis on **spirituality** as a feature of people's lives (and, indeed, of their dying). This focus on maintaining a thread of meaning is helpful in supporting people in facing death and their loved ones in dealing with the grief associated with their loss. Other branches of social work clearly have a lot to learn from this aspect of hospice philosophy (Moss, 2005).

A traditional weakness of the hospice movement has been its narrow focus on individuals without taking adequate account of the wider social context and such relevant factors as poverty, racism and sexism. There are, however, signs that this situation is now changing (see Bevan, 1998, 2002; Bevan and Thompson, 2003; Desai and Bevan, 2002; Riches, 2002).

human services This is a term used to describe a range of 'people professions'. It incorporates the traditional caring professions of social work, counselling, health care and so on, but is also broader than this. Moss offers helpful comment when he states that:

'Human services practitioners' is a phrase which has become more widely used in recent years to include the whole range of professional people who work in a formal caring capacity. These include social workers; probation officers; youth workers; advice workers; counsellors; criminal and community justice workers; and all who work in a health care capacity. Although not the most elegant of phrases, it is intended to be a comprehensive and inclusive term which captures the essence of the work across many disciplines. We are dealing with *human* services which are dealing with *human* problems and concerns all the time.
(2005, p. 4)

This is an important term for (at least) two reasons:

> As Moss points out, it emphasizes the *human* dimension of our work – we are people working with people. This may sound obvious, but it very easy for this important point to be lost in the pressures of the job. Busy practitioners often complain that the pressures of the work can lead to the heart of social work being forgotten, with a mechanistic approach to getting through a heavy workload taking its place (see Neil Thompson, 2004).
> Social work is only one branch of the human services among many. We need to remember that we are part of a multidisciplinary network and must therefore not act in isolation. This is an important part of the social work value of **partnership**.

partnership, see p. 199

NOS Key Role 2

Plan, carry out, review and evaluate social work practice, with individuals, families, carers, groups, communities, and other professionals

humility Humility is the quality of being humble. This means being able to recognize the limitations of what we are able to achieve. Social work can and does achieve a lot of success, but it would be entirely unrealistic (and unreasonable) to expect success in all cases.

The profession of social work involves dealing with deeply rooted problems – deeply rooted in the social and political fabric of the broader social context and also often deeply rooted in well-established family dynamics, personal habits and attitudes as well as each person's sense of identity. Given the deep-rooted nature of the issues we are dealing with, it would be naïve to expect major changes in all the cases we take on. This is not to say that major positive change is not possible – history has taught us that it is. Rather, it is a matter of being realistic and accepting that there will be limits to what we can achieve in terms of positive outcomes and how often we achieve them. **social context, see p. 69**

Humility is important for (at least) three reasons:

1 *Motivation and workload management.* If we have unrealistic expectations of what we can achieve, it will be difficult to sustain our motivation in the face of a range of situations where we cannot make progress. This, in turn, is significant in terms of managing a heavy workload. If we allow an unrealistic attitude to demotivate us, then we will struggle to maintain the energy levels required to rise to the challenges that social work practice presents.

NOS Key Role 5

Manage and be accountable, with supervision and support, for your own social work practice within your organization

2 *Self-care.* Similarly, if we have unrealistic expectations, we do ourselves a disservice as far as **self-care** is concerned. Unrealistic expectations can be a major source of stress (Thompson et al., 1994), whether these expectations come from others or from ourselves. We therefore have to be careful to make sure that we do not add to the existing pressures of social work by unnecessarily giving ourselves unachievable expectations as an additional burden.

3 *Empowerment* If the people we are trying to help feel that we are expecting too much by setting our sights too high, we run the risk of reducing their motivation and confidence rather than boosting them. In this respect we would be contributing more to disempowerment than empowerment (see **goal setting**).

task-centred practice see p. XXX

Principle 7 **Self-management**

Setting ourselves unrealistic targets or expectations is contrary to the principle of self-management in so far as it undermines self-care.

institutionalization This is a term that is used in two senses, both of which are important in social work. First, it refers to a historical approach to welfare policy which had the effect of segregating people – particularly those who were seen as a danger to society in some way (for example, because of mental health problems or what was then known as 'mental handicap' – that is, learning disabilities). This was achieved by placing people in large institutional settings, often far removed from local communities on the basis of 'out of sight, out of mind'. Over the years this was challenged and today's community care policy is largely a reaction to the problems associated with the earlier emphasis on institutional care (Stainton, Welshman and Walmsley, 2005).

The policy had detrimental effects, in so far as it made people dependent (see **dependency**) by getting them accustomed to institutional regimes that did not involve making decisions for themselves or having to take responsibility for earning a living and so on. The regime also took away individual choice and was therefore very disempowering. Furthermore, it was a very stigmatizing regime (see **stigma**).

The second meaning of institutionalization refers to the process by which social patterns become established as norms and thus part of a culture (including an organizational culture). For example, 'institutional racism' refers to discriminatory processes and assumptions that have become so deeply ingrained in patterns of behaviour that they become the norm. This may be to the extent that even people who have no racist beliefs (or may even be strongly committed to anti-racism) may contribute to racist outcomes by following these institutional patterns unthinkingly – not realizing the unfair consequences, because the racist norms are so well established that they are just taken for granted. However, you should note that it is not just racism that can be institutionalized. It can apply to any form of discrimination (**heterosexism**, for example) and to other social and cultural processes.

What both meanings of the term have in common is an emphasis on patterns of behaviour and assumptions that become dangerous and unhelpful in some way. Clearly both are significant problems for social workers to avoid.

learning disability This is an umbrella term for a wide range of conditions, all of which are about intellectual impairment of some form and degree. It includes Down's Syndrome, autistic spectrum disorder (see **autism**) and various others. As with all wide-ranging terms, it can mask the range of conditions within it, and the extent to which they can differ in terms of their consequences. For some people, having a learning disability can mean being totally dependent on others for every aspect of their lives, while others might experience some form of specific difficulty, but otherwise be able to live largely independently.

There has been a significant change over the past half-century in terms of how people with intellectual impairments have been conceptualized and supported. Historically there has been a tendency to fear and marginalize them, and such ideas were reinforced by the 'eugenics' movement (that is, the movement which argued that social worth should be judged on genetic make-up, with people who were not genetically 'pure' being seen as second-class citizens). This approach was prevalent in the early twentieth century and promoted the idea that people with learning disabilities were a 'threat' to society.

Segregation and institutional life (see **institutionalization**) remained the order of the day for many people until policy making began to be challenged in the 1970s by the 'normalization' model (see **social role valorization**). This attempt to challenge the perception of people with learning disabilities as different and inferior by promoting their social inclusion has not been without its critics, but it has laid the foundations for a further challenge based on a rights approach. In theory, citizenship endows people with a right to have their voice heard, but putting such ideas into practice relies on people with learning disabilities being conceptualized as being full citizens in the first place.

NOS Key Role 3

Support individuals to represent their needs, views and circumstances

The term 'learning difficulties' is often used as an alternative to 'learning disabilities'. Both terms were introduced to replace the former term of 'mental handicap' which had become stigmatized and quite problematic.

linguistic sensitivity Language plays a central role in social life, and so it should come as no surprise to learn that it is equally important in social work. The language we use can at times be crucial in determining the outcome of our involvement. Language can bring people together or it can set them apart. The ability to match the form of language to the circumstances is an important part of good practice. For example, using overly formal language in talking to clients and carers could alienate them, while using very informal language in, say, a court hearing could seriously undermine our professional credibility. Having a sensitivity to language and how it can affect situations is therefore part and parcel of the essential requirements of effective social work.

Linguistic sensitivity is also important in relation to tackling discrimination and promoting equality. This is because language not only reflects reality, it also constructs that reality, in the sense that, if we use discriminatory forms of language, we are actively constructing unequal social relations and thereby making the problem worse. Unfortunately, however, approaches to the potential for language to do harm have tended to be crude and simplistic, often taking the form of lists of 'taboo' words that are deemed 'politically incorrect', with little or no opportunity to look at *why* or *in what circumstances* a particular term may be inappropriate. This reductionist approach has had the effect of making many people very wary and defensive about language issues, raising anxiety levels and hampering debate, discussion and learning about these complex matters.

What is needed is a balance between the two destructive extremes of, on the one hand, paying little or no attention to the role of language and, on the other hand, a simplistic PC approach that does not do justice to the complexities and which has a tendency to do more harm than good (see Neil Thompson, 2003b). Linguistic sensitivity is not something that can be developed overnight, but it is a skill that is important enough to devote time and effort to developing over time.

locus of control This is a psychological term. 'Locus' means place (as in 'location' and 'locality'), and so the concept of 'locus of control' is concerned with the question of where an individual perceives control to lie. There are, according to this theory, two types of people, those with an internal locus of control ('internals') and those with an external locus ('externals'). This difference is very significant in terms of how we tackle life and its challenges:

> *Internals* have greater confidence and are more proactive in how they deal with the situations they become involved in. They are empowered and feel that they have a great deal of control over their lives and circumstances.
> *Externals* perceive control to lie elsewhere – with other people, in forces beyond their control, 'fate' and so on. They have lower levels of confidence, and tend to be reactive rather than proactive. They do not feel empowered and feel that circumstances are largely beyond their control.

The reality is that no one has complete control over their lives and no one has no control at all. We are all somewhere in between those two extremes. Where we are on that continuum will depend in part on our attitude, on whether we see ourselves as having more or less control (that is, having a more internal or more external locus of control).

Principle 7 **Self-management**
An internal locus of control is very helpful when it comes to self-management.

Principle 2 **Empowerment and Partnership**
An internal locus of control is also very helpful in relation to empowerment.

Locus of control is an important concept in relation to stress. People with an internal locus of control are likely to be better equipped to deal with the pressures they face, as they are more likely to take a proactive approach (Thompson et al., 1994). This is significant in terms of **self-care** (being able to protect ourselves from **stress**) and, more broadly, in terms of practice, as stress is an important issue for the people we are seeking to help, as well as for our own health and well-being.

The concept can be seen as an important part of empowerment, as the efforts we make to support an internal locus of control can help people to address pressures, can be an important part of building a platform for helping people gain greater control of their lives. As we shall see in Part 4, empowerment is partly about removing, weakening or circumnavigating external, sociological obstacles to taking control of our lives (discrimination and oppression, for example), and partly about dealing with internal, psychological obstacles. The concept of locus of control can help us with the latter.

NOS Key Role 3
Support individuals to represent their needs, views and circumstances

looked-after children Child care law and policy are premised on a commitment to keeping children with their families wherever possible and safe to do so, and to returning children to their families as soon as reasonably possible if they do have to be removed from home at any point. However, there are circumstances where children and young people need to be removed from home and placed in substitute care (whether in a children's home or with foster carers – see **fostering**). Such children are said to be 'looked after' and are protected by regulations designed to safeguard them from harm – the looked-after children system (LAC) which requires social workers to keep records of assessments, care plans and actions taken.

Prior to the implementation of the Children Act 1989, a distinction was drawn between voluntary and statutory (or compulsory) care. The former referred to situations where parents agreed to their children being placed in substitute care and the latter to situations where officialdom had intervened in terms of a care order or emergency protection order having been made by a court, or the child or young person being remanded in care as part of criminal proceedings in the youth court. This distinction no longer applies, as 'in care' is a term reserved only for the latter category and children being looked after on a voluntary basis are said to be 'accommodated'. 'Looked-after children' is the term used to describe both children 'in care' and those 'accommodated' – in other words, children in substitute care.

The main reasons for children being looked after are:

> *Child protection.* Children may be looked after away from home to protect them from abuse – where serious abuse has taken place or where there is serious concern that abuse is likely to occur.
> *Family breakdown.* Families may not be able to stay together for a variety of reasons – for example, when children are placed in substitute care because their behaviour is seriously beyond the control of their parents and is placing them (or others) at serious risk of harm.
> *Parental non-availability.* This may occur in a single parent household when the parent becomes ill or is otherwise indisposed (for example, as a result of a drink problem).

In all cases the social worker concerned will seek family alternatives (grandparents, for example) before making arrangements for a child to become 'looked after'. This is part of the child care philososphy and policy of supporting family life as a better alternative than state provision.

`mediation` **Conflict** is very commonly encountered in social work, and a skilled and experienced social worker will have many conflict management tools up his or her sleeve. Mediation is one such tool. It is used when two or more people cannot come to an agreement about something important and the lack of agreement is causing problems in some ways (for example, in relation to parental contact for children following a divorce).

Principle 4 `Knowledge, Skills and Values`

Mediation and conflict management skills are important parts of an effective social worker's skills repertoire, although they have often been neglected in social work education over the years.

The basis of mediation is the use of a neutral facilitator. This terminology is very important:

> *Neutral.* The mediator must remain impartial throughout. If either party feels the mediator is biased, the process is likely to fail.
> *Facilitator.* It is not the mediator's responsibility to resolve the dispute, but rather to facilitate the parties in finding their own resolution. In this way, mediation is a form of empowerment, in so far as it is geared to helping people resolve their own problems rather than do it for them in a way that may create **dependency**.

Principle 2 `Empowerment and Partnership`

Mediation needs to be seen as a form of empowerment in so far as it helps people resolve their own conflicts rather than seeks to resolve the conflicts for them

There will be some stylistic differences in terms of how different mediators approach the task, but a very common pattern is that the people involved in the dispute are given the opportunity to 'state their case', as it were, to present the situation as they see it. The other party(ies) are not allowed to interrupt (on the understanding that, when it is their turn to speak soon, they will be free from interruption). Once each party has given their side of the story the mediator can choose to continue working with them together to try to reach an agreement or he or she can use the 'caucus' approach.

A 'caucus' is a one-to-one meeting, out of earshot of the other party. This amounts to a form of 'shuttle diplomacy' in which the mediator has confidential one-to-one discussions with the parties, helping them to edge forward to finding a mutually satisfactory way forward. When the time is right, the mediator will bring the parties together again to prepare the way for finalizing an agreement.

Mediation is a voluntary process, and there is no point trying to pressurize people into accepting it as a way forward, as it is highly unlikely to work if it is not entered into in a committed way. It is also a highly skilled undertaking, but one with a very high success rate in achieving positive outcomes.

NOS Key Role 3

Support individuals to represent their needs, views and circumstances

mental health problems This is a highly contested term. Traditionally it has been used to refer to 'mental illness' – in other words, it has been conceptualized as part of a medical model, although this approach has come under increasing challenge in recent years. The medical model discusses 'illnesses', such as **schizophrenia**, **depression**, **bipolar disorder** as well as various 'neurotic' or nervous disorders. The response to the problems associated with these conditions is predominantly a medical one, with extensive use of medication and occasionally electro-convulsive therapy and/or surgery – although counselling and psychosocial interventions are also used to a certain extent.

There have been many critiques of the medical model of mental health problems, beginning with the work of Szasz (1961) and the anti-psychiatry movement (Laing, 1965; Laing and Cooper, 1971) followed by poststructuralist approaches (Foucault, 1967), feminist analyses (Fawcett and Karban, 2005) and other critical perspectives (Pilgrim and Rogers, 2005; Neil Thompson, 2003a). There have also been approaches that have been highly critical of traditional medical perspectives, but have remained within a medical frame of reference – for example, in continuing to refer to mental 'illnesses' (for example, Bentall, 2003; Bracken and Thomas, 2005; Laurance, 2003). What these critiques have in common is the recognition that people who are experiencing mental distress and related problems are not best helped by a model of intervention that conceives of the situation as an illness in need of treatment, as this amounts to a reductionist approach (see **reductionism**) that neglects both the complex psychological

dynamics of mental health problems and the equally complex (if not more so) set of social, economic and political issues that play a part in shaping the experience of mental distress.

Principle 1 Social Context

It is important that social workers do not neglect the social context of mental health problems.

Mental health problems are very important in social work. This is because there is an important set of duties for specialist mental health workers in helping people with mental health problems deal with the personal, social and existential challenges they face. There is also the significance of mental health issues for social workers more generally and not just specialist mental health workers. This is because mental health issues can apply in any social work situation, whether in child care, community care with adults or any other branch of practice.

multidisciplinary working It is not uncommon for social workers to work as members of a multidisciplinary team, rather than as part of a team where all colleagues are social workers or social work assistants. For example, team colleagues might be nurses, occupational therapists and/or physiotherapists, doctors, psychologists, play therapists, members of the police force or education system or indeed anyone involved in people work. Often, the rationale for having multidisciplinary teams is to facilitate the provision of a holistic service. A common way of trying to achieve this is a system whereby service users are allocated a key worker or care co-ordinator whose role it is to draw upon the expertise of others in the team and, in partnership with the service user, co-ordinate 'packages' of care and support. As a social worker you might be a key worker, but not all key workers are social workers.

The diversity of perspectives which comes with multidisciplinary working can be beneficial, as can the more direct channels of communication between disciplines.

NOS Key Role 2

Plan, carry out, review and evaluate social work practice, with individuals, families, carers, groups, communities, and other professionals

Many teams operate very successfully in this way, but there is the potential for difficulties to arise in situations where:

> there is a clash in terms of **occupational culture** – for example, if workers from a profession allied to medicine work to a medical model approach and social workers adopt a social model approach there may be some tension if it is felt that some important values are not being taken seriously, or a particular perspective disrespected. Expectations about work levels, autonomy of decision making, professional development and so on can be very different, and these can lead to misunderstandings and even resentment within teams, especially where one occupational culture is dominant over others;

> role boundaries are not clearly defined – in some settings there can a degree of overlap between team members from different disciplines. For example, there are sometimes situations which could be just as easily and competently resolved by a community psychiatric nurse as by a social worker and vice versa. However, there are clearly major differences of emphasis between their roles and so it is important that these are clearly understood and respected if service users are to receive the best input that each can offer and to not have responses either duplicated or overlooked;

> the team is managed by someone from a discipline other than social work, unless that manager has a very good grasp of social work, its promise and its constraints;

> ground rules are not in place or only loosely observed – for example, **confidentiality** and consent will always be important issues and there needs to be agreement about what are and are not appropriate policy and behaviour;

> communication networks are inefficient – this is especially so where colleagues from different disciplines work to different time schedules and are used to different communication systems;

> there is no clearly defined and agreed framework for decision making or for resolving disputes, particularly in terms of contentious issues such as **risk** taking; and

> there are significant differences in terms of professional codes of ethics and behaviour.

We have not meant to be unduly negative here, as multidisciplinary working has a good deal to offer and there are many examples of initiatives that work very well. The above are merely points to bear in mind if you are invited or expected to work in this way. Flying the flag for social work can be difficult in some circumstances but also extremely rewarding, especially when you can recognize and highlight to others what the team, and those with whom it works, would miss out on if a social work perspective were lacking.

neglect This is a term that has a long history in child care social work, but is also now part of the emerging body of knowledge relating to the **protection of vulnerable adults**. In relation to children it is seen as a form of abuse, as 'neglect' is a short-hand term for 'neglect of children's needs'. These include the basic physical needs of food, drink and shelter (and medical attention when needed) as well as psychological needs, such as love, affection and acceptance. Neglect would therefore be seen to apply in situations where parents (or other carers) are failing to meet children's needs in one or more of these areas.

Neglect can arise for various reasons, not least the following:

> The parents/carers may not have an adequate understanding of children's needs (for example, as a result of a learning disability – although it should not be assumed that parents with learning disabilities will necessarily be neglectful).

> The parents/carers may have mental health needs that prevent them from caring adequately (depression, for example).

> Social factors, such as poverty and poor housing may make it difficult if not impossible to meet children's needs in those circumstances.

> The child may have special needs that the parents/carers are not well-equipped to meet.

> There is a deliberate attempt to harm the child (for whatever reason) through neglect.

Neglect can be difficult to detect at times as the effects are slow and gradual and the presenting signs may be due to other reasons, such as an underlying undiagnosed medical condition (see **failure to thrive**). It can also be difficult to draw a line between poor (but legal) parenting and (abusive) neglect, but it should be remembered that, in all cases of child abuse, the appropriate procedures should be followed and the matter dealt with collectively on a multidisciplinary basis, rather than 'solo'.

Neglect in relation to protecting adults has much in common with neglect as a form of child abuse. It relates to situations in which people are in a position of **dependency** and therefore rely on others for their basic needs to be met. Neglect occurs when these needs are not met and, as with child neglect, there can be various reasons as to why this might occur. Also, as with child neglect, situations involving the neglect (or suspicion of neglect) of vulnerable adults need to be dealt with in accordance with the appropriate procedures.

NOS Key Role 4

Manage risk to individuals, families, carers, groups, communities, self and colleagues

networking This is a term that applies in two senses or at two levels. First, it refers to the recognition that social workers are part of a multidisciplinary system and need to work in partnership (Principle 2: Empowerment and Partnership). We need to make the effort to form helpful working relationships with colleagues in the appropriate agencies: community nurses, health visitors, GPs, police officers, housing officers, probation staff, youth workers, teachers and so on. There are skills involved in positive networking in this way, and the importance of partnership as a social work value means that it is important to develop these skills.

Second, networking can be a feature of direct practice in terms of drawing on existing social and community networks to meet needs and address problems, as well as strengthening those networks where possible (see **signposting** and **community social work**). It involves recognizing that social work is not simply a matter of providing or commissioning services, and can be usefully carried out through the appropriate use of networks of informal, voluntary and private provision.

Jack offers a helpful definition:

A *social support network* is a set of interconnected relationships among a group of people which provides help in coping with the demands of daily living. The members of social support networks may include relatives, friends, neighbours, work colleagues, volunteers and professionals.
(2000, p. 328)

He goes on to make some important observations about networking:

In the socially impoverished environments in which social workers are usually to be found, residents are likely to benefit from the creation and maintenance of a wide range of socially supportive network relationships in the locality. A community orientation, rather than a purely individualistic approach, is indicated, which helps people to participate in such activities as play groups, youth clubs, women's groups, food co-operatives, luncheon clubs and adult education classes. The relationships formed can help individuals to develop competence, build self-esteem, participate in reciprocal exchanges and provide a sense of belonging, all of which are likely to improve their health and well-being in significant ways.
(Jack, 2000, p. 329)

Networking skills, in both senses of the term are therefore important parts of the social worker's repertoire and should therefore be taken very seriously.

oppression Neil Thompson defines oppression as:

Inhuman or degrading treatment of individuals or groups; hardship or injustice brought about by the dominance of one group over another; the negative and demeaning use of power. It often involves disregarding the rights of an individual or group and is thus a denial of citizenship.
(2006c, p. 40)

Reference was made earlier in Part 3 to discrimination as a process of identifying differences and treating certain people unfairly as a result of those differences. It was also pointed out that such discrimination often leads to oppression. It can therefore be helpful to see discrimination as the process, and oppression as the outcome (which is why the terms anti-discriminatory practice and anti-oppressive practice are so often used interchangeably). That is, oppression arises primarily because particular individuals or groups are discriminated against because they are part of a marginalized, devalued or stigmatized minority.

Oppression is a very important concept in social work because:

1. Our practice so often involves the exercise of power. Oppression can arise from the inappropriate use of such power – whether through the deliberate abuse of power or the unwitting misuse of it (Neil Thompson, 2003a). It is to be hoped that social workers would not use their powers deliberately to oppress others (although there are sadly many cases on record of this happening), but the unwitting misuse of power is an ever-present possibility for any practitioner.

NOS Key Role 6

Demonstrate professional competence in social work practice

For example, a social worker may oppress a disabled person by relying on a stereotype that disabled people are not able to make decisions for themselves (Oliver and Sapey, 2006). We therefore have to make sure that our actions (and inactions) do not have detrimental effects for the people we are seeking to help.

2. Social work's clientele experiences more than its fair share of oppression. That is, the people we are seeking to help come predominantly from groups who are subject to 'inhuman or degrading treatment' as a result of power relations in society being largely stacked against them. It is important to note that social work does not involve dealing with the 'general public', but rather with those sectors of the general populace who are disadvantaged in one or more ways (as a result of poverty and deprivation, stigmatization, social exclusion and so on).

3. Social justice is a key social work value, and we cannot reconcile a commitment to social justice with actions and attitudes that contribute to or condone oppression.

partnership Partnership literally means working with other people, but it is important that we use it in more than just a literal sense. This is because, for the most part, we would find it difficult to get through a working day without working with other people in a direct, literal sense. If all it means is working with other people in a literal sense (as opposed to working in isolation), then it becomes a meaningless concept.

As a social work value, partnership means moving away from the traditional, elitist notion of professionalism in which the professional 'knows best' and has the power to decide unilaterally what to do. Partnership involves moving towards a more empowering form of professionalism in which professionals, clients and carers work together to identify: (i) what problems need to be addressed; and (ii) how best to tackle them. In this way, social work should be seen as a shared process, a collective endeavour with people, rather than something we do *to* them or *for* them.

NOS Key Role 1

Prepare for, and work with, individuals, families, carers, groups and communities to assess their needs and circumstances

This can be a difficult goal to achieve, especially for people who are long-standing users of services and/or people who are resistant to receiving help. However, the benefits are generally worth the effort expended, as a failure to work in partnership can be very costly (creating mistrust or even hostility at one extreme and **dependency** at the other). Sometimes, partnership working may not be possible, and it may be necessary to rely on the use of statutory powers (in relation to child abuse or serious mental health problems, for example). However, giving up on partnership should be seen as a last resort and it should not be abandoned lightly, at the first sign of any difficulties.

A good example of working in partnership is illustrated by the use of the 'exchange model' of assessment, as developed by Smale and colleagues:

THE EXCHANGE MODEL

Assumes that people:

> Are expert in themselves.

Assumes that the worker:

> has expertise in the *process* of problem solving with others;

> understands and shares perceptions of problems with their management;

> gets agreement about who will do what to support whom;

> takes responsibility for arriving at the optimum resolution of problems within the constraints of available resources and the willingness of participants to contribute.

(Smale et al., 1993, p. 18)

Being able to work in partnership can be a real test of the social worker's skills in terms of communication, forming a rapport, being clear and focused, managing conflict constructively and so on.

physical abuse This refers to the type of abuse inflicted by physical harm – in effect, an assault. Formerly referred to as 'non-accidental injury', it can arise from excessive physical chastisement (for example, when a parent does not intend to cause harm to a child, but uses excessive force and thus causes injury) or from deliberate intention to inflict an injury. Note, however, that the physical chastisement of children is not, of itself, considered to be abusive officially – although there is a strong 'anti-smacking' lobby that argues it should be.

The term 'physical abuse' has its roots in the field of child protection, but is now firmly established as part of the vocabulary of the abuse of vulnerable adults – see **protection of vulnerable adults**. Such abuse can be cold and calculating, where the perpetrator is in full control of their actions and is intentionally acting in what we might describe as a sadistic way. Alternatively, the abuse may arise when an individual is overstressed or has lost his or her temper as a result of one or more frustrations.

For many years doctors and other health professionals have been trained in recognizing signs of physical abuse in children and young people, but it is only relatively recently that the question of abuse of vulnerable adults has begun to gain the attention it deserves. An important factor is not just the injuries themselves (these may have been caused by an accident), but rather, any possible discrepancy between the nature of any injury and its explanation. Where someone gives an explanation that is not consistent with the injury, then this is likely to set alarm bells ringing and lead to the relevant protection procedures being invoked.

Physical abuse is significant, not only because of the physical harm it does, but also because of the psychological effects. It can be a very **traumatic** experience and can have long-term adverse effects, as well as do a lot of harm in the short term.

politicization The notion that 'the personal is political' has become a well-established idea in feminism (Segal, 1999). However, it can be extended beyond gender-related oppression to apply to any situation characterized by inequality and disadvantage. Although the problems experienced by social work clients can be deeply personal, they are also political to a certain extent at least – that is, they are connected to broader patterns of power relations, social structures and so on. 'Politicization' refers to the process of helping people see their problems as part of the broader political backcloth, so that they can recognize that the problems are not their own fault – and so that they can have the opportunity to link up with people in similar circumstances and support one another through shared experiences of adversity.

This approach was part of radical social work which developed in the late 1960s and early 1970s. In its earliest incarnation it was often done very crudely and in ways that did not necessarily help or empower people (Fook, 2002). Gradually it became apparent that simply making people aware of the political context of their problems did not necessarily move the situation forward. It was realized that a more sophisticated approach to these issues was called for.

However, despite more sophisticated approaches to this beginning to develop, the process has become far less common than was previously the case (although it was never a mainstream social work tool). It has largely been replaced as a specific practice tool by a broader emphasis on empowerment (see Part 4) which incorporates a political dimension.

Politicization developed as part of radical social work. Powell points out that the strength of this movement was its emphasis on environmental factors and a strong ethical stance, but he also indicates that: 'Its weakness is its problem with connecting its critique to the predominantly individualised nature of social work intervention' (2001, p. 69).

Politicization has much in common with Freire's (1972) notion of 'conscientization' which refers to forms of education that are geared towards developing a critical consciousness rather than simply filling people with facts and figures (what Freire calls the 'banking' model of education). This is an approach that can be translated into a social work context, presenting social work practice as a process that has the potential for 'consciousness raising'.

post-traumatic stress disorder This is a condition which can develop when someone witnesses or experiences something which is severely traumatic and during which they experience intense fear and often helplessness (see **trauma**). Examples of such events might include seeing someone killed or severely injured, suffering torture or seeing someone tortured, suffering or witnessing a physical or sexual attack and so on. While it is to be expected that people will feel distressed after experiencing or witnessing a traumatic episode, what characterizes post-traumatic stress disorder (PTSD) is that the distress persists long after the event, sometimes for months or even years. The ways in which the condition manifests itself are varied but can include:

> *Flashbacks*. The images, memories and associated emotions recur, sometimes in the form of vivid dreams, but often just taking over one's thoughts, so that the distress is relived over and over again.
> *Feelings of detachment* from the world and people around oneself, sometimes described as emotional numbness – also feelings of low mood and pessimism.
> *Irritability* and increased 'watchfulness', which can affect sleep patterns and concentration.

While there has been a good deal of debate over recent years about PTSD, it is increasingly becoming recognized that emotional responses to major trauma can be quite severe and prolonged. There has also been a recognition that individuals working in occupations such as firefighting, rescue, police work and paramedics may be affected by repeated or severe exposure to life-threatening situations, trauma and death itself – this is known as 'secondary traumatization'.

Some social workers will work in specialist settings where PTSD is a major feature of their work. However, it is a condition that may occur on the caseload of any social worker, as no one is immune from the effects of exposure to traumatic incidents – they can happen to anyone at any time.

NOS Key Role 4
Manage risk to individuals, families, carers, groups, communities, self and colleagues

poverty Poverty has long been a contested issue. That is, there are competing views about what constitutes poverty and whether it should be measured in absolute or relative terms. Absolute poverty refers to subsistence levels and whether one has the resources to keep oneself alive. What constitutes 'basic needs' is also contested, but the absolute poverty approach still embraces the notion that minimum needs are definable. This definition of poverty underpins eligibility for social security benefits, in that those people with an income less than that calculated by the government as being sufficient to meet basic needs, are officially defined as being below the 'poverty line'.

Relative poverty, on the other hand, takes into account that standards and expectations change over time, so that the dividing line between poverty and affluence will be a moveable one, relative to the expectations of the culture in which we live. And so, if most people have televisions and annual holidays and can afford to travel to work or school, then those unable to afford these things would be considered to be poor *in relation* to the majority who can and in relation to the prevailing social standards. In this respect, relative poverty is closely related to social exclusion, in so far as poverty of this kind may not be life-threatening, but it does adversely affect people's participation in mainstream society and their sense of belonging.

The potential for you to be working with people experiencing poverty is very high (Jones and Novak, 1999), and you will do your clients a disservice if you fail to appreciate what that means to them in terms of social exclusion, stress, stigma and adverse effects on health, educational achievements and so on.

Unfortunately, many people are judgemental about people living in poverty and assume that it is their own fault due to idleness. However, this is a grossly oversimplified view that fails to take account of the sociological dimensions and causes of poverty – thereby failing to uphold Principle 1: Social Context.

Potentially anyone can be prone to poverty, but some groups of people feature more frequently in the poverty statistics than others. For example, members of ethnic minorities, older people and disabled people are more likely to be living in poverty than people in the general population. This clearly has major implications for social work policy and practice.

see Social Trends: www.statistics.gov.uk/socialtrends

Social work practice can address poverty by: (i) taking it into consideration in assessments so that we do not underestimate its significance as a limiting factor in people's lives; (ii) providing or **signposting** welfare rights advice in order to maximize income; (iii) seek to address the possible negative effects of poverty (low self-esteem, for example); and (iv) contribute in whatever ways possible to political processes geared towards tackling poverty and deprivation.

power This is one of those terms that is widely used, but which is very difficult to pin down. It is often defined in terms of having the ability to achieve one's ends – the wherewithal to make the progress we seek. While this is a good starting point, its main drawback is that it implies that power is a characteristic of individuals, when the reality is much more complex than this. Power can be an individual matter, but it can also be seen to apply at other levels, not least the following:

> *Interpersonal.* A person's individual skills and characteristics can give him or her considerable power. However, this is constrained by the skills and characteristics of others – that is, power is not just a *personal* matter, it is also *interpersonal*.

> *Group.* Membership of particular groups can bestow power, as if the group's power is loaned to the individual member.

> *Discourse.* Poststructuralist theory (see Part 4) emphasizes the importance of 'discourses', frameworks of language, meaning and action that shape individual actions, interpersonal relations and social processes. Such discourses are major sites of power.

> *Organizational.* A person's position within an organization can be very significant in terms of power, but so too can organizational culture. A culture within an organization can be very influential in shaping all manner of process and event and is therefore very significant in the study of power.

> *Structural location.* Social divisions play an important role in allocating power and 'life chances' or opportunities. Like discourses, structural relations are major sites of power.

social divisions, see p. 70

Power is such a central theme of society in general and social work in particular that it would be very unwise for any social worker not to develop a sensitivity to the operations of power and a good understanding of how they influence the lives of clients and carers and our relations with them.

projection This is a concept deriving from the work of Freud. It is one of the processes used as a 'defence mechanism' or means of maintaining the integrity of identity. It refers to the process of 'projecting' one's own feelings on to others – that is, assuming that someone shares the same feelings at that time, regardless of whether they do or not. For example, someone who is very anxious about a situation may assume that others involved are equally anxious. Their own feelings are so predominant that they overextend them to other people. Conversely, someone who is not anxious about a situation may not notice that other people are. He or she 'projects' his or her lack of anxiety onto others.

Projection can be quite a subtle mechanism and it can easily be missed. For example, someone who feels jealous in a particular set of circumstances may not face up to their own feelings of jealousy by attributing them to someone else – that is, to misread the situation as if it is someone else who is actually jealous. In this way, projection can be seen as a form of **avoidance behaviour**.

The person who is projecting one or more feelings onto others may not realize that they are having such feelings themselves. For example, someone who feels guilty, but does not recognize that this is what they are experiencing, may project guilt onto one or more other people without having the self-awareness to recognize their own feelings. In this way, they are protecting themselves from the painful and uncomfortable feeling of guilt, hence the idea that projection is a 'defence mechanism'.

Projection is also incorporated into Gestalt therapy. Panning describes it as one of the five forms of 'resistance' that therapists need to work through:

> Projection is the confusion of self and others that results in attributing to the outside world something that truly belongs to self. A part of the self or feeling about self is experienced, but not understood or owned as self, and is attributed to another person outside the body. Projection in its unhealthy form is blaming, and not taking responsibility for self or one's own actions. Psychological growth suffers when one is unable to own 'unacceptable' parts of the self.
>
> (2002, pp. 150–1)

Projection is an important process for social workers to be able to recognize, as it can at times be very significant in shaping the situations we are dealing with or an individual's reaction to that situation.

protection of vulnerable adults In recent years we have seen the development of what have come to be known as PoVA (Protection of Vulnerable Adults) procedures, parallel in many ways with the long-standing child protection procedures. These apply to 'vulnerable' adults in general (including people with physical and learning disabilities and/or mental health problems), rather than specifically older people, but do incorporate issues relating to elder abuse, as discussed above. The procedures provide advice on what practitioners should do if abuse comes to light or is suspected. Although developed locally in each local authority area, they tend to have much in common. They also generally include organizational guidance on such matters as the screening of prospective employees, multi-agency working and so on. In terms of employees, the Department of Health introduced a 'PoVA list' in 2004. This list includes the names of people who have harmed vulnerable adults as part of their employment in a social care setting. This is part of a concerted effort to protect vulnerable adults from abuse.

For a very long time the abuse of adults has not received the attention it deserves. Although there has been some degree of media coverage, this has not been at anywhere near the magnitude or extent of that relating to child abuse. For many years practitioners had no guidance on how to proceed if they suspected abuse was taking place. It is also likely that much abuse was missed because levels of awareness were previously not as high as they are now (although levels of awareness can still be quite low in some places).

Responding to the challenge of protecting vulnerable adults can be quite a daunting undertaking, but it is an important area of practice and, like child protection, is a shared undertaking.

racism Cashmore discusses the definition of racism in the following terms:

> Up to the late 1960s most dictionaries and textbooks defined it as a doctrine, dogma, ideology, or set of beliefs. The core element in this doctrine was that 'race' determined culture. And from this were derived claims of racial superiority. In the 1960s the word was used in an expanded sense to incorporate practices and attitudes as well as beliefs and in this sense racism denotes the whole complex of factors which produce racial discrimination ...   (1996, p. 308)

This is an important definition because many

people still associate racism with a set of specific beliefs. This can lead to an assumption that 'Because I do not believe in racial superiority, my actions will not be racist'. However, this is an oversimplification. It is perfectly possible not to have racist beliefs, but for our actions none the less to result in racist outcomes. That is, we may unwittingly behave in a way that results in a person or group being treated less favourably (to 'suffer a detriment', to use the legal term). For example, we may make assumptions based on stereotypes without realizing we are doing so, because the stereotype(s) concerned are so strongly embedded in our culture and thus our upbringing. Racism, like other forms of discrimination is a matter of outcomes, rather than intentions. We can have perfectly good (if perhaps naïve or complacent at times) intentions, but still produce unfair outcomes.

Racism is a very important issue in social work, as it is very easy for social work assessments and interventions at a minimum to fail to address the significance of racism in many people's lives and, at worst, to exacerbate the problems. The development of anti-racist forms of practice is therefore quite rightly high up the agenda in terms of social work education and practice as part of a broader commitment to an anti-discriminatory or emancipatory approach to social work.

Issues relating to anti-racism have been dealt with in a very confrontational way in some places in the past, leading to a high level of anxiety and defensiveness (see Neil Thompson, 2003a and 2005b, for a discussion of this). It is important that we do not allow this to discourage people from taking seriously the very important challenge of anti-racism.

reductionism This is a form of oversimplification where something of complexity that operates on a number of different levels is accounted for by an explanation that reduces it to only one of its many aspects. As Sibeon puts it, reductionist theories:

> wrongly attempt to reduce the complexity of social life to a single unifying principle of explanation, such as 'the actions of individuals', or 'structured necessities' bound up with 'the needs of system' or with

the so-called 'interests of capitalism' or the 'interests of patriarchy'. (1996, p. 34)

Reductionism can be a problem in terms of both theory and practice. Approaches to social work theory that fail to do justice to the complexity and multi-layered nature of the topic can result in dangerous distortions. For example, to locate an explanation of age discrimination solely at the level of individual prejudice can be said to be reductionist, because it fails to account for institutional **ageism**, such as the rationing of life-enhancing health care treatments on the grounds of age or media representations which promote negative stereotypes of older people.

Approaches to social work practice that do not recognize that the situations we encounter are complex and multi-layered risk doing more harm than good. Reductionism will also limit opportunities for creative and appropriate intervention if the complexity of the issues is not appreciated.

A reductionist approach can be seen as the opposite of a holistic one. A holistic approach is one that attempts to incorporate the whole picture and does not present a partial or distorted view. In the complex world of social work, a holistic approach is clearly preferable to a reductionist one. We therefore need to beware of falling into the trap of trying to make sense of complex, multi-level phenomena by reference to a simple, single-level explanation.

NOS Key Role 1

Prepare for, and work with, individuals, families, carers, groups and communities to assess their needs and circumstances

Human actions and interactions operate at a number of levels (for example, personal, cultural and structural), and therefore need to be understood at different levels. The task of both the theorist and the practitioner is to make sense of social work situations by drawing on all the various levels, rather than oversimplifying by relying on one alone.

residential care This is a term that is used in both child care and adult services. It refers to the provision of accommodation and care in institutions known as 'homes'. Historically, children's homes were very large (consider, for example, the large establishments set up by Dr Barnardo in the latter part of the nineteenth century), but this approach was not very satisfactory as it did not offer personalized levels of care to nurture the children's development. Children's homes today tend to be much smaller and modelled on family units. The philosophy of child care is now firmly in the direction of supporting family care (see **family support**) and so: (i) fewer children are now being accommodated in substitute care; and (ii) where substitute care is required, preference is given to **foster care**. Consequently, residential care for children and young people is now a much smaller enterprise than was once the case.

The residential care of adults has also changed significantly over the years, especially for people with mental health problems and/or learning disabilities. The policy of **community care** has meant a strong switch of emphasis from large-scale institutions (the psychiatric and 'mental handicap' hospitals of yesteryear) towards: (i) care in people's own homes where possible; and (ii) care in small-scale supported accommodation when (i) is not feasible. For older people, the situation is less clear cut. While there has certainly been a strong switch of emphasis towards community-based support as an alternative to residential care, large residential homes for older people are still quite common. The failure to devote sufficient resources to the provision of more appropriate forms of accommodation can be seen as an example of institutional **ageism**, in so far as older people have received less investment of funds in developing more flexible forms of residential care.

A further important point to note in relation to adult residential care is that the term is used in two slightly different ways. Sometimes 'residential care' is used as an all-encompassing term that includes both nursing home care and care in 'rest homes'. At other times, 'residential care' is used to mean non-nursing care (social care as opposed to nursing care – although it is not always easy to draw a line between the two).

resilience This is a term often used in child care, but which can be equally applicable to adults. It refers to the ability to 'bounce back' after a setback and perhaps even to be all the stronger for having gone through a difficult experience. It is like a form of elasticity – the ability to be 'stretched' by a difficult and demanding experience or set of experiences, but without 'snapping'.

Promoting resilience in children who have been abused or have experienced other problems or deprivations is increasingly being recognized as an important part of social work with children, young people and their families. It involves focusing on strengths and building up positives, rather than dwelling on negatives – strengthening skills and problem-solving strategies, exploring the lessons learned and how these can be used positively in facing future problems and challenges.

NOS Key Role 2

Plan, carry out, review and evaluate social work practice, with individuals, families, carers, groups, communities, and other professionals

The approach can also be applied to adults – for example, in relation to people who have been experiencing mental health problems. Instead of feeling sorry for people who have experienced difficulties, we should be looking at how we can help to recognize and strengthen resilience.

Experiences of loss can be a source of resilience. For example, Schneider (2000) makes the important point that we should not confuse grieving with depression. The latter is a negative state that brings significant problems, while grieving can be seen as a process of 'healing' (albeit in a spiritual rather than a medical sense) that can also bring positives. In particular, an experience of loss can be an opportunity for personal growth, opening up new ways of coping with adversity and appreciating what strengths and personal and social resources we have. This is not to deny the pain and suffering that can be so acute in times of significant loss, but rather to balance the picture out – to recognize that the pain can be part of strengthening our ability to deal with the challenges we face in our lives.

This shows how loss and grief issues have positive potential – see also transformational grief.

Promoting resilience can therefore be seen as an important social work task, giving us a role in empowering people by helping them to realize the strengths they have and exploring how they can be capitalized upon and developed still further.

Fostering resilience can be significant in promoting empowerment – see Thompson, 2007.

Support individuals to represent their needs, views and circumstances

resources 'Resources' is a broad term used to refer the wherewithal to provide help and support. It incorporates physical resources (buildings, such as day centres, for example), financial resources (access to budgets), information resources and human resources (that is, people and the efforts they expend). 'Resource shortfall' is the term used to refer to situations in which demand exceeds supply. This is a very common situation in social work, as resources are finite, and so an important part of the social worker's repertoire is the ability to make the best use of available resources. Also important is the ability to press for more resources, to draw on negotiation and influencing skills where possible.

The allocation of resources is a political process that incorporates a number of different considerations and operates at a number of levels (ranging from individual cases to national budgets). All four types of resources have an important part to play, but in particular we should not underestimate the significance of human resources. As the slogan goes, 'an organization's most important resource is its human resource – its people'. This relates to the long-standing concept in social work of 'use of self' – that is, the ability to use one's personal resources as a helping tool.

Plan, carry out, review and evaluate social work practice, with individuals, families, carers, groups, communities, and other professionals

Such personal resources include the ability to deal with the emotional pressures and demands of the work (see **resilience**).

rights The Webster's *Third New International Dictionary* defines a right as:

> 1: an ethical or moral quality that constitutes the ideal of moral propriety and involved various attributes (as adherence to duty, obedience to lawful authority …): something morally just … 2: something to which one has a just claim.

Rights are important in social work because safeguarding and promoting people's rights is part of the social work role – part of the commitment to empowerment (see Part 4). For example, if an elderly person is living at a high level of risk of harm in the community, we may come under considerable pressure (from relatives, neighbours and even other professionals) to place the person concerned in **residential care**, even if he or she does not want to leave home. In such circumstances, we have to not only respect the individual's right to remain in their own home (despite the level of risk), but also protect that right by supporting the individual's wishes, rather than trying to persuade or coerce him or her into accepting a residential place. Rights are an important part of citizenship. **citizen rights, see p. 8**

The question of rights is a very complex one, as rights can conflict with one another (one person exercising his or her rights may, in doing so, be infringing someone else's rights – for example, one person's right to freedom of expression may conflict with another person's right not to be insulted). Rights are therefore often a source of dilemmas and need to be balanced – for example, the need to balance the right to take risks against the right to protection or the right to family life against the right of children to be protected from abuse. Rights also need to be balanced with responsibilities – they are, in effect, two sides of the same coin (one person's right is another person's responsibility).

The Human Rights Act 1998 is an important piece of legislation in the UK. It builds on the commitment expressed by The United Nations Charter of 1945, when the modern conception of human rights came into its own, and makes the European Convention on Human Rights part of domestic law. Individuals who feel that their human rights have been infringed can seek redress through the legal system without having to make application to the European Court of Human Rights in Strasbourg (the latter process being a very lengthy and costly one).

risk assessment Risk assessment refers to a process of identifying the risks involved in a particular situation, considering how likely it is that particular untoward events will occur (abuse, self-harm or suicide, for example) and their likely or possible impact if they do occur. Risk assessment can form part of an overall assessment (as discussed in Chapter 2.1) or can be undertaken in its own right when it is felt appropriate to do so. An example of the former would be a community care assessment with an older person where the social worker, as part of the overall process of identifying needs and possible ways of meeting them, also considers the risk factors involved (relating to the possible adverse consequences of dementia perhaps). An example of the latter would be a situation where an assessment was done at the beginning of the process of being involved (in relation to supporting a family with a child or young person in need perhaps), but where new information comes to light to suggest there may be additional factors to be considered (suspicions that illegal drugs are being used, for example).

Risk assessment is not an exact science, but there are systematic frameworks available that can be used to guide the practitioner – for example, the Brearley risk model (Brearley, 1982). It is important that risk assessments are seen as important tools of professional practice and not as bureaucratic processes. It is dangerous to 'go through the motions' as if it is simply a routine procedure, and not undertake a focused, well-thought out assessment, as we may miss something very significant – perhaps with disastrous consequences.

Manage risk to individuals, families, carers, groups, communities, self and colleagues

However, it is also important to recognize that no risk assessment is foolproof. Even an excellent risk assessment may not enable us to prevent things going wrong. Human beings are complex and often unpredictable, so there can never be a complete guarantee that risk assessment will be an accurate predictor of events. None the less, we should not allow this to make us defeatist, but rather to recognize the limitations of risk assessment and acknowledge that the process reduces the likelihood of harm but can never remove the dangers altogether.

It is likely that risk assessment tools will become more sophisticated over time, but it is unlikely that we will ever reach a point that they are so well developed that they are guaranteed to work in all cases. However, whatever the quality of the tools available to us, it is important that we use them and not leave risk factors entirely to chance.

risk management Risk is part and parcel of everyday life, but it is especially to the fore in social work. This is because we are generally helping people to deal with problems and difficulties in their lives – and these problems often: (i) bring additional risks above and beyond everyday risk factors; and (ii) can also intensify the everyday risks faced. An example of (i) would be suicide risks in dealing with people who are severely depressed or in an unstable frame of mind, for whatever reason. An example of (ii) would be the risk of fire. All households have a certain degree of risk of fire, but a household where a person with dementia lives carries a higher level of risk of fire.

Once a **risk assessment** has been carried out, a decision needs to be made about how the situation is to be managed. If the level of risk is deemed to be quite low, the decision may be made not to intervene further. However, if a significant level of risk is identified, it will be important to establish:

> How can the *likelihood* of harm occurring be minimized (or, in some cases, removed altogether)? For example, if an autistic

child becomes very violent when taken near water (rivers, lakes or seaside), how can such situations be avoided (at least in the short term while efforts are made to help the child concerned to learn to cope with expanses of water)?

> How can the *impact* of harm be minimized? For example, if an elderly person is prone to falling over, can sharp edges or other potentially very harmful items be covered up, cushioned or removed?

> Are there any contingency measures that need to be put in place in case problems do arise? For example, if someone is likely to have an epileptic convulsion, have carers been trained in how to deal with the situation?

> How will the situation be monitored? For example, are there family members, neighbours and/or home care staff who can keep an eye on the situation and report any significant changes? Are they aware of the risks identified by the risk assessment and have they been briefed on what they should do if the situation takes a turn for the worse?

The point was made earlier that risk assessments cannot be foolproof, and it is similarly the case that risk management cannot be guaranteed to work. Even if we have done everything we reasonably can, things can still go wrong, and it is important that we have a balanced view of this and do not have unrealistic expectations of what can be achieved in high-risk situations. We can do our best and no more.

schizophrenia This is a very contested concept – that is, there are strongly divergent views about it. Traditionally it has been thought of as a 'mental illness', and therefore very much a medical matter. However, there is also a school of thought that regards the degree of certainty implicit in the medical model conception as inappropriate, and questions the very validity of schizophrenia as a concept (see, for example, Bentall, 2003). Read makes apt comment when he argues that:

> the heightened sensitivity, unusual experiences, distress, despair, confusion and disorganization that are currently labelled 'schizophrenic' are not symptoms

of an illness. The notion that 'mental illness is an illness like any other', promulgated by biological psychiatry and the pharmaceutical industry, is not supported by research and is extremely damaging to those with this most stigmatizing of psychiatric labels. It is responsible for unwarranted and destructive pessimism about the chances of 'recovery', and has ignored – or even actively discouraged discussion of – what is actually going on in these people's lives, in their families, and in the societies in which they live.

(Read, 2005, p. 596)

Schizophrenia is often misunderstood and assumed to refer to a 'split' personality, whereas it actually refers more accurately to a *shattered* personality – that is, an identity that lacks coherence and unity. People with schizophrenia generally have difficulty in sustaining a meaningful sense of self. It tends to manifest itself in the following characteristics:

> *Hearing voices* – auditory illusions;
> *Delusions* – believing things about oneself that are untrue (that one has superhuman abilities, for example); and/or
> *Thought disorder* – communicating ideas that do not appear to make sense.

People with schizophrenia often display other 'symptoms', such as lethargy, apathy and depression, although it is possible that some signs that are said to denote schizophrenia are actually side-effects of the anti-psychotic medication commonly used.

The effects of schizophrenia can be very disabling for the person concerned, and so the social work role often involves helping people cope with day-to-day pressures and life demands. There can also be a statutory role in circumstances where the condition is such that the person concerned is a danger to him- or herself or to others and may be in need of being removed to a place of safety (a psychiatric hospital, for example) on a compulsory basis.

self-care As Principle 6: Realism and Challenge helps us to understand, social work is a demanding and challenging occupation. It can bring great rewards in return, but we have to be realistic and recognize that the pressures of the work can be immense and have the potential to do us harm if they are allowed to become excessive (see **stress**). Employers have a duty of staff care under the health and safety legislation, and so they have an obligation to take all reasonable steps to try and ensure that levels of pressure do not reach a harmful level. However, that legislation combines with professional good sense to place a duty also on each member of staff – and that is a duty of *self-care*. That is, each of us shares a responsibility with our employers to make sure that the work we are doing is not harming our physical or mental health or our well-being.

NOS Key Role 5

Manage and be accountable, with supervision and support, for your own social work practice within your organization

Important self-care practices include:

> Exercising our time and workload management skills as effectively as we can.
> Making good use of supervision and the support it offers.
> Making good use of **teamwork** and the support that offers too.
> Informing our line manager if we feel pressures are getting unrealistically or dangerously high.
> Raising workload pressure issues at a team meeting if necessary.
> Not having unrealistic expectations of ourselves – we cannot meet everybody's needs and solve everybody's problems; if we do not accept this, then we are setting ourselves up to fail.
> Making sure we take our leave entitlement and any time off in lieu that has accrued – many people lose part of their leave entitlement because they do not take the time off in the period allowed (in effect, this amounts to 'donating' part of your holiday entitlement to working for your employer free of charge when you should be using that time to recharge your batteries – an overworked and overstretched social worker can easily do more harm than good).

Self-care is something that needs to be taken very seriously. Your employer has an important part to play in making sure that your work pressures do not reach levels that are harmful to you. However, whether or not your employer fulfils that responsibility as fully as they should, it does not take away staff members' responsibility to play their part – both individually and collectively.

self-esteem Our sense of self (or 'self concept') can be seen to comprise a number of elements, including self-image (how we perceive ourselves, based partly on how other people perceive us) and self-esteem (how we value ourselves and that too is based partly on the perceptions of others and how other people value us), also often referred to as self-worth. The two tend to influence each other – for example, a poor self-image will make low self-esteem more likely and vice versa. Self-esteem is closely linked to confidence – the higher a person's self-esteem, the higher their confidence is likely to be and, conversely, someone who lacks self-esteem is likely to lack confidence.

Self-esteem is an important concept in relation to human development. It is particularly significant in relation to children and the development of **resilience**, as there is evidence to suggest that self-esteem is a very important factor for children in promoting resilience and thus insulating themselves from stress (Durkin, 1995). However, it is a concept that applies across the life course, not just in childhood. Events at any stage in our lives can either strengthen or undermine our self-esteem.

It can also be an important concept in relation to mental health. For example, psychiatry has long recognized links between low self-esteem and **depression**. And, indeed, mental health social workers will regularly encounter examples of low self-esteem, which is perhaps not surprising, given the corrosive and undermining nature of **mental health problems**.

Social workers need to be aware of self-esteem because:

1 It is something that can have a bearing on many of the issues we deal with in practice – it is never far away.

2 It is not fixed once and for all, but will vary, depending on the circumstances (see **essentialism**). Our actions can therefore be pivotal at times – that is, we may boost or

undermine self-esteem, depending on how we treat people.

self-harm People can cause themselves harm for a variety of reasons and in a variety of ways. The most common form of self-harm relates to cuts and scratches, especially to the arms and wrists. Such actions can cause significant harm, but are generally not likely to lead to serious injury. However, they can be indicative of serious underlying problems and can also lead to further problems – for example, where an individual with scars on his or her wrists as a result of cutting or scratching may be stigmatized, marginalized and/or bullied. This can lead to a vicious circle developing: negative attention attracted by people's response to self-harm can lead to increased pressure and strain which, in turn, can lead to further self-harm, thereby beginning a spiral of problems.

Self-harm can arise in various ways and for various reasons. For example, self-harm can arise as a result of experiencing a **trauma** (including **physical**, **sexual** or **emotional abuse**). A common theme is low **self-esteem**, or a relative absence of self-worth, a tendency to devalue oneself. It is as if the individual concerned is punishing him- or herself. Trauma can lead to both low self-esteem and self-harm.

Self-harm can also manifest itself as head banging for children and adults with learning disabilities, especially for those with communication difficulties and/or who are frustrated or unsettled for some other reason. It can take considerable attention and reassurance to persuade someone who is engaging in this behaviour to cease doing so – and can be quite distressing for all concerned.

Self-harm can occur in any class or ethnic group, but it is more prevalent in women than in men, especially young women. The most serious form of self-harm is when the urge to self-injure amounts to a **suicide** attempt. Taking one's own life is, of course, an extreme form of self-harm. However, it is important to note that people who self-harm through cutting, scratching or head banging are not necessarily likely to attempt suicide. Risks of suicide need to be assessed and managed carefully on an individual basis

and do not lend themselves to a blanket or generalized approach.

NOS Key Role 4

Manage risk to individuals, families, carers, groups, communities, self and colleagues

sex offenders This is a term used to identify people who commit rape, sexual assault or other forms of **sexual abuse**. The vast majority of sex offenders are adult males, although we should not allow this fact to prevent us from recognizing that some women and some young people can and do commit sexual offences. While many sex offenders will have been abused themselves during their childhood, many will not have been (just as many children who have been abused do not grow up to become abusers – the relationship between abusing and being abused is a complex one).

In terms of how sex offenders can be helped not to re-offend, Cavadino comments as follows:

> Measures which can reduce reoffending include supervision by the probation service: 93 per cent of offenders and 96 per cent of those resident in probation hostels are not reconvicted for sexual or other violent offences during the course of supervision or residence. Well-designed sex offender treatment programmes can also significantly reduce the likelihood of reconviction for a sexual offence.
>
> Sex offenders employ distorted patterns of thinking which allow them to rationalize their behaviour. The attitudes include, for example, the view that children can consent to sex with an adult, and that victims are responsible for being sexually assaulted. Treatment programmes for sex offenders seek to tackle and change these distorted attitudes.
>
> (Cavadino, 2000, p. 315)

It is interesting to note the use of the word, 'treatment', indicating that this is an area of practice still strongly influenced by a medical model.

One significant factor is that of **risk assessment**. Even if an offender receives a lengthy prison sentence, he or she is not going to be in prison permanently, and so the question arises of how much of a risk does this person present to children (or other vulnerable people) when in the community. It is therefore necessary to undertake a risk assessment (and update it from time to time) to establish the nature and extent of the risk posed and thus make a judgement about what needs to be done to minimize the risk of re-offending. There is, of course, no definitive 'scientific' way of assessing risk that will guarantee that nothing will go wrong – human existence is far too complex for that. It is therefore a question of making the best assessment we can, based on the information available to us.

NOS Key Role 4

Manage risk to individuals, families, carers, groups, communities, self and colleagues

sexism Cranny-Francis and colleagues explain the significance of gender in contemporary society:

> Gender divides humans into two categories: male and female. It is a system which organises virtually every realm of our lives; whether we are sleeping, eating, watching TV, shopping or reading, gender is at work. Yet, because it is everywhere, it is sometimes difficult to see it in operation. Imagine trying to escape the division of gender in our lives – without the birth certificate which records our gender, we could not get a passport or driver's licence (which also record our gender). But say we had managed to get by without paperwork. Every trip to a public toilet would demand that we declare our gender by which door we choose. Every human body in modern societies is assigned to a place in a binary structure of gender.
>
> (Cranny-Francis, 2003, p. 1).

This passage highlights well the prevalence of gender differences. However, it is the next sentence in what Cranny-Francis and colleagues have to say that is crucial: 'Not only does the system of gender divide the human race into two categories, it privileges the male over the female' (2003, p. 1). This is where sexism comes in. It is not simply a matter of gender differences, but rather of gender inequalities. In the vast majority of cases it is women who are in the less privileged position, although the specifics of each situation may vary quite considerably.

Like racism, sexism has been the subject of considerable oversimplification over the years and this has discouraged many people from taking the issues seriously (women and men). However, regardless of this, we do have to recognize that there are significant patterns of gender inequality in society in general and – importantly, in social work. For example, it is very easy to fall into sexist assumptions and, if we are not careful, reinforce such dangerous and unhelpful ideas that caring is women's work, that emotions are 'off limits' for men, and so on.

Both women and men can find dealing with sexism challenging, as the development of anti-sexist practice involves 'unlearning' much of what our society has taught us about 'proper' roles for men and women. However, it is important that we work together to take these issues forward and strive for a more egalitarian approach to gender issues, so that neither women nor men are treated unfairly because of their gender.

sexual abuse This is a form of abuse that involves abusive behaviour of a sexual nature, and is generally manifested in one or more of the following:

> Sexual contact with a child or young person under the age of 16 (including, but not limited to, full intercourse).

> Exposing a child or young person under the age of 16 to pornographic or otherwise sexually inappropriate material.

> Speaking to a child or young person under the age of 16 in a sexually explicit or otherwise sexually inappropriate way.

> Taking sexual advantage of someone (adult or child) who is not able to give informed consent (for example, as a result of a severe learning disability).

> Using force to obtain sexual contact with a vulnerable adult – see **protection of vulnerable adults**.

> Using emotional pressure or other such forms of manipulation to obtain sexual contact with a vulnerable adult.

Note that, in cases of sexual abuse relating to children and young people, it is not necessary for the actions of the perpetrator to involve force for them to count as abusive. Regardless of whether a child consents to (or, even on relatively rare occasions, initiates) sexual contact, this amounts to abuse. This is because it is taken that children are not in a position to give informed consent to such matters.

Sexual abuse, whether of children or vulnerable adults, can be very **traumatic** for the person concerned and can do lasting psychological harm. Where there is evidence or suspicion of sexual abuse, it is therefore important that the matter is dealt with appropriately in accordance with either **child protection** or **protection of vulnerable adults** procedures. And, of course, such matters need to be dealt with very carefully and sensitively. We should beware, though, of the very significant danger of discrediting sexual abuse – of thinking 'No, that can't possibly be happening'. History has taught us that it can happen – that it often does, and that being incredulous can be a serious mistake.

NOS Key Role 6

Demonstrate professional competence in social work practice

`sexuality` This is a term that is used in two senses: (i) sexual orientation or identity; and (ii) expression of sexual or sensual needs. The latter can be a significant issue at times – for example, in working with older or disabled people in a residential setting, as it should not be assumed that particular people do not have sexual feelings or needs. The former is also a significant issue in a number of ways:

> Gay men, lesbians and bisexual people can experience discrimination because of their sexual identity. We should ensure that our actions do not reinforce this and, where possible, challenge it.
> Some people experience difficulties in clarifying and feeling comfortable in establishing their own sexual identity. Young gay people may be distressed by having sexual feelings that are stigmatized and may need help in sorting out their own feelings and sense of personal direction. For example, a young person leaving care may need social work support, not only in terms of practical living arrangements and social and life skills,

but also in dealing any anxieties or confusions relating to his or her own sexual identity.
> Sexual identity can also feature as an issue in terms of family conflict and can be very relevant in terms of family therapy.

Sexuality, in both senses of the word, can be seen as part of our identity, what makes us who we are. It is therefore important to have awareness of this so that we do not act oppressively by disrespecting someone's sense of self.

Gay affirmative therapy is an approach that has been developed by Davies and Neal (1996). It is an approach to counselling and related disciplines that emphasizes the importance of taking account of sexuality issues and not falling foul of stereotypes or other aspects of discrimination. Davies makes apt comment when he argues that: 'The gay affirmative therapist affirms a lesbian, gay or bisexual identity as an equally positive human experience and expression to heterosexual identity' (1996, p. 25) and goes on to emphasize that:

> Gay affirmative therapists are those whose beliefs and values appreciate homosexuality – and bisexuality – as valid and rich orientations in their own right and who perceive *homophobia*, not diverse sexualities, as pathological.
>
> (Davies, 1996, p. 40)

`signposting` In the late 1960s and early 1970s when Social Services Departments were established in England and Wales and Social Work Departments in Scotland, there was a sense of optimism and the sense of a dawning of a new era for social welfare. This was partly because, in combining the previous children's departments, welfare and mental welfare departments into the larger, multipurpose departments, it was believed that a more unified and comprehensive approach to social needs could be developed. It was almost as if the new departments were expected to be 'one-stop shops'.

With hindsight we can now see that this was an overly optimistic view, and that even the combined resources of the new, larger departments would not be able to meet everyone's needs. Indeed, we can now see that the depth and breadth of social need are such that social services can only be part of a broader picture of welfare provision that must also incorporate voluntary bodies and private sector provision. This web of 'welfare pluralism', as it has become known, means that part of a social worker's role is referring people on to other sources of help – hence the term, 'signposting'.

In order to be able to do this we need to:

> Have at least a basic knowledge of the local services and facilities: statutory, voluntary and private.
> Know how to find out more about what is available (it is unrealistic to expect to be able to have comprehensive knowledge).
> Have the humility to recognize that we cannot be all things to all people and thus be prepared to refer on where necessary.

Have a clear understanding of the social work role so that we do not attempt to help in ways that are better suited to other agencies.

NOS Key Role 5

Manage and be accountable, with supervision and support, for your own social work practice within your organization

social exclusion This is the process, or more accurately a set of processes, by which individuals are denied full participation in the society and communities in which they live. It is linked with the notion of citizenship and has much in common with the notion of relative poverty (see **poverty**) in that it highlights how people can be prevented from participating in the social norms and expectations, aspirations and so on that allow people to feel that they are part of their society and belong to it.

While poverty itself plays a big part in excluding many people from the mainstream of society, it is not the only reason, as Williams (1998) comments:

In the poverty studies tradition in Britain, much of the emphasis has been on lack of access to material resources, whereas the concept of social exclusion provides a framework to look at the social relations of power and control, the processes of marginalization and exclusion, and the complex and multi-faceted ways in which these operate. In other words, whereas

poverty studies emphasised class and distributional issues, social exclusion allows us to look at issues to do with social and cultural injustices generated by inequalities of gender, race, ethnicity, sexuality, age and disability, and the ways these may intersect and be compounded by issues of distribution.

(Williams, 1998, p. 15)

This extends the concept to include, for example, those pushed to the margins because of:

> assumptions about old age and the capacity to lead 'useful' lives (see **ageism**);
> barriers that prevent people with disabilities from being able to operate in societies structured around the needs of non-disabled citizens (see **disability**);
> social processes that exclude members of ethnic minorities (for example, racist assumptions about educational or other capabilities);
> sexist assumptions about what is an appropriate male or female role (and the sanctions – ridicule or disapproval, for example – that are brought to bear when people depart from such gender expectations);
> discrimination on the grounds of sexual orientation: 'heterosexism'.

Social exclusion is an important issue at both a macro and a micro level At the macro level each of us may not be able to play a significant part in what is essentially a social and political policy issue (no more than any other citizen), but collectively as a profession we can continue to draw attention to social exclusion and the need for it to be addressed. At a micro level we can take account of social exclusion on day-to-day basis as a feature of the assessments we carry out and the interventions we propose as a result of them.

NOS Key Role 6

Demonstrate professional competence in social work practice

social justice The development of anti-discriminatory practice in social work has meant that social justice as a social work value has received increasing attention. This is because a central feature of anti-discriminatory practice is the recognition of extensive and deeply ingrained social inequalities. Social work is in a pivotal position with regard to such inequalities, in so far as our actions can either challenge or reinforce the inherent unfairness. A commitment to social justice is therefore a commitment to making sure that we are tackling inequalities as far as we reasonably can, rather than adding to them. This involves recognizing the inherent injustices in a social system characterized by **poverty** and deprivation, **racism**, **sexism**, **ageism**, **disablism**, **heterosexism** and other such forms of discrimination.

It is important to recognize that, while full social justice in the short term may be an unachievable goal, social work can make a positive and valuable contribution to moving in the right direction in the longer term. We can be part of the solution, rather than part of the problem. This is an important point to emphasize, as some people have rejected social justice as a value, on the grounds that it is unrealistic. Social justice is an idealistic notion, in the sense of an ideal to work towards, rather than something that can be dismissed as 'utopian' or out of touch with reality.

The term *social* justice is used rather than simply justice to show that it is more than a matter of individual fairness (although that too is very important); rather, it is a matter of understanding how social processes and institutions systematically combine to produce unfair outcomes. Social justice is therefore a *sociopolitical* matter, rather than simply an issue of personal **ethics**. It reflects the *social* nature of social work and its links with wider social and political issues. unfair outcomes, see pp. 70, 131–2 sociopolitical issues, see p. 69

social role valorization This approach grew out of the earlier widely used concept of 'normalization'. It is premised on the idea that if people with learning disabilities are encouraged and allowed to take up roles within their communities which are socially valued, then this will help to counteract entrenched negative stereotypes which associate them with being 'different', dependent and even dangerous. It is most often associated with the work of Wolfensberger (see Flynn and Nitsch, 1980) and,

although it has its critics, is still an influential model which continues to inform social work practice. Over the last 20 years or so, policy has been directed towards integrating people with learning difficulties into their communities and helping them to live, as far as is possible, the life of their choosing. One well-known and well-used piece of guidance for practitioners in this field is the *Framework for Accomplishments* (O'Brien and Lyle, 1987). It highlights the following as areas to promote:

> *physical presence* – being able to access those community facilities which others take for granted but have been denied to those living in institutions;
> *choice* – in all aspects of life;
> *competence* – being expected to have the potential for development;
> *respect* – being a valued member of the community; and
> *participation* – being part of, rather than apart from, social networks.

While such frameworks have played a major part in challenging the stigmatization of people with learning disabilities and in moving policy away from segregation and dependency towards empowerment and citizenship, it has attracted criticism because of its reliance on the concept of 'normality'. Promoting the idea that someone who used to be considered 'deviant' can be allowed to 'pass as normal' by entering the mainstream would seem to assume that 'the mainstream' and 'normality' are one and the same thing. However, the positive emphasis on helping people with learning disabilities overcome aspects of discrimination is clearly something to be welcomed.

spirituality Canda and Furman define spirituality as:

> The search for meaning, purpose and morally fulfilling relation with self, other people, the encompassing universe, and ultimate reality, however a person understands it … it was explained that spirituality can be 'expressed through religious forms but is not limited to them'.
> (Canda and Furman, 1999, p. 9, cited in Moss, 2005, p. 11)

The basic idea behind spirituality is that we all need a sense of meaning and purpose, a means of understanding ourselves and our relationships with others and with the wider world. Without that sense of meaning we will feel unfulfilled, cast adrift and ill at ease. For many people religion provides this sense of meaning and connection, but it is not necessary to be religious to be spiritual. Religion and spirituality overlap in many ways, but they are not the same thing.

This is an important concept for social work because many people we encounter in professional practice will be struggling with their spirituality, their sense of who they are and how they connect with others and so on. For example, many people who experience mental health problems report a feeling of 'disconnection', as if they feel uneasy with the very basis of their being. Also, children and young people growing up may need help in finding a sense of meaning, direction and how they fit into the wider adult world.

In addition, as Moss (2005) points out, spirituality can be a significant issue when people are grieving. A major loss can leave us feeling very insecure, unsure of where we now stand. It is no coincidence that one of the major theoretical approaches to loss and grief is called 'meaning reconstruction theory' (Neimeyer, 2001), as it is at times of loss that we can feel that our sense of meaning and connectedness has been undermined, if not shattered altogether – temporarily at least.

Principle 5 Loss and Grief

Experiences of loss throw issues of spirituality into sharp relief.

If the person(s) we are trying to help belongs to a particular faith community, we can, of course, consider the implications of this for how we can best provide help and support. But, if those we seek to help do not have a religious outlook on life, we should not make the mistake of thinking that issues of spirituality will not apply. Spirituality is part of the challenge of being human and therefore applies to every single one of us.

stereotypes Stereotyping is a form of categorization – that is, assigning people to groups who share particular characteristics. Given the important role of culture in society, we can see the value of categorization up to a point. That is, it is reasonable to expect that certain characteristics will be shared by members of a culture – for example, that people will display patterns of behaviour that have been part of their cultural upbringing (what sociologists refer to as 'folkways', such as French people kissing each other on the cheek as a greeting). However, a stereotype is a set of expectations of a group of people that remains fixed, despite evidence to suggest that it is inaccurate or inappropriate. Stereotypes are therefore very much to be avoided.

Problems of stereotyping arise when:

> The categories used to refer to groups of people are unduly negative or demeaning – for example, racist stereotypes based on notions of inferiority.
> The categories are inaccurate or biased – for example, stereotypical assumptions about gender roles that are restricting for women and men (women have no role to play in the tough world of senior management; men are not cut out for child care roles).
> The categories become overgeneralized. For example, while it may be reasonable to associate Australians with a love of cricket, it would be a mistake to assume that *every* Australian loves cricket.
> Applying a category becomes rigid and resistant to change. For example, someone working with people with learning disabilities stereotypically continues to see them as presenting a high level of threat, even though he or she has extensive experience and evidence to show that this expectation is very inaccurate.

Stereotyping involves assuming that an individual possesses the set of characteristics associated with the stereotype. That is, it is assumed that all members of a group share the characteristics of the stereotype. For example, there is a stereotype of older people being deaf, and so it is quite common for younger people to raise their voices to them, even when this is not necessary. The incidence of hearing loss in old age is indeed higher than in the general population. However, on this basis, simply to assume that an older person is hard of hearing, simply because they are old, is to rely on an inaccurate, misleading

...tially dangerous stereotype. In this ...ereotypes distort reality.

NOS Key Role 1

Prepare for, and work with, individuals, families, carers, groups and communities to assess their needs and circumstances

There is an extensive psychological literature on stereotypes. However, we should also note that they are a *sociological* phenomenon too – that is, they are closely linked with power relations, ideology and social processes and institutions (see Chapter 2.2).

stigma A stigma is literally a mark. However, it is generally used to refer to a specific type of mark, namely a mark of shame or dishonour. To be stigmatized means to be looked down upon, to be regarded as inferior or of lesser worth for some reason. It can occur on an individual basis (that is, specific circumstances can lead to a particular individual being stigmatized). However, we also have to recognize that there is a sociological dimension to stigma, in so far as the distribution of stigma is not random, but rather follows distinct social patterns – for example, members of socially marginalized groups (**travellers**, people with mental health problems, members of ethnic minorities and so on) are likely to be stigmatized as a group regardless of their individual actions. Stigma is therefore closely linked with notions of **discrimination** and **oppression**.

Stigma is closely associated with the notion of 'labelling'. Labels, such as 'tearaway', 'looney', 'deviant' or 'druggie' highlight the people concerned as 'different', and with this come negative attitudes and the assumption that people who are different are necessarily inferior (or, in some situations, a threat). The media can influence public opinion by using such labels and thus play a part in stigmatizing large numbers of people.

However, it is often the case that, while social workers should not be attaching offensive labels to people, we none the less need to apply some sort of label in order to be able to establish a particular client as being eligible for support and services which are based on an assessment of need. For example, some services may not be available to the general public at large, but rather reserved for people with learning disabilities. If we are working with someone who has quite a low level of intelligence, but who has not been officially assessed or diagnosed as having a learning disability, we may have to go through the process of having that label attached if the service concerned is what this person needs or something he or she could benefit from considerably. In such circumstances we have to be very careful and sensitive in the use of such labels and make sure, as far as we reasonably can, that they are not used in a negative and stigmatizing way.

Social workers can play a broader role in challenging stigmatization. For example, when working as part of a multidisciplinary network, we may need to challenge (sensitively and constructively) any reliance on stigmatization that colleagues may present. Similarly, we can challenge (also sensitively and constructively) any internalization of negative attitudes that we encounter in clients who are subject to stigmatization – for example, by promoting **self-esteem** and building on strengths.

Stigma is particularly important in social work because most if not all of the people we work with will be subject to stigmatization of one form or another (simply being the client of a social worker is often enough to attract stigma).

the strengths perspective Social work, by its very nature, involves dealing with people with problems and unmet needs – people who are often vulnerable and at a low ebb. If we are not careful we can allow this to lead us into adopting a negative approach to the people we are trying to help, to focus on weak points, problems and difficulties and perhaps lose sight of the strengths that people can bring to the situation.

'The strengths perspective' is a term used to describe efforts to promote an emphasis on the need to recognize and develop strengths. It is the opposite of a long-standing criticism of some forms of traditional social work – namely that they are 'pathologizing', presenting the problems people face as if they represent inadequacies within the individual concerned (an example of **reductionism**).

Ligon captures the idea well in stating that:

Social work practice from a strengths perspective recognizes that there are resources that can be tapped in both the social worker and the client. Therefore, the relationship is approached as collaborative and avoids hierarchy; the intent is to empower, not disempower, the client. A strengths perspective acknowledges that the client possesses knowledge, abilities, resilience, coping, and problem-solving skills that are there to be employed. Certainly people get stuck, become overwhelmed, or experience events that render them unable to fully utilize their strengths. It is important to identify and amplify these strengths so that clients can go back and rediscover what has already worked for them in the past. ... Therefore, the role of the social worker is to facilitate the process, to serve as a bridge to the client's own resources, to move ahead and seek solutions. (2002, p. 99)

There are clear links between this idea and: (i) **resilience** (drawing on people's coping resources and ability to 'bounce back' after an experience of adversity); (ii) solution-focused approaches (concentrating on what has worked before in tackling problems); (iii) empowerment (helping people gain greater control over their lives, rather than fostering dependency); (iv) narrative approaches (helping people 're-author' problematic aspects of their lives); and (v) existentialism (helping people develop 'authentic' approaches to their lives and the challenges involved). Note that (ii) to (v) inclusive are discussed in Part 4.

The strengths perspective helps us to move away from traditional approaches to practice that have often had the effect of reinforcing some people's sense of 'inadequacy' (for example, in the use of disempowering language, involving such terms as 'maladjusted', 'dysfunctional' or 'problem families'). It presents a much more positive, partnership-based practice that avoids such criticisms.

NOS Key Role 3

Support individuals to represent their needs, views and circumstances

stress The Health and Safety Executive (HSE) define stress as: 'the adverse reaction people have to excessive pressure or other types of demand placed on them'. As the HSE goes on to say: 'Pressure is part and parcel of all work and helps to keep us motivated. But excessive pressure can lead to stress which undermines performance, is costly to employers and can make people ill'. www.hse.gov.uk

Some people adopt the approach that stress is inevitable in social work, that it is an inherently stressful occupation. However, this is a misunderstanding of stress. Social work is inherently a *pressurized* occupation, but it is not inevitable that such pressures will overspill into harmful stress. Stress can be avoided by good management (including good self-management – Principle 7) – for example, by being realistic in what we can achieve. If we expect to be able to meet everybody's needs and solve everybody's problems, then we are not only setting ourselves up to fail, but also setting ourselves up for stress – Principle 6: Realism and Challenge.

NOS Key Role 5

Manage and be accountable, with supervision and support, for your own social work practice within your organization

Stress is an important concept in social work because it can apply to:

> *Clients/service users.* It is often the case that the people we are seeking to help are experiencing stress, and so this needs to be part of our assessment and borne in mind in our intervention.
> *Carers.* The pressures of caregiving can be immense and can potentially lead to serious stress problems. It is important that we do not neglect this issue in working with carers.
> *Staff.* If we are not careful, the not insignificant pressures of social work can spill over into stress. It is therefore important that we guard against this and seek support whenever we need it (seeking support should not be seen as a sign of weakness).
> *Managers.* People in management positions generally have to find a balance between the needs of service users and the staff working with them, on the one hand, and the limitations of the budget on the other. This

...is part and parcel of management, ... can prove extremely difficult at times and may lead to stress if not managed properly.

Unfortunately, stress is often seen as a sign of a weak individual (a 'poor coper'), but this is a very inaccurate, misleading and potentially dangerous approach to the subject. Stress is a multidimensional phenomenon – that is, it has personal/psychological aspects to it, but it also has organizational and sociological aspects to it as well. To concentrate on the individual level without considering the wider organizational and social context is a dangerous oversimplification (although sadly a very common one). Stress is a complex problem and needs a careful, well-thought out approach, rather than a simplistic tendency to be judgemental and 'blame the victim' or think that breathing exercises are the answer.

suicide To take one's own life is something that can happen in a variety of circumstances, mainly the following:

> After an extended period of severe **depression**.
> In circumstances where the person concerned feels there is no way out of the situation (severe debts, for example) or, at least, no honourable way out of it (a situation characterized by intense shame, for example).
> Where the person concerned is terminally ill or has a degenerative illness.
> In response to experiencing a major **trauma**.
> Where **serious mental health** problems are being experienced.
> As a result of the influence of drugs (including alcohol).

Suicide is also strongly associated with unemployment. It can occur in any age group, although ageist assumptions can lead practitioners working with older people into thinking that this is not an issue for them to consider.

While some people may give warning (directly or indirectly) that they are planning to take their own lives, it is often the case that the event comes as a complete surprise. People close to the person concerned may well have understood that all was not well, but not realized what was to happen. Conversely, many people who are seen as high risk in terms of the danger that they may take their own lives may remain that way

for a long time but not actually commit suicide. There is therefore no definitive way to predict the degree of suicide risk a person faces, although social workers, alongside others involved should none the less remain alert to the possibility.

Suicide is a highly stigmatized form of death and can lead to **disenfranchised** grief (that is, a form of grief that is not socially sanctioned or openly acknowledged – Doka, 2001). Social workers helping people cope in the aftermath of a suicide need to take account of this. Grollman makes apt comment when he points out that:

> With self-inflicted death, the emotions are intensified to unbelievable and unbearable proportions. People with suicidal intentions are under intense mental strain which they feel incapable of resolving. If they succeed in taking their life, those left behind experience not only the pain of separation but aggravated feelings of guilt, shame, anger, and self-blame. The act of self-destruction raises the obvious questions 'Why?' and 'What could I have done to prevent it?' Anxious and grief-stricken, each survivor asks: 'How can I face my friends? What will they think of me?' Death is a robber. Death by suicide, however, represents the greatest of all affronts to those who remain.
> (Grollman, 1988, p. 1)

supervision Supervision is a term that is used in two senses in social work. On the one hand, it can refer to the process by which social workers monitor and seek to influence the behaviour of particular individuals. This relates to offenders (including young offenders and perpetrators of abuse); children whose school attendance is giving cause for concern (see **education social work** above); children in need of care and/or protection; people with mental health problems (especially those who have been psychiatric in-patients on a compulsory basis over an extended period of time) and other similar situations where there is concern about risk of harm to self or others. The process involves regular contact (for example, through home visits) to assess and manage levels of risk and take whatever reasonable steps are necessary to prevent a deterioration in the situation and bring about positive changes.

On the other hand, it can refer to the process by which managers and others (for example, practice teachers and mentors) have oversight of an individual's work and the related issues of staff development and well-being. This aspect of supervision is discussed in some detail in Part 2 above. It is a vitally important part of effective social work as the complex demands of social work make support and guidance a necessity.

NOS Key Role 5

Manage and be accountable, with supervision and support, for your own social work practice within your organization

teamwork Most social workers work in teams, either social work teams or multidisciplinary teams involving colleagues from other agencies. Whichever type of team we belong to, the relationship is a two-way one, in the sense that we can (and should) both give and receive. Giving involves playing a part in supporting team colleagues – for example, when they face particular difficulties. Such support can be practical (helping with particular tasks), professional (engaging in a case discussion and perhaps suggesting possible ways forward) and emotional or moral (letting your colleague know there is someone concerned about their well-being).

Receiving is the converse of giving. Just as you should be prepared to give support when one or more colleagues need it, so should you be prepared to accept it when you need it. Ideally, it will be offered, but in some situations you may need to seek it out, and you should not hold back from asking for help. Receiving support is just as much a part of teamwork as giving it.

Principle 7 **Self-management**

Effective self-management involves being prepared to use support and not see asking for help as a sign of weakness,

Having a supportive team like this can be an enormous benefit, boosting confidence and morale, fending off stress and making for a much more pleasant working environment. It also provides a strong foundation for learning. Teams that have members who help and support one another are much more likely to provide good environments for learning – fertile soil for developing your knowledge and skills and deepening your understanding of values issues.

Of course, teamwork is not just about peer support. There will also be a team leader or team manager who has a primary responsibility for: (i) supporting individual staff (both informally on a day-to-day basis and formally through structured supervision sessions on a regular basis); and (ii) leading the whole team and playing a key role in developing and maintaining a culture of commitment to high-quality practice, support and learning.

NOS Key Role 5

Manage and be accountable, with supervision and support, for your own social work practice within your organization

Good teamwork depends on:

> *Effective communication* – poor or non-existent patterns of communication will severely undermine teamwork.
> *Openness, honesty and integrity* – a willingness to deal with matters openly and constructively and not 'sweep issues under the carpet'.
> *A willingness to tackle problems together* – no team will be immune to problems, but good teams will deal with their problems (rather than indulge in **avoidance behaviour**) and do so together (not in a fragmented way).

trafficking Trafficking is an illegal, but lucrative trade, mostly in weapons and drugs, but also people (usually women and young girls). Human trafficking is a process which allows for profit to be made from the enticement or forceful removal of people from their homes and families and into situations where they are made to work against their will. Fröschl captures the point well when she cites the following passage from LEFÖ (1996, p. 20):

We talk of trafficking in women whenever women migrate on the basis of deception and false promises on the part of intermediaries, when they incur high debts for this purpose, and as a consequence are in a desperate situation in the target country. When women, because of this, are forced to perform activities and render services against their will, forced into slavery-like exploitative work, or are deprived of their personal freedom and sexual integrity by husbands or employers.

(Fröschl, 2002, p. 60)

Often, the people concerned are trying to escape poverty or discrimination in their own countries and believe the traffickers to be recruitment agents who will help them to find well-paid work or educational opportunities in more prosperous economies. In reality, these opportunities rarely materialise and they find themselves forced into prostitution and other unregulated and dangerous forms of work for little or no wages. Exploitation is easy because these people have little on which to exist in a foreign country or to repay what has supposedly been invested by the trafficker on their behalf. It is not uncommon for travel documents, including passports, to be confiscated by the traffickers. The process has elements in common with the illegal smuggling of people, but trafficking itself is defined by the use of violence as a means of ensuring that those caught up in the trade remain compliant.

This is, of course, a human rights issue but those involved tend, by definition, to be hidden from the view of those who could help. Given that many of those involved are young and vulnerable, there is a likelihood of referral to social services agencies from police officers, accident and emergency departments and others who become aware of their existence and plight. Social workers need to at least be aware of the existence of this trade, especially those working with young adults in the fields of drug misuse, prostitution and so on.

transference This is a concept deriving from the work of Freud. It refers to the process by which an individual may transfer their feelings towards one person to another, say from Person A to Person B. This generally arises where Person B reminds the individual concerned of Person A (in physical appearance, mannerisms, accent or whatever). This can be a positive transfer or a negative one. That is, if the individual feels positive towards Person A, he or she may then feel positive towards Person B. Conversely, if

there are negative feelings towards Person A, then a degree of negativity and even hostility can be transferred to Person B. Positive transfer may be captured in comments like: 'I immediately warmed to Karen when I met her; it was as if I had known her for ages', while a negative transfer may result in comments like: 'When I met Richard I immediately felt uncomfortable; there was just something about him I didn't like, but I couldn't quite put my finger on it'.

Transference, whether positive or negative, can be quite problematic when it arises. Positive transfer means that we may trust someone we meet because they remind us of a trustworthy person we know or have known, whereas our trust in the person we have just met may not be well placed. Conversely, negative transfer can lead us into treating people unfairly, not giving people a chance, treating them negatively because they remind us of somebody who has hurt or mistreated us in the past.

Transference can arise in situations where a client may see a social worker as a parent figure, because we remind them in some way of their mother or father. This can lead to their expectations of us being inappropriate – that is, expecting that we will 'parent' them, rather than support them in solving their problems. When handled skilfully, though, transference can be used positively – for example, as a means of encouraging self-awareness by carefully and sensitively highlighting the processes of transference that are taking place.

In later forms of psychoanalytical thinking (the work of Lacan, for example), transference is associated with the use of language and is understood as a means by which a client attributes special knowledge and authority to the worker. By not accepting this position and helping the client to challenge it, the worker can help the client move forward by developing their own understanding and knowledge.

NOS Key Role 3

Support individuals to represent their needs, views and circumstances

trauma 'Trauma' is the Greek word for wound. It is used in a literal sense in the medical profession to refer to physical wounds, but in the human services more broadly, including social work, it is used in a more metaphorical sense to refer to psychological wounds. The term can apply to a wide range of situations, including, but not limited to, the following:

> being the victim of a serious crime, particularly one involving violence and/or violation of decency or intimacy;
> experiencing multiple losses – either cumulatively (one after the other over a relatively short period of time) or singly (several members of a family being killed in a car crash or an explosion, for example).
> being involved in a public disaster (a plane crash or a major fire or flood, for example).
> engaging in armed combat in the armed forces;
> having a near-death experience; and
> prolonged exposure to stressful circumstances.

Principle 5 Loss and Grief

Trauma issues are closely linked to loss and grief.

Roberts and Greene define trauma as:

Experience involving actual or threat of death, serious injury, or loss of physical integrity to which the person responds with fear, helplessness or horror. These experiences involve distressing physical or psychological incidents outside a person's usual range of experience. (2002, p. 848)

Experiencing a trauma can have a major detrimental effect on someone's life and well-being. The stress involved can produce a range of psychological reactions as well as physical symptoms (headaches, stomach pains, anorexia). There can also be significant social implications – for example, someone affected by trauma may lose their job because they no longer feel able to function well enough within it. There can also be significant implications for relatives, friends and colleagues, as significant trauma can cause considerable distress throughout a network of people.

Social workers can play a significant role in helping people adjust to a situation where they have experienced a trauma and seek to minimize the negative effects. A wide variety of methods

can be used in this regard, depending on a careful assessment of the situation.

It is also important to note that the term 'trauma' is often used very loosely in everyday speech: 'I saw a very sad film last night – it was quite traumatic.' We have to be careful not to confuse this loose usage of the term with a genuine trauma. Experiencing a trauma is much more than just being distressed. See also **post-traumatic stress disorder**.

travellers This term is used to describe communities that are associated with travelling or nomadic lifestyles and includes, amongst others, Gypsies, New (Age) Travellers and those who travel with fairgrounds and circuses. Such groups are often made unwelcome by the communities in which they wish to take up temporary residence and attract negative stereotypes which tend to associate them with unlawful behaviour, lack of hygiene and a low take up of education. Travelling communities and their advocates would argue that any difficulties they face in these areas result from the discrimination they face, rather than from inherent traits. The discrimination can be:

> *direct* – as when individuals or groups are denied entry to a building or service purely on the grounds that they are members of a travelling community and presumed to live up to the negative stereotypes associated with that community; or
> *indirect* – such as when conditions for an entitlement for a service are set with the knowledge that they cannot be met by members of a travelling community.

Those following a nomadic lifestyle need cooperation at the levels of both national and local government if there is to be any sort of continuity in terms of healthcare and education, but these rights can be difficult to access and form part of the agenda for change proposed by campaigners. Despite there being anti-discrimination laws, the legal system does not necessarily work to the advantage of all Travellers. For example, Gypsies are recognised as an ethnic minority group for the purposes of the Race Relations Act 1976, but New (Age) Travellers are not. And, while the Human Rights Act 1998 makes reference to 'respect for family and private life', the Criminal Justice and Public Order Act 1994 removed the duty on local authorities to provide campsites, and increased powers to evict those camping without permission.

Travellers argue that they are not being allowed to live the lifestyle of their choosing and that the lack of facilities and understanding seriously undermine their social structure and traditions, based as they are on a system of networking which is increasingly difficult to maintain.

Social workers can have a role at the micro level in promoting the education and welfare of members of the community (this is likely to be especially true for social workers working at a community level – see **community social work**), and, at a macro level, in terms of trying to influence policies so that discrimination issues can be tackled.

unconditional positive regard We are called on as social workers to work with people whose attitudes and behaviour we might not like or agree with but, if we allow ourselves to make judgements about them and their contribution to society, we run the risk of compromising our professionalism.

NOS Key Role 1

Prepare for, and work with, individuals, families, carers, groups and communities to assess their needs and circumstances

The term 'unconditional positive regard' was introduced to the social work vocabulary by Carl Rogers (1961) and refers to the need to do the best we can for whoever we are called on to work with, regardless of how we feel towards them. We must be positive towards them in our efforts to help them, and this must be unconditional (hence the term 'unconditional positive regard'), rather than dependent upon whether we like the individual concerned, approve of them and so on. Being judgemental puts us in the position of 'claiming the moral high ground', and so is to be avoided if we are committed to working in partnership to effect change, as adopting such an approach is likely to make partnership harder to achieve rather than easier.

As people working with people, our own feelings inevitably have an impact on what we do, and it is not always easy to work in situations where our own values are challenged. However, picking and choosing clients on the basis of their assumed 'worth' is not compatible with social work values, and so those feelings need to be dealt with, so that they do not get in the way of achieving the best possible outcomes from our interventions.

Unconditional positive regard is therefore an important values issue. However, it is also a practical issue. That is, we need unconditional positive regard in order to be effective. For example, if we are working with a sex offender, we may object strongly to the abuse that he or she has perpetrated. However, if we allow our feelings to get in the way of helping that offender and offer him or her a lower level of service, then we are reducing the likelihood of a positive outcome. In this way, we are therefore making it more likely that he or she will re-offend. In this case, a lack of unconditional positive regard is making a negative, rather than positive, contribution to child protection and our efforts to safeguard children from harm.

vulnerability Vulnerability is a concept that is often oversimplified. Equating it with helplessness, frailty or an inability to cope can justify a response that is based on paternalism rather than **partnership** (EDF, 1999). As discussed in relation to **stigma**, it is sometimes necessary to be labelled 'vulnerable' in order to become eligible for services, but this can amplify unequal power relationships between service users and providers if the following issues are not taken into account:

> *Vulnerability is not necessarily a constant state.* People who do not normally need any extra help can find themselves vulnerable under a particular set of circumstances. For example, a person with a mild learning disability may have been leading an independent life until he or she is made redundant, so that normal routines and coping mechanisms are thrown into disarray and self-confidence is undermined. It is something most of us experience at one time or another, and so treating someone as inherently and permanently vulnerable runs the risk of denying them their strengths

and laying the foundations for dependency. Vulnerability, then, is not a characteristic of an individual, but rather of the circumstances people find themselves in at times.

> *It is not necessarily about individual 'failing'.* In the same way that disability can be said to be socially constructed (see **disability**), it can be argued that vulnerability can be caused or made worse by the way society is organized and the way it operates. For example, it could be argued that insufficiently staffing of care facilities for older people can lead to vulnerability in terms of an increased likelihood of falls, malnutrition, abuse, neglect and so on. Similarly, putting a deaf person in a position where no-one understands his or her method of communicating (perhaps in an immigration office, courtroom or hospital) and makes no adjustment, can be said to cause that person to be vulnerable when they would not normally be so, or to that degree. If vulnerability were down to individual failing, then that person would need help in all circumstances and this is obviously not the case with most deaf people. While some people, for various reasons, may find themselves in vulnerable circumstances more often than others, this does not justify being judgemental in seeing the individual as inherently vulnerable.

> *The protection versus rights dilemma.* Whatever the cause, there will always be people who need to be protected from exploitation. For example, someone whose understanding is compromised by a severe learning disability or dementia may need to have some decisions made on their behalf and in what is perceived to be their 'best interests'. In such situations the social work role is not to label the person concerned as 'vulnerable' and take over. Rather, it is a matter of balancing rights and risk and helping people gain as much control of their circumstances as they can in spite of the limiting factors.

NOS Key Role 3

Support individuals to represent their needs, views and circumstances

welfare rights This is a form of advocacy for helping people experiencing poverty and related problems to understand their entitlements under the law relating to social security, housing, employment and so on, and to assist them in claiming those entitlements. The social security system is a complex and fast-changing one and it is not easy to understand its terminology or processes or to keep track of new legislation and directives. Welfare rights workers focus in two main areas:

> *a micro-level focus* – helping individuals to maximize their income through their entitlement to state benefits and highlighting other forms of welfare provision, including supporting them to challenge what are perceived as unfair judgements; and

> *a macro-level focus* – raising awareness of poverty and anti-poverty initiatives and contributing to policy making.

There is some debate as to whether this should be part of a social worker's role, or independent of it (Bateman, 2000), but the aims do seem to fit well with social work's anti-oppressive stance. Indeed, in some instances, such as where financial charges for services are levied by local authorities, it can be difficult for those involved in brokerage and care management not to become embroiled in welfare rights issues because social security benefits can form part of the payment for local authority services. Given that poverty is likely to feature very highly in the lives of many with whom we work, we are well placed to undertake a welfare rights role ourselves, especially where the role requires us to investigate someone's capacity to afford charges. Where we become aware of poverty or a lack of take-up of entitlements, as social workers we have the skills to advise or advocate. However, it also serves to highlight the tension within social work about having two sets of interests to promote – those of an under-resourced government and those of an impoverished population. For this reason, some social workers and agencies feel it is more appropriate to refer clients to specialist welfare rights workers who, as well as being impartial, may also be able to spend more time on building up a specialist knowledge base and to digest the very frequent changes to the system and their implications.

youth justice It has long been recognized politically and professionally that it is important to invest in steering young people away from crime. Early theories of criminal behaviour located the problem within the individual, as if crime were a form of pathology affecting only certain types of individual (Muncie, 2001). More sophisticated theories have taken account of sociological factors, such as poverty and deprivation, social exclusion and so on, recognizing that, while individuals do carry responsibility for their actions (including any criminal actions), an adequate understanding of crime must also take account of contextual influences as well as individual actions.

While the state invests a significant amount of money in dealing with crime (although many would argue it is far from enough), there is a special emphasis on services for young people, on the understanding that tackling offending behaviour at an earlier age will pay dividends in the long run in terms of reducing adult offending.

This emphasis on youth crime is explained in the following passage from Farrington:

Official records and 'self-report' studies also show that individuals more often break the law when they are young. The 'peak' ages at which they are most likely to be found guilty or cautioned are between 15 and 19. Criminal involvement typically starts before the age of 15, but declines markedly once young people reach their 20s. However, young people who become involved in crime at the earliest ages – before they are 14 – tend to become the most persistent offenders, with longer criminal careers. (Farrington, 2002, pp. 425–6).

This special emphasis includes the following elements;

> Youth courts that operate separately from the main criminal courts, with specially trained magistrates.
> Sentencing options available for young offenders that do not apply to adults.
> Extensive use of informal warnings and formal cautions to prevent children and young people being drawn into the criminal justice system.
> The existence of multidisciplinary youth offending teams devoted specifically to reducing youth crime.

A major part of the social work response to youth offending is the recognition that criminal behaviour is often closely linked with social problems, such as abuse, drug misuse, social exclusion, family tensions and difficulties, racism and so on. The primary aim is to draw on social work knowledge, skills, values and methods to help young people avoid or move out of offending behaviour.

points to ponder

> Which terms or concepts have you found most interesting? Why?
> Which terms or concepts have you found most useful? Why?
> Which terms or concepts surprised you? Why?
> Which terms or concepts would you like to know more about? How can you find out?
> Have you been able to note any patterns or interconnections across concepts? If so, which ones?

suggestions for further reading

accountability

Thompson, N. (2005) *Understanding Social Work: Preparing for Practice*, 2nd edn, Basingstoke, Palgrave Macmillan.
Accountability is a theme which runs through this work.

See also:
Banks, S. (2002) 'Professional Values and Accountabilities', in Adams et al. (2002b).
Doel, M. and Shardlow, S. (2005) *Modern Social Work Practice: Teaching and Learning in Practice Settings*, Aldershot, Ashgate, ch. 11.

adoption

Hart, A. and Luckock, B. (2004) *Developing Adoption Support and Therapy: Neutral Approaches for Practice*, London, Jessica Kingsley.
Kirton, D. (2000) *Race, Ethnicity and Adoption*, Buckingham, Open University Press.
Logan, J. and Smith, C (2005) 'Face-to-Face Contact Post Adoption: Views from the Triangles', *British Journal of Social Work*, **35**(1).
Zeitlin, H. (2002) 'Adoption of Children from Minority Groups', in Dwivedi and Varma (2002).

advocacy

Bateman, N. (2000) *Advocacy Skills for Health and Social Care Professionals*, London, Jessica Kingsley.
Dalrymple, J. (2003) 'Professional Advocacy as a Force for Resistance in Child Welfare' *British Journal of Social Work*, **33**(8).
Forbat, L. and Atkinson, D. (2005) 'Advocacy in Practice: The Troubled Position of Advocates in Adult Services', *British Journal of Social Work*, **35**(3).

See also Chapter 14 of Payne (2005).

ageism

Kingston, P. (1999) *Ageism in History*, London, NT Books.
Pugh, S. (2003) 'Working with Older People to Challenge Ageism', in Horwath and Shardlow (2003).
Thompson, N. (1995) *Age and Dignity: Working with Older People*, Aldershot, Arena.
Thompson, S. (2005) *Age Discrimination*, Lyme Regis, Russell House Publishing.

alcohol abuse

Alcohol Concern (2002) *100% Proof: Research for Action on Alcohol*, London, Alcohol Concern.
Collins, S. and Keene, J. (2000) *Alcohol, Social Work and Community Care*, Birmingham, Venture Press.
Sutherland, I. (2004) *Adolescent Substance Misuse*, Lyme Regis, Russell House Publishing,

asylum seekers and refugees

Marfleet, P. (2006) *Refugees in a Global Era*, Basingstoke, Palgrave Macmillan.

Whittaker, D. J. (2005) *Asylum Seekers and Refugees in the Contemporary World*, London, Routledge.

attachment

Dallos, R. (2006) *Attachment Narrative Therapy*, Maidenhead, Open University Press.

Howe, D. (1995) *Attachment Theory for Social Work Practice*, Basingstoke, Macmillan – now Palgrave Macmillan.

Howe, D., Brandon, M., Hinings, D. and Schofield, G. (1999) *Attachment Theory, Child Maltreatment and Family Support: A Practice and Assessment Model*, Basingstoke, Palgrave Macmillan.

Nash, M., Munford, R. and O'Donoghue, K. (eds) (2005) *Social Work Theories in Action*, London, Jessica Kingsley, Part 4.

autistic spectrum

Aarons, M. and Gittens, T. (1999) *The Handbook of Autism: A Guide for Parents and Professionals*, London, Routledge.

O'Neill, J. L. (1999) *Through the Eyes of Aliens: A Book about Autistic People*, London, Jessica Kingsley.

Overton, J. (2003) *Snapshots of Autism: A Family Album*, London, Jessica Kingsley.

Wall, K. (2004) *Autism and Early Years Practice: A Guide for Early Years Professionals, Teachers and Parents*, London, Paul Chapman.

avoidance behaviour

Thompson, N. (2006) *People Problems*, Basingstoke, Palgrave Macmillan.

bipolar disorder

Jamison, K. R. (1997) *An Unquiet Mind: A Memoir of Moods and Madness*, London, Picador.

Maj, M., Akiskal, H. S, Lopez-Ibor, J. J. and Sartorious, N. (eds) (2002) *Bipolar Disorder*, Chichester, John Wiley and Sons.

brokerage

See care management.

burnout

Miller, D. (2000) *Dying to Care?: Work, Stress and Burnout in HIV/AIDS*, London, Routledge.
The first part of this book sets the scene in fairly general terms and is therefore of interest to a wider readership than those who work in the HIV/AIDS field.

Thompson, N. (1999) *Stress Matters: A Personal Guide*, Birmingham, Pepar Publications.

Thompson, N., Murphy, M. and Stradling, S. (1994) *Dealing with Stress*, Basingstoke, Macmillan – now Palgrave Macmillan.

care management

Bradley, G. (2005) 'Movers and Stayers in Care Management in Adult Services', *British Journal of Social Work*, **35**(4).

Gormon, H. and Postle, K. (2003) *Transforming Community Care: A Distorted Vision?*, Birmingham, Venture Press.

Lloyd, M. (2002) 'Care Management', in Adams et al. (2002b)

Postle, K. (2002) 'Working "Between the Idea and the Reality": Ambiguity and Tensions in Care Managers' Work', *British Journal of Social Work*, **32**(3).

Thompson, N. and Thompson, S. (2005) *Community Care*, Lyme Regis, Russell House Publishing.

carers

Clements, L. (2005) *Carers and Their Rights: The Law Relating to Carers*, London, Carers UK.

Douek, S. (2003) 'Collaboration or Confusion? The Carers' Perspective', in Weinstein et al. (2003).

Frank, J. (2002) *Making it Work: Good Practice with Young Carers and Their Families*, London, The Children's Society and The Princess Royal Trust for Carers.

Hepworth, D. (2005) 'Asian Carers' Perceptions of Care Assessment and Support in the Community, *British Journal of Social Work*, **35**(3).

Heron, C. (2003) 'Working with Carers: A Specialism that Crosses Boundaries', in Horwarth and Shardlow (2003).

Manthorpe, J. (2003) 'Nearest and Dearest? The Neglect of Lesbians in Caring Relationships', *British Journal of Social Work*, **33**(6).

case conference

Amiel, S. (2003) 'The Child Protection Case Conference' in Amiel and Heath (2003).
  This is in a collection on family violence written from a primary care perspective.

Murphy, M. (2004) *Developing Collaborative Relationships in Interagency Child Protection Work*, Lyme Regis, Russell House Publishing.

child protection

Corby, B. (2005) *Child Abuse: Towards a Knowledge Base*, 3rd edn, Buckingham, Open University Press.

Ferguson, H. (2004) *Protecting Children in Time: Child Abuse, Child Protection and the Consequences of Modernity*, Basingstoke, Palgrave Macmillan.

Franklin, B. and Parton, N. (2001) 'Press-ganged! Media Reporting of Social Work and Child Abuse', in May et al. (2001).

Murphy, M. (2004) *Developing Collaborative Relationships in Interagency Child Protection Work*, Lyme Regis, Russell House Publishing.

Parton, N. (2005) *Safeguarding Children: Early Intervention and Surveillance in a Late Modern Society*, Basingstoke, Palgrave Macmillan.

Pinkerton, J. (2002) 'Child Protection', in Adams (2002b).

Pritchard, C. (2004) *The Child Abusers: Research and Controversy*, Buckingham, Open University Press.

community care

Ahmad, W. I. U. and Atkin, K. (eds) (1996) *'Race' and Community Care*, Buckingham, Open University Press.

Bowl, R. (2001) 'Men and Community Care', in Christie (2001).

Hudson, J. (2002) 'Community Care in the Information Age', in Bytheway et al. (2002).

Lymbery, M. (2004) 'Managerialism and Care Management Practice with Older People', in Lymbery and Butler (2004).

Means, R., Richards, S. and Smith, R. (2003) *Community Care: Policy and Practice*, 3rd edn, Basingstoke, Palgrave Macmillan.

Thompson, N. and Thompson, S. (2005) *Community Care*, Lyme Regis, Russell House Publishing.

community social work

Banks, S., Butcher, H. L., Henderson, P. and Roberts and Robertson J. (eds) (2003) *Managing Community Practice: Principles, Policies and Programmes*, Bristol, The Policy Press.

Stepney, P. and Evans, D. (2000) 'Community Social Work: Towards an Integrative Model of Practice', in Stepney and Ford (2002).

conflict

Braithewaite, R. (2001) *Managing Aggression*, London, Routledge.

Booker, O. (1999) *Averting Aggression*, Lyme Regis, Russell House Publishing.

Newhill, C. E. (2003) *Client Violence in Social Work Practice: Prevention, Intervention, and Research*, London, The Guilford Press.

Thompson, N. (2002) *People Skills*, Basinsgtoke, Palgrave Macmillan.

counselling

Brown, H. C. (2002) 'Counselling', in Adams (2002a).

Geldard, K. and Geldard, D. (2003) *Counselling Skills in Everyday Life*, Basingstoke, Palgrave Macmillan.

Heron, J. (2001) *Helping the Client: A Creative Practical Guide*, 5th edn, London, Sage.

Nelson-Jones, R. (2005) *Introduction to Counselling Skills: Texts and Activities*, 2nd edn, London, Sage.

cultural competence

Burford, B. (2001) 'The Cultural Competence Model', in Baxter (2001).

Gunaratnam, Y. (2002) 'Whiteness and Emotions in Social Care', in Bytheway et al.

Parekh, B. (2006) *Rethinking Multiculturalism: Cultural Diversity and Political Theory*, 2nd edn, Basingstoke, Palgrave Macmillan.

debt

Edwards, S. (2003) *In Too Deep: CAB Clients' Experience of Debt*, CAB/Citizens' Advice Scotland.

Kober, C. (2005) *In the Balance: Disabled People's Experience of Debt*, London, Leonard Cheshire.

dementia

Adams, T. and Manthorpe, J. (eds) (2003) *Dementia Care*, London, Arnold.

Kitwood, T. M. (1997) *Dementia Reconsidered: The Person Comes First*, Buckingham, Open University Press.

Manthorpe, J., Illife, S. and Eden, A. (2004) 'Early Recognition of and Responses to Dementia: Health Professionals' Views of Social Services Role and Performance', *British Journal of Social Work*, **34**(3).

dependency

Goble, C. (2004) 'Dependence, Independence and Normality', in Swain et al. (2004).

Leece, J. and Bornat, J. (2006) *Developments in Direct Payments*, Bristol, The Policy Press.

Lustbader, W. (1991) *Counting on Kindness: The Dilemmas of Dependency*, New York, The Free Press.

Sapey, B., Stewart, J. and Harris, J. (2001) 'Disability: Constructing Dependency through Social Policy', in Baxter (2001).

depression

Brown, G. W. (2000) 'Life Events, Loss and Depressive Disorders', in Heller et al. (2000).

Godfrey, M. and Denby, T. (2004) *Depression and Older People: Towards Securing Well-being in Later Life*, Bristol, The Policy Press/Help the Aged.

Rowe, D. (2003) *Depression: The Way Out of Your Prison*, Hove, Brunner Routledge.

Sheppard, M. and Kelly, N. (2001) *Social Work Practice with Depressed Mothers in Child and Family Care*, London, Stationery Office.

Stoppard, J. M. (2000) *Understanding Depression: Feminist Social Constructionist Approaches*, London, Routledge.

disability

Barnes, C. and Mercer, G. (2006) *Independent Futures: Creating User-Led Disability Services in a Disabling Society*, Bristol, The Policy Press.

Hubbard, A. (2002) 'On Becoming a Disabled Person', in Bytheway et al. (2002).

Oliver, M. and Sapey, B. (2006) *Social Work with Disabled People*, 3rd edn, Basingstoke, Palgrave Macmillan.

Swain, J., French, S. and Cameron, C. (2003) *Controversial Issues in a Disabling Society*, Buckingham, Open University Press.

Swain, J., French, S., Barnes, C. and Thomas, C (eds) (2004) *Disabling Barriers – Enabling Environments*, 2nd edn, London, Sage.

discrimination

Donnison, D. (1998) *Policies for a Just Society*, Basingstoke, Macmillan – now Palgrave Macmillan.

Fook, J. (2002) *Social Work: Critical Theory and Practice*, London, Sage.

Thompson, N. (2003) *Promoting Equality: Tackling Discrimination and Oppression*, 2nd edn, Basingstoke, Palgrave Macmillan.

Thompson, N. (2006) *Anti-Discriminatory Practice*, 4th edn, Basingstoke, Palgrave Macmillan.

Tomlinson, D. and Trew, W. (eds) (2001) *Equalising Opportunities, Minimising Oppression*, London, Routledge.

disenfranchised grief

Cave, D. (2000) 'Gay and Lesbian Bereavement', in Dickenson et al. (2000).

Doka, K. (ed.) (2001) *Disenfranchised Grief*, 3rd edn, New York, Lexington.

Oswin, M. (1991) *Am I Allowed to Cry? A Study of Bereavement Amongst People Who Have Learning Difficulties*, London, Human Horizons.

Thompson, S. (2002) 'Older People', in Thompson (2002).

domestic violence

Blyth, L. (2005) 'Not Behind Closed Doors: Working in Partnership against Domestic Violence', in Carnwell and Buchanan (2005).

Hearn, J. (2001) 'Men, Social Work and Men's Violence to Women', in Christie (2001).

Humphreys, C. and Mullender, A. (2003) 'Assessment and Role Across Social Work Specialisms in Working with Domestic Violence', in Horwath and Shardlow (2003).

Mullender, A., Hague, G., Imam, U., Kelly, L., Malos, E. and Regan, L. (2002) *Children's Perspectives on Domestic Violence*, London, Sage.

drug misuse

Buchanan, J. and Corby, B. (2005) 'Drug Misuse and Safeguarding Children: A Multi-Agency Approach', in Carnwell and Buchanan (2005).

Harbin, F. and Murphy, M. (eds) (2006) *Secret Lives: Growing with Substance*, Lyme Regis, Russell House Publishing.

Harris, P. (2005) *Drug Induced*, Lyme Regis, Russell House Publishing.

Kroll, B. and Taylor, A. (2003) *Parental Substance Misuse and Child Welfare*, London, Jessica Kingsley.

Neale, J. (2004) 'Gender and Illicit Drug Use', *British Journal of Social Work*, **34**(6).

education social work

Blyth, E. and Milner, J. (1997) *Social Work with Children: The Educational Perspective*, Harlow, Longman.

Huxtable, M. and Blyth, E. (eds) (2000) *School Social Work Worldwide*, Washington DC, National Association of Social Work.

elder abuse

Amiel, S. and Heath, I. (eds) (2003) *Family Violence in Primary Care*, Oxford, Oxford University Press, Part 4.

Kingston, P. (2006) *Adult Protection in Perspective*, Maidenhead, Open University Press.

Pritchard, J. (2001) *Male Victims of Elder Abuse: Their Experience and Needs*, London, Jessica Kingsley.

Pritchard, J. (ed.) (2001) *Good Practice with Vulnerable Adults*, London, Jessica Kingsley.

essentialism

Bertens, H. (1995) *The Idea of the Postmodern: A History*, London, Routledge.

Burr, V. (2003) *Social Constructionism*, 2nd edn, London, Routledge.

Thompson, N. (2000) 'Existentialist Practice', in Stepney and Ford (2000).

ethics

Banks, S. (2004) *Ethics, Accountability and Social Professions*, Basingstoke, Palgrave, Macmillan.

Dean, H. (ed.) (2004) *The Ethics of Welfare: Human Rights, Dependency and Responsibility*, Bristol, The Policy Press.

Leathard, A. and McLaren, S. (2007?) *Ethics: Contemporary Challenges in Health and Social Care*, Bristol, The Policy Press.

Moss, B. (2006) *Values*, Lyme Regis, Russell House Publishing.

Osmo, R. and Landau, R. (2001) 'The Need for Explicit Argumentation in Ethical Decision Making in Social Work', *Social Work Education*, **20**(4).

ethnocentricity

Barn, R. (1999) *Working with Black Children and Adolescents in Need*, London, BAAF.

Devore, W. and Schlesinger, E. G. (1999) *Ethnic Sensitive Social Work Practice*, 5th edn, London, Allyn & Bacon.

Dominelli, L., Lorenz, W. and Soydan, H. (2001) *Beyond Racial Divides: Ethnicities in Social Work Practice*, Aldershot, Ashgate.

Graham, M. (2002) *Social Work and African-Centred Worldviews*, Birmingham, Venture Press.

failure to thrive

Iwaniec, D. (2004) *Children Who Fail to Thrive: A Practical Guide*, Chichester, John Wiley.

Wynne, J. (2003) 'Physical Symptoms and Signs of Child Abuse', in Amiel and Heath (2003).

family support

Canavan, J., Dolan, P. and Pinkerton, J. (eds) (2000) *Family Support: Directions from Diversity*, London, Jessica Kingsley.

Dolan, P., Canavan, J. and Pinkerton, J. (eds) (2006) *Family Support as Reflective Practice*, London, Jessica Kingsley.

Gardner, R. (2003) *Supporting Families: Child Protection in the Community*, Chichester, John Wiley.

Katz, I., Pinkerton, J. and Birkin, M. (eds) (2003) *Evaluating Family Support: Thinking Internationally, Thinking Critically*, Chichester, John Wiley.

Vanclay, L. (2003) 'Supporting Families: An Interprofessional Approach?', in Leathard A. (ed.), *Interprofessional Collaboration: From Policy to Practice in Health and Social Care*, Hove and New York, Brunner-Routledge .

fostering

Brown, H. C. (2002) 'Fostering and Adoption', in Adams et al. (2002b).

Padbury, P. and Frost, N. (2002) *Solving Problems in Foster Care: Key Issues for Young People, Foster Carers and Social Services*, London, The Children's Society.

Wheal, A. and Mehmet, M. (2006) *The Foster Carers' Handbook*, 3rd edn, Lyme Regis, Russell House Publishing.

Wilson, K., Petrie, S. and Sinclair, I. (2003) 'A Kind of Loving': A Model of Effective Foster Care', *British Journal of Social Work*, **33**(8).

goal setting

Marsh, P. and Doel, M. (2005) *The Task Centred Book*, London, Routledge.

Pinnock, M. and Dimmock, B. (2003) 'Managing for Outcomes', in Henderson and Atkinson (2003).

Thompson, N. (2002) *People Skills*, 2nd edn, Basingstoke, Palgrave Macmillan, see Part 3.

good enough parenting

Wheal A. (ed.) (1999) *Working with Parents: Learning From Other People's Experience*, Lyme Regis, Russell House Publishing.

Woodcock, J. (2003) 'The Social Assessment of Parenting: An Exploration', *British Journal of Social Work*, **33**(1).

heterosexism and homophobia

Brown, H. C. (1998) *Social Work and Sexuality: Working with Lesbians and Gay Men*, Basingstoke, Macmillan – now Palgrave Macmillan.

Carabine, J. (ed.) (2004) *Sexualities: Personal Lives and Social Policy*, Bristol, The Policy Press.

Davies, D. and Neale, C. (eds) (1996) *Pink Therapy: A Guide for Counsellors and Therapists Working with Lesbian, Gay and Bisexual Clients*, Buckingham, Open University Press.

Moreland, I. and Willox, A. (eds) (2005) *Queer Theory*, Basingstoke, Palgrave Macmillan.

hospice

Lucas, S. (2003) *Palliative Care and HIV/AIDS: Worlds Apart or a Vision Shared?* – available from www. hospiceinformation.info.

Philp, I. (2006) *A New Ambition for Old Age: Next Steps in Implementing the National Service Framework for Older People*, London, Department of Health.

Saunders, C. (2002) 'The Philosophy of Hospice', in Thompson (2002c).

Worswick, J. (1993) *A House Called Helen: The Story of the First Hospice for Children*, London, HarperCollins.

institutionalization

Goffman. I. (1961) *Asylums: Essays on the Social Situation of Mental Patients and Other Inmates*, Harmondsworth, Penguin – a classic text in this field.

Stainton, T., Welshman, J. and Walmsley, J (2005) *Pressures for Change* – Unit 14 of Open University Course K202 (Care, Welfare and Community), 2nd edn, Milton Keynes. Open University.

learning disability

Clarke, J. (2006) *Just Ordinary People: William Francis Blunn 'Our Bill'*, Liverpool, MOWLL.

May, D (ed.) (2001) *Transition and Change in the Lives of People with Intellectual Disabilities*, London, Jessica Kingsley.

Race, D. (2002) *Learning Disability: A Social Approach*, London, Routledge.

Stainton, T. (2002) 'Learning Disability', in Adams et al. (2002b).

Wolfensberger, W. and Tulman, S (1989) 'A Brief Outline of the Principle of Normalization', in Brechin and Walmsley (1989).

linguistic sensitivity

Drakeford, M. and Morris, S. (1998) 'Social Work with Linguistic Minorities' in Williams et al. (1998).

Thompson, N. (2003) *Communication and Language: A Handbook of Theory and Practice*, Basingstoke, Palgrave Macmillan.

locus of control

Cardwell, M., Clark, L. and Meldrun, C. (2004) *Psychology for A Level*, London, Harper Collins.

mediation

Craig, Y. J. (ed.) (1998) *Advocacy, Counselling and Mediation in Casework*, London, Jessica Kingsley.

Leibman, M. (ed.) (2000) *Mediation in Context*, London, Jessica Kingsley.

Lindstein, T. and Meteyard, B. (1996) *What Works in Family Mediation: Mediating Residence and Contact Disputes*, Lyme Regis, Russell House Publishing.

mental health problems

Dwivedi, K. N. and Harper, P. B. (2004) *Promoting the Emotional Well-being of Children and Adolescents and Preventing their Mental Ill-Health: A Handbook*, London, Jessica Kingsley.

Gilbert, P. (2003) *The Value of Everything: Social Work and its Importance in the Field of Mental Health*, Lyme Regis, Russell House Publishing.

Heller, T., Reynolds, J., Gomm, R., Muston, R. and Pattison, S. (eds) (2000) *Mental Health Matters: A Reader*, 2nd edn, Basingstoke, Palgrave Macmillan.

Rogers, A. and Pilgrim, D. (2003) *Mental Health and Inequality*, Basingstoke, Palgrave Macmillan.

multidisciplinary working

Leathard, A. (ed.) (2003) *Interprofessional Collaboration: From Policy to Practice in Health and Social Care*, Hove, Brunner-Routledge.

Murphy, M. (2004) *Developing Collaborative Relationships in Interagency Child Protection Work*, Lyme Regis, Russell House Publishing.

Weinstein, J., Whittington, C. and Leiba, T. (eds) (2003) *Collaboration in Social Work Practice*, London, Jessica Kingsley.

neglect

Bennett, G., Kingston, P. and Penhale, B. (1997) *The Dimensions of Elder Abuse: Perspectives for Practitioners*, Basingstoke, Palgrave Macmillan,

Howe, D. (2005) *Child Abuse and Neglect: Attachment, Development and Intervention*, Basingstoke, Palgrave Macmillan.

networking

Carnwell, R. and Buchanan, J. (eds) (2005) *Effective Practice in Health and Social Care: A Partnership Approach*, Maidenhead, Open University Press.

Thompson, N. (2002) *Building the Future: Social Work with Children, Young People and Their Families*, Lyme Regis, Russell House Publishing, Chapter 3.

Folgheraiter, F. (2004) *Relational Social Work: Towards Networking and Societal Practices*, London, Jessica Kingsley.

oppression

Fook, J. (2002) *Social Work: Critical Theory and Practice*, London, Sage.

Mullally, B. (2002) *Challenging Oppression: A Critical Social Work Approach*, Oxford, Oxford University Press.

Thompson, N. (2003) *Promoting Equality: Tackling Discrimination and Oppression*, 2nd edn, Basingstoke, Palgrave Macmillan.

Thompson, N. (2006) *Anti-Discriminatory Practice*, 4th edn, Basingstoke, Palgrave Macmillan.

partnership

Carnwell, R. and Buchanan, J. (eds) (2005) *Effective Practice in Health and Social Care: A Partnership Approach*, Maidenhead, Open University Press.

Harrison, R., Mann, G., Murphy, M., Taylor, A. and Thompson, N. (2003) *Partnership Made Painless*, Lyme Regis, Russell House Publishing.

Social Care Institute for Excellence (2004) Position Paper 3: *Has Service User Involvement Made a Difference to Social Care Services?*: London, SCIE – available from www.scie.org.uk

Sullivan, H. and Skelcher, C. (2002) *Working Across Boundaries: Collaboration in Social Services*, Basingstoke, Palgrave Macmillan.

politicization

Jordan, B. (2004) 'Emancipatory Social Work? Opportunity or Oxymoron?', *British Journal of Social Work*, **34**(1)

Freire, P. (1972) *Pedagogy of the Oppressed*, Harmondsworth, Penguin.

Langan, M. (2002) *The Legacy of Radical Social Work*, Basingstoke, Palgrave Macmillan.

Powell, F. (2001) *The Politics of Social Work*, London, Sage.

post-traumatic stress disorder

Joseph, S. et al. (1997) *Understanding Post-Traumatic Stress: A Psychosocial Perspective on PTSD and Treatment*, Chichester, Wiley.

Scott, M. J. and Palmer, S. (eds) (2000) *Trauma and Post-Traumatic Stress Disorder*, London, Sage.

Yule, W. (ed.) (1999) *Post Traumatic Stress Disorder: Concepts and Therapy*, Chichester, Wiley.

Also see 'trauma'.

poverty

Davis, A. and Wainwright, S. (2005) 'Combating Poverty and Social Exclusion: Implications for Social Work Education', *Social Work Education*, **4**(3).

George, V. and Wilding, P. (2002) *Globalisation and Human Welfare*, Basingstoke, Palgrave Macmillan, Chs 4, 5 and 6.

Jones, C. and Novak, T. (1999) *Poverty, Welfare and the Disciplinary State*, London, Routledge.

Lister, R. (2004) *Poverty*, Oxford, Blackwell.

power

Bar-On, A. (2002) 'Restoring Power to Social Work Practice', *The British Journal of Social Work*, **32**(8).

Fook, J. (2002) *Social Work: Critical Theory and Practice*, London, Sage.

Thompson, N. (2007) *Power and Empowerment*, Lyme Regis, Russell House Publishing.

Westwood, S. (2002) *Power and the Social*, London, Routledge.

protection of vulnerable adults

Kingston, P. (2006) *Adult Protection in Perspective*, Buckingham, Open University Press.

Martin, J. (2007) *Safeguarding Adults*, Lyme Regis, Russell House Publishing.

Penhale, B. and Parker, J. (2003) 'The Protection of Vulnerable Adults: The Role of Social Work', in Horwath and Shardlow (2003).

Pritchard, J. (2001) *Good Practice with Vulnerable Adults*, London, Jessica Kingsley.

racism

Back, L. and Solomos, J. (eds) (2000) *Theories of Race and Racism: A Reader*, London, Routledge.

Bhavnani, R. Mirza, H. S. and Meetoo, V. (2005) *Tackling the Roots of Racism: Lessons for Success*, Bristol, The Policy Press/Joseph Rowntree Foundation.

Penketh, L. (2000) *Tackling Institutional Racism: Anti-Racist Policies and Social Work Education and Training*, Bristol, The Policy Press/Joseph Rowntree Foundation

Pilkington, A. (2003) *Racial Disadvantage and Ethnic Diversity in Britain*, Basingstoke, Palgrave Macmillan.

Solomos, J (2003) *Race and Racism in Britain*, 3rd edn, Basingstoke, Palgrave Macmillan.

residential care

Crimmens, D. and Pitts, J. (eds) (2000) *Positive Residential Practice: Learning the Lessons of the 1990s*, Lyme Regis, Russell House Publishing.

DOH (2001) *Care Homes for Older People: National Minimum Standards*, 3rd edn, London, HMSO.

Mehra, H. (2002) 'Residential Care for Ethnic Minority Children', in Dwivedi et al. (2002)

Thompson, N. (2004) *Group Care with Children and Young People*, 2nd edn, Lyme Regis, Russell House Publishing.

resilience

Gilligan, R. (2000) *Promoting Resilience: A Resource Guide on Working with Children in the Care System*, London, BAAF.

Gilligan, R. (2004) 'Promoting Resilience in Child and Family Social Work: Issues for Social Work Practice, Education and Policy', *Social Work Education*, **23**(1).

rights

Clarke, C. (2002) 'Identity, Individual Rights and Social Justice', in Adams et al. (2002b).

Clements, L. and Young, J. R. (1999) *Human Rights: Changing the Culture*, Oxford, Blackwell.

Ife, J. (2001) *Human Rights and Social Work: Towards Rights-Based Practice*, Cambridge, Cambridge University Press.

Kallen, E. (2004) *Social Inequality and Social Injustice: A Human Rights Perspective*, Basingstoke, Palgrave Macmillan.

Watson, J. and Woolf, M. (2003) *Human Rights Toolkit*, London, Legal Action Group.

risk assessment and management

Harding, T. (2005) *Rights and Risk: Older People and Human Rights*, London, Help the Aged.

Kemshall, H. (2002) *Risk, Social Policy and Welfare*, Birmingham, Open University Press.

Langan, J. and Lindow, V. (2004) *Living with Risk: Mental Health Service User Involvement in Risk Assessment and Management*, Bristol, The Policy Press/Joseph Rowntree Foundation.

O'Sullivan, T. (2002) 'Managing Risk and Decision Making', in Adams et al. (2002b).

schizophrenia

Bentall, R. P. and Beck, A.T. (2003) *Madness Explained: Psychosis and Human Nature*, Harmondsworth, Penguin.

Boyle, M. (2002) '"Schizophrenia" Re-evaluated', in Heller et al. (2000).

self-care

Hawkins, P. and Shohet, R. (2000) *Supervision in the Helping Professions: An Individual, Group and Organizational Approach*, 2nd edn, Maidenhead, Open University Press.

Phillipson, J. (2002) 'Supervision and Being Supervised', in Adams et al. (2002b).

Thompson, N. (1999) *Stress Matters*, Birmingham, Pepar.

self-esteem

Blair, M. and Wilson, L. (2002) *C is for Confidence: A Guide to Running Confidence-Building Courses for Women of All Ages*, Lyme Regis, Russell House Publishing.

Wilson, L., Blair, M. and Armstrong, P. (2002) *D is for Direction: A Guide to Running Confidence-Building Courses for Men of All Ages*, Lyme Regis, Russell House Publishing.

Self-esteem is mentioned in many introductory psychology textbooks, where development of the self, self-regard or self-concept are discussed. See, for example, Gross, R. D. (2005) *The Science of Mind and Behaviour*, 5th edn, London, Hodder Arnold.

See also 'attachment'.

self-harm

Babiker, G. and Arnold, L. (1997) *The Language of Injury: Comprehending Self-Mutilation*, Leicester, The British Psychological Society.

Fox, C. and Hawton, K. (eds) (2004) *Deliberate Self-Harm in Adolescence*, London, Jessica Kingsley.

sex offenders

Kemshall, H. (2002) *Risk Assessment and Management of Serious Violent and Sexual Offenders: A Review of Current Issues*, Edinburgh, Scottish Executive Social Research.

Matravers, A. (2003) *Sex Offenders in the Community: Managing and Reducing the Risks*, Cullompton, Willan.

sexism

Bryson, V. (1999) *Feminist Debates: Issues of Theory and Political Practice*, Basingstoke, Macmillan – now Palgrave Macmillan.

Connell, R. W. (2002) *Gender*, Cambridge, Policy Press.

Gruber, C. and Stefanov, H. (eds) (2002) *Gender in Social Work: Promoting Equality*, Lyme Regis, Russell House Publishing.

Oakley, A. (ed.) (2005) *Gender, Women and Social Science*, Bristol, The Policy Press.

sexuality

Bhattacharyya, G. (2002) *Sexuality and Society: An Introduction*, London, Routledge.

Brown, H. C. (1998) *Social Work and Sexuality: Working with Lesbians and Gay Men*, Basingstoke, Macmillan – now Palgrave Macmillan.

Carabine, J. (ed.) (2004) *Sexualities: Personal Lives and Social Policy*, Bristol, The Policy Press/Open University

Saraga, E. (1998) 'Abnormal, Unnatural and Immoral?', in Saraga (1998).

social exclusion

Barry, M. and Hallet, C. (eds) (1998) *Social Exclusion and Social Work: Issues of Theory, Policy and Practice*, Lyme Regis, Russell House Publishing.

Lister, R. (2004) *Poverty*, Cambridge, Polity Press.

Smale, G., Tucson, G. and Statham, D. (2000) *Social Work and Social Problems: Working Towards Social Inclusion and Social Change*, Basingstoke, Macmillan – now Palgrave Macmillan.

social justice

Craig, G. (2002) 'Poverty, Social Work and Social Justice', *British Journal of Social Work*, **32**(6).

Jordan, B. (1998) *The New Politics of Welfare: Social Justice in a Global Context*, London, Sage.

Kallen, E. (2004) *Social Inequality and Social Justice: A Human Rights Perspective*, Basingstoke, Palgrave Macmillan.

social role valorization

Brown, H. and Walmsley, J. (1997) 'When Ordinary is Not Enough: a Review of the Concept of Normalisation', in Bornat et al. (1997).

Walmsley, J. (2005) 'Normal lives or Different Lives' – Unit 7 of Open University Course K202, 2nd edn, Milton Keynes, Open University.

spirituality

Furman, L. D., Benson, P. W., Grimwood, C. and Canda, E. (2004) 'Religion and Spirituality in Social Work

Education and Direct Practice at the Millennium: a Survey of UK Social Workers', *British Journal of Social Work*, **34**(6).

Hodge, D. R. (2005) 'Spirituality in Social work Education: A Development and Discussion of Goals that Flow from the Profession's Ethical Mandates', *Social Work Education*, **24**(1).

Mackinlay, E. (2001) *The Spiritual Dimension of Ageing*, London, Jessica Kingsley.

Moss, B. (2005) *Religion and Spirituality*, Lyme Regis, Russell House Publishing.

stereotypes

Pickering, M. (2001) *Stereotyping: The Politics of Representation*, Basingstoke, Palgrave Macmillan.

stigma

Burke, P. and Parker, J. (eds) (2006) *Social Work and Disadvantage: Addressing the Roots of Stigma through Association*, London, Jessica Kingsley.

Goffman, E. (1963) *Stigma: Notes on the Management of a Spoiled Identity*, Englewood Cliifs, NJ, Prentice-Hall.

the strengths perspective

Healy, K. (2005) *Social Work Theories in Context: Creating Frameworks for Practice*, Basingstoke, Palgrave Macmillan.

Munford, R. and Sanders, J. (2005) 'Working with Families: Strengths-based Approaches', in Nash et al. (2005).

stress

Coffey, M., Dugdill, L. and Tattersall, A. (2004) 'Stress in Social Services: Mental Well-Being, Constraints and Job Satisfaction', *British Journal of Social Work*, **34**(5).

Thompson, N. (1999) *Stress Matters*, Birmingham, Pepar Publications.

Thompson, N., Murphy, M. and Stradling, S (1996) *Meeting the Stress Challenge*, Lyme Regis, Russell House Publishing.

suicide

Harvey, J. H. (2002) *Perspectives on Loss and Trauma: Assaults on the Self*, London, Sage.

Taylor, S. and Gilmour, A. (2002) 'Towards Understanding Suicide', in Heller et al. (2000)

Wertheimer, A. (2001) *A Special Scar: The Experience of People Bereaved by Suicide*, London, Routledge.

supervision

Hughes, L. and Pengelly, P. (1997) *Staff Supervision in a Turbulent Environment*, London, Jessica Kingsley.

Morrison, T. (2005) *Supervision Skills: An Action Learning Approach*, 3rd edn, Brighton, Pavilion.

Thompson, N. (2002) *People Skills*, 2nd edn, Basingstoke, Palgrave Macmillan.

teamwork

Onyett, S. (2003) *Teamworking in Mental Health*, Basingstoke, Palgrave Macmillan.

Payne, M. (2000) *Teamwork in Multi-Professional Care*, London, Lyceum Books/Macmillan.

Payne, M. (2002) 'Coordination and Teamwork', in Adams et al. (2002b).

trafficking

van den Anker, C. and Doomernik, J. (eds) (2006) *Trafficking and Women's Rights*, Basingstoke, Palgrave Macmillan.

Froschl, E. (2002) 'Trafficking in Women', in Gruber, C. and Stefanov, H. (eds) (2002) *Gender in Social Work: Promoting Equality*, Lyme Regis, Russell House.

trauma

Gibson, M. (2006) *Order from Chaos: Responding to Traumatic Events*, 3rd edn, Bristol, The Policy Press.

Scott, M. J. and Palmer, S. (eds) (2000) *Trauma and Post-Traumatic Stress Disorder*, London, Sage.

Spiers, T. (ed.) (2001) *Trauma: A Practitioners' Guide to Counselling*, Hove, Brunner Routledge.

Tomlinson, P. (2004) *Therapeutic Approaches to Work with Traumatized Children and Young People: Theory and Practice*, London, Jessica Kingsley.

See also 'Post-traumatic stress disorder'

travellers

Fay, R. (2001) 'Health and Racism: A Traveller Perspective', in Farrell, and Watt (2001).

Roberts, A. (2005) 'Working With Gypsy Travellers: A. Partnership Approach', in Carnwell and Buchanan (2005).

unconditional positive regard

Means, D. and Thorne, B. (1999) *Person-Centred Counselling in Action*, London, Sage.

Rogers, C. (1961) *On Becoming a Person: A Therapist's View of Psychotherapy*, London, Constable.

Olan, J. (2003) *Skills in Person-Centred Counselling and Psychotherapy*, London, Sage.

vulnerability

Brown, H. (2005) 'Vulnerability and Protection' – Unit 18 of Course K202 (Care, Welfare and Community), 2nd edn, Milton Keynes, The Open University.

Pritchard, J. (2001) *Good Practice with Vulnerable Adults*, London, Jessica Kingsley.

welfare rights

Bateman, N. (2003) *Welfare Rights*, London, Care and Health.

Walker, R. (2005) *Social Security and Welfare: Concepts and Comparisons*, Maidenhead, Open University Press.

See also the books on specific social security benefits which are regularly updated and published by the Child Poverty Action Group.

youth justice

Bateman, T. and Pitts, J. (eds) (2004) *The RHP Companion to Youth Justice*, Lyme Regis, Russell House Publishing.

Canton, R. and Eadie, T. (2004) 'Social Work with Young Offenders: Practising in a Context of Ambivalence', in Lymbery and Butler (2004).

Muncie, J., Hughes, G. and McLaughlin, E. (eds) (2002) *Youth Justice, Critical Readings*, London, Sage.

Smith, R. (2003) *Youth Justice: Ideas, Policy and Practice*, Cullompton, Willan Publishing.

4

4.1 introduction

Social work practice is based on an extensive knowledge base developed over a considerable number of years. That knowledge base comprises not only 'practice wisdom' passed from generation to generation, but also theoretical understandings and related research findings. We shall examine the importance of research as an underpinning of practice in Part 5, but here our concern is with the important role of theory in providing an understanding of the complex issues we face in practice and the various ways we can attempt to address those issues. As we noted in Chapter 2.7 when discussing reflective practice, theory is an important basis of practice and one that we neglect at our peril. Developing a good understanding of the theoretical underpinnings of contemporary social work is therefore an important task. This part of the book is intended to assist you in that task. integrating theory and practice, see p. 142

Part 4 contains short accounts of 22 key theories and theorists in order to help you appreciate the wide range of ideas and theoretical perspectives that have shaped current thinking and that are likely to influence the development of our thinking and practice in the coming years. The list is not, of course, exhaustive, as the wellspring from which social work thinking has drawn over the years is far too vast for that.

Some of the ideas have developed within social work itself, while others have a much broader basis and have been developed to address wider aspects of society, rather than just social work itself. This part of the book therefore makes reference to the works of some thinkers and writers who did not concern themselves directly with social work, but whose ideas have none the less been adapted to cast light on the social work world.

As with Part 3, the ideas presented here should be seen as forming a gateway to further study, a beginning or development of your knowledge and understanding of these issues, rather than a sufficient understanding in its own right or a definitive statement on the subject concerned. The 'Suggestions for further reading' at the end of this part of the book should be very helpful in guiding you further in following up on those particular ideas or approaches that interest or appeal to you.

4.2 theories and theorists

introduction

The 22 areas of theory are presented in alphabetical order to prevent any significance being attached to the relative merits of the ideas being presented according to the order in which they appear. Naturally, we are more sympathetic towards some ideas and perspectives than others, but we have none the less tried to be fair in how we have presented all the theories. In the limited space available to us we cannot realistically present a thorough introduction to the various theoretical frameworks discussed here. We have to settle for the more modest aim of presenting a short summary to give a 'flavour' of the particular approach. This should give you enough to begin to appreciate what each perspective has to offer and thus give you a foundation on which to develop a fuller and deeper knowledge over time.

anti-discriminatory practice Social work's clientele is prone to being discriminated against – looked down upon, treated as second-class citizens and thus treated unfairly (see the discussion of discrimination in Part 3). It is therefore important that, as social workers, we are aware of this and its implications for our practice.

In the early days of anti-discriminatory practice, the major focus was on anti-racism. Since then, while anti-racism continues to be a major issue and a central part of anti-discriminatory practice, the focus has been broadened to include discrimination in relation to gender (sexism), age (ageism), disability (disablism) sexual identity (heterosexism) and other such forms of disadvantage. But, of course, in reality, anti-discriminatory practice is even broader than a finite list such as this, as it involves challenging unacceptable practices in relation to any group or individual singled out for unfair treatment.

Anti-discriminatory practice can be seen to involve:

> Recognizing the significance of discrimination in people's lives – especially in the lives of

those disadvantaged groups we commonly encounter in social work – and how oppressive this can be. Often what appear to be 'personal' problems will have their roots, in part at least, in wider social issues of discrimination. For example, many of the difficulties people with mental health problems encounter can be linked with discrimination – for example, difficulties in obtaining housing and employment. This can have a significant effect, as a lack of housing and employment are significant factors in preventing people with mental health problems dealing with the pressures they encounter.

Principle 1 Social Context

Discrimination is a key feature of the social context.

> At a minimum, making sure that our own practice does not reinforce or add to such discrimination. Discrimination is a matter of outcomes, not intentions. That is, if an individual or group is treated unfairly because they are perceived as different, the important issue is the outcome (their being treated

unfairly and thus placed at a disadvantage), regardless of the intentions. Much discrimination is unintentional (for example, as a result of unwittingly relying on a stereotype), but that does not alter the fact that it is discrimination and thus unacceptable. Anti-discriminatory practice therefore involves a degree of self-awareness and recognizing whether any aspects of our practice unwittingly reinforce discrimination – unlearning assumptions or established patterns of behaviour based on unfairness (for example, being patronizing towards disabled people by being too eager to 'look after' them, rather than support them in increasing their level of independence).

> Trying to tackle discrimination and its adverse effects. The roots of discrimination are very deep indeed and are to be found in cultural formations and structural power relations as well as personal beliefs and attitudes. In this sense, discrimination can be *institutional* – that is, built into systems and institutionalized patterns of behaviour or assumptions. We cannot therefore expect to remove discrimination altogether without radically altering the social terrain in which it finds such 'fertile soil'. This is a long-term project and one that social work can only play a part in over the years. Our immediate concerns therefore need to focus on more modest aims of doing whatever we reasonably can to prevent, counteract and remove discrimination and the oppression it leads to. For example, in helping a black family deal with and challenge the racism they are encountering in the mental health system, a social worker can play an important part in countering racism for that particular family (which could be a very significant help for them), while also making a small contribution to challenging racism in society more broadly.

NOS Key Role 6

Demonstrate professional competence in social work practice

Principle 6 Realism and Challenge

Anti-discriminatory practice is a challenging aspect of social work, but failing to address it can be highly problematic.

Anti-discriminatory practice is not a specialist approach that only applies in certain circumstances (for example, when a white social worker is working with a black client). Rather, it is a fundamental building block of good practice. It needs to be incorporated across the board and should not be seen as an 'add on' as and when required. As such, it is a major challenge. We therefore have to have a degree of humility in this regard and recognize that we will get it wrong sometimes, but it is vitally important that we rise to the challenge as best we can – both individually and collectively.

Some approaches to anti-discriminatory practice have been confrontational, dogmatic and simplistic and have failed to appreciate the complexities involved. They have also, in doing so, alienated many potential supporters of an anti-discriminatory approach. It is therefore essential that future efforts in this direction are not allowed to fall into this trap. Education and training for anti-discriminatory practice should not be about making feel people feel guilty for their upbringing, but rather an educational process geared towards helping people 'unlearn' the often discriminatory assumptions they have been brought up to believe and to adopt more empowering approaches to working with difference.

Principle 2 Empowerment and Partnership

Anti-discriminatory practice and empowerment need to go hand in hand.

Some writers define anti-discriminatory practice in very narrow, individualistic terms and reserve the term 'anti-oppressive practice' for the wider, more sociologically informed approach to discrimination and oppression. However, we base our understanding here on the work of Neil Thompson (2003a, 2006c), who argues that discrimination is the process that leads to oppression. Attempts to tackle oppression therefore need to focus on tackling discrimination – discrimination and oppression are two sides of the same coin. Anti-discriminatory practice, as used here, should therefore not be confused with the diluted, individualistic notion of tackling discrimination that some writers allude to.

cognitive-behavioural approaches

This approach has its roots in behavioural psychology. The school of behaviourism is premised on the idea that all behaviour is learned and that, therefore, behaviour can be changed through sophisticated programmes of re-learning or 'behaviour modification'. At one time this was seen as a useful approach to social work and was widely used, especially in the mental health and learning disabilities fields, although it had many strong critics who were unhappy about the way in which it treated people as entities that could be manipulated. It was thus seen by many as a dehumanizing and therefore unethical approach, although these concerns did not prevent it from featuring a great deal, as it was seen to be very effective in promoting behaviour change in many circumstances.

In addition to the ethical objections to behaviour modification, there were also theoretical objections. Behavioural psychology denied the significance of subjective processes and concentrated primarily if not exclusively on observable behaviour (looking at what events triggered particular behaviours and what 'rewards' reinforced them). There was no room in this theory for subjective factors, such as thoughts or beliefs. Over time, then, behaviourist psychology mellowed and started to adopt a less 'hard-line' approach to subjective factors, especially cognitive ones – that is, issues relating to thinking, memory and belief. From this, a 'cognitive-behavioural' approach developed, a theoretical perspective and practice method that still placed significant emphasis on behavioural factors, but also recognized that these are mediated by cognitive factors – that is, it was recognized that how a person behaves depends in part at least on his or her beliefs and understandings and, in order to change behaviour, it is often necessary to change a person's beliefs. For example, if someone believes that they have nothing worth living for, the result may be depression. In order to help with this depression, it will be necessary to change the belief that the person concerned has nothing to live for.

Cognitive-behavioural work can be used in a variety of situations, including: depression, anxiety, problems in controlling anger, drug and alcohol problems, behaviour management difficulties with children and offending behaviour. With its roots in 'scientific' psychology, the theoretical perspective is concerned with adopting a rigorous approach that involves, for example, measuring a 'baseline' of behaviour (the starting point) and then measuring any subsequent progress by reference to that baseline. This allows cognitive-behavioural practitioners to be in a strong position to measure the success of the intervention. It has a record of a high success rate and is thus often associated with evidence-based practice as it supports the 'what works' agenda that has developed in social work in recent years.

evidence-based practice, see p. 280

Methods used as part of this approach include: cognitive restructuring (helping people change their patterns of thought); skills training (social skills, communication skills, assertiveness and so on); modelling (showing methods of coping, for example); and coaching.

The main strength of the approach is that it is able to demonstrate a high level of success. However, the main criticism it attracts is that it does not address wider issues. For example, if someone's self-defeating beliefs and associated behaviour arise as a result of racist ideology, a cognitive-behavioural approach may enable the individual concerned to change his or her beliefs and behaviour, but will not necessarily make a dent on the racist processes that led to the situation. This does not mean that it is not a valuable approach, but it does mean that it should not be used in isolation, but rather as part of a broader-based approach that includes other more socially informed elements.

Principle 1 Social Context

We need to be wary of approaches that neglect the social context.

communicative action theory

This is an approach associated with the work of the social theorist, Jürgen Habermas (1972, 1984, 1987). His work is in the tradition of the critical theory associated with the Frankfurt School, although he developed their ideas in a number of ways. The Frankfurt School was interested in combining the insights of broad structural thinking (as evidenced in the works of Marx) and the narrower concerns of individual-oriented psychology (for example, psychodynamics). Habermas shares this interest in linking individual concerns with the wider structural context, but he has shown particular interest in how communication and language bridge the two areas. His thinking is very broad ranging and not all of it is necessarily relevant to social work, although his ideas around 'communicative action' clearly are.

Habermas is interested in developing rational social and political systems based on forms of communication free of domination. He argued that communication and knowledge are linked with what he called 'interests' – that is, communication and knowledge are not unbiased. Habermas introduced the notion of an 'ideal speech situation', by which he meant a situation in which each participant has an equal chance to take part in an unconstrained and undistorted dialogue. This is a useful concept because, by having such an ideal in mind, we can see how actual communications differ from it, and thus identify any distortions or inequalities involved.

Habermas's work explores how knowledge 'may not be neutral or value-free but may instead reflect the sectional interests of particular groups and embody relations of unequal power' (Tew, 2002, p. 85). A good example of his view of knowledge and interests is his rejection of positivism in social science – that is, the notion that social scientists can be neutral and value-free in their work and uncover objective truths about culture and society. He argues that social science is inevitably undertaken from a position of interest (what he called 'knowledge-constitutive interests').

The same argument can, of course, be applied to social work. Social work practice cannot be undertaken from a neutral point of view and therefore reflects particular interests and power relations – not without a radical reworking of the rationality on which society is based.

Critical reflection is a further aspect of Habermas's work that has relevance for social work. As noted in Chapter 2.8, reflective practice is an important part of good practice. Habermas sees critical reflection as an alternative to the positivist notion of uncovering an underlying truth. Instead, critical reflection is concerned

with the meanings involved in social interactions (including social work practice) – identifying assumptions, the operation of power relations and so on.

Principle 3 Critical Analysis

Habermas's approach is consistent with critical analysis.

Another significant aspect of Habermas's work is the important distinction between lifeworld and system. Lorenz explains this in the following terms:

> These concepts refer together to a given state of society; 'lifeworld' captures those aspects and processes in which people experience themselves as communicating actors capable of expressing intentions and giving meanings to their world, whereas 'system' denotes what are in fact the structural consequences of those actions and which ensure the material reproduction of society via the media of power and money. (2004, pp. 146–7)

Principle 1 Social Context

Habermas's approach is also consistent with an emphasis on the social context.

Lorenz goes on to argue that the origins of social work lie in both domains, and it can be seen that it acts as an intermediary between the two. This is because social work can influence, up to a point, both elements and also be influenced by them. In this respect, there is a parallel with the existentialist notion of the 'dialectic of subjectivity and objectivity' (see Neil Thompson, 2000c) – that is, the interplay between the actions of human actors and the wider social networks and circumstances in which we operate. This again highlights Habermas's emphasis on communicative action, as it is in large part through communication that lifeworld and system interact.

community work In contrast to the predominantly individualist focus of the largest part of social work practice, community work (or community development work, as it has also been known), seeks to tackle problems at the community level. This involves:

- developing good working relationships with key players in local communities (see networking in Part 3) to identify problems to be solved and strengths to be built on;
- drawing on the informal resources available by mobilizing community support and interest where possible;
- identifying, harnessing and utilizing statutory and voluntary sector resources in the area (social services, health, housing, education, leisure and libraries, and so on);
- seeking additional sources of help and funding – for example, through charitable funding sources;
- making sure that local people have the opportunity to participate in developments (see **user development** below), especially individuals or groups who are marginalized and/or excluded in some way;
- contributing to local and regional policy making and related political processes; and'capacity building' – that is, helping to promote the knowledge, skills and confidence necessary for people to play an active part in their community, to build on its strengths and help tackle its problems.

NOS Key Role 2

Plan, carry out, review and evaluate social work practice, with individuals, families, carers, groups, communities, and other professionals

In community work the traditional emphasis in social work on individual casework is replaced with a concern for developing schemes and projects that tackle the issues at the broader community level. Community work projects might typically include:

- Campaigning for a welfare rights centre to be established in a particular area with high levels of poverty and deprivation – for example, by using the local council's anti-poverty strategy as a lever to promote the development of such a centre.
- Working with the local education authority to support the development of after-school clubs to ensure that children are safely looked after while giving parents (especially single parents) the opportunity to pursue paid employment.
- Supporting the local race equality network

to promote anti-racism and provide help for people who experience racial attacks, intimidation or victimization.
- Working with voluntary bodies to develop volunteering schemes – for example, to befriend and support isolated older people in the community.

These are just some of the wide range of possibilities that come under the broad heading of community development work.

Munford and Walsh-Tapiata make helpful comment when they argue that:

We view community development as a process and a way of perceiving the world. Community development should not be viewed as just a 'job' but as a 'mindset' that characterizes a particular perspective on the world. While many workers will be employed as community development workers, others (for example, social workers) will be able to use community development principles in their daily work and to use these principles and community development practices to analyze and identify how the individual situations of social services clients can transformed.

(Munford and Walsh-Tapiata, 2005, p. 98)

Unfortunately, community work is not as prevalent as it once was, and is in need of a significant investment of resources if its potential is to be realized. The influence of community development thinking on social work practice varies considerably from area to area. In some settings a community approach is in evidence in a number of ways (liaison committees with local communities, for example), while in others there is little or no trace. The development of community social work (see Part 3) has been strongly influenced by community development theory and practice, but once again there is considerable variation from area to area in the extent to which this approach can be seen to be in evidence.

crisis intervention A crisis is defined as a turning point in somebody's life, a critical moment where the situation will either get better or get worse, but it will (by definition) not stay the same. The term is commonly confused with an emergency, a situation that needs to be addressed urgently. However, while the two terms, 'crisis' and 'emergency' can overlap at times, it is important to recognize the significant differences between them.

A crisis is the 'point of no return', the pivotal point at which a situation changes. To understand a crisis, we first need to understand its opposite, 'homeostasis'. This refers to the state of psychological equilibrium or balance that characterizes most people most of the time. It is when we are coping with the demands being made upon us without experiencing a significant strain. Homeostasis incorporates a continuum of coping – from a low level (when we are having a bad day, for example) to a high level (when things are going well for us). Provided our level of coping remains within this broad continuum, we can be said to be 'in homeostasis'. A crisis, then, occurs when homeostasis breaks down, when our everyday coping resources are overwhelmed for some reason and we are forced into adopting a new approach. The new approach may be better than our previous approach or worse – hence the idea that a crisis is a turning point, a situation that is either an improvement on what went before or a worsening. In the former case we can be said to have learned and grown from the crisis – it has strengthened us and taken us in a positive direction, while in the latter case, it will have weakened us and taken us in a negative direction. The aim of crisis intervention, then, is to maximize the positive potential of the situation, to do what we reasonably can to help the client(s) involved in the crisis turn it into a point of growth, rather than a diminution of their ability to cope.

Principle 2 Empowerment and Partnership

Crises have the potential for empowerment.

This is very different from an emergency which, by definition, is a situation requiring an urgent response. Many emergencies are not crises at all, in the sense that they do not involve a person's coping resources being overwhelmed or amount to a 'turning point' situation. They may well become a crisis if they are not attended to urgently, and so they may be seen as potential crisis points, rather than necessarily actual crisis moments.

We should also note that a crisis may contain no element of emergency whatsoever. A crisis may be something that develops over time and is anticipated well in advance, rather than an emergency situation. For example, someone whose partner is terminally ill may be well aware of his or her impending death, with no element of urgency or surprise whatsoever, but the actual death when it comes may none the less trigger a major crisis reaction if the intensity of grief overwhelms that person's coping abilities.

Principle 5 Loss and Grief

Crises can produce a significant grief reaction.

Crisis intervention, as a theoretical perspective, does not offer any predefined methods of intervention. Rather, it leaves the situation open to a wide variety of possible responses – but whatever the response we choose, it needs to be geared towards maximizing the positive potential of the crisis if it is to be consistent with crisis theory. Note the emphasis on the positive potential – crisis intervention should not be confused with 'crisis survival' which concerns itself with helping people weather the storm of the crisis. Crisis intervention is much more than just a survival strategy, as it offers the potential to help people secure major positive changes in their lives.

NOS Key Role 2

Plan, carry out, review and evaluate social work practice, with individuals, families, carers, groups, communities, and other professionals

empowerment   The basis of empowerment is helping people gain greater control over their lives. Literally, the term means 'to give power to', but it can be misleading to interpret it too literally. Power is not normally a gift one person can give to another. Rather, it is a case of helping people develop their own power by increasing the control they have over their lives.

Neil Thompson argues that this can be done at three levels:

> › *Personal.* Individuals can be helped gain greater control over their lives in a variety of ways – for example, through the enhancement of confidence and self-esteem.
> › *Cultural.* Discriminatory assumptions and stereotypes can be challenged in an attempt

to break down an oppressive culture in which the values and interests of dominant groups are presented as normal and natural. Empowerment at this level is therefore concerned with 'consciousness-raising', becoming aware of ideologies premised on inequality.

> *Structural.* Power relations are rooted in the structure of society and so empowerment at this level must involve the eradication, in the long term, of structured inequalities. This involves a collective political response, a concerted programme of action for social change.   (2003a , p. 77)

Principle 1 Social Context

Empowerment is not just an individual process – it has significant social roots.

Strategies for promoting empowerment would include:

> *Personal.* Boosting confidence and self-esteem; developing skills; identifying and, where possible, removing, obstacles to personal development; avoiding the creation of dependency; focusing on strengths and abilities; and promoting resilience.

> *Cultural.* Challenging discriminatory stereotypes that can have disempowering effects on people (for example, the notion that it is acceptable to make decisions on behalf of older people without consulting them); challenging internalized oppression (where individuals have taken on board negative assumptions about themselves – for example, a person with a learning disability who sees only limitations and not possibilities); using forms of language that do not reinforce discrimination or negativity.

> *Structural.* Recognizing the significance of structural power relations and the fact that we do not start from a position of a 'level playing-field'; taking account of factors relating to class, race, gender and so on, and how these can influence the situations we are dealing with; connecting the personal with the political – for example, helping a depressed woman understand her circumstances in terms of the role of women in society, rather than simply seeing depression as an illness.

Empowerment can therefore be seen to involve helping people resolve their own difficulties as far as possible, by avoiding dependency creation and by learning how to deal with future problems and challenges.

NOS Key Role 3

Support individuals to represent their needs, views and circumstances

As Principle 3 shows, empowerment is closely connected with partnership (see Part 3), in so far as it involves doing things *with* people as far as possible, rather than *to* or *for* them. To be in a strong position to promote empowering forms of social work, it is therefore necessary to have a good understanding of what is involved in working in partnership.

An important point to recognize is that some people may not want to be empowered. This can be for various reasons, including the following:

> They are very anxious, and the idea of taking control of their lives may add to that anxiety.

> They have a history of dependency (see Part 3), and can therefore see no benefit in empowerment.

> They mistakenly see empowerment as an excuse by the social worker not to do what they are supposed to do – that is, they expect to receive a service, rather than receive help in avoiding the need for a service.

> There is a reluctance to engage with the social worker, or even outright hostility.

In such situations, we need to be careful to make sure that we avoid the destructive extremes of: (i) simply giving up on empowerment ('If they don't want to be empowered, why should I bother?'); and (ii) trying to impose empowerment ('I'm going to empower you whether you like it or not'). The former is unduly defeatist, while the latter is clearly quite oppressive. Finding the balance between these two extremes can be very challenging work, but this is where the social worker's skills come into their own. Helping people move towards empowerment is a highly skilled undertaking, but one that is well worth the effort required for the skill development involved.

4

Principle 6 `Realism and Challenge`

*Avoiding defeatism and cynicism
is a key part of realism.*

Finally, it is important to note that
empowerment should be seen in the context
of anti-discriminatory practice. This is
because discrimination is a major source of
disempowerment, and empowerment is a
significant way of tackling discrimination and
oppression.

`existentialism` Existentialism is a very complex
philosophy but it can be summed up in one
sentence: 'existence precedes essence' (Sartre,
1958). Existence refers to human actions, and is
therefore fluid and changeable. Essence, by
contrast, refers to the idea of an underlying
nature and is thus seen as fixed and immutable.
The common-sense view tends to be that our
actions (existence) are based on our nature
(essence). Existentialism reverses this in
arguing that we are what we become. This places
choice at the heart of human existence.
Existentialism argues that choice – that is, the
need to choose and the ability to choose – is
absolute, in the sense that we cannot not
choose. Sartre, one of the most famous
existentialists, gives the example of a prisoner in
a cell. While the prisoner's range of options is
severely limited by imprisonment, the prisoner
still has the ability to choose. For example, in
receiving a meal on a tray, the prisoner may
choose to eat it, to throw it at the wall or
whatever. Choice, in the sense of the action of
choosing, is therefore *absolute*. Choice, in the
sense of the range of options available, is
relative, relative to our social circumstances,
for example.

Another important concept in existentialism
is the notion that 'we are what we make of what
is made of us' (Sartre, 1976). What this means
is that:

> Human agency and decision making
> are to the fore. Human existence is not
> characterized by determinism. The context
> shapes and constrains, but it is not the
> context that decides.
> We need to understand the notion of agency
> or the ability to choose in the sociopolitical

context that is grounded in sociological
reality, not a naïve individualism that fails to
take account of wider social and structural
factors. While each of us not only can choose,
but also has to choose, what we are able to
choose will depend on a wide range of factors,
often beyond our control, such as class, race
and gender.

> Human existence can be seen as a journey
> (note the link here with spirituality). This
> can be compared with the famous saying
> from Marx (1962) – that is, that people make
> history but not in circumstances of their
> own choosing.

Principle 1 `Social Context`

*Existentialism incorporates both
individual and social factors.*

The 'progressive-regressive method' is a concept
emerging from existentialism that can be
usefully applied to social work. It draws on the
idea that our present is not simply the outcome
of the past (as, for example, the behaviourist
notion of 'conditioning' would have us believe).
Our present position is shaped in part by
previous experiences and learning, but also by
our future aspirations or intentions. The present,
then, owes much to the future (progressive)
and the past (regressive) and how we make
sense of these influences. In order to understand
an individual now, we need to take account of:
(i) future aspirations (and possibly how these
may be being obstructed – for example, by
depression); (ii) past experiences; and (iii) how
the individual concerned is interpreting these.

A further important element of existentialism
is the notion of bad faith. The fact that we have
to choose, that we are responsible for our
own decisions and actions means that many
people try to avoid personal responsibility by
seeking refuge in determinism (biological,
environmental and so on) – that is, they try to
deny responsibility for their own actions.

Principle 2 `Empowerment and Partnership`

*Tackling bad faith can be an important
contribution to empowerment.*

Social work from an existentialist point of
view can therefore be seen as the attempt to
help people overcome bad faith and achieve

authenticity. In this respect, it is a form of empowerment. It helps people to understand what they have control over, what they must take responsibility for and helps them to learn how to carry that responsibility without bad faith. It is a very powerful approach, but unfortunately not one that is widely used.

family therapy This is an approach that grew out of **systems theory** (see below). In fact, the theory underpinning family therapy was at one time referred to as 'family systems theory', although these days it is influenced by a wider range of theoretical perspectives.

The basic idea behind family therapy is that the problems individuals experience should not be seen in isolation, but rather as signs of underlying problems in the family and its dynamics – that is, the interactions between family members. What is often presented as problem behaviour in an individual can, according to family therapy, be understood as a 'symptom' of 'dysfunctions' within the family system.

Traditionally, family therapy has been divided into four main 'schools' or approaches:

> *Structural.* This is based on the idea that family structure can be at the heart of problems being experienced. The task of the family therapist is to help create a family structure that functions more effectively. It owes much to Minuchin's (1974) idea that, by changing the family structure, it is possible to change the behaviour and psychological responses of the members of that family. A key concept is boundaries – for example, between parental roles and the roles of children. The therapist helps to renegotiate boundaries in order to make progress in dealing with the family's difficulties.

> *Strategic.* This approach is so called because it involves developing specific strategies for promoting change in a family's dynamics. In particular, it is concerned with identifying barriers to change, or what is referred to as 'resistance'. Emphasis is placed on making sure that family members do not lose face in the process of resolving their difficulties. Also important is the notion that the 'symptoms' being displayed are an adaptive response to the family situation, rather than problems in their own right. To remove the symptoms, you need to change the family circumstances. Strategic family therapy is an extension of structural family therapy rather than an alternative to it.

> *Milan.* This school of family therapy takes an approach to family change characterized by neutrality. It is concerned with listening to each family member's views of the situation in an unbiased way and helping to identify ways of moving forward. It draws on techniques, such as 'hypothesizing' and 'circular questioning'. It involves a consideration of first order cybernetics (interactions within the family) and second order cybernetics (interactions between the family and the therapist/s).

> *Bowen.* A key concept in Bowen's (1978) approach is that of anxiety. It is presented, though, not so much as an individual psychological concept, as a variable within the family system. Bowen conceives of the therapist as a 'coach', helping family members control their reactions to situations (based on the idea that one person's reactions will influence the reactions of others within the family). 'Differentiation of self' is an important part of this. It refers to the ability to maintain a balance between thinking and feeling and not allowing emotions to take over.

However, in recent years, new approaches influenced by social constructionist and postmodernist thinking have emerged. These have arisen in response to criticisms of traditional approaches that they pay inadequate attention to power dynamics (for example, gender relations within families) and wider issues of social processes. A key feature of more recent developments is a reliance on the concept of 'narratives' – the stories that are a key feature of how we make sense of our lives – for example, the post-Milan approach which emphasizes the role of narrative (Flaskas, 2002). (See also **narrative approaches** below.) In some ways this can be seen as a development of the traditional family therapy concept of 'family scripts' – the idea that families establish patterns of behaviour based on institutionalized meanings (that is, meanings that have built up over time and become firmly entrenched).

Principle 1 Social Context

Earlier forms of family therapy neglected the social context.

Some social workers will work in settings that specialize in family therapy (child and adolescent mental health services typically draw heavily on family therapy), while many others may use it as one tool among many. Additionally, a large number of social workers will not necessarily use formal family therapy methodology, but may none the less draw on family therapy understandings as part of their work.

groupwork Social work has a long history of individual casework – that is, interventions geared towards working on a one-to one basis with individual clients. Given that each client is a unique individual in their own right and the problems they face will be largely unique to them, a personalized, 'tailor-made' approach is clearly one that has much to commend it. However, while the uniqueness of the individual is an important value, we should not allow this to blind us to the fact that clients often have much in common in terms of both the problems they encounter and the possible solutions available to them. Groupwork seeks to exploit this in a positive way by bringing people together to identify shared problems and explore the possibility of shared solutions where the individuals concerned can support one another in making progress. As Doel and Sawdon comment:

> Groups can provide a more effective environment to experience empowerment because they can be used to replicate or simulate the larger society; in many respects they are microcosms of the wider society, but more amenable to change, at both a personal and a group level.　　　　(1999, p. 13)

Groupwork typically involves a series of sessions at fixed intervals (say, weekly) involving a small number of people who have similar problems or who are in similar circumstances. The sessions are facilitated by one or two staff who will try to:

> - develop a good atmosphere in the groups where people can relax and focus on the important issues;
> - enable people to bond with one another as far as possible to create a basis for mutual support;
> - influence the group dynamics in a positive way;
> - use the group process as a means of identifying: (i) common problems; and (ii) potential shared solutions; and
> - exploit opportunities to boost confidence and develop skills.

The sessions can vary from being quite structured at one extreme to very free-floating at the other. The theoretical underpinnings can also vary considerably, including psychodynamic, behavioural and task centred. Groupwork can also vary in terms of the following:

> - *The purpose of the group.* Why has the group been set up? What are you hoping to achieve? Is there scope for negotiation with group members or is the group's purpose pre-defined?
> - *The size of the group.* Groups can range in size from three or four to over 20, although at the top end of this range, it is unlikely that the groups will get maximum benefit from the process. Six to 12 is normally a good range to aim for.
> - *Whether it is open or closed.* Are you restricting membership to those who are part of the group to begin with or will you allow new members to join at a later stage? There is no easy answer to this question. A lot will depend on the nature and character of the group and: (i) how responsive they are likely to be to new members; (ii) whether one or more new members will significantly (and detrimentally) alter the group dynamics; and (iii) whether the proposed new member is ready for joining the group in terms of where it is up to and whether it is likely to be of benefit to him or her.
> - *The timescales involved.* Groups can be set up for a fixed period of time – for example, a parenting skills group over, say, an eight-week period. Alternatively, they can be ongoing (a support group for people who attend a mental

health day centre, for example), with no finite finishing point.

> *Membership of the group.* Who will be eligible to be a member? What criteria will be used to decide? What difference might it make to the group in terms of its overall composition?

> *The range of activities.* Will it be primarily a discussion group or will there be other activities used? If the latter, what will their purpose be? What form will they take?

Groupwork is not as widely used as it once was, but it is none the less a very valuable approach that can have a lot of success. We should not allow the current strong emphasis on individualist approaches to discourage us from considering a groupwork approach.

humanistic/person-centred approaches

This is a broad-based approach that draws on a number of theoretical perspectives, including the human potential movement (Heron, 2001; Maslow, 1970) and the work of Carl Rogers (1951, 1961). Rogers' work has been particularly influential in counselling and psychotherapy as well as in social work. The basic idea underpinning this approach is that people have great potential for growth and development, but that this potential needs to be nurtured and supported if it is to be realized – a process often referred to as 'self-actualization'.

According to humanist or person-centred approaches, the social work role is that of helping individuals fulfil their potential – for example, by identifying obstacles to progress and personal growth and exploring ways of removing or sidestepping them or, failing that, reducing their impact. Important principles are:

> *Genuineness.* Being genuine means not putting on an act, allowing one's own personality and values to be the basis of our approach. It involves not being manipulative or 'playing games'.

> *Empathy.* Having the skills of 'empathy' means being able to recognize, and respond appropriately to, other people's feelings. This is contrasted with 'sympathy', which means actually sharing those feelings.

> *A non-directive approach.* The role of the social worker involves helping people realize their potential and this cannot be done by

giving directions or instructions. It is a matter of helping people find their own way forward.

> *Self-determination.* Clients need to take responsibility for their own actions and recognize the choices they need to make and the actions they need to take. This is the other side of the coin to a non-directive approach.

> *Warmth.* Working relationships need to be based on warmth. Cold, clinical relationships are doomed to failure as these will not motivate people to move forward, and so it is important that we show warmth – and, linked to the comments above, this needs to be genuine warmth.

To put this approach into practice requires us to be able to recognize what factors in a situation are holding people back when it comes to solving their own problems or healing their own wounds, as it were.

NOS Key Role 3

Support individuals to represent their needs, views and circumstances

It has much in common with the strengths perspective, as discussed in Part 3, in so far as it involves avoiding seeing people as weak and 'inadequate' and, instead, focusing on how the potential for growth and development can be realized. Although this approach developed long before the language of empowerment was brought into use, it can be seen as an important part of developing empowering forms of practice.

Humanistic and person-centred approaches are often linked with existentialist theory, and there are certainly degrees of overlap in places. However, there are two key differences. The first is that humanism is based on the idea that people are fundamentally good and that it is other factors (the influence of negative, harmful experiences, of other people or of society more broadly, for example) that lead people away from that essentially good nature. Existentialism rejects this as essentialist and argues instead that there is no fixed human nature – rather, it is a case of human behaviour being dependent on the interaction of the choices we make and the influence of the circumstances in which we make them and *not* predetermined by any inherent 'goodness'. The second key difference is that existentialism is deeply rooted in a *sociopolitical* understanding of human existence and the need for practice to be informed by an understanding of wider issues, such as social structures, power relations, cultural formations and so on. This is in stark contrast to the individualism of humanistic or person-centred approaches which traditionally neglect the wider context.

narrative approaches The basis of narrative approaches is the idea that social reality is maintained through a set of stories or 'narratives'. These are partly rooted in culture and society around us (see **social constructionism** below), but are also partly created in and by our interactions with one another and our own sense of identity. Narratives can be helpful and empowering, but they can also be self-defeating and negative, a barrier to progress. The crux of narrative approaches to helping is working with people to assist them in 'rewriting' negative or problematic narratives and replacing them with positive, life-enhancing ones.

Principle 2 Empowerment and Partnership
Narrative approaches focus very closely on empowerment and partnership through the idea of co-authoring new narratives.

Problematic narratives include:

> *Self-blame.* Blaming oneself without taking account of the wider social circumstances or the role of others.

> *'Victim' mentality.* Not challenging other people's tendency to put the label of 'victim' on some people in certain circumstances.

> *'It's not my place'.* Internalized assumptions about gender roles can hold people (especially women) back from pursuing particular opportunities.

> *'What do you expect at your age?'.* Ageist assumptions can be very inhibiting in terms of the limitations they bring, and older people themselves are not immune from ageist influences and can therefore be disempowered by them.

These are just a small selection of the 'stories' that can both contribute to the problems people experience and hold them back from dealing with them.

One form of narrative approach is 'constructive social work' (Parton and O'Byrne, 2000). It makes good use of the narrative concept, as the following passage indicates:

> Women of all ages frequently complain of depression. As *constructive social workers* we have a problem with this as we feel it is a story imposed on people by a discourse based on pathology being the explanation of problems and expertise being required to diagnose and treat them. Even if such treatment works the person is left in a dependent role, still unable to have control of their own life. Addiction to Prozac is only another kind of misery; urges may be muffled but one can still be out of touch with one's own body. As Furman and Ahola (1992) say, these diagnoses can be self-verifying and 'watchful wording' is needed to develop an alternative story of self-control.
> (Parton and O'Byrne, 2000, p. 168)

As we have emphasized, social work arises from the interaction between individuals and the social context. This is just as true in terms of narrative approaches, as the narratives arise partly from a personal interpretation of the circumstances the individual concerned encounters and partly from the cultural formations of the wider society – the narratives or discourses that go to make up the cultural level of the society of which we form a part.

Social work practice based on a narrative approach would involve helping people to understand their problems in terms of the narratives they have developed and thus to look for ways of 're-authoring' those narratives that are unhelpful and help translate them into more positive, affirming narratives in which they have greater control. The expertise of the worker is not that of an expert solution finder, but rather of someone who has expertise in supporting people in moving from internalized negative, restrictive narratives towards more empowering ones.

Principle 1 The Social Context
While narratives are deeply personal, they also have their roots in the social sphere.

This approach is being used more and more in social work, in particular in mental health, in work with people who have been abused and, as we noted earlier, family therapy. However, there is no reason why it needs to be restricted to these fields. Indeed, it can be a useful basis for empowering forms of practice across a wide range of settings. For example, the use of meaning reconstruction theory (Neimeyer and Anderson, 2002) in working with people who have experienced major losses is further evidence of how the concept of narrative can be of great help.

Principle 5 Loss and Grief

Narratives provide a way of making sense of a major loss in a person's life.

Narrative approaches, with their roots in social constructionism, draw on the philosophical discipline of phenomenology and are therefore compatible with existentialism, as discussed earlier.

postmodernism This is a very complex set of philosophical ideas, and is used in very different ways by different theorists across different disciplines (including sociology, political theory, literary criticism, media studies and architecture). Basically it can be understood as the historical development of ideas from, first of all, an age of superstition and irrational beliefs prior to the Enlightenment (a seventeenth- and eighteenth-century intellectual movement that celebrated the use of reason and the development of knowledge). Following the Enlightenment, we had the Age of Reason characterized by an emphasis on science rather than religion. At this time, it was felt that there would be progress through science – for example, through medical science having a major impact on ill health and disease. This new era of rationalism and science became known as modernity.

Postmodernism is based on the idea that we are now entering a period of 'postmodernity'. This approach challenges the notion that science will bring inevitable progress. It contends that this belief in the power of rationality is a myth. It argues that society is characterized by what it calls 'fragmentation', a splintering into subsections with no overall, overarching connection through science or rationality. Consider, for example, the Internet, the multiple sources of information that are so varied,

disparate and dispersed. This is a good example of fragmentation, the notion of a steady march of progress being replaced with the idea of modern life or, rather, postmodern life being characterized by difference, multiplicity and diversity.

Postmodernism is critical of grand theories or 'metanarratives'. Postmodernist theory tries to be more situated or specific, smaller and less ambitious in its scope in terms of what it tries to achieve. It is very suspicious of overarching theories like marxism and functionalism that try to incorporate too much into their scope.

Postmodernism can be divided into two main schools: weak and strong. This distinction is particularly significant in relation to anti-discriminatory practice. This is because the strong version is not compatible with anti-discriminatory practice (or indeed social work as a whole), as it argues that progress in terms of emancipation is not possible, that it is a 'modernist myth'. The weak form of postmodernism is less rejecting of the idea of emancipatory progress, but it none the less places limits on how much can be achieved through human efforts to make progress. As Pease and Fook put it:

> we side with those expressions of postmodern thinking that do not totally abandon the values of modernity and the Enlightenment project of human emancipation. Only 'strong' or 'extreme' forms of postmodern theory reject normative criticism and the usefulness of any forms of commonality underlying diversity. We believe that a 'weak' form of postmodernism informed by critical theory can contribute effectively to the construction of an emancipatory politics concerned with political action and social justice.   (Pease and Fook, 1999a, p. 12)

Postmodernism has become an influential school of thought, although: (i) it is often confused with poststructuralism (to be discussed below); and (ii) the implications for practice are only barely sketched out at present and are to a large extent shrouded in confusion. It has become a very fashionable school of thought, but there are already signs that it is on the wane – see Sibeon, 2004.

One important aspect of postmodernist thought is its rejection of what is known as 'foundationalism', the idea that there are underlying foundations of truth that shape reality. The anti-foundationalism inherent in postmodernist thought is based on the idea that social reality is fluid and free-floating, not rooted in essentialist fundamental truths. This has implications for social work in terms of recognizing that the values on which our work is based are entities that we see as important and need to promote, not underlying realities that will emerge without our efforts to make them a reality.

poststructuralism This is an approach to theory closely linked with postmodernism. In essence, it is a reaction to, and rejection of, earlier theories of structuralism which were associated with thinkers like Lévi-Strauss who believed that underlying deep structures (for example, kinship relationships) had profound influences on different cultures – that is, while the surface manifestations of cultures may be different, there may be some elements of underlying similarity. This structuralist approach was dominant for a long time, particularly in anthropology. However, with the development of thought by such writers as Foucault (Faubion, 2002), this structuralism has been increasingly challenged.

Petersen and colleagues explain poststructuralism in the following terms:

> When we use the term poststructuralism here, we take it to mean that school of thought which is opposed to and seeks to move beyond the premises of structuralism, to develop new models of thought, writing and subjectivity. As Best and Kellner explain, structuralism focuses in the underlying rules which organise phenomena into a social system and aims at objectivity, coherence, rigour and truth. Structuralists seek to describe social phenomena in terms of linguistic and social structures, rules, codes and systems, and to develop grand, synthesising theories (Best and Kellner 1991: 19). Examples of structuralist analysis include Marxism and functionalist sociology. Poststructuralists, on the other hand, focus on the inextricable and diffuse linkages between power and knowledge, and on how individuals are constructed as subjects and given unified identities or

subject positions. That is, they focus on micro politics and on subjectivity, difference and everyday life. (1999, p. 3)

Foucault wrote of 'discourses'. Literally a discourse is a conversation. Foucault used it in a wider sense to mean pieces of language and, indeed, reactions associated with those uses of language which form 'sets' and which are very influential in how we see the world. A discourse, then, is a powerful framework of meaning, as, for example, in the case of 'managerialist discourse', in which certain concepts (the importance of measurement, for example) become established as taken-for-granted assumptions. This concept of discourse is also widely used by postmodernists, although Foucault himself explicitly rejected the label of 'postmodernist'.

Tew offers helpful comment:

> A discourse may comprise a body of related writings or conversations that construct a particular mode of understanding – for example, the strictures around correct discipline to be found in late nineteenth-century childcare manuals (see Miller 1983). It may comprise non-linguistic forms, such as the representation of women in Pre-Raphaelite art, or the symbolisation of the state and the party within Soviet architecture. It may also comprise sets of practices that signify certain meanings, for example, the rituals around medical consultations which construct doctor as expert and patient as passive recipient. All such discourses have the potential to situate people in particular (power) relationships to one another, or to specific social institutions or apparatuses. (Tew, 2002, p. 69)

In terms of the implications for social work, poststructuralism means that we should be asking ourselves: What discourses are operating here? How are people's perceptions of the situation being shaped by dominant forms of thought and language use? For example, in dealing with someone with mental health problems, to assume that they are suffering from a mental illness is to adopt what Foucault would call a medical discourse, with such powerful underlying notions as 'doctor knows best' and 'doctor's orders'. An alternative discourse would be to see such matters as being in the realms of an individual experiencing mental distress as a result of wider social pressures (discrimination, for example). Another example of the significance of the notion of discourse would be in relation to dependency. Social work has long been criticized for 'looking after' people (disabled people, for example) rather than helping them to achieve their rights. We can therefore see that, over the years, social work has moved from a discourse of dependency to a discourse of rights and empowerment.

psychodynamics This is a term that originates in a work of Sigmund Freud, but has been developed over the years by many others – for example, Erikson, Klein and Lacan. To understand what the term means, it is helpful to break it down into its component parts. This is 'psycho', which comes from the Greek word 'psyche', meaning mind, and 'dynamics' which means the interactions of different elements which influence each other. So, in short, psychodynamics is the study of how different elements within the mind influence one another.

Freud's theory was based on the idea of three particular elements within the mind, id, ego and superego. The id is a collection of desires and drives comprising what we know as Eros (or libido) and Thanatos (or destructive urges – sometimes also referred to as the 'death instinct'). Eros is about the translation of sexual energies into everyday activities. The theory behind Eros is that the libido is primarily a sexual force which becomes 'sublimated' into energy directed in other ways. Sublimation is the process of making basically socially unacceptable sexual drives acceptable by redirecting them into work, study, the arts, sport, politics and so on. Thanatos is the other side of the coin, in so far as it refers to drives that are destructive in nature. The combination of Eros and Thanatos makes up the id.

Alongside the id is the superego. This is a term that refers to what is often known as the conscience. It represents the internalization of one's parents and the values and expectations they have instilled in us over the years. As we are brought up, we develop a conscience, as if the voice of our parents were in our head, telling us what we can and cannot do in order to be

accepted within society. The superego is therefore in some respects a counterbalance to the id. The id is selfish, in the sense that it is concerned with our own needs and wishes, perhaps at the expense of others. The superego, by contrast, is concerned with ensuring that we are able to live side by side with one another in society or, as Freud called it, 'civilization'. The ego is the balancing mechanism between the id and the superego. That is, if we understand the workings of the human mind as being to some extent a battle between personal drives and wishes, and the requirements of broader society for order, co-operation and so on, then we can see the role of the ego as being the referee, as it were. It seeks to produce a balanced individual, someone who is not overly concerned with their own wishes and feelings, but nor someone who neglects those for the wider concerns of the conscience.

A phrase commonly associate with Freud's work is: 'where id was, there shall ego be'. This is because Freud felt that many of the problems people encountered in their lives were due to their id being too strong and uncontrolled. Too strong an id can lead to antisocial behaviour due to a lack of self-control and therefore a tendency towards self-indulgence, perhaps at society's expense. This can also be manifested in terms of over-indulgence – for example, in the development of alcohol problems. It can also be argued that child abuse, particularly sexual abuse, is due to too strong an id on the part of the abuser, that he or she feels unable to control their basic urges. However, according to this theory, psychological problems can also arise where the superego is too strong. This can manifest itself in terms of neurotic, over-anxious behaviour and a lack of confidence.

Within psychodynamics, then, the role of the social worker is to boost the functioning of the ego, to make sure that neither id nor superego dominate, but rather provide a balance.

Another key part of Freud's theory of psychodynamics is the role of the unconscious. By this he means that we may be acting on id drives without realizing we are doing so. This has become a very influential notion now often taken for granted and sometimes used uncritically. The basic idea behind the unconscious is that some aspects of the human mind are easily understandable to the individual concerned, whereas other aspects, like the iceberg, remain below the surface and can only be accessed with the help of someone who understands how psychodynamics works (a psychoanalyst, for example).

There have been some efforts to link psychodynamics with a sociological perspective (for example, Mitchell's, 2000, work on feminism) but this has been largely undeveloped. Sartre (1958) has written about psychodynamics from an existentialist perspective, but this is a very different approach from that of Freud and the psychodynamics used in social work.

Freudian psychodynamics can be criticized for a serious lack of attention to the social context. This is a major weakness.

Psychodynamics was at one time a very dominant approach to social work and, while its dominance has long since waned, it still remains a significant influence in a number of ways.

radical social work First generation radical social work developed in the late 1960s and early 1970s. It was a reaction against the highly individualized psychodynamically oriented social work prevalent at that time. Radical social work laid the foundations for anti-discriminatory practice by emphasizing the social roots of many of the difficulties that clients faced. It adopted an explicitly political approach, arguing that social work needed to ally itself with oppressed groups against the forces in society that served to keep them in positions of subservience and relative powerlessness.

Principal 1 Social Context

The emergence of radical social work played a significant part in the development of a more sociologically informed approach to theory and practice.

The term 'radical' refers to an approach that seeks to tackle problems 'at the roots' – that is, at a sociopolitical level, rather than at the level of the individual or family. This perspective was therefore critical of individual casework and set much more store by groupwork and community development methods – approaches that are basically collective in nature. Informed primarily

by marxist theory, radical social work never became a dominant approach, although it was quite influential in a number of ways. In terms of the long-standing 'reform vs. revolution' debate in politics, radical social work came down very clearly in favour of revolution, in so far as it recognized that social problems are rooted in social structures and processes, rather than in personal inadequacies that require casework. Politicization (see Part 3) was one of its main tools and contributing to social change was its major aim.

However, the original version of this approach has been heavily criticized for being too simplistic and failing to recognize the subtleties and complexities of the social (work) world. It did, none the less, provide an important platform for the later development of emancipatory forms of practice and a clearer focus on the political and sociological dimensions of social work. The need to move from the earlier, first generation radical social work towards the more sophisticated forms of anti-discriminatory practice we have today is captured in Jan Fook's comments:

> As a young social worker in the 1970s, I graduated with an awareness that casework was seen as inherently conservative and that community work was seen as the 'right-minded' path to follow. Yet this simple dichotomy did not seem to fit the world of my early practice. I worked with people in my first job who, although strong and empowered volunteers – some of them trailblazers in the field of intellectual disability services – still needed emotional support, and sometimes more explicit counselling, to help them cope with the daily stresses of parenting children with intellectual disabilities.
>
> (Pease and Fook, 1999a, pp. 4–5)

What this passage illustrates well is the importance of *incorporating* an understanding of wider structural factors into social work's psychosocial tradition, rather than using political and sociological insights to *displace* other important aspects of the knowledge base.

Second generation radical social work is often referred to as 'critical practice', based on the tradition of critical theory which Tew defines in the following terms:

The term 'critical theory' has been used in a variety of contexts with different meanings, but always indicating an approach which seeks not to take things at face value, but to probe beneath the surface in order to find what may lie hidden there.   (2002, p. 17)

Principle 3 `Critical Analysis`

Radical social work also contributed to a focus on critical analysis in social work practice.

In relation to radical social work, what can be seen to lie 'beneath the surface' is a complex web of social and political factors that play a significant role in shaping the problems clients experience and which can act as barriers to dealing with those problems.

NOS Key Role 1

Prepare for, and work with, individuals, families, carers, groups and communities to assess their needs and circumstances

Although the term 'radical social work' is rarely used these days, second-generation radicalism in the form of anti-discriminatory practice can be seen as a significant development of the earlier approach, incorporating its strengths in terms of the need to draw on political and sociological insights, but without falling into the trap of the reductionism and oversimplification that characterized the first incarnation of this approach.

`social constructionism` This refers to an approach to theorizing rather than a specific theory itself. It can be characterized by four main themes:

1. *Reality is 'socially constructed'.* Berger and Luckmann (1967) is generally recognized as a classic text of social constructionism. The authors argued that reality is not simply 'given' in any direct sense. Our understanding of reality is something we have to build up ('construct') partly through subjective understandings of the world. However, those subjective perceptions have their roots in society, in so far as they are in large part shaped by culture.
2. *Knowledge is historically and culturally specific.* What counts for 'knowledge' will

vary over time and from culture to culture. That is, our understanding of the world will depend on the historical circumstances we find ourselves in (for example, we no longer think of the world as being flat) and our cultural background (for example, cultural values will shape our perception of the outside world – cultures draw attention to certain aspects of reality, but mask or overlook others). This means that there can be no definitive understanding of a fixed 'human nature'. Society is constantly changing and our ways of understanding change with it.

3. *Knowledge and action are interrelated.* What we know influences what we do. What we do influences what we know. This applies both individually and socially. This is important in terms of how we regard social problems – what constitutes a social problem is socially defined. That is, social problems are socially constructed. Burr illustrates this in the following example:

> before the Temperance movement, drunks were seen as entirely responsible for their behaviour, and therefore blameworthy. A typical response was therefore imprisonment. However, there has been a movement away from seeing drunkenness as a crime and towards thinking of it as a sickness, a kind of addiction. 'Alcoholics' are not seen as totally responsible for their behaviour, since they are the victims of a kind of drug addiction. The social action appropriate to understanding drunkenness in this way is to offer medical and psychological treatment, not imprisonment.   (Burr, 1995, p. 5)

In this respect, social constructionism has much in common with Foucault's notion of discourse – see the discussion of **poststructuralism** earlier in this chapter.

4. *Language plays a key role.* Language acts as an intermediary between individuals and society. It is not only a system of communication, but also a system of social representation and, as such, is very influential in shaping how we see the world (that is, in constructing our reality).

The situation is nicely summed up in the following passage:

> If language is a central means by which we carry on our lives together – carrying the past into the present to create the future – then our ways of talking and writing become key targets of concern.
> (Gergen, 1999, p. 62)

In some respects, social constructionism overlaps with other theoretical perspectives discussed in this chapter, namely existentialism, postmodernism and poststructuralism.

This is a perspective that has significant implications for social work, not least the following:

> ❯ We cannot assume that the way a social worker sees the world and the way the individuals we are trying to help see it will be the same – they may be vastly different, and in some ways incompatible.

NOS Key Role 1

Prepare for, and work with, individuals, families, carers, groups and communities to assess their needs and circumstances

> ❯ We therefore need to take account of how each of us sees the situation we are working on if we are to be able to work in partnership.
> ❯ The meanings people attach to events will be very significant. Practice involves not only offering 'objective' services, but also engaging with subjective understandings.
> ❯ The best help we may be able to give people is to assist them in renegotiating (or 're-authoring') the meanings they attach to parts of their lives (oppressive, disempowering meanings, for example – see **narrative approaches** above).

solution-focused therapy This is an approach associated primarily with the work of de Shazer (1982, 1985, 1991). It has much in common with **the strengths perspective** discussed in Part 3 and with **narrative approaches** discussed above. It is concerned with helping people make progress in dealing with their problems by focusing on the 'exceptions' – those times when the problem does not apply, when it could have been present but ~~~ , or when it is experienced less frequently

or less intensely. For example, in dealing with a problem of anxiety, the helper would assist the person concerned in identifying situations when he or she does not feel anxious or feels less anxious. This then provides a foundation from which possible solutions can be developed – for example, by establishing what is different in those circumstances when the problem features less (or not at all) and trying to use such differences as a way forward. It can be used to enable people to look at the strengths they have and how they can draw on these more fully to resolve their difficulties.

Solution-focused therapy is in large part a reaction to psychodynamically oriented theories that seek solutions from developing a detailed knowledge of the problems and their roots. De Shazer's view is that the solution does not need to be related to the problem. For example, the reasons why somebody became a person prone to anxiety do not really matter if that person can construct a solution to the problem of anxiety.

'Constructing a solution' is a key part of this approach and, as language is the means by which such construction takes place, language issues become very important (hence the link with narrative therapy). A common technique is what is known as the 'miracle question', which is explained by Parton and O'Byrne:

> According to this approach an important technique in helping people formulate goals, to express what they want and to start looking to the future, is the 'miracle question'. It goes like this:
>
> > 'Suppose that when you leave here, you go out and do what you are having to do, you get home, have something to eat and later go to bed; and while you are asleep something miraculous/magical happens and the problems that brought you here vanish, in the click of a finger; but because you were asleep you don't know this has happened. When you wake up in the morning what will be the first thing you will notice that will tell you that this has happened?' (Based on various versions from de Shazer and Berg)
>
> ... In this way the solution is constructed without discussing the problem or how it can

be overcome. People's affect can undergo a major change, as they describe and construct with the worker an alternative way of being. This is often the beginning of the hope that is necessary to get things started. The most important thing this question does is that it disconnects the problem from the solution and as other people's reactions are talked about it generates interactional descriptions; talking about other people's reactions and conversation reinforces the changes and their possibility. (Parton and O'Byrne, 2000, p. 103)

This is an approach that has much to offer, as it can be very effective. It focuses on strengths and can therefore be an important part of empowerment, as it is a matter of helping people solve their own problems, rather than trying to do it for them. As social workers we can use this approach by helping people identify 'exceptions' and from this map out possible ways of constructing alternative scenarios and thus possible solutions. Solution-focused therapy is part of a broader school of 'brief therapy' which is concerned with methods of resolving difficulties and making progress that do not rely on long-term programmes of intervention.

Principle 2 Empowerment and Partnership

The focus on strengths and potential solutions makes this a potentially very empowering approach.

systematic practice This is a long-standing approach to practice that emphasizes the importance of clarity of focus. It recognizes that the pressures of work can lead practitioners to 'lose the plot', to become unfocused and drift because they have lost sight of the purpose of their intervention. In dealing with the messy, complicated situations that are so common in social work it is not surprising that there is a very real danger of losing our focus and getting drawn into other dynamics that can lead us away from our role. For example, if we are not careful, we can become 'general family helpers' and end up encouraging dependency unwittingly because we have allowed the pressures we face to confuse the issues and thus blur our vision of why we are involved and what outcomes we are supposed to be working towards.

Neil Thompson (2002b) discusses systematic practice and proposes a framework for using this approach. It involves addressing the following three questions:

> ❭ *What are you trying to achieve?* What outcomes are you aiming for? What needs are to be met? What problems need to be solved?
> ❭ *How are you going to achieve it?* What steps need to be taken? What needs to change? What resources need to be drawn on?
> ❭ *How will you know when you have achieved it?* What will success look like? How will you know that no further work is needed? How will you know when to celebrate success and congratulate clients on their achievements?

The first question helps us to make sure that we are clear about the purpose of our intervention – it is very easy for this to become muddled and very fuzzy in the 'swampy lowlands' of practice, as Schön (1983) calls them, with competing and multiple demands (some of which are compatible with the social work role, some of which are not). The second question helps us to establish a plan, to be clear about what specific steps need to be taken, by whom, when and so on. These are both important questions. However, the third question is particularly important as it helps to make sure that we have answered the first two appropriately. This is because, if we have been too vague or unfocused in answering the first two questions, we will struggle to answer the third.

NOS Key Role 2

Plan, carry out, review and evaluate social work practice, with individuals, families, carers, groups, communities, and other professionals

The third question will also enable us to determine when we can conclude our involvement. This is important in terms of empowerment, as we should be very careful to ensure that we do not stay involved longer than is necessary and thereby encourage dependency (and also waste important social work resources).

Principle 2 Empowerment and Partnership

The focus on clear goals avoids dependency and provides a sound basis for empowerment.

It is important to note that this approach is intended to be carried out in partnership. That is, it is not simply a matter of the social worker deciding what is to be achieved, how it will be achieved and so on. Rather, these are matters to be addressed together, to be negotiated rather than imposed.

There are (at least) three clear benefits to systematic practice:

> The clarity and focus can be a source of confidence and security for clients, as they can help bring a sense of order to what are often chaotic circumstances.
> The clarity and focus can be a source of confidence and security for the worker also. Social work is a demanding activity, characterized by considerable complexity and variability, as well as dilemmas and contradictions. We therefore need to make good use of approaches that offer a means of managing the complexity without descending into chaos.
> It provides a firm basis for professional practice in terms of accountability – systematic practice offers a transparent approach to social work tasks.

This is not intended to be a rigid approach. While the three key questions provide a useful framework to guide practice, there is no reason why it cannot be used flexibly – that is, the questions should be reviewed from time to time to check that they are still applicable.

importance of review, see p. 49

Principle 6 Realism and Challenge

Systematic practice helps to prepare us for the significant challenges involved in social work.

systems theory This is a theoretical approach that has been widely used in social work across a variety of settings and client groups, although it is not without its critics. Its main tenet is that the social world is made up of a set of interconnected systems and subsystems. In order to promote change in one part of the system it may be necessary to change another part of the system, and so 'systemic' social work is concerned with influencing the workings of systems (as *family therapy* does in intervening

in family systems). The types of systems to be considered include:

> family (current family arrangements and family of origin);
> friends and social contacts;
> workplace networks;
> community groups; and
> social systems, such as health care, social security and education

The roots of systems theory are in biology (the human body being seen as a set of interacting systems – the nervous system, the musculo-skeletal system and so on) and forms of sociology influenced by biological analogies (primarily the structural-functionalism of Talcott Parsons, 1967). Problems in one part of the system (or in one subsystem) can have a detrimental effect on another part of the system (or another subsystem).

The strengths of systems theory are: (i) it broadens the focus beyond the individual and thus moves away from individualistic models that can 'pathologize' clients by assuming that the problems lie within the individual; and (ii) it provides a platform for developing a more sociological approach. Its drawbacks, by contrast are: (i) it fails to fulfil its potential for addressing sociological issues – in particular, it does not take account of power relations and related concepts of discrimination and oppression; and (ii) it has a tendency to be dehumanizing – losing track of the people dimension of social work. In this regard, Forte is critical of the 'mechanistic imagery' in the descriptions of society that systems theory uses:

Society and its subsystems are not best conceived of as sets of 'forces' or 'imperatives' determining collective and individual behaviour. Other common systems concepts like 'inputs', 'outputs', 'throughputs', 'gearing', 'function' and push-pull notions of communication also seem alien and dehumanizing. These are ideas that are borrowed from 'models that are foreign to the social sciences' (Joas, 1996, p. 231). Furthermore, these terms suggest a theory without real people (Wolfe, 1992).

(Forte, 2001, p. 221)

Since the 1970s systems theory has been enormously influential in social work (and elsewhere too – for example, in management theory). In fact, it has over the years been taken for granted in many quarters as a basic foundation of social work thinking. However, its dominance is now clearly waning, as its roots in the inherently conservative model of structural-functionalism make it ill-equipped to respond to the challenges of anti-discriminatory practice. The growth of interest in postmodernist and poststructuralist approaches has also added to the growing dissatisfaction with systems approaches.

Despite its shortcomings, the legacy of systems theory is a positive one, in so far as it has played a part in helping us move away from the psychodynamic emphasis on the individual towards a more sociologically adequate approach. However, it is not sufficiently sophisticated to take that journey to its conclusion. As Neil Thompson comments:

> In short, the irony of the systems approach's model of society is that it does not account for the macro-level systems which operate in society. It has gone beyond the level of individual pathology but does not go far enough.   (1992, p. 99)

One development from systems theory has been the growth of interest in what have become known as 'ecological' approaches. These involve linking social work issues to wider environmental issues. Jack and Jack (2000) argue that ecological approaches have the potential to incorporate an understanding of social structural issues. However, it would seem that such a venture can be successful only by detaching itself from the inherent conservatism of systems theory and its biological roots.

Principle 1 Social Context

Although systems theory addresses aspects of the social context, it also neglects significant elements of it.

task-centred practice The basic idea behind task-centred practice is that people can be helped to tackle their problems and achieve their goals through a structured process of identifying the steps that need to be taken to get them to their required destination. It basically involves three stages:

① *What is the current situation?* This involves assessing the current set of circumstances and establishing what is problematic about them – that is, being clear about why this situation is unhelpful, undesirable or painful. What is it that is motivating us to want to make changes to the current arrangements?

② *What situation do we want to be in?* What is our desired destination? In other words, what situation would we be happy to be in and how does it differ from the one we are in? in this way we are mapping out what needs to change.

③ *What tasks need to be completed to get us from where we are now to where we want to be?* What steps do we need to take to make progress from a problematic situation to one that we are happy with?

Effective practice with this method involves:

❯ Being clear about precisely what is problematic; a vague or unfocused approach is unlikely to work.

❯ Similarly, being clear about what is desirable, what outcomes we are working towards.

❯ Identifying specific tasks and being clear about what order they should be carried out in (it is wise to begin with easily achievable tasks to boost confidence and gain a sense of momentum).

❯ Agreeing to share or exchange tasks to develop a clear basis of partnership – this can help to develop a sense of security and again boost confidence and contribute to a sense of momentum.

❯ Making careful use of timescales – too tight a timescale will demotivate and set people up to fail, while too long a timescale may means that momentum is not built up and the situation is allowed to drift.

❯ Well-developed negotiation skills – it would be naïve to assume that there will always be a coincidence of interests between client and worker (for example, the worker m statutory obligations – in relation protection, perhaps – that conflic wishes of one or more members o

4

theories and theori

Task-centred practice is based on three important factors: motivation, security and partnership. Being clear about what is problematic, what situation is preferable, what needs to change and the specifics of how it can change can stimulate a great deal of motivation by: (i) identifying desirable targets to aim for and a means of achieving them; (ii) boosting the confidence needed to move forward. This approach also helps to create an important sense of security, often replacing feelings of confusion, uncertainty, isolation and defeatism with a sense of purpose and direction, renewed confidence and feelings of being supported.

NOS Key Role 2

Plan, carry out, review and evaluate social work practice, with individuals, families, carers, groups, communities, and other professionals

Task-centred practice is also founded on partnership and empowerment, as the whole process involves working together on the basis of establishing agreement about what needs to be done, who is going to do it, by when and so on. It therefore provides a basis for empowerment, as effective task-centred practice can boost problem-solving skills and thus give people greater control over their lives.

NOS Key Role 3

Support individuals to represent their needs, views and circumstances

A common misunderstanding of task-centred practice is that it is simply a matter of 'doing tasks' – a so-called 'pragmatic' approach that involves uncritically and non-reflectively doing whatever practical tasks seem to need doing at any given time. This is far removed from the structured and focused approach of task-centred practice which involves providing a framework for motivating and reassuring people in times of difficulty and for building confidence. The appropriate use of the approach also provides a good opportunity for clients to be helped in learning problem-solving skills – for example, through modelling.

transactional analysis This approach derives from the work of Berne (1970, 1975). It has its roots in a combination of psychodynamic and humanistic thinking and has proved very useful as a means of promoting effective communication and improving interpersonal relations. A major part of this approach is the attempt to understand interactions between people in terms of three 'ego states': parent (behaviour modelled on one or both of our parents), adult (responding to the here and now) or child (using patterns of behaviour or 'scripts' that we learned in childhood). Depending on what ego state a person adopts at a given time, this gives us various combinations when two people interact – for example, the following:

> *Parent–parent.* This represents a power struggle, where each participant is trying to dominate the other.
> *Parent–child.* In this combination, one person 'parents' the other. The person occupying the 'child' ego state leaves responsibility with the 'parent'.
> *Adult–adult.* This is a positive relationship, based on mutual respect, and is therefore something to aim for.
> *Child–child.* In this combination neither party is prepared to take (adult) responsibility – for example, when two people express dissatisfaction with a situation, but neither is prepared to do anything about it, as if waiting for a 'parent' to solve the problem for them.

These 'ego states' have a strong parallel with Freud's id (child), ego (adult) and superego (parent) – see the discussion of **psychodynamics** above. The main difference, however, is that, as the name implies, psychodynamics is concerned with interactions *within* the individual, whereas the focus of transactional analysis is interactions *between* people.

A further aspect of transactional analysis (or TA for short) is the use of the concept of 'strokes'. These can be positive (praise, encouragement and so on) or negative (criticism, discouragement and so on), and can be very influential in shaping how interactions (or 'transactions' as TA calls them) develop. Positive strokes are seen as an important part of meeting people's needs for recognition and thus self-esteem (see Part 3). This gives us a further useful concept to understand the complex dynamics of interpersonal interactions.

TA is also concerned with the notion of 'games'

in interpersonal interactions (one of the classic texts of TA is entitled *Games People Play* – Berne, 1970). Games are typical patterns of transaction that are unhelpful or destructive. For example, someone may patronize or even bully another person by characteristically adopting a parent–child approach to him or her.

Games, scripts and ego states can all influence what Harris (1995) calls 'life positions', of which there are four, as follows:

> *I'm OK – You're OK.* Your attitude to yourself and to others is positive. This is a good position to be in.
> *I'm OK – You're not OK.* Your attitude towards yourself is positive, but you have a negative attitude towards others. This means that you are likely to be critical of others, perhaps unfairly so.
> *I'm not OK – You're OK.* You have a negative attitude towards yourself, but are positive towards others. This may make you feel inferior and/or incompetent.
> *I'm not OK – You're not OK.* You have a negative attitude towards both yourself and others. This will tend to make you very critical of both yourself and others – a very negative mindset.

This is a further dimension of how TA can be used to analyse (and thus make sense of) complex interactions between people.

Transactional analysis can be used as a means of making sense of interactions that are going wrong in some way (creating tensions or failing to achieve effective communication, for example). This then gives us a foundation from which to explore the possibilities of helping to change those interactions. TA has much in common with humanist approaches, in so far as it is concerned with human potential and helping clients to develop their abilities by abandoning unhelpful 'child' scripts (ways of understanding situations and responding to them that we developed in our formative years) and adopting more 'adult' ones.

TA has good potential for **empowerment**, given its emphasis on human potential and the development of personal autonomy. However, it has little to say about the influence of broader social structures, culture and so on, although the potential does exist for developing the theory in that direction.

user involvement This is a general approach or underpinning philosophy rather than a specific technique. In recognizing and drawing on the expertise of users of services, it fits well with social work's value base, particularly in terms of empowerment and partnership. Involving service users in the planning and delivery of services was promoted as good practice as far back as the Seebohm Report in 1968 and, with a growing emphasis on rights, the movement in general has continued to gather strength over the last few decades, although not evenly across all client groups (Carter and Beresford, 2000; Evans and Banton, 2001; Thornton and Tozer, 1994). The NHS and Community Care Act 1990 imposed a duty on local authorities to include service users in the planning and delivery of services but, as with many concepts that are enshrined in law, involvement is a term that is open to interpretation and responses can be tokenistic while still adhering to legal requirements. For example, there is a big difference in terms of power sharing between, at one extreme, asking for feedback about decisions already made and, at the other, passing over control to service users in some form, and yet all points along this participation continuum (a term used by Hickey, 1994) have been claimed as user involvement initiatives.

Beresford, in discussing user participation in research, makes the following comment on what he sees as the dominant approach to user involvement:

> I'd headline this approach as a managerialist/consumerist one ... It has been presented as a non-political neutral technique for information gathering from service users, to provide a fuller picture on which to base policy and provision. Its role has never been framed in terms of altering the distribution of power or who makes the decisions.
>
> (Beresford, 2003, p. 3)

Addressing the power imbalance is something which goes beyond the practice of individuals. That is not to say that individuals cannot play an important part in the process – indeed, as we say elsewhere, working *with* people and drawing on *their* strengths are cornerstones of good practice. Rather, it is to say that this is not enough on its own. For there to be change at the level of organizational policy, there needs to be a change at the level of organizational culture – that is an acceptance that clients have a right to be involved in decisions which affect the welfare provision that is made available to them. If commitment to user involvement is not part of the value base of an organization, then it is unlikely that the changes which would allow for user involvement to become an integral part of the organization's philosophy and working practices (rather than an afterthought or response to a directive) would be made. Beresford and Croft highlighted the moral argument for user involvement when they wrote: 'having a say is also important in its own right. It shouldn't need any justifications. It reflects the value an agency or organisation places on people' (1993, p. 19).

NOS Key Role 3

Support individuals to represent their needs, views and circumstances

And so, while individual social workers drawing on the expertise and strengths of individual clients is a major part of what social work is about, this approach would argue that there is also much to be gained from addressing the unequal power imbalance at a broader level.

Proponents of user involvement would highlight the following types of initiative as indicative of a move away from an 'us and them' mindset:

> Having service user representation on interview panels in the selection process for social work degree courses.
> Inviting service users to take part in skills training on social work courses, rather than simulating through the use of role play.
> Involving service users at the level of planning and policy making rather than 'after the event', so that consultation is meaningful and the commitment to partnership genuine. While having a service user representative on committees and the like is a step in the right direction, it can be tokenistic, in the sense that it is unlikely to take account of the diversity within client groups.
> Incorporating a service user perspective in the assessment of competence of social work students on placement.

While there have been clear steps in the right direction in recent years, we still have a long way to go before this aspect of partnership working is given the attention it deserves.

Principle 2 Empowerment and Partnership

User involvement is a vitally important part of both empowerment and partnership.

4.3 conclusion

Part 4 cannot, of course, provide a detailed and comprehensive account of the theoretical underpinnings of social work. Our aim has been the much more modest one of providing a 'taster' of various aspects of the wide range of ideas and frameworks that inform social work practice across various settings. We hope that you have found our offerings both interesting and useful.

We have presented the 22 approaches in alphabetical order, but you may have noticed that some of them have interconnections and form part of particular 'schools' of thought. For example, social constructionism, narrative approaches and solution-focused approaches have a lot in common. However, such groupings of theoretical perspectives are neither simple nor clear cut. For example, we have included solution-focused approaches alongside social constructionism and narrative approaches, but they can also be linked with task-centred practice and systematic practice. Links can also be misleading. For example, systems theory and existentialism are both sociologically informed approaches, and yet they are poles apart in terms of how they address social issues. In short, then, attempts to connect theoretical positions together can lead us into a minefield of complex issues.

Perhaps what is more important than linking theories together is the task of linking them to practice. For some approaches, the links between theory and practice are quite clear, as with task-centred practice which offers a helpful practice method. With others, the links are more indirect and require a greater use of our reflective practice skills. However, what all the theoretical perspectives outlined here have in common is that they can all cast some degree of light on the challenges of practice that we face. Theory will not provide ready-made solutions or prescriptions for practice, but what it can do is provide the raw materials for us to make sense of the complex realities of social work.

theory and practice, see p. 142

NOS Key Role 6

Demonstrate professional competence in social work practice

Finally, we would remind you that both the 'Suggestions for further reading' overleaf and Part 7, the 'Guide to further learning', should be drawn upon as a gateway to further study. What we have presented here is only a beginning, and we wish you well in taking your learning forward by reading in more depth and detail about the important knowledge base that is available to us to make sure that our practice is *informed* practice.

> Why is theory important as a basis for practice?
> Which theoretical perspectives have you found most interesting? Why?
> Which theoretical perspectives have you found most useful? Why?
> Which theoretical perspectives surprised you? Why?
> Have you been able to note any patterns or interconnections across perspectives? If so, which ones?

suggestions for further reading

general texts about theory

Healy, K. (2005) *Social Work Theories in Context: Creating Frameworks for Practice*, Basingstoke, Palgrave Macmillan.

Payne, M. (2005) *Modern Social Work Theory*, 3rd edn, Basingstoke, Palgrave Macmillan.

Thompson, N. (2000) *Theory and Practice in Human Services*, 2nd edn, Buckingham, Open University Press.

anti-discriminatory practice

Bates, J. (2005) 'Embracing Diversity and Working in Partnership', in Carnwell and Buchanan (2005).

Brown, H. C. (1998) *Social Work and Sexuality: Working With Lesbians and Gay Men*, Basingstoke, Macmillan – now Palgrave Macmillan.

Daatland, S. O. and Biggs, S. (2006) *Ageing and Diversity: Multiple Pathways and Cultural Migrations*, Bristol, The Policy Press.

Fook, J. (2002) *Social Work: Critical Theory and Practice*, London, Sage.

Foster, J. (2001) 'Women in the Caring Professions: A Case in Point', in Baxter (2001).

Healy, K. (2005) *Social Work Theories in Context: Creating Frameworks for Practice*, Basingstoke, Palgrave Macmillan – Ch. 9 in particular.

Sapey, B., Stewart, J. and Harris, J. (2001) 'Disability: Constructing Dependency through Social Policy', in Baxter (2001).

Solomos, J. (2003) *Race and Racism in Britain*, 3rd edn, Basingstoke, Palgrave Macmillan.

Thompson, N. (2003) *Promoting Equality: Tackling Discrimination and Oppression*, 2nd edn, Basingstoke, Palgrave Macmillan.

Thompson, N. (2006) *Anti-Discriminatory Practice*, 4th edn, Basingstoke, Palgrave Macmillan.

Thompson, N. (2007) *Power and Empowerment*, Lyme Regis, Russell House Publishing.

Thompson, S. (2005) *Age Discrimination*, Lyme Regis, Russell House Publishing.

cognitive-behavioural approaches

Cigno, K. and Bourn, D. (eds) (1998) *Cognitive-Behavioural Social Work in Practice*, Aldershot, Ashgate.

Payne, M. (2005) *Modern Social Work Theory*, 3rd edn, Basingstoke, Palgrave Macmillan.

Sheldon, B (1995) *Cognitive-Behavioural Therapy: Research, Practice and Philosophy*, London, Routledge.

communicative action theory

Crossley, N. and Roberts, J. M. (eds)(2004) *After Habermas: New Perspectives on the Public Sphere*, Oxford, Blackwell Publishing.

Habermas, J. (1972) *Knowledge and Human Interests*, London, Heinemann.

Habermas, J. (1984) *Theory of Communicative Action*, Boston, MA, Beacon Press.

Habermas, J. (1987) *The Theory of Communicative Action Vol 2: Lifeworld and the Rationalization of Society*, Boston, MA, Beacon Press.

community work

Dominelli, L. (2006) *Women and Community Action*, Bristol, The Policy Press.

Popple, K. (2002) 'Community Work', in Adams et al. (2002b).

Twelvetrees, A. (2001) *Community Work*, 3rd edn, Basingstoke, Palgrave.

Harris, K. (ed.) (2007) *Respect in the Neighbourhood: Why Neighbourliness Matters*, Lyme Regis, Russell House Publishing.

crisis intervention

Gibson, M. (2006) *Order from Chaos: Responding to Traumatic Events*, 3rd edn, Bristol, The Policy Press.

Roberts, A. R. (2005) *Crisis Intervention Handbook: Assessment Treatment and Research*, 3rd edn, Oxford, Oxford University Press.

Thompson, N. (1991) *Crisis Intervention Revisited*, Birmingham, Pepar Publications.

empowerment

Adams, R. (2003) *Social Work and Empowerment*, 3rd edn, Basingstoke, Palgrave Macmillan.

Fook, J. (2002) *Social Work: Critical Theory and Practice*, London, Sage

Humphries, B. (ed.) (1996) *Critical Perspectives on Empowerment*, Birmingham, Venture Press.

Thompson, N. (2007) *Power and Empowerment*, Lyme Regis, Russell House Publishing.

existentialism

Butt, T. (2004) *Understanding People*, Basingstoke, Palgrave Macmillan.

Thompson, N. (1992) *Existentialism and Social Work*, Aldershot, Avebury.

Thompson, N. (2000) 'Existentialist Practice', in Stepney and Ford (2000).

Van Deurzen, E. and Arnold-Baker, C. (eds) (2005) *Existential Perspectives on Human Issues: A Handbook for Therapeutic Practice*, Basingstoke, Palgrave Macmillan.

family therapy

Barnes, G. (2004) *Family Therapy in Changing Times*, Basingstoke, Palgrave Macmillan.

Carr, A. (2000) *Family Therapy: Concepts, Process and Practice*, Chichester, John Wiley and Sons.

Nichols, M. P. and Schwartz, R. C. (2001) *The Essentials of Family Therapy*, Boston, Allyn & Bacon.

Vetere, A. and Dowling, E. (2005) *Narrative Therapies with Children and Their Families: A Practitioner's Guide to Concepts and Approaches*, Hove, Routledge.

groupwork

Doel, M. and Sawdon, C. (1999) *The Essential Groupworker: Teaching and Learning Creative Groupwork*, London, Jessica Kingsley.

Doel, M. (2005) *Using Groupwork*, London, Routledge.

Ward, D. (2002) 'Groupwork', in Adams et al. (2002a).

Ward, D. (2006) *Working in Group Care: Social Work and Social Care in Residential and Daycare Settings*, Bristol, The Policy Press.

humanist/person-centred approaches

Heron, J. (2001) *Helping the Client: A Creative Practical Guide*, 5th edn, London, Sage.

Merry, B. and Lusty, B. (2002) *Learning and Being in Person-Centred Counselling*, Ross-on-Wye, PCCS Books.

Payne, M. (2005) *Modern Social Work Theory*, 3rd edn, Basingstoke, Palgrave Macmillan.

Rogers, C. R. (1961) *On Becoming a Person: A Therapist's View of Psychotherapy*, London, Constable.

narrative approaches

Chamberlayne, P., Bornat, J. and Apitzsch, U. (2004) *Biographical Methods and Professional Practice: An International Perspective*, Bristol, The Policy Press.

Mills, M. A. (1999) 'Using the Narrative in Dementia Care', in Bornat (1999).

Milner, J. (2001) *Women and Social Work: A Narrative Approach*, Basingstoke, Palgrave Macmillan.

postmodernism

Bertens, H. and Natoli, J. (eds) (2002) *Postmodernism: The Key Figures*, Oxford, Blackwell.

Drolet, M. (ed.) (2004) *The Postmodern Reader: Foundational Texts*, London, Routledge.

Fawcett, B., Featherstone, B., Fook, J. and Rossiter, A. (2000) *Practice and Research in Social Work: Postmodern Feminist Perspectives*, London, Routledge.

Fook, J. (2002) *Social Work: Critical Theory and Practice*, London, Sage.

Parton, N. (2000) 'Postmodern and Constructionist Approaches to Social Work', in Adams et al. (2002a).

Pease, B. and Fook, J. (1999) *Transforming Social Work Practice: Postmodern Critical Perspectives*, London, Routledge.

poststructuralism

Healy, K. (2000) *Social Work Practices: Contemporary Perspectives on Change*, London, Sage.

Fook, J. (2002) *Social Work: Critical Theory and Practice*, London, Sage.

Petersen, A., Barns, I., Dudley, J. and Harris, P. (1999) *Poststructuralism, Citizenship and Social Policy*, London, Routledge.

Tew, J. (2002) *Social Theory, Power and Practice*, Basingstoke, Palgrave Macmillan.

psychodynamics

Cardwell, M., Clark, L. and Meldrun, C. (2004) *Psychology for A Level*, 3rd edn, London, Harper Collins.

Davison, G. C., Neal, J. M. and Kring, A. M. (2003) *Abnormal Psychology*, 9th edn, Chichester, John Wiley and Son.

Payne, M. (2005) *Modern Social Work Theory*, 3rd edn, Basingstoke, Palgrave Macmillan.

Storr, A. (2001) *Freud: A Very Short Introduction*, Oxford, Oxford University Press.

radical social work

Bailey, R. and Brake, M. (eds) (1980) *Radical Social Work and Practice*, London, Edward Arnold.

Fook, J. (2002) *Social Work: Critical Theory and Practice*, London, Sage.

Jones, C. and Novak, T. (1999) *Poverty, Welfare and the Disciplinary State*, London, Routledge.

Langan, M. (2002) 'The Legacy of Radical Social Work', in Adams et al. (2002a).

social constructionism

Burr, V. (2003) *Social Constructionism*, 2nd edn, London, Routledge.

Gergen, K. J. (1999) *An Invitation to Social Construction*, London, Sage.

Parton, N. and O'Byrne, P. (2000) *Constructive Social Work: Towards a New Practice*, Basingstoke, Macmillan – now Palgrave Macmillan.

solution-focused therapy

Myers, S. (2007) *Solution-Focused Approaches*, Lyme Regis, Russell House Publishing.

Parton, N. and O' Byrne, P. (2000) *Constructive Social Work: Towards a New Practice*, Basingstoke, Macmillan.

Shazer, S. de (1985) *Keys to Solutions in Brief Therapy*, New York, Norton.

Shazer, S. de (1991) *Putting Difference to Work*, New York, Norton.

systematic practice

Egan, G. (2002) *The Skilled Helper: A Problem-Management Approach to Helping*, 7th edn, Pacific Grove, CA, Brookes Cole.

Pinnock, M. and Dimmock, B. (2003) 'Managing for Outcomes', in Henderson and Atkinson (2003).

Thompson, N. (2002) *People Skills*, 2nd edn, Basingstoke, Palgrave Macmillan.

systems theory

Healy, K. (2005) *Social Work Theories in Context: Creating Frameworks for Practice*, Basingstoke, Palgrave Macmillan.

Jack, G. and Jack, D. (2000) 'Ecological Social Work: The Application of a Systems Model of Development in Context', in Stepney and Ford (2000).

Payne, M. (2005) *Modern Social Work Theory*, 3rd edn, Basingstoke, Palgrave Macmillan.

task-centred practice

Doel, M. (2000) 'Task-centred Work', in Adams (2002a).

Ford, P. and Postle, K. (2000) 'Task- Centred Practice and Care Management', in Stepney and Ford (2000).

Healy, K. (2005) *Social Work Theories in Context: Creating Frameworks for Practice*, Basingstoke, Palgrave Macmillan.

Marsh, P. and Doel, M. (2005) *The Task-Centred Book*, London, Routledge.

transactional analysis

Berne, E. (1961) *Transactional Analysis in Psychotherapy*, New York, Grove Press.

Berne, E. (1970) *Games People Play: The Psychology of Interpersonal Relationships*, Harmondsworth, Penguin.

Berne, E. (1975) *What Do You Say After You Say Hello*, London, Corgi Books.

Harris, T. (1995) *I'm OK, You're OK*, London, Arrow.

Pitman, E. (1983) *Transactional Analysis for Social Workers*, London, Routledge & Kegan Paul.

user involvement

Beresford, P. (2003) *It's Our Lives: A Short Theory of Knowledge, Distance and Experience*, London, Citizen Press in association with Shaping Our Lives.

Kemshall, H. and Littlechild, R. (eds) (2000) *User Involvement and Participation in Social Care: Research Informing Practice*, London, Jessica Kingsley.

Minhas, A. (2005) 'Dependent upon Outside Help: Reflections from a Service User', in Carnwell and Buchanan (2005).

Social Care Institute for Excellence (2004) *Position Paper 3: Has Service User Involvement Made a Difference to Social Care Services?*, London, SCIE – available from www.scie.org.uk.

Shaping Our Lives National User Network (2003) *Shaping Our Lives: What People Think of the Social Care Services They Use*, York, Joseph Rowntree Foundation.

Thompson, N. (2007) *Power and Empowerment*, Lyme Regis, Russell House Publishing.

drawing on research

5

introduction

Our experience with social work students over the years has taught us that the notion of research can cause considerable anxiety and self-doubt. But, you need to remember that you are not expected to be an expert in matters relating to research. Rather, you are required to have an understanding of why research is important and how it relates to practice.

> The majority of health and social care practitioners do not have, nor necessarily need, the skills required to undertake a research project. What we all need, however, are the skills and knowledge to appreciate, understand and use research and evidence in order to provide the highest quality and most effective care possible for our patients, clients and service users. It should be a natural activity for health and social care practitioners to keep up to date and use research findings and evidence in their work, and being 'research literate' should be one of the basic skills of all these professional groups. (Hek, Judd and Moule, 2002, p. 2)

Part 5 of the book is divided into three main chapters. Chapter 5.1 is entitled 'Why is research important?' It looks at the important issues of, firstly, what is research? What exactly do we mean when we use this rather anxiety-provoking term? It will then look at research-minded practice. This is an important concept developed in the early 1990s which is still very relevant to today's social work world. It emphasizes the importance of research as an underpinning basis of reflective practice. Following on from this, we shall explore issues relating to evidence-based practice, an approach to social work which has developed a considerable following in recent years, but one which is not entirely unflawed. We shall therefore present a critical perspective on evidence-based practice. Finally, in this chapter, we shall make brief comment about the importance of critical evaluation skills when it comes to addressing research issues.

Principle 3 Critical Analysis

An uncritical acceptance of 'evidence' can be very problematic. We therefore need to recognize that evidence-based practice is not an alternative to critical analysis.

Chapter 5.2 is entitled 'Understanding research methods and process', and is intended to give an overview of what is involved in actual research practice. It begins by looking at the principles of good research and follows this with a discussion of important issues relating to research design and methods. There is also in this chapter a discussion of the very important topic of research ethics and also the equally important question of how do we evaluate research?

Chapter 5.3 is entitled 'Incorporating research into practice'. Our task in this chapter is to present some ideas on how practitioners and managers can draw links between the world of research and the world of practice, as it is vitally important that we do not have a situation in which research and practice are not interconnected. This chapter, therefore, explores important issues relating to finding research materials, relating such research to practice, and maintaining a research-based culture. Chapter 5.4 provides a short conclusion.

5.1 why is research important?

In Chapter 2.7 the discussion of reflective practice emphasizes the importance of linking day-to-day practice to our professional knowledge base. Much of this professional knowledge base comes from a tradition of research. If we are to promote reflective practice, we therefore need to have an understanding of what research is, how it influences our work and the dangers of neglecting the research dimension.

Two decades ago, Jeff Hopkins wrote of the importance of 'sensitive and informed practice' (Hopkins, 1986). Here we wish to emphasize the *informed* element of Hopkins' approach. It is argued that social work is too important to rely on guesswork when this is not necessary or to fail to draw on the knowledge base available.

NOS Key Role 6

Demonstrate professional competence in social work practice

As we see it, there are two main options. We can deal with each new practice situation as if it were entirely new, or we can draw on what we already know about:

> social problems and social needs
> human development
> family dynamics
> processes of discrimination and oppression
> how power operates
> and so on.

When we practise, we are indeed encountering unique situations, but even the unique circumstances we meet have things in common with other situations. Therefore, we do not have to start from scratch or reinvent the wheel; we have a wealth of previous experience and the knowledge distilled from it to draw upon. In many ways, this is what research is. It is a distillation of previous experience and the lessons that can be learned from it.

And, as we shall see below in relation to the discussion of research-minded practice, the discipline involved in research methodology provides a very good basis for developing a focused and systematic approach to practice. That is, if we are to avoid the stereotype of a social worker as being somebody who is vague and woolly minded, then it is vitally important that we adopt a disciplined approach to what we are doing, with clarity about our aims and so on. Having a good understanding of research methodology and the rigour on which it is based will not automatically make us effective, focused practitioners with good, analytical skills, but it will certainly be a step in the right direction. systematic practice, see p. XXX

Principle 3 **Critical Analysis**

An understanding of research methodology can help us to develop our critical analysis skills.

what is research?

At its simplest, research can be defined as the pursuit of scientific knowledge, but this begs three questions (or sets of questions):

❶ *What counts as pursuit?* That is, what counts as valid or legitimate research?

❷ *What do we mean by scientific?* How does social science differ from the natural sciences?

❸ *What counts as knowledge?* Does this imply certainty and truth? If so, is this realistic?

Each of these questions could form the basis of a book in its own right but, given our modest space allowance here to address these issues, we shall limit ourselves to the following comments:

❶ *What counts as valid research?* There are a number of recognized methods and procedures that are accepted within the academic community as the basis of good practice in research. We shall explore these in outline in Chapter 5.2.

❷ *What do we mean by scientific?* Social science is very different from the natural sciences which seek to establish laws of nature. The natural science approach is referred to as 'positivism'. Social science involves going beyond positivism – that is, the naïve view that people and society can be understood according to scientific laws parallel with the laws of nature with which the natural sciences concern themselves. In the social sciences, scientific endeavours are concerned with people, not things; meanings, not laws.

❸ *What counts as knowledge?* The social sciences rarely produce definitive certainty. However, what social scientific research can produce is a greater degree of probability.

It is important to recognize that research can be very helpful in a number of ways. It can:

❯ Enable us to get the bigger picture, to see how what we are dealing with connects with the wider world of knowledge and understanding and, indeed, as mentioned earlier, with the experiences of others in the field that have gone before us.

❯ Give us a more informed basis for practice. There are considerable dangers in relying on an uninformed approach to practice which can be very detrimental.

❯ Provide a platform for further learning and development.

Having considered some of the key issues relating to what is research, we are now able to move on to consider an approach to these issues which has come to be known as research-minded practice, as this approach will help us to achieve the three aims we have just outlined.

In 1992, an important book under the title of *Applied Research for Better Practice* was published. Its authors, Everitt and colleagues, made a significant contribution to our understanding of the significance of research and how it can and should relate to high-quality practice:

> Research-minded practice is concerned with the analytical assessment of social need and resources, and the development, implementation and evaluation of strategies to meet the need ... The taken-for-granted becomes subject to critical scrutiny. An examination of research methodology and exploration of research methods is fundamental to such practice. (1992, p. 4)

The positive characteristics of research-minded practice have been summarized in the following passage:

Thus, research-minded practitioners:
> will be constantly defining and making explicit their objectives and hypotheses;
> will treat their explanations of the social world as hypotheses – that is, as tentative and open to be tested against evidence;
> will be aware of their expertise and knowledge and that of others;
> will bring to the fore theories that help make sense of social need, resources and assist in decision making with regard to strategies;
> will be thoughtful, reflecting on data and theory and contributing to their development and refinement;
> will scrutinise and be analytical of available data and information;
> will be mindful of the pervasiveness of ideology and values in the way we see and understand the world.

(Everitt et al., 1992, pp. 4–5)

Reflective practice teaches us that it is not enough to rely on guesswork and habit. Given that social work involves dealing with people who are distressed, vulnerable and/or subject to discrimination and oppression, it is dangerous not to make sure that what we are doing in response to their needs and problems is based on a thorough understanding of the issues concerned. Research (and research-minded practice) can clearly help us in this regard.

NOS Key Role 4

Manage risk to individuals, families, carers, groups, communities, self and colleagues

Another important issue is that of the need to cut through ideology which Berger and Luckmann (1967) define as 'ideas serving as weapons of social interest'. Research helps us to see through the ideological gloss that is often put over the underlying reality. In this regard, it is part and parcel of the development of a critical perspective. Research-minded practice provides:

> An emphasis on making sure our actions are informed by research as far as it is reasonably possible.
> A warning about the dangers of taking things at face value.

> A basis for critical analysis, enabling us to draw on the discipline involved in research methodology.

Here we can draw a link with professionalism, as discussed in Part 2 in relation to law and policy. There, a distinction was drawn between the traditional elitist professional role where the professional is seen as an expert who draws on science, and the more participative and empowering approach to professionalism that is to be preferred. In a research context, feminist and critical approaches to research have helped us to appreciate that it is important to go beyond traditional positivist models of science and research which again place the professional (whether researcher or practitioner) in an elitist position (see Truman and Humphries, 1999). It is important to move away from this towards the empowering form of professionalism discussed earlier. In this way, we can also promote empowering forms of research; that is, using research-based knowledge to empower people, not to increase our differentials; to work more closely with people (that is, in partnership), not push them further away.

Principle 2 **Empowerment and Partnership**

Research has the power to be empowering or disempowering.
It is important that we aim for the former.

evidence-based practice

Evidence-based practice in social work has arisen as a development of evidence-based medicine. The medical profession is now devoting considerable effort and expense to ensuring that the treatments offered have been adequately tested to try to ensure that they will be effective. This arose following concerns raised about a number of medications that, on further testing, were found to be ineffective if not actually counterproductive. That is, there was the embarrassing revelation that the medical profession had been devoting huge sums of money to the use of particular drug treatments without any adequate assurance that these were effective in what they sought to achieve. Following this difficult transition from medicine based on assumption and faith to one based on hard evidence, there has been a major focus on the use of scientific research to ensure that no further funds are wasted on ineffective treatment.

In recent years, social work has moved very much in this direction, asking questions about 'what works'. In many ways, this is a positive move forward as it enables us to question traditional, taken-for-granted assumptions about what is or what is not effective in terms of the actions taken by social workers. It has made us more aware of not only the risk of investing time, effort and energy into ineffective practices, but also the danger of doing harm:

> it is perfectly possible for good-hearted, well-meaning, reasonably clever, hard-working staff, employing the most promising contemporary approaches available to them, to make no difference at all to (or even on occasion to worsen) the condition of those whom they seek to assist. (Sheldon and Chilvers, 2000, p. 2)

The question of whether social work can do harm is a very important one. If we adopt the traditional approach of basing our interventions on faith and traditional intervention styles, then we have no way of knowing whether we are not only failing to do good, but are actually doing harm.

NOS Key Role 4

Manage risk to individuals, families, carers, groups, communities, self and colleagues

Appreciating the possibility that our work may inadvertently do harm is, in our view, a significant move forward, as there has long been a neglect of this aspect of our practice. For example, some years ago, one of the present authors was approached by the manager of a social work team. The manager had devised a questionnaire to be filled in by clients of the team. It was intended that this questionnaire would seek the clients' views on the effectiveness, or otherwise, of the help they had received from members of the team. The questionnaire included various topics and then a rating scale from 1, low, to 6, high, in terms of how helpful the social work interventions had been. It was necessary to point out to the manager concerned that this questionnaire did not take account of the possibility that the interventions had actually done harm. It was therefore suggested that the ratings scale should be from, say, minus 6 to plus 6, making it clear to people filling in the form that allowance was being made for the possibility that attempts to help may not only have failed to improve the situation, but may actually have made it worse. If we are not basing our work on evidence, how do we know that our efforts are not doing harm?

The concept of 'evidence-based practice' is one that has had a great deal of influence in health care theory and practice and is now receiving a lot of attention in social work and social care. The basic premiss of evidence-based practice is that it is wise to make sure, as far as reasonably possible, that the work we undertake is based on empirical evidence as to its effectiveness. Macdonald captures the point well when she argues that:

> The underpinning principle of evidence-based practice appears relatively uncontroversial: that when professionals intervene in people's lives they do so on the basis of the best available evidence regarding the likely consequences of that intervention. They should be as confident as it is possible to be that what they do will bring about the changes sought and will do so with the minimum of adverse consequences.   (Macdonald, 2002, p. 424)

While we would agree that this basic principle is relatively uncontroversial, how it is translated into reality is far from uncontroversial (see, for example, the debate between Stephen Webb and Brian Sheldon – Webb, 2001; Sheldon, 2001). The concept of evidence-based practice raises a number of complex questions about the nature of science, the nature of evidence, the role of research and the relationship between theory and practice (Neil Thompson, 2000b). The development of evidence-based practice is therefore not as simple or clear cut as many people would have us believe. It none the less has value in raising awareness of the importance of being clear about: (i) the evidence on which our interventions are based; and (ii) the impact of such interventions.

NOS Key Role 2

Plan, carry out, review and evaluate social work practice, with individuals, families, carers, groups, communities, and other professionals

Frost makes the important point that:

> a dogmatic adherence to evidence-based practice immediately dismantles the possibility of any partnership approach to working with service users. ... If we do indeed base all our practice on 'evidence', then by default any room for negotiation, partnership and compromise with the service user is lost.
>
> Indeed, the proponents of evidence-led practice tend to privilege RCTs [randomized controlled trials] (Macdonald, 1996), which by definition tends to exclude any user involvement in the research and evaluation process. (Frost, 2004, p. 50)

The situation is also very complex in so far as:

1. There is a lack of clarity about what counts as evidence. See, for example, the comments of Trinder (2000, p. 237) to the effect that the 'definition of evidence should be broadened' and the 'claims of evidence-based practice should be narrowed' (cited in D'Cruz and Jones, 2004, p. 9).

2. Much of what we do in social work is not directly amenable to being evidenced – for example, we do not follow set protocols, as distinct from pharmacological interventions in the medical profession. In line with Schön's (1983) comments about the swampy lowlands of practice, often what we do is messy and indeterminate, and it is therefore not entirely clear in many cases how research evidence could be of direct assistance to us.

We can identify two phases in the development of evidence-based practice: strong and weak. The strong version is based on the notion that we have to place major emphasis on research evidence about what works, and the implication of this is that forms of intervention for which there is no sound research base should not be pursued or funded. The weak form of evidence-based practice is not quite so extreme. Its basic argument is that we should draw on research evidence where possible but recognizes that: (a) research evidence will not always be available; and (b) it is not the only type of evidence to be taken into account. As Becker and Bryman (2004, p. 55) comment:

> Research, particularly where it is trustworthy and robust, is a key source of evidence for policy and practice. But again it must be remembered that it is only one source, only one way of knowing, and that political imperatives, resources and other considerations also need to be taken into account by policymakers and especially by government: 'Rather, research evidence is just one influence on the policy process and, while the research community is free to argue that it should receive greater attention, it would be anti-democratic to insist that research evidence should be the prime consideration' (Walker, 2000, p. 163). (Becker and Bryman, 2004, p. 55)

critical evaluation skills

It is important to re-emphasize the point that social workers are not expected necessarily to be researchers themselves (although there is much learning to be gained from actually undertaking research). However, to be users or consumers of research, we need to have some idea of what is involved in research, what makes for good research, and so on. This means that we have to have critical evaluation skills or, in other words, the ability to recognize what is legitimate research and what is not. This means having at least a basic understanding of the rules, as it were, of good research practice. This is particularly important now that we are operating in an era where, because of the internet, information is more readily accessible than it used to be and where it can be difficult to find the source of that information and judge its reliability. These rules will be discussed in Chapter 5.2, and so it will be important to bear in mind when you are reading that chapter that the information provided there forms the platform from which you can develop the critical evaluation skills you need to be an informed consumer of research.

> **practice focus**
>
> **5.1**
>
> While reading the course programme Ida had been surprised to see that there was a module devoted to research issues. At first she couldn't see what this had to do with social work and told a fellow student that if she'd wanted to be a researcher she wouldn't have applied to do a social work degree. However, after an experience on her first placement, she began to understand why it was included in the curriculum. While working within a community living project for adults with learning disabilities, she came across an article which hailed the success 'in a number of cases' of a particular and innovative form of therapy. The therapy was quite intense and raised some ethical dilemmas for Ida and so she put this on the agenda for discussion at her next meeting with her supervisor. When they looked more closely at the article she realized that, while the researchers made a big thing about the 'successes' they had left it for the reader to work out that there must have been a significantly higher number of cases where the therapy had not made a difference or, indeed, may have done some harm. Moreover, there was little discussion about how the researchers had defined 'success'. Ida thought back to her earlier thoughts on reading the programme and realized that, had her supervisor not raised those points, she might well have been drawn into accepting the 'benefits' of the therapy in an uncritical way which could have had potentially harmful consequences. After this experience she could understand the rhetoric behind equipping social workers with the skills to at least evaluate, if not undertake research. If she was going to keep abreast of developments in her field, she would need to take on board a lot of new information and learn how not to take things for granted. Seeing this as a gap in her knowledge and skills base, she began to welcome the time that had been put aside for research topics.

We shall return to these issues in Chapter 5.2 under the heading of 'Evaluating research'.

points to ponder

> ❯ Why is research important for practice?
> ❯ What steps do you need to take to develop research-minded practice?
> ❯ What do you understand by the term 'scientific'? Can social work be scientific?
> ❯ What types of evidence need to be considered in relation to social work?
> ❯ How can you get access to evidence relating to service user perspectives?

5.2 **understanding research methods and process**

introduction

If we are to develop a good and useful understanding of research, then it is important that we are not afraid of it, that its tendency to provoke anxiety is dealt with. It is to be hoped that this chapter can play a part in that by providing an overview of what is involved in research and, in that way, demystifying it to a certain extent.

It is important to avoid two destructive extremes. On the one hand we wish to move away from the sort of intellectual game playing that puts so many people off the academic world and what it has to offer in terms of learning and development. While certain people's careers in the academic world may depend on research output and may involve the use of obscure jargon in order to be a member of that academic club, we should not allow this to put us off the benefits of research. At the other extreme, we should not adopt an anti-intellectual approach – that is, one that drives a wedge between the world of theory, understanding and learning from that of the world of actual practice. As we noted in relation to reflective practice, it is vitally important that we integrate the two, the thinking and the doing. This chapter is intended to help in that regard.

the principles of good research

It is very important that research is rigorous – that is, based on an approach that is disciplined and systematic, allowing little room for problems to arise. This is a very useful general principle, as it means that people undertaking research have to be careful that they are not allowing bias to creep into their work (or at least are keeping bias to a minimum, making it explicit where it does occur).

Another principle of research is that of validity. This applies in two senses. There is the everyday sense of the term that research needs to be valid or legitimate; in other words, this is another term for rigour. However, it is also used in a more specific sense within research, to refer to the need to ensure that the tools used as part of the research process are appropriate to the task at hand. For example, if in a study of stress the results are based on people's own reports of their experiences of stress, then it would be important, in terms of validity for the researchers, to make it clear that what they are reporting on is self-perceptions of stress and not necessarily stress itself. If they were to claim that their study measured stress, this would be an example of a lack of validity. In other words, the criterion of validity means that researchers have to make sure that they are actually measuring or testing what they say they are seeking to measure or test, and they have to be quite precise about this (another example of rigour).

A related principle is that of reliability. A reliable research study is one which has internal consistency. For example, if another researcher were to carry out the same study using the same methods, how likely is it that similar results would be achieved? If the results were to be significantly different with all other variables remaining the same, this would strongly suggest that the research lacks reliability.

Objectivity is often quoted as an important principle of research, but this is a very complex matter. This is because studies cannot be entirely objective, in the sense of being entirely free of subjective elements. If we are talking about social science and therefore a science of people, it is inevitable that there will be a subjective dimension. An alternative term that is perhaps more accurate is that of 'openness'. This refers to the need to make sure that the basic premises of the research, such as the process, rationale and outcomes, are open to critical inquiry – that is, they are not hidden or out of reach.

explanatory power

The aim of research is to develop our understanding, to cast light on areas that need further understanding. It is therefore important that research has the ability to explain. A research study that does not help to explain is of little or no value. Note, however, that even where a study fails to confirm its hypothesis, this does not mean that it lacks explanatory power. Learning that something is not as we expected it to be can help in terms of explaining that particular phenomenon or set of phenomena.

While it is important to try and adhere to the principles of research, we need to recognize that research is inevitably a political process with a subjective element to it. In other words, power issues are likely to arise, and no researcher, however hard they try, can be entirely free of a subjective perspective. For example, simply the choice of research topic involves a subjective element of choice and may well be influenced by broader political factors.

Principle 1 **Social Context**

Research does not take place in a social vacuum – the social context is therefore an important consideration.

research design

This refers to the way in which research is organized, the way in which the process takes place as it were. It involves, amongst other things, addressing the following questions:

What is the research question? This involves looking at what are you trying to cast light on? What are you trying to test? Ultimately, it is about establishing what the research is intended to achieve.

What type of research would be most appropriate? There are a number of distinctions that can be made here that can help us decide which is the most appropriate research approach for our purposes. First there is the major distinction between quantitative and qualitative research. The former refers to types of research that involve precise measurement (use of questionnaires, for example, where the data generated can be subjected to detailed statistical analysis). Qualitative is not so focused on numerical data; it would include methods such as interviewing, where a helpful picture that casts light on the subject under review can be gained but without the same precise mathematical detail.

There is also an important distinction between deductive and inductive research. Deductive research is based on the idea of a hypothesis. That is, a proposition is put forward and the research then sets out to test it. Inductive research, by contrast, is where there is no specific hypothesis or proposal to be tested, but where the researcher takes an overall perspective on a situation and tries to identify patterns that emerge from this. This is closely linked to the idea of grounded theory.

Research can be either participative or non-participative. Participative research is where the researcher or researchers are involved directly in that which they are studying. For example, a method known as participant observation involves one or more researchers working alongside a particular group of people and noting key issues that arise. An example of this would be a researcher working with a group of young people at a youth club over a period of time and seeking to identify key patterns and issues that arise from their observations. Most research, however, is non-participative, in the sense that it involves a researcher trying to remain neutral and external to the processes they are examining.

Research can also be either exploratory or substantive. Exploratory refers to the type of research where little is known about a particular subject and the research project is, in a sense, dipping its toe in the water to try and get a better understanding. This is usually as a forerunner to more substantive research, to more extensive work on that particular topic. Exploratory research is often very useful as a forerunner to more substantive studies and can suggest new directions for research activity.

What specific method would be most appropriate? There are various methods available to researchers and which specific method would be most appropriate is an important question that the researchers must ask in establishing how best to proceed. Different methods will have different advantages and disadvantages, and so it is important that there is a careful matching between the method chosen and the desired outcomes.

Common research methods are questionnaires, interviews, biographical methods (or life story work) and so on.

How will you process the data? A problem often encountered by inexperienced researchers is that they generate a large amount of data, but then are not clear about what they are going to do with it. They can, in effect, become overwhelmed with large amounts of data and have little clear idea about how this is to be processed. An effective researcher will therefore clarify in advance what is to be done with the data generated from a particular study. This involves asking questions like: what type of data will be generated? How can it be analysed? How can conclusions be drawn from it? and so on. Leaving this until the end of the process can be very problematic indeed.

ethnography

This is a well-established approach to research that involves trying to get an understanding of real-life experiences. It can be well summarized in the following passage:

> This involves the careful collection of *qualitative* evidence (that is, detailed evidence on a few people) through involvement in the lives of those studied. The point is to see them in the context in which their lives take place and try to reconstruct their experiences, beliefs, understandings from their own standpoint. This attempt at empathy is always fraught with

A related approach is that of biographical methods or life story work. This involves working with particular people in a specific setting to discuss their experiences of life throughout their life course, to see what patterns emerge in terms of changes that have occurred over time. For example, there have been a number of studies which examine the experiences of older people that have allowed us to identify both significant changes over time that have affected this group of people, and significant issues relating to how older people are treated in our society (Malone et al., 2005).

interviewing

This is an important and widely used technique. It is similar to interviewing in the social work sense (that is, a structured, focused discussion with a client), but it has a subtly different purpose when it comes to research.

Interviews can be used as an additional method to, for example, a questionnaire study or may be used as a method in its own right. Where it is used as an additional study, it is generally implemented as a means of focusing on particular themes identified in the primary study. For example, a questionnaire about people's experiences of receiving bereavement counselling may identify particular themes that can then be followed up in more depth with a set of interviews with a selection of the people who initially completed the questionnaire form.

Principle 5 Loss and Grief

There is an extensive body of research on loss and grief issues
that can cast a great deal of light on social work practice.

What interviews offer is depth rather than breadth. That is, because of the time-consuming nature of interviewing as a method (this involves preparation, the interview itself, transcribing the interview, analysing it and so on), it is not possible to have large numbers of interviewees involved in a study. We cannot, therefore, achieve the same breadth as, say, a questionnaire study, but that breadth is traded for the depth of knowledge and insight that can come from interview work.

Interviews are normally based on what is known as an 'interview schedule'. This refers to a number of questions to be asked. These questions are normally fixed in the sense that there is a structure to them and each person who is interviewed will be asked the same questions in the same sequence in order to achieve a degree of order and uniformity. However, the most common form of interview is what is known as a semi-structured interview. This is where there are the usual number of fixed questions, but where supplementary questions are allowed. That is, if an interviewee, in responding to one question, raises an interesting issue that the researcher wishes to pursue, then the researcher is permitted to ask additional questions about the matter arising. The researcher is none the less expected to return to the fixed structure when this is suitable, rather than have an unstructured, free-flowing interview which would be difficult to compare with other interviews as part of the same study.

questionnaires

We are very familiar with the idea of questionnaires because they are widely used in formal research as well as in more informal activities, such as popular magazines. The advantages of questionnaires are that they provide breadth (it is possible to circulate questionnaires to large numbers of people at relatively low cost) and a degree of uniformity across variants. That is, because of the fixed structure of the questionnaire, we have a certain amount of reassurance that people will be tackling the questions in broadly the same way. Little scope is allowed for people to go in their own direction.

However, this is also a disadvantage of questionnaires that while having a degree of fixity and uniformity gives us a basis for easy comparison across large numbers of people, the limited response options on a question mean that sometimes the responses may not be particularly helpful. For example, if people are asked to choose between a yes or no answer, they may feel that their actual response should be less rigid than this, but if the questionnaire has too many options, then it may become unwieldy and therefore make it less likely that people will actually fill it in. A further disadvantage of questionnaires is their lack of depth. They are, in effect, a mirror image of interviewing. The advantages of interviewing are the disadvantages of a questionnaire study and vice versa. This is why, as mentioned earlier, the two are often used in tandem.

Questionnaires are undoubtedly of some value in providing a broad overview of a situation, but we do need to recognize their limitations. They leave a lot unsaid and, because of their relative inflexibility (which is an advantage in terms of rigour), we pay the price of losing certain advantages in terms of flexibility and qualitative understanding.

A key issue with questionnaires is the importance of getting sampling right. That is, if a questionnaire study is to be of benefit, then the people chosen to complete it must be representative of the group of people being studied. We must move away from the problem associated with a number of traditional studies, for example, in psychology where the sample was predominantly a group of US college students. Much of our psychological knowledge is based on studies primarily or exclusively comprising US college students. This clearly raises questions about how representative of wider social groups any findings are.

textual analysis

This is an approach that is linked with the notion of discourse. A discourse literally means a conversation, but has come to be used as a broader term to refer to not only structures of language, but also structures of power and social interaction that accompany such language forms. A textual analysis involves a finely detailed analysis of texts to identify patterns, biases and taken-for-granted assumptions. In this way, a textual analysis can identify, for example, issues relating to the role of power and how power is exercised through language.

This can be a very helpful method for examining, for example, social work records to see what particular topics feature, what assumptions are being made, and so on. It is a technique widely used in media studies, but has broader application across other disciplines as well.

the ethics of research

Research involves a certain amount of power in terms of: (i) the social standing of researchers being associated with universities and so on; and (ii) the later publication of research and the significance of this in terms of the effect that it can have on people's lives (for example, where an issue that was previously in the private domain becomes part of the public domain through being published in a research report). In the exercise of power, it is important to recognize the significance of ethics to ensure that it is a responsible exercise of power.

This involves asking such questions as: Will this research harm people? For example, some forms of medical research may harm people through withholding medical treatment that could be of assistance to them. Does the research break any ethical principles such as confidentiality? Does it exploit people? These are all important issues to address in ensuring that the research is ethical. It is important to remember, though, that these are not just abstract issues or only relevant to professional researchers in the academic world – codes of ethics relating to research apply to practitioner research and student projects too.

Proposals for research normally have to be approved by an ethics committee at a university, within a health authority or wherever the research is to take place. This is an important safeguard, and it is clearly not a matter to be taken lightly. It is therefore important that, whether as an undergraduate or at a later stage of your career, if you are planning on undertaking research, you obtain the appropriate ethical approval. If in doubt, seek advice from a tutor or other appropriate adviser.

NOS Key Role 5

Manage and be accountable, with supervision and support, for your own social work practice within your organization

One important point to emphasize is that feminist approaches to research have brought an extra dimension to the notion of research ethics. Feminist and critical approaches to research (see, for example, Humphries, 2000) have argued the case for research studies to be empowering, to treat people as subjects, not objects. Traditionally, research in the social sciences has involved powerful researchers undertaking studies of relatively powerless groups in society – and this is particularly the case in research relating to social work. For example, while there have been many studies by academics of disabled people, how many studies of academics have been undertaken by disabled people?

A final point in relation to the ethics of research is the question of funding. Who is providing funding for the particular study? Is there any conflict of interest here? Is there any potential bias as a result of the funding source? This is something that needs to be taken into consideration in relation to not only the ethics of research but also its legitimacy. How useful is the research study when it appears to have been funded by a body that has a vested interest in particular outcomes arising from that research?

practice focus

5.2

evaluating research

The point was made earlier that most social workers will not engage in actually doing research, but it is to be hoped that we will be consumers of research, that we will be prepared to gain the benefits of having an understanding of what research tells us about the area of practice we are concerned with.

In order to evaluate research as a consumer of it, we need to address the following questions:

> *Does it do what it sets out to do?* This may seem a strange question to ask, but it is surprising how many studies do not actually do what they set out to do. They may claim to address a particular topic in a particular way, but the actual detail of the research may reveal that their claim of what they were doing is not entirely accurate.

> *Does it use acceptable methodology?* There are debates and different schools of thought about what constitutes acceptable methodology. For example, there are some relatively hard-line people who feel that qualitative methods are inferior to quantitative methods. However, these debates aside, there are still clear issues about can we be satisfied that the methods used were appropriate in the circumstances? Where, for example, a researcher has drawn generalizations from the responses given by a sample of people interviewed on a city street, you might want to question whether the number of people interviewed was large enough to be representative of the wider population claimed. Using an extreme example to make the point, claiming that three-quarters of people think that social workers do a good job when you only asked four people and three of them gave that response, would obviously not be creditable research! Getting a big enough response to be able to generalize from often presents practical problem in terms of scale and suggests the need to consider a methodology other than direct interviews in those circumstances.

> *Is it ethical?* Does it meet the requirements of research ethics or are there problems

related to this? However, realistically this issue will not occur very often because of the scrutiny in most cases of a research ethics committee prior to the research starting. None the less, we should not be complacent and assume that such scrutiny has ensured that all ethical issues have been satisfactorily covered.

> *Do its conclusions follow?* It is sadly sometimes the case that people undertake very good quality studies, but then draw conclusions illogically from them. We therefore have to ask ourselves: are the conclusions drawn justified by the actual research study, or are the authors of the research study overstepping the mark in terms of the valid lessons that can be learned from the study?

> *Is the discussion of findings balanced?* For example, does it omit key issues or overemphasize others? While there may have been no bias in terms of carrying out the study, there may well be an element of bias in terms of how the findings are interpreted and presented. This is not to accuse researchers of trying to be deceptive, but rather being realistic and accepting that, in any social science undertaking, we can never eradicate subjectivity altogether. This returns us to the point made earlier about the need for openness, to be clear about any particular bias that may be applying.

> *Are the findings still relevant today?* You may come across research that was carried out many decades ago and yet is still being drawn on to support particular claims, even though those claims have attracted criticism, or the findings are no longer relevant. For example, to compile statistics about levels of poverty requires a definition of what constitutes poverty and so results obtained from data compiled in the last century need to be analysed in that particular context, rather than in terms of how poverty is defined today. It is therefore important to consider when, as well as why and how research is undertaken.

conclusion

This chapter has only given a very brief overview of a very complex set of issues. There is clearly a great deal more to be learned about research and you are advised to consult the guide to further learning in Part 7, as it is important for your development that you continue to learn about these complex but vitally important issues.

The good news is that the more you read about research, the more comfortable you will be. We have worked with many people in social work – students and practitioners – who have initially found the idea of using research quite daunting but, in a relatively short period of time, they have managed to get over the initial hurdles to have demystified the subject and have started to feel much more comfortable with it. So, it is reassuring to recognize that research matters are not inevitably anxiety provoking.

In addition, it is important to recognize that drawing on research and benefiting from it is a shared responsibility and is not just a personal matter for individual social workers. Many teams, for example, have a culture of sharing knowledge, understanding and news of research developments. This is a topic to which we shall return in Chapter 5.3.

A final point of reassurance on the subject of tackling the complexities of research is that it is highly likely that part of your professional training towards a social work qualification will include input about research methods and their importance as an underpinning of high-quality professional social work practice.

> What is meant by research 'rigour'?
> What is meant by research 'reliability'?
> What is an 'ethnographic' approach to research?
> Why are ethics important in relation to research?
> What is involved in critically evaluating research?

5

5.3 incorporating research into practice

introduction

The whole of Part 5 of the book has been geared towards emphasizing the importance of research. In this chapter, our aim is to draw links between the world of research and the world of actual practice. We therefore concern ourselves with looking at how social work practice can actually draw upon the benefits associated with a research base. As we noted in relation to evidence-based practice in Chapter 5.1, there are clear dangers associated with going about our important business in social work without at least some reassurance that there is a positive benefit to be gained from our actions. We owe it to the people we serve, our profession and to ourselves, to make sure that what we offer is based as fully as possible on a well-informed approach, and this clearly involves being able to draw upon the wealth of research that applies to social work and related matters.

evidence-based practice, see p. 280

NOS Key Role 6

Demonstrate professional competence in social work practice

In this chapter, we shall explore issues relating to finding research. How do we actually get hold of the relevant information? And, linked to this, will be the question of how do we find the time to do so? We will then move on to look at relating research to practice, to consider what is involved in this process. Finally, we shall explore the very important topic of maintaining a research-based culture.

finding research

These days we are very lucky to have the benefit of the Internet as a major source of information. It is important to recognize, however, that there is a huge difference between what is available in terms of research from the Internet generally – that is, for any user of the World Wide Web, and the additional services available through colleges and universities. University and college libraries invest significant sums of money in subscription services to a number of databases under the sources of information that are not available to the general user of the Internet. This is particularly important for social work students, as there is a strong tendency for many to rely on their connection to the Internet at home to download relevant information. While there is nothing wrong with this in principle, it does mean that there is a huge source of additional information available from the college or university system that is not being taken advantage of. Also, it is worth bearing in mind that these resources are likely to have been 'vetted' to some degree in terms of whether the information has a reliable source – something you will have to be wary of if surfing the Internet yourself. While some people may be feeling overawed by the size and complexity of the library system, it is well worth trying to get over this because of the huge benefits that can be gained in accessing relevant information.

Also in relation to the use of the Internet, there is much to be gained by the use of bookmarking, or the 'My Favourites' facility. This means that, when you find a site that is useful to you for your studies, you can then include it in a list of favourites, so that you do not have to look it up again, you can simply click on it and access it directly from your web browser. Our advice is that you make extensive use of this facility. Whenever you encounter a site that may be of benefit, include it in your favourites list, as it is very easy to forget where you found a particular piece of information or how to get back to a particular site. The bookmarking facility makes this a lot easier for you and prevents any such problems of forgetting.

Another important source of research information can be research groups. These may exist within a particular employing organization or on a regional basis. It is well worth your while making enquiries about whether research groups are in operation in your area and, if so, how you can get access to the information that they generate.

Other major sources of research information are the academic and professional journals. These are a vitally important source of information on research studies. We are fortunate in social work to have a wide variety of relevant journals. There are not only those that apply generically to social work, such as the *Journal of Social Work*, but also more specialist journals relating to each field of practice. You may be surprised to find out just how many journals are available in relation to a particular topic. It is therefore well worth making the effort to find out what are the journals that relate to your particular field of interest and where they are available from.

There are also important research organizations – for example, the Rowntree Foundation. This foundation provides excellent research studies on social policy and related issues and is able to provide free summaries of their work.

Rowntree Foundation, see p. 344

Some magazines and newspapers can also be useful for providing summaries of research, particularly the quality newspapers such as *The Guardian, The Independent* and *The Times*, and other such papers in other countries.

Training courses can also help with research at times. For example, a training facilitator may make reference to a relevant piece of research and you may then have the opportunity to follow up on this if you feel it is helpful to you in your practice.

There are also professional organizations that, although not specifically set up for the purposes of research, can be a useful inroad to gain research information. These include generic organizations, such as the Social Care Institute of Excellence (SCIE) and more specialist areas within each particular field – for example, BASPCAN in relation to child protection.

It is clearly important to be research minded here, to be sensitive to the potential sources of research. Research findings will not seek you out, so it is important that you do whatever is necessary to seek them out. Do remember, however, that the responsibility for research-minded practice is a shared responsibility. This is not just down to you alone to find research information, it is a responsibility you can share with colleagues.

Manage and be accountable, with supervision and support, for
your own social work practice within your organization

Also important in relation to finding research is the question of finding time. Some people argue that they do not have time to find and read research. However, this is basically a false economy. The time that is invested in having a more informed, more confident, more professional approach to practice, is easily repaid in terms of the benefits gained. We should be wary, then, of falling into the trap of assuming that using research is a drain on our time resources – it is in fact a very effective and worthwhile use of our scarce time resources. time and workload management, see p. 111

relating research to practice

We noted earlier in Chapter 5.1 that it is important to adopt a critical approach to the use of research. It is not simply a matter of letting research dictate practice. Therefore, in relating research to practice, we have to do it in a way that allows us to engage our critical faculties. It is certainly not simply a matter of 'the research says X', therefore we must do X. That is a wholly unsatisfactory, grossly oversimplified understanding of the links between research and practice.

The relationship between research and practice is a complex one, but we can make steps forward by trying to establish a balance between, on the one hand, the unhelpful extreme of disregarding research and, on the other, the perhaps equally unhelpful extreme of an uncritical use of research.

Using research is very much about the use of best evidence, but this still requires professional and analytical skills. Again, we must emphasize that research is not a set of prescriptions for practice. We have to ask such questions as: does the research apply in the situation I am dealing with? How strong is the research? Is it just one isolated study, or are there sets of studies that have similar findings? How extensive is the research? Is it of limited scope or does it apply more broadly? Is it the contrary research that challenges the findings that are of interest to you? These are all important questions that will help us form links between the research base and our actual practice.

We cannot emphasize enough the importance of not jumping to conclusions. Research is rarely, if ever, definitive. Research generally talks about suggesting or showing rather than proving. We have to realize that the nature of social work is very complex, very prone to considerable uncertainty, and what research can do is limited to casting light on certain areas. Research will rarely provide a definitive approach to a topic and it would be dangerous at times to assume that it does.

There are significant links also with the discussion in Chapter 5.1 of evidence-based practice. We noted there that there are other kinds of evidence as well as research. What is important is the ability to integrate different types of evidence – not only research evidence but what we can learn from the input and perceptions of clients and carers, for example. This is an important connection with reflective practice, as discussed in Chapter 2.7, where what is required of us as professionals is to integrate various sources of knowledge. It is therefore about maintaining a suitable balance whereby research evidence is part of the knowledge we integrate, but it is not the whole story. It would be dangerous to rely too heavily on research in that way.

The point has been emphasized that the responsibility for drawing on the research knowledge available to us is a shared one. To maintain it as a shared responsibility, it needs to become part of the workplace culture in which you work (or will be working). A major question, therefore, is how do we maintain a research-based culture? How do we make research part and parcel of our day-to-day work, rather than something that fades into the background or is only touched upon from time to time?

There is no short or easy answer to this, but we would argue that the following elements are very important in this. If you wish to play an important part in maintaining a research-based culture, you will need to:

> *Read.* An important part of reflective practice is to continue to read about social work and related matters. If we fall into the trap of assuming that reading is something you do when you have to in order to get your qualification, and can promptly be forgotten once you qualify, then we are on thin ice and run the risk of failing to develop high-quality reflective practice. Continuing to read as part of ongoing professional development is therefore crucial, and so the reading of research reports and summaries should be part of that reading (Neil Thompson, 2002b).

> *Discuss.* For research to become part of a workplace culture, it needs to be discussed at team meetings, away-days and so on. One possible way forward here is what is known as a 'learning set'. This involves a group of people meeting from time to time (say, on a monthly basis) to develop an understanding of particular issues, so if you are working in a team of social workers dealing with older people and their needs, for example, it may be possible to set up a learning set of interested parties to review current research and the implications of it for working with older people – for example in relation to elder abuse.

> *Challenge anti-intellectualism.* It is unfortunately the case that we have a tradition (albeit thankfully a dwindling tradition) of regarding social work as simply a practical activity unconnected with matters of learning, thinking and intellect. This is a dangerous tendency, and one that needs to be challenged. To maintain a culture focused on research, it is important that any instances of anti-intellectualism are challenged constructively, but firmly.

> *Attend training and other such events.* While training courses may not be specifically focused on research, often they are based on research findings, either directly or indirectly.

> *Subscribe* – for example, to databases, either personally or institutionally. There are such services as Social Work Alliance, for example, which, for a modest fee, provide significant amounts of information about new developments in the social work field including research developments. If your employer does not subscribe to such a service, you may wish to either invest in it yourself from your own funds or try to put pressure on your employer to take out a subscription on behalf of you and your colleagues.

> *Think.* Social work is a pressurized activity, and so it is very easy for people to get into a mentality of 'head down and get on with it'. This will bypass research and the benefits a well-informed approach to practice can bring. We therefore have to make sure that we are taking the opportunity to use our thinking capacity.

> *Engage.* This means not simply taking research at face value, but thinking about its implications, linking one research study with other research studies, drawing out the implications for practice (sometimes researchers will do this, but very often they do not). Remember again, though, that this is a shared responsibility; it is about groups of people engaging rather than just individuals. You can support each other in this endeavour.

> *Support.* It is to be hoped that social workers will support one another in the various demands made upon them, and why should the demand of being well-informed by research be any different? It is well worth looking at how people can support one another in making sure that their practice is well-informed practice.

Principle 3 `Critical Analysis`

Anti-intellectualism is dangerous because it discourages a critical perspective.

practice focus

5.3

Graham had found being a practice teacher a very satisfying experience. His latest student, Irene, had been a keen student who often asked him and his team colleagues about the pros and cons of the particular approaches they used. Sometimes he couldn't answer her questions and realized that he was in danger of losing that critical edge to his thinking which had made him ask those questions himself at an earlier point in his social work career. This realization spurred him on to do something he had meant to do for a long time now but had never made the space for in his demanding schedule. He sent a memo to his colleagues inviting them to put aside just one hour each month to get together to think about their practice and their professional development and was pleased when all replied positively. To get the ball rolling he brought an article he had seen which had cast some doubt on the effectiveness of a particular form of therapy. Several colleagues were not aware of this and the session provoked a good deal of debate about whether they needed to revisit the effectiveness of the approaches that they favoured. It became clear that some people kept themselves up to date with developments but that others were also in danger of losing sight of the changes that were going on around them as they applied themselves to their busy workloads. The monthly sessions continued to be well attended and became a focus not only for information sharing, but also for helping each other to access and understand research.

conclusion

We have seen that research is not a matter of providing definitive truth. It is not that simple. More realistically, research is a tool to promote informed, reflective practice. It reduces the amount of uncertainty, the gaps in our knowledge. We have argued that, in keeping with Principle 3: Critical Analysis, we need to take a critical approach to this, because to give too much respect to the findings of research without questioning them, can lead to difficulties.

We have also emphasized that the use of research is a shared responsibility. It is not just about individual social workers ploughing a lonely furrow in splendid isolation; rather, it is a case of groups of social workers and their managers recognizing that professional practice needs to be informed practice, and that means paying due regard to what the wider research community has to say about the important issues we address in our practice.

However, we have also seen that there is no need to panic. The skills and knowledge we have touched on in this part of the book can be developed over time. No-one is expected to be fully competent in the use of research overnight. However, we need to make sure that we do not go to the other extreme of losing focus and allowing research issues to drift and fade away. We see it as part of every social worker's professional responsibility to make sure that their work is well informed, including well informed by research. If each of us takes that responsibility seriously, and supports others in doing so, we have the foundations for building a much more professional approach to social work practice.

points to ponder

> In what ways can you gain access to research evidence?
> What is involved in adopting a 'critical' approach to research?
> What are the key elements of a research-based culture?
> What sources of support are available to you in relation to incorporating research into practice?
> How can research help to promote reflective practice?

5.4 **conclusion**

The use of research is certainly no panacea. However, there is no doubt considerable scope for making greater use of the insights that research can offer us. As we noted earlier, it has long been recognized that social work practice needs to be *informed* practice – we do our clients a considerable disservice if we simply base our efforts to help them on habit, routine, guesswork and copying others rather than on research-minded practice as part of a broader commitment to reflective practice. We therefore need to take the research dimension of social work very seriously and give it the attention that it deserves. This means getting past the anxiety about research that is commonly encountered and 'demystifying' the subject so that we can all feel more confident in tackling it and drawing on the benefits it has to offer. It is to be hoped that our discussions in Part 5 will have played at least a small part in demystifying research and thus taking away some of the anxiety that can discourage people from embracing the research world.

We are in favour of the development of evidence-based practice but we are cautious about the dangers of: (i) attaching too great a degree of significance to the role to research evidence, at the expense of other forms of evidence that we need to take into account (the perspective of clients and carers, for example); and (ii) re-introducing a positivist model with an oversimplified understanding of the relationship between (social) science and society (Neil Thompson, 2000b). What we need, then, is a balanced approach – one that avoids the destructive extremes of, on the one hand, rejecting the value of research and the evidence it produces and, on the other, overestimating the role that research evidence can play and thereby failing to take sufficient account of the other important factors that should be informing our work.

NOS Key Role 4

Manage risk to individuals, families, carers, groups, communities, self and colleagues

Sometimes research evidence will be presented to you 'on a plate', as it were – for example, through a training course or other such development event. However, at other times you will need to seek the evidence out. It is therefore important that you should remember the guidance given in Chapter 5.4 about developing and maintaining a culture of research-minded practice. The point was made that this is a shared responsibility. This means that you should not be isolated in this activity and should have the support of colleagues to draw upon. However, it also means that you have to play your part and take whatever reasonable steps you can to put research on the agenda and make sure that it does not get forgotten in the pressures of the workaday world. If you are fortunate enough to find yourself in a culture in which research-minded practice and reflective practice more broadly are supported and valued, you can look at how you can make the most of this. If you are not fortunate enough to be in such a workplace culture, you can consider how best you can develop good practice despite the lack of cultural support and, when you are sufficiently well established and confident in your role, you may wish to consider how you can influence (collectively with like-minded colleagues where possible) the culture to try and make it more conducive to good practice and continuous learning.

suggestions for further reading

5.1 why is research important?

Becker, S. and Bryman, A. (eds) (2004) *Understanding Research for Social Policy and Practice: Themes, Methods and Approaches*, Bristol, The Policy Press.

Hek, G., Judd, M. and Moule, P. (2002) *Making Sense of Research: An Introduction for Health and Social Care Practitioners*, 2nd edn, London, Continuum.

Sheldon, B and Chilvers, R. (2000) *Evidence-Based Social Care: A Study of Prospects and Problems*, Lyme Regis, Russell House Publishing.

Thompson, N. (2000) *Theory and Practice in Human Services*, 2nd edn, Buckingham, Open University Press.

5.2 understanding research methods and process

Becker, S. and Bryman, A. (eds) (2004) *Understanding Research for Social Policy and Practice: Themes, Methods, and Approaches*, Bristol, The Policy Press.

Chamberlayne, P., Bornat, J. and Apitzsch, U. (eds) (2004) *Biographical Methods and Professional Practice: An International Perspective*, Bristol, the Policy Press.

D'Cruz, H. and Jones, M. (2004) *Social Work Research: Ethical and Political Contexts*, London, Sage.

Everitt, A. and Hardiker, P. (2004) *Evaluating for Good Practice*, Basingstoke, Palgrave Macmillan.

Gomm, R. (2003) *Social Research Methodology: A Critical Introduction*, Basingstoke, Palgrave Macmillan

Robson, C. (2002) *Real World Research: A Resource for Social Scientists and Practitoner-Researchers*, 2nd edn, Oxford, Blackwell.

Singh, G. and Johnson, M. R. D. (1998) 'Research with Ethnic Minority Groups in Health and Social Welfare', in Williams, Soydan and Johnson (1998).

Smith, M. J. (1998) *Social Science in Question*, London, Sage.

5.3 incorporating research into practice

Becker, S. and Bryman, A. (eds) (2004) *Understanding Research for Social Policy and Practice: Themes, Methods and Approaches*, Bristol, The Policy Press.

Chamberlayne, P., Bornat, J. and Apitzsch, U. (eds) (2004) *Biographical Methods and Professional Practice: An International Perspective*, Bristol, The Policy Press.

D'Cruz, H. and Jones, M. (2004) *Social Work Research: Ethical and Political Contexts*, London, Sage.

Fuller, R and Petch, A. (1995) *Practitioner Research: The Reflexive Social Worker*, Buckingham, Open University Press.

Gomm, R. (2003) *Social Research Methodology: A Critical Introduction*, Basingstoke, Palgrave Macmillan.

Hek, G., Judd, M. and Moule, P. (2002) *Making Sense of Research: An Introduction for Health and Social Care Practitioners*, 2nd edn, London, Continuum.

Humphries, B. (2003) 'What Else Counts as Evidence in Evidence-based Practice', *Social Work Education*, **22**(1).

Lewis, J. (2003) 'The Contribution of Research Findings to Practice Change', in Reynolds et al. (2003).

Sheldon, B. and Chilvers, R. (2000) *Evidence-Based Social Care: A Study of Prospects and Problems*, Lyme Regis, Russell House Publishing.

career pathways

6

introduction

Social work is more than just a job, and so the notion of career is a very important one to consider. To many people, the idea of career implies working towards promotion. However, it is important to see the idea of 'career' in much broader terms than this. A career is a course of development, regardless of whether that involves moving up to the next rung on the ladder. 'Career' implies the opposite of being stuck in a rut of just following routines year in, year out. The notion of career is therefore very closely linked to the idea of continuous professional development (a point we shall discuss in some detail below), and job satisfaction. Given that social work is a professional activity, it is necessary for practitioners to be involved in an ongoing development of their knowledge and skills to make sure that they are learning from their experience, so that, as time goes on, they have more and more to offer their clientele.

NOS Key Role 6

Demonstrate professional competence in social work practice

We are very fortunate in social work that there is a wide range of career pathways available to us and a wide range of opportunities for continuous professional development within those pathways. In Chapter 6.1, we shall therefore examine the range of career opportunities available to qualified social workers. This includes practice, management and education. From this we will move on, in Chapter 6.2, to look at issues to do with continuous learning and the implications of this for continued registration as a social worker. In Chapter 6.3 we shall examine what is involved in applying for jobs and will offer advice and guidance on completing an application and how best to present yourself at an interview. Chapter 6.4 provides a short concluding discussion.

6.1 **career opportunities across settings**

Career opportunities in social work can be divided up into various categories. For example, some people draw a distinction between social work itself and social care, with the latter including careers in, for example, residential work. There is also a distinction to be drawn between social work and community justice work. At one time working with offenders (whether adult offenders or youth offenders) was clearly seen as part of social work. However, developments in the last decade or so have led in some areas (in England and Wales, for example, but not in Scotland or Northern Ireland) to an increasing separation of community justice issues from the mainstream of social work, although many people within the community justice field remain committed to a social work model, and there are some indications at least that there will be an increasing rapprochement between social work and community justice in the future. This section applies a broad brush to these issues and includes reference to a wide variety of possible careers that are open to a qualified social worker. It therefore includes fields that are not necessarily seen as traditionally social work specifically, such as residential work, or the community justice field.

statutory sector

This is predominantly local authority departments. In recent years, the relationship between social work and local authority departments has become increasingly complicated and we have seen an increase in the diversity of configurations. At one point, it was relatively straightforward that England and Wales had Social Services Departments, Scotland had Social Work Departments and Northern Ireland had Social Services as part of health trusts and boards. However, we are now seeing a diversification of this, whereby there is an increasing split between children's services (for example, in the amalgamation of Education Departments and the children and families sector of Social Services Departments) and adult services. In many areas the latter are joining forces with health colleagues or remaining as relatively autonomous units, but distinct from what were previously Social Services Departments that incorporated children's services as well. The position, then, is clearly very complicated, but one thing is quite clear: local authorities employ large numbers of social workers, and so there are very many opportunities for employment within this sector.

In addition to local authority departments, there are opportunities for social work in health-related work. This includes hospitals, health centres and multidisciplinary teams (for example, in relation to physical and/or mental health). The specific opportunities vary from area to area; for example in some areas there are social workers attached to

GP surgeries, but in other areas no such provision exists and therefore there will be no employment opportunities in these areas.

CAFCASS (the Children and Family Court Advisory and Support Service) also provides employment opportunities for qualified social workers www.cafcass.gov.uk

In addition, there is the field of community justice to consider. The Probation Service and equivalent bodies in other countries of the UK and further afield provide opportunities for qualified social workers although, as mentioned above, the inclusion of probation work under the heading of social work is a contentious one these days. None the less, social workers are not excluded from the field of community justice, especially in relation to working with young offenders where social work skills in working with young people are still strongly recognized.

the voluntary sector

While it is clear that the statutory sector is by far the biggest employer of social workers, we should not neglect the voluntary sector. Some people tend to equate social work with the statutory sector, but this is a significant mistake, as a great deal of high-quality practice goes on in the voluntary world. There are two main types of voluntary sector organization. There are large, often national, organizations that are often very well known – for example, the NSPCC and Barnardo's in the child care field, and bodies such as Age Concern, Mind and so on in other fields. There are also smaller, often local or regional, voluntary bodies that have a lower profile, but none the less can do some excellent work in their particular field. In terms of employment opportunities, the picture is quite complex. Some of the voluntary organizations such as the NSPCC employ large numbers of qualified social workers, whereas other voluntary sector organizations often do not have the funding infrastructure to do this and sometimes have to rely on the efforts of unqualified workers.

Some voluntary organizations employ teams of social workers, while others may have just one post. For example, large hospices may have a team of social workers, while small hospices may have only one social worker as part of the multidisciplinary team (or indeed may not have a social worker at all).

Terms and conditions of employment can vary across a voluntary sector. Many voluntary sector employers use more or less identical terms and conditions to the statutory sector, whereas others may offer terms that differ in significant ways – for example, in terms of salary and other conditions. If you have experience of working in the statutory sector and are considering a switch to the voluntary sector, you should not assume that any post available will be offering the same terms and conditions as your previous employment. Similarly, if you are approaching the voluntary sector as your first post in social work, then you need to be aware of the significant differences that can sometimes apply in terms of what is on offer to you as an employee. This is not to say that the statutory sector is necessarily better than the voluntary sector; in fact, our experience of working across a wide variety of social work settings is that staff in the voluntary sector often display much higher levels of job satisfaction although they may face similar frustrations and constraints as their statutory sector colleagues, and may also have extra uncertainties relating to funding contracts.

the private sector

This is an important sector too. On the whole, it is a smaller sector than certainly the statutory sector but also the voluntary sector. Much of the work in the private sector relates to residential care and the provision of domestic services such as home care. The scope for employment of qualified social workers is relatively limited compared with especially the statutory sector, but there are still significant opportunities within the private sector.

One important point to consider in terms of private sector employment opportunities is that this sector is often stereotyped as being 'just about profit, not about care'. It is important to recognize that this is a stereotype and that organizations and establishments within the private sector vary enormously (as indeed they do in the statutory and voluntary sectors). It is certainly untrue and unfair to tar all private sector organizations with the notion that their sole or primary pursuit is profit, even if this is at the expense of quality of service provision.

independent practice

This is a small but growing sector of the career market. Independent practitioners are a small group of specialist workers. One such group, for example, is children's guardians (or guardians *ad litem*, as they were known until fairly recently). These are specialist child care workers who work within the court system. This type of work does not present opportunities for newly qualified staff, as there is a clear expectation that somebody acting as a children's guardian would be a very experienced and qualified worker.

children's guardians, see p. 171

The independent sphere also includes people who offer training and consultancy services. Social work organizations generally provide their own in-house training, whether it is directly provided by their own training staff or bought in by independent training providers. Similarly, social work organizations are increasingly drawing on consultancy support where they face a particular set of issues or challenges. They may feel that it is a worthwhile investment of money to bring in an independent consultant to offer a fresh perspective and an additional layer of expertise in tackling perhaps some of the more thorny aspects of social work policy and practice.

There are also opportunities in terms of independent practice for people to investigate complaints. Many social work organizations have a panel of independent complaints investigators so that, on the occasion of a serious complaint arising, they can ask somebody from their panel to undertake an independent investigation on their behalf.

There are also limited opportunities in independent practice for people to be involved in social work education – for example, as a long-arm or off-site facilitator of practice learning (practice teacher). These are people who have a background in social work education, who are skilled at facilitating learning and provide backing to students who are on placement with organizations that do not employ somebody who is suitably qualified to act as a practice learning facilitator.

The independent practice sector does not offer opportunities for newly qualified staff. People in the early stages of their career may well have an aspiration towards operating in this sphere and that is perfectly legitimate but they need to be realistic in terms of how soon they can enter this type of work, given that it relies on a considerable body of experience and expertise.

> **the voice of experience 2**
>
> 'It took an awful lot of courage to give up my job and launch my own business as an independent social worker. However, I knew of others who had successfully made the transition, so I took comfort in that. It is just over a year now since I took the plunge and, while I still feel uneasy at times, I am really enjoying what I am doing. Being well organized has proven to be essential, as I have no boss to give me a nudge if I start to get careless', Cara, independent social worker.

occupational social work

This is not a widely used term in the UK. In America the term occupational social work is used to refer to the use of social workers in industry. For example, some large companies employ social workers to deal with workplace problems. These include problems associated with alcohol and drug abuse, mental health problems, stress, conflict and so on. The idea behind occupational social work is that companies who invest in providing social work services will be seen as good employers and this will justify the investment in looking after their staff and their specific needs. The idea has relatively limited application at present, although the potential for growth and development in this field is enormous.

Also within this field of what can broadly be called occupational social work is the work of such organizations as the Soldiers, Sailors Airmen and Families Association, or SSAFA for short. Bodies such as SSAFA provide support for individuals and families without the need for the involvement of social services on a more formal basis, but may work closely alongside more formal systems where this is required.

Opportunities for this type of work are likely to remain limited for the foreseeable future, but it is none the less a possible option for some people at least.

social work education and research

The vast majority of people employed in colleges and universities to teach social work have a background in social work themselves. That is, they have careers that have involved being a social work practitioner and possibly also a manager before going on to become a tutor or lecturer in the subject of social work. Again, this is something that is not really an option for somebody in the early stages of their career, but at a later stage, social work education provides a number of opportunities for people to remain within the social work field but with a new emphasis and focus to their work, the opportunity to learn new skills and broaden their horizons accordingly. Universities and research institutes and sometimes employing organizations also offer opportunities for qualified social workers to engage in research work. While this does not necessarily involve direct social work practice skills, it is none the less an important part of the career pathway network available to qualified social workers.

As a stepping stone to a career in social work education or research, many social workers contribute to social work education either through being practice learning facilitators/practice teachers, or by being a guest speaker or part-time lecturer on a social work degree or related programme.

management

While it is not strictly necessary to be a qualified social worker in order to be a social work or social care manager, having a social work qualification can be a major asset for those people seeking a management career.

Management is a broad term. It can apply to first-level management – for example, people who are team managers or group leaders in residential care perhaps. There are also middle managers, people involved at various levels in an organization relating to the management of that organization but who are not directly supervising staff, but nor are they senior managers at a strategic level. And of course, finally, there is the level of senior management. While it may take quite some time for somebody to get from being a newly qualified social worker to being a senior manager, it does happen, and so we should not rule out the possibility of reaching the dizzy heights of senior management.

There are also managerial posts indirectly associated with social work. For example, some local authorities employ policy advisers who have a partly managerial, partly research role. They may be involved in dealing with particular projects or advising on particular initiatives.

training and development

The majority of social work organizations employ staff as training officers or managers or staff development officers (the terms vary widely). There are also people involved in this field who are involved in related roles as, for example, S/NVQ assessors and mentors. This means that developing a training or staff development aspect to one's career portfolio can be a realistic option for some people.

Marcus had been in the same post for many years, as a social worker based at an inner-city hospital. He thoroughly enjoyed the varied nature of the work and felt that, while he was comfortable in the role, it still offered him the challenges he relished. One day he set some time aside to prepare a presentation he had been asked to make to a group of trainee medical and nursing staff on the role of the social worker. He didn't expect it to take long, as he just needed to think about what his role entailed and how to get that across to others in a positive light and without being jargonistic. But when he applied himself to the task he realized that his planned focus was actually a very narrow and, in some ways, a misrepresentative one. Having been in his own particular social work environment for a number of years he had come to equate his social work role with *the* social work role. When he thought about all of the possible environments he could be working in, he remembered that, while there would be similarities in terms of

practice focus

6.1

core social work skills, values and dilemmas, there could also be significant differences in terms of such aspects as working environment, obligation to employer, job security and personal safety, and expectations of role and outcome. He decided that not only would he broaden out the presentation to incorporate a wider perspective on social work, but he would also try to make time to visit colleagues in other disciplines in order to enrich his own experience and contribute to his own understanding of what social workers do and face in different contexts. While not planning to move out of his current role he could see that this would be a useful process in terms of his continuing professional development within it.

Principle 6 **Realism and Challenge**

Whichever branch of social work you pursue your career in, realism and challenge will be a part of it.

conclusion

It should be clear from our comments above that there is a wide and varied network of career opportunities. The vast majority of qualified social workers are employed as practitioners in direct service provision and assessment. However, there are also significant numbers of qualified social workers who are involved in important roles in relation to education, training, management, policy development, and so on. It is therefore possible to have a full, varied and satisfying career within the social work field. However, to return to our earlier point that we should not equate career development necessarily with promotion, it is worth emphasizing that social work is such a varied and demanding and challenging occupation that it is quite possible to remain as a practitioner for an extended period of time, but still to maintain a clear career path in terms of constantly learning and developing, growing in the role as it were. We are not trying to discourage people from seeking promotion in due course. Indeed, the effective working of social work systems depends on having good people in senior positions, but what we are seeking to emphasize is that it is a mistake to equate career development with promotion. The two can go together, but they do not have to.

points to ponder

> Do you know which sector you would prefer to work in (statutory, voluntary or private)? Why?
> What makes the other sectors less attractive to you? Are you possibly making assumptions about them that are inaccurate (for example, that the private sector is interested only in profit)?
> Have you considered becoming a practice teacher at some point in your career?
> What strengths do you feel you have that can help you take your learning forward?
> Who do you trust to give you guidance on career development?

6.2 **continuous professional development**

In 2005, the necessity for qualified social workers to be registered in the UK with the General Social Care Council (GSCC) was a significant development in the history of social work professionalism. For many years, people in social work in the UK have bemoaned the absence of any formal recognition of the value and significance of social work and have been concerned at the lack of a mechanism for excluding inappropriate people from the profession. The introduction of registration has therefore been a major landmark in the historical development of UK social work. It can be seen as a major contribution towards taking us forward.

One key aspect of registration is the requirement for continuous professional development. That is, once somebody has become registered as a social worker, they will need to keep a record of their continuous professional development so that, after a further three years, when it is necessary for them to re-register, they will be obliged to provide evidence of the fact that they have devoted time, effort and energy to their own learning and development.

NOS Key Role 5

Manage and be accountable, with supervision and support, for your own social work practice within your organization

This in itself is a major development because, in the past, the commitment to continuous professional development has been patchy. While many people have had a major commitment and have contributed tirelessly to the learning development of themselves and their colleagues, others have neglected this aspect of their professional duties and have been satisfied to adopt the 'head down, get on with it' mentality that can be very dangerous. It is to be hoped that the registration system will encourage people in the former group, while presenting obstacles and difficulties in the latter.

In this chapter, we shall explore what is involved in various aspects of continuous professional development (or CPD for short). We shall begin by looking at what are known as postqualifying arrangements. From this, we shall move on to look at the role of in-service training before considering issues related to learning from experience more broadly. Finally, we shall examine some key issues relating to the important role of higher education.

postqualifying awards

For some years now social workers in the UK have had access to additional training and professional recognition under the postqualifying (or 'PQ') awards scheme. This has included awards in child care, community care, mental health and practice teaching. It is likely that newly qualified workers will receive details of the opportunities available in their area. If not, we would recommend that you make the necessary enquiries to find out what possible options you might have.

in-service training

Most, if not all, social work employers offer some level of in-service training. Generally this is a programme of one or two-day courses (although more extensive courses may be available at times). Such courses tend to cover a range of issues, including:

> *Changes in the law and policy.* By the time you qualify as a social worker you should have a good grasp of the key issues relating to law and policy but, of course, these issues do not stand still. You may well find that major changes occur before too long in your professional career and that you therefore need professional updating on the key aspects of the changes and how they may have an impact on your practice.

> *Professional updates and gap filling.* These, too, are important aspects of in-service training. While there may be changes in law and policy that need updates, there could well be other changes in our professional knowledge base or in our approach to issues that require update-related training. For example, issues relating to what constitutes good practice develop over time. A new approach that offers exciting opportunities for improved practice may develop that requires the need for training for practitioners to become at least basically proficient in them. Similarly, even someone who has learned a great deal from their professional training will not know all there is to know about their particular field. This is what we mean when we use the term gap filling. It does not matter how well informed, how experienced or how competent you are, there will always be gaps in your knowledge. Such is the vast expanse and complexity of the field of social work. Training relating to such gaps can therefore be invaluable although, unfortunately, some people take the arrogant view that once they are qualified, they do not need such training.

> *New approaches and ideas.* At one time social work practice paid little or no attention to anti-discriminatory practice. Once the ideas started to become embedded in social work education, new generations of social workers came into practice with relatively well developed ideas on such matters, such was the emphasis on anti-discriminatory practice on professional training courses. However, there were many practitioners who have qualified prior to the development of anti-discriminatory practice as a social work value, and they therefore needed training on this new approach. A more recent example would be the development of evidence-based practice where more and more people are appreciating the need for their work to be underpinned by evidence, but are not familiar with the ideas behind the theory of evidence-based practice and therefore welcome training on the subject.

Principle 4 `Knowledge, Skills and Values`

In-service training can help to maintain, develop and update knowledge, skills and values.

learning from experience

This takes us back to the topic of reflective practice. We noted in Chapter 2.7 that it is not enough simply to try and follow instructions or develop habits or base our practice on guesswork, we need to have a well-informed, analytical approach that enables us to learn from our experience and grow and develop over time.

NOS Key Role 6

Demonstrate professional competence in social work practice

In order to do this, we need to have a major emphasis on learning from experience. This refers back to the point made earlier about the significance of career. Career should not be equated with promotion but, rather, with ongoing development (which may or may not lead to promotion at a later date).

Learning from experience can be enhanced in a number of ways. First, we have the important role of supervision and appraisal. These are both employment-related practices that can have enormous benefit in helping people to learn from their experience. For example, supervision can help to identify key learning points from actual day-to-day practice. Appraisal every six or 12 months (depending on the particular scheme of your employer) can help to identify broader learning needs and potential ways of addressing those needs.

Some organizations have what are known as learning sets. These are meetings held on a regular basis by a group of people who are interested in developing their knowledge and understanding of a particular topic.

---

the voice of experience 3

'When I first qualified I worked in a team where the idea of continuing to learn was a bit of a joke. The team manager took the unhelpful view that, "If you've got time to learn, you haven't got enough work to do." I quickly moved on to another team – one that had a reputation for being keen on learning from experience. I have never looked back. Life was so much better after I made the move', Chris, care manager in an older people's team.

In addition, we should not neglect the significance of personal study and/or research. Ideally, social workers should be enthused by the work they do. They should gain pleasure from the learning involved. Neil Thompson (2000b) talks of 'the adventure of theory' and, by this, he means the pleasures and joys that can be gained from engaging with the challenging work we undertake and appreciating the complexities and subtleties involved, gaining some satisfaction from our ability to understand them and deal with them. The practitioner who prefers to simply learn the basics and then just put everything else down to experience is missing out on enormous potential benefits in terms of job satisfaction and further learning.

---

practice focus

6.2

Naomi felt very positive when she started her first job as a social worker in a multidisciplinary team. As a student she had been introduced to the concept of registration and understood it as a means to ensure that she maintained the standard of professional competence she had reached in order to be granted the title of qualified social worker. She was somewhat surprised, then, to hear one of her new colleagues discussing registration in very negative terms, using phrases like 'it's a real bind' and 'as if we haven't got enough to do already'. She could understand that, for many, this was something new that needed to be incorporated into an established way of thinking and working, but for her the requirements fitted very well with her aspirations. She could see that the world in general was changing all the time, and her studies had highlighted that the social work role was too. Indeed the social work profession itself had been under threat on more than one occasion and could never be taken for granted. The prospect of working in a multidisciplinary team had prompted Naomi to think carefully about what she could contribute to the team and how her role would be different from that of other colleagues. She wondered whether revisiting this regularly might serve as a good basis from which to build in terms of how she could demonstrate continuing competence. Like her colleague she knew that she would regularly be called on to account for how she guarded against complacency and to prove that she remained competent to practise in a changing world, but she welcomed, rather than resented, the duty placed on her by the registration process.

higher education

Not everyone in social work will wish to pursue higher education. Undertaking the initial qualification, engaging in in-service training and, perhaps, postqualifying awards, plus engaging in regular supervision combined with a personal commitment to continuous learning, can be a great success. Others, however, will want to go beyond this and will want to register at a college or university to undertake a course of study geared towards obtaining a further qualification, perhaps a specialist certificate or diploma. What is available varies across the country but, in certain areas at least, there will be opportunities to take advanced courses in relevant topics such as child protection, counselling, family therapy, gerontology and management.

Beyond the specialist certificates and diplomas, there will also be opportunities to register for higher degrees such as Master's programmes and even doctorates. Master's degrees take two main forms. There are taught Master's degrees which are similar to a first degree programme in terms of how they are run but are offered at a more advanced level and usually involve some sort of dissertation or extended essay as a final piece of work. These can be undertaken on a full-time or a part-time basis. More often than not in social work, they are taken on a part-time basis to fit in with a career in social work. The other type of Master's degree is a research-based Master's degree. This involves working closely with a nominated supervisor, proposing a course of research which will be undertaken and written up according to the prescribed regulations. Both types of Master's degree are a significant undertaking. The latter type perhaps involves a greater reliance on self-discipline, but both types will involve immense effort and resilience.

NOS Key Role 5

Manage and be accountable, with supervision and support, for your own social work practice within your organization

People interested in very advanced study can consider registering for a doctorate, for example a PhD. A PhD or equivalent involves making a new contribution to the knowledge base. It is possible to obtain a Master's degree by showing an advanced level of knowledge, but without necessarily contributing to that knowledge itself. A doctorate, by contrast, has as its basic criterion for success that the candidate must have made an original and substantial contribution to the knowledge base. This is clearly a major undertaking that requires a lot of careful consideration and planning.

conclusion

Continuous professional development is clearly an important part of the career pathways network relating to social work. There are numerous opportunities available to members of the social work profession to sustain their learning, to grow as professionals in the process, and to gain the benefits of continuous learning. Such learning can require a significant investment of time and energy, but in the vast majority of cases that investment is more than repaid by the benefits that are to be gained from it. We would therefore strongly recommend that, as you progress through your career, you keep an open mind about the learning opportunities available to you and make the most of what comes your way in terms of chances to capitalize on the learning available.

points to ponder

> What is meant by 'continuous professional development'? Why is it important?
> What roles does in-service training fulfil?
> How can you make sure you learn from your experience over time?
> What is a learning set?
> How can supervision help you to learn?

6.3 applying for jobs

introduction

You cannot have a career without first having a job! Is it just down to luck whether you get a particular job or not, or can you influence the process in your favour? We believe it is the latter. It is a matter of selling yourself, convincing potential employers that you are a worthwhile investment. This chapter provides you with advice and guidance on how to work your way through the difficult process of applying for a job. It is broken down into four parts. The first part is entitled 'First things first', and is concerned with the preliminaries to take care of before you do anything else. We then move on to look at the issues involved in making application for a job. Thirdly, we explore issues relating to the interview and what is involved in this often nerve-racking process. Finally, we examine the matters arising in relation to what we have called 'After the event' – that is, issues to do with how to respond to disappointment if you do not get the job and how best to manage the situation if you are offered the post.

first things first

Before actually making application for a job, there are certain things you can do as preliminary preparation. First, you need to know where the jobs that you may be interested in are advertised. Many local authorities advertise in national publications, such as *Community Care* and *The Guardian* in the UK, but not all employers do this. If you are wanting to work with a particular employer and your only source of information about jobs is the national media, you may be missing out on important information about jobs. If you are not sure where a particular organization is likely to advertise any jobs, you may wish to contact them to ask that question. If the organization concerned has a web site that may be a good starting point for you.

The next important question to ask yourself is: what job do you want? As we have seen in the earlier chapters in Part 6 of the book, there is a vast network of career pathways that can be pursued. Are you wanting to pursue a particular type of career within social work? Do you wish to specialize in a particular area, or do you want to have breadth of experience before considering a specialism? What geographical area are you prepared to consider for jobs? For example, if you are not prepared to move house, how far are you prepared to travel on a daily basis? In this way, you can establish your 'catchment area'.

Next, you need to ask yourself: do you want this job? That is, when you see a particular job advertised, it is important that, in your anxiety to achieve employment, you should not jump in, as it were, before you are ready. It is important to do your homework to find out what precisely is involved in the job concerned. What sort of set up is there? Is it really something you want to go for? Sometimes people's anxiety to get paid work can lead them to applying for any vacancy that arises. Are you sure you need to do this, or can you relax a little and apply for only those jobs that particularly appeal to you? It can be a big mistake to go for the first paid employment you see and then find that, once you have started the job, it is not really satisfying you or taking you in the direction you want to go.

It is also important to ask yourself: is it feasible for you to do this particular job? Are there any essential requirements that you may not be able to meet? For example, in some areas, it is feasible to be a field social worker without the need to drive, but in other areas, the rural nature of the patch would not allow a person who cannot drive to be able to cover the necessary territory. Similarly, in terms of the distance from your home to the place of work, how long would it take you to get there in the rush hour? It is important to check this out because what can be a 30-minute journey in time for a 2 p.m. interview, may be an hour and 15 minutes journey in the rush hour.

There is also the issue of informal discussion with prospective employers to consider. Some employers encourage this and give the name and contact details of a person they would like you to speak to (because it is not in their interests to have applications from people who are not going to be suitable for the post). You may find it a bit daunting to ring up a potential employer and have an informal chat with them, but we would encourage you to do so none the less, because: (a) you can gain invaluable information about whether you actually want to apply for the post; and (b) if you do, you may gain important insights that will help you strengthen your application.

We wish to emphasize the importance of doing your preparatory work. It can be a significant mistake to launch straight into applying for a job without first thinking through the issues that we have raised here. We would therefore urge you to consider these issues very carefully before proceeding to the next step.

making application

When you apply for a job, it is highly likely that it will be a competitive situation. That is, it is not simply a case of: are you good enough to do the job?, but rather: are you the best person to do the job? It is therefore important that you 'sell yourself' – that is, that you make your strengths clearly visible. Selectors are not mind readers; they will not know, unless you tell them, precisely what you have to offer, what benefits they will have from employing you, and why it is in their interests to offer you a post. Some people struggle with this and it goes against the grain for them to put themselves forward in such a positive way. Given the way men and women are brought up differently in our society, this can be an issue especially for women. Many men are taught how to be competitive and how to put themselves forward as favourably as possible, but for significant numbers of women (but not necessarily all women), this can be more difficult, because it does not fit with their upbringing. None the less, man or woman, it is important to get over any anxieties about putting yourself in as positive a light as possible. It is a matter of putting yourself in the shop window. You are highly unlikely to be able to compete successfully with others who adopt this 'sell yourself' approach if you are sitting back and hoping that the employers will give you the post anyway.

*Self-management skills can be very helpful when it comes
to 'selling yourself' to a possible employer.*

It is important to get the balance right. We want to avoid the unhelpful extremes of, on the one hand, being so modest that you hide your light under a bushel, that you fail to put across just what strengths you would bring to the job, compared with, on the other hand, an arrogant approach that comes across as somebody who is not going to be a pleasant person to work with. We would advise you to think carefully about this balance and how you can achieve it.

the voice of experience 5

'I showed my completed application form to my partner, but was surprised by the response: "You've been far too modest. How do you expect to compete successfully against other candidates if you play down your strengths?" I didn't like the idea of having to blow my own trumpet, but I realized that I would have to if I was to stand a chance of getting the job', Sam, a final-year student.

We are able to offer some practical tips on making applications. We suggest you read these carefully and, when the time comes to complete an application form, you revisit this section of the book to remind yourself of the key issues raised:

> *Photocopy the form.* It is surprising how many people spill coffee on the application form and then have to panic and ask the personnel section to send them another copy urgently. Our advice therefore is to photocopy the form when it arrives. You can then, if you wish, use the photocopy to do a rough draft of your application before proceeding to your final draft to be submitted.

> *Read the form carefully.* Make sure you fill it in properly and actually provide the correct information. We have experience of a number of situations where people have not done themselves favours by providing the wrong information on a form. A simple example of this is where a form asks, for example, for a date of birth. The person concerned provides that day's date (although increasingly employers are not asking for dates of birth to avoid claims of age discrimination). None the less, it is very important that you concentrate and fill in the form carefully and accurately. You will not be impressing anybody if you fail to do this basic thing.

> *Apply for the specific job.* The job should involve specific duties that are provided on a job specification form or equivalent. If you want to convince the selectors that you are not only a suitable candidate for the job, but are actually likely to be the best candidate for the job, then you need to address the specific issues. For example, if a particular job involves court work (although many social work posts do not), you would need to address this issue directly and show how you are suitable for tackling court work. Even if you have no experience in this area, you may want to make a positive comment about how you are keen to learn and develop the necessary skills. General application for 'a social work post' will not be sufficient for convincing the selectors about why you are suitable for this specific job.

> *Identify your strengths explicitly.* As mentioned above, selectors are not mind readers. You have to make it perfectly clear what it is you have to offer. Part of the

process of making application is the attempt to secure an interview – that is, to be short listed. If you do not make your strengths sufficiently clear, you run the risk that you will not be short-listed, even though you may actually have more to offer than candidates who are short-listed. It is therefore vitally important that you do not understate what you have to offer. One of the present authors once received an application form from an applicant and, in the space allotted to provide details of experience and so on, the candidate had simply written 'to be discussed at interview'. Of course, this did not occur, because the candidate had not done sufficiently well to justify being short-listed.

> *Don't tell lies.* It is important to be positive and to sell yourself, as we have emphasized, but we must draw the line at relying on untrue matters. Not only are there ethical issues involved in obtaining a job on false pretences, but also there is the practicality that, if you are found out, either during the application process itself or after being appointed, this is likely to backfire on you. If, for example, it emerges during the selection procedure, you may have ruined any chances of obtaining any future posts with that employer. If it emerges after you have been appointed that there was an untruth on your application form, you may find yourself being dismissed for that, which is not going to do your long-term career prospects much good at all.

> *Don't shoot yourself in the foot.* It is very important to be positive. You should not, therefore, identify any weak points. It is up to the selectors to look for any potential weaknesses, but it does not help you to put any specific weaknesses directly in front of them, as this may undermine your overall positive impression. Again, it is important that you should not tell lies. If there are any aspects of your past or current situation that could be deemed a weakness, and it is necessary for you to make reference to this for some reason, then we would advise you to put this across in as positive a set of terms as you can. For example, you could comment on how much you have learned from the errors you have made or the difficulties you have experienced, or whatever, and/or you can express a commitment to learning about these issues to improve in this area. But basically, you should not shoot yourself in the foot by giving people reason to think less highly of you, nor should you give them ammunition to do so themselves.

> *Express yourself clearly and neatly.* Do not rush filling in the application form, as you run the risk of presenting a garbled message to the selectors. Think carefully about what you are trying to say (this is where a rough draft beforehand can be helpful) and especially if you are producing the form in handwriting, make sure that it is neat and legible. First impressions are very important and if the impression you give is that you cannot be bothered to try and make a good impression, this is not likely to go down well.

> *Choose your referees carefully.* Most employers ask for a reference from a current or most recent employer, and so you will have little choice in this matter. However, in terms of other referees, you will need to think carefully about who is likely to support your application and how credible that person will be as a referee. For example, we have seen references from people who argue that the candidate would make an excellent social worker, but we have been left wondering how the referee would know this, given that the referee concerned does not have a background in, or connection with, social work. So you will need to think carefully about who is

the best person to approach. Do not automatically assume that: (a) you will get a good reference from this person; and (b) that this person's credibility will be well established in the eyes of the selectors.

a note on CVs

Some employers ask for a curriculum vitae instead of, or as well as, an application form. If you have not completed a CV before, you will need to look carefully at what needs to be included. We would also encourage you to ask people you know who may have produced CVs of their own, whether you can have a look at their CV to get an idea of what to include, how to present it, what not to include and so on. The more experienced and established such people are in their careers, the more impressive their CVs are likely to be, and so the more you can gain by asking to see them. You will need to be sensitive about this, of course, because a person's CV could be seen as a private matter, so choose carefully the people you are going to ask about this to make sure that your request is not seen as intrusive or inappropriate.

When it comes time to prepare your own CV, make sure you lay it out as impressively as possible. As with the application form, first impressions count, so do not give people the impression that you are untidy, disorderly and unconcerned with how you come across to other people.

interviews

By the time you get to the interview stage, you have already had some degree of success, and so it is important to recognize your strengths in achieving this. We recognize that interviews can be anxiety-provoking situations but, not for the first time in this book, our advice is: don't panic. It is a matter of keeping your nerves under control for a relatively short period of time. In the period leading up to the interview and the interview itself, it is understandable that you will feel nervous, but selectors will know this and, to a certain extent, will make allowances for it. However, what they will be interested to see is whether despite a certain degree of nervousness, you still manage to keep yourself under control and put yourself across positively.

> **the voice of experience 6**
>
> 'All four candidates were clearly very nervous. It was interesting to note, though, that two of the candidates managed to keep their nerves under control and came across very positively, while the other two clearly let themselves down by letting their nerves get the better of them. These candidates might have been able to do a good job but we weren't able to take the risk. What if their nerves got the better of them in practice situations?', Andrea, a team manager.

In an interview situation, it is important to let your personality come shining through, to let them see what they would be getting for their money. They will not, or should not, be trying to catch you out, but you may trip yourself up if you let your nerves get the better of you so that they do not see the 'real' person underneath. They just see the surface impression of an anxious person.

Given the significance of interview nerves, what might help you in preparation is to think about what helps you relax. What makes you feel comfortable? What makes you feel confident? Can you draw on these in the period leading up to the interview? What is very important to avoid is an escalation situation where your initial nervousness makes you worry about the situation and then you start to panic. Once you start to panic you feel more nervous, and so on, risking a vicious circle arising. The interview situation is one where you are trying to sell yourself as the best candidate for the job. You are trying to put yourself across very positively and you are bound to feel at least a little bit nervous (if not *very* nervous!), but remember that it is all in a good cause and that, at the end of the day, provided that you do not allow nerves to get out of hand, selectors will not penalize people simply for being nervous. It is par for the course.

It is worth remembering that an interview is a two-way process. They are trying to assess your suitability for the job in question, but there is also an important element of you assessing whether this is an organization you would want to work for and this is the specific job you want. Issues may arise during the interview that lead you to reconsider your earlier perspective on the situation. You should therefore feel free to ask them questions about issues that concern you (you will probably be invited to do this at the end of the interview, but other opportunities may arise during the course of the interview).

As with the process of completing an application form, there are some practical tips that we can give you that we hope you will find useful. Certainly students that we have presented these tips to in the past have given us very positive feedback to the effect that they found these extremely helpful. We would recommend that you read these carefully now, and then, when interview time comes round, re-read them to keep them uppermost in your mind at the time when you need them most.

practical tips

> *Preparation.* We advise you to re-read your application on the day of the interview, or at least the day before, so it is fresh in your mind what you have said about yourself, what approach you took, what sort of impression you have been trying to put across. It can pay dividends to think ahead for the interview, to do some preparatory work. Remind yourself of what experience, knowledge, skills and values you have that make you suitable for the post. If this is not clear and fresh in your mind, then you have got a struggle ahead of you to convince others of what you have to offer. Try not to go into too much detail, though, in your thinking and planning, as it is important that you do not tire yourself out and turn up for the interview in an overtired or stressed state. Once again, it is important to get the balance right.

> *Dress formally but comfortably.* Interviews are formal occasions and even in work settings where people normally dress casually, there is generally an expectation that interviewees will recognize the rules, as it were, and turn up suitably dressed in a reasonably formal outfit. Note, though, our emphasis on dressing comfortably also. You will want to be as relaxed as you can be in these circumstances and, having clothing that is too tight or shoes that are not comfortable, will not help you in that regard.

> *Remember the importance of non-verbal communication.* Smiling, making eye contact, and so on, can all be important aspects of a successful interview. People interviewing you may also feel nervous (it is a responsible job appointing a new

member of staff), and so you may help in putting them at their ease if you use appropriate body language, and this can only help in terms of making a favourable impression. Beware, however, of going over the top. Just use the sort of non-verbal communication you would use in trying to put somebody at their ease in meeting somebody for the first time, and so on.

> *Engage with people.* Make connection where you can. An important part of social work is being able to engage with people, to make connections and so, if you can manage to do this in the early stages of an interview situation, then you will put yourself in a very strong position. It is particularly important to begin and end well. So, on first meeting people, be prepared to shake hands, to make eye contact and so on. Similarly, at the end of the interview, smile and thank people for taking the time to consider your application, and again be ready to shake hands.

> *Show enthusiasm.* Employers will not want somebody who just tolerates the job. They will want somebody who is keen to do their best and so, if you are able to show enthusiasm right from the off, then this puts you in a stronger position than would otherwise be the case. However, it is important not to overdo this too. If you come across as unrealistically enthusiastic or overzealous, this could easily be put down to you playing a game to try and impress. It is important to be genuine about these matters, as selectors are generally not unintelligent people and will be able to see through any game playing.

> *Concentrate and listen carefully.* This is another example of how it is important not to let your nerves get the better of you. You need to be on your mettle and if you find this difficult, bear in mind that it is for a relatively short period of time. You can relax in a little while but for now, while the interview is taking place, you need to be very focused, concentrating on what you are being asked, what the selectors are looking for and how best to respond to their questions. It is also important in a social work context to show that you are able to listen carefully and appropriately, even in difficult or anxiety-provoking situations, as this is the sort of practice challenge that social workers regularly face.

> *Think before you answer.* There is no rush. It can be a significant mistake to allow your anxiety or your eagerness to get the interview over with, to push you into providing an ill-thought-through answer. Think carefully about what you have been asked and about the best way of answering it. Of course, you do not want to take too long and come across as somebody who is too ponderous and slow to be suitable for social work but, again, it is a matter of balance. A successful balance will be one where you give yourself some thinking time but without overdoing it.

> *Speak clearly.* Again, nervousness can be a factor here. It is interesting to note how many people tend to mumble and speak indistinctly when they are nervous. It is almost as if our nerves are trying to stop us from speaking clearly because, if people cannot make out what we are saying, they cannot criticize us or attack us for what we have said. Of course, the reality is that, if we mumble, not only do we make the interview experience difficult for all concerned, but we give ourselves a negative representation. In other words, we do not do any favours for our application if we mumble. It is therefore very important to make sure that we speak clearly, even if we are nervous.

> *Be honest but positive.* As with the application process where we advised that any issues which may be seen as potentially negative, our advice is to turn these

into learning gains wherever you can. If it is inevitable that you have to mention in response to a question, for example, that you have previously made a mistake or not done particularly well at something, do not allow this to become something that undermines you. Try and turn it into a positive by showing the selectors what you have learned from that experience (for example, what you would do differently in future or have done differently since those matters arose) or what learning you hope to gain about these matters in future.

> *Give examples where appropriate.* The selectors will be trying to form a picture of you. Giving short basic answers to their questions will not help in this regard, but if you can give, where appropriate, an example or two to back up what you are saying, this will give them a clearer picture of who you are, where you are coming from, and what you have to offer.

> *Don't waffle.* We are back to nerves again. It is commonly the case that people who are nervous do not know when to stop talking. They start to provide an answer and then, once they have given the information they needed to, instead of stopping, smiling and waiting for the next question, they continue to provide more and more information, perhaps unnecessary information and, in the process, give the selectors the message that they lack communication skills in a pressurized situation – not a good message to be giving potential social work employers.

> *Don't try and answer questions you don't understand.* It can be a nerve-racking experience for interviewers too, and this may mean that they ask questions that are not very clear or well formed, or it may be that they are asking you a question on the assumption that you have certain information which you do not have. It can be again nerve racking to be asked a question that you do not understand, and you may feel uncomfortable about asking for the question to be repeated or rephrased, but that is nothing compared with the problems you can get yourself into if you try and provide an answer to a question you do not really understand. Of course, only a fool would try and provide a sensible answer to a question they do not understand, so do not allow yourself to come across as a fool by falling into this trap. If you find yourself in this difficult situation, that is unfortunate, but the best way out of it is to take a deep breath, say simply but clearly, 'I'm sorry I don't understand the question', or words to that effect.

> *Think about what questions you want to ask.* It is generally the case that interviews conclude with a member of the interview panel saying to you: do you have any questions you want to ask us? It can be a very negative ending to an interview simply to say: 'No, I don't think so'. This can be a bit of an anti-climax, particularly if you have done very well so far and then you spoil it with such a limp answer. We would therefore strongly suggest that, as part of your preparation for the interview, you think about what questions you would like to ask. This may be about such issues as: what training is likely to be offered? What would the supervision arrangements be? And so on, and so forth. We suggest that you also consider writing these questions down and taking them in with you to the interview. Then, if you are asked if you have any questions, you can refer to your notes and, if any of the questions you have planned to ask have already been answered in the course of the interview, you can simply (and impressively) say: 'You've answered some of my questions but the ones you haven't answered are these', and then launch carefully into asking those questions. This well-organized, focused approach can help to impress potential

employers, whereas fumbling and stumbling around possible questions, or not having anything to ask, comes across in a very negative way in most situations.

> *Think about what you haven't had chance to say.* Many interviewers also ask (in addition to 'Have you any questions to ask?'): 'Is there anything you want to add? Is there anything you want to tell us about yourself that you haven't had the opportunity to say so far?' The short answer to this should be: yes. This is an ideal opportunity to fill any gaps. If you wanted, for example, to convince the panel of your expert skills in a particular aspect of practice or your enthusiasm for a particular matter, but this has not come up in the interview so far, then you can say words to the effect of: 'Yes, I had hoped to talk to you about my skills and experience in x but that hasn't come up so far', and then you can give them a potted version of what it is you offer in that field. Again, you may find it helpful to make some notes to this effect before the interview and take them into the interview with you so that, if called upon to do so, you can have a quick look at your notes and, if there are any gaps, any issues that have not been covered, you can raise them there and then. This can be doubly effective because: (a) it means you have the opportunity to impress on issues you would not otherwise have had the opportunity to impress on: and (b) the fact that you have come prepared and actually identified the strengths you would bring to the job, is impressive in itself.

> *When or how will they let you know?* As we have seen, there is a lot of anxiety that can go into an interview situation, but it can be even more anxiety provoking to be kept waiting to know the outcome. In fact, many people find that not knowing the outcome is more anxiety provoking than the interview itself. If you are not going to know for a fortnight, for example, then knowing that you will not get the result for a further two weeks, can make it a less pressurized experience, rather than spending two weeks constantly waiting for the phone to ring or for a letter to drop through the letterbox. So, to prevent yourself from having any unnecessary anxiety, it is perfectly legitimate for you to ask (if you have not been told already) when you are likely to be informed of the decision and what form that communication will take (telephone call, letter or whatever).

practice focus
6.3

Darren was becoming demoralized because, while virtually every job application he had submitted since qualifying had led to an interview, he had still not been successful in securing himself a job. He knew that his performance on the day usually failed to live up to the good impression he made in a written submission. He put this down to extreme nervousness at the first interview and seemed unable to overcome the association between interviews and failure. With each unsuccessful interview he became more nervous at the prospect of going through the process again and began to find it difficult to put himself across in a positive light when he had the opportunity to do so in person. He realized that he needed to find a strategy for addressing this problem and asked himself how he might approach the issue if he was working with an unconfident service user. It occurred to him that 'reframing' the experience might work and began to think of the interview as an opportunity to share information and expectations rather than as a test. He knew that he had proved his competence in such contexts before, having performed well in meetings and interviews with service users, managers and colleagues, and so decided to think of job interviews as opportunities rather than threats. This made all the difference on the day at his next interview and, while he was 'pipped at the post' by a more experienced candidate, he was elated at the feedback which suggested that he would have been appointed had there been two posts to be filled. He now felt that getting the social work post he wanted was a matter of time rather than competence, and realized that he was able to welcome, rather than dread, the next opportunity.

after the event

There are two main outcomes to an interview situation once the decision has been made: bad news or good news. If it is bad news, the first thing to bear in mind is that you should not take it personally. The selectors will be looking for the person they consider to be the best candidate for the job. The fact that they have not chosen you as the best candidate, should not be interpreted as a failure on your part. This is for two reasons. First, the fact that they consider somebody else to be better suited to the job does not means that you are unsuitable. Perhaps if that person had not applied, they would have been happy to give you this job. Second, the decision is based on their opinion and it may well turn out, in the long run, that you would have been a better candidate for the post. However, job selection is not an exact science, and there are many cases on record of selectors who have basically got it wrong and subsequently regretted their decision, wishing they had appointed an alternative candidate. It is therefore vitally important that you do not take this personally and see it as a sign of failure or inadequacy on your part.

Linked to this is the importance of asking for feedback. It may be that you did superbly well in both your application and your interview, but it just turned out that somebody else did even better. However, there may have been aspects of your application or your interview that detracted from how impressive you were. It can be quite daunting to ask for feedback on performance, particularly as that feedback may involve an element of criticism, although such criticism should be constructive. We would strongly advise you to ask for feedback. Not all employers will give it but if you are lucky enough to have been interviewed by an employer who will give feedback, you may learn some important tips for your next interview. You went through a very anxious situation, the least you can get out of it is some benefit in tips on improving your performance next time round.

If it is good news, then congratulations, but this is not the end of the story. There are still some issues to address. First of all, you need to ask yourself: do you still want the job? Has anything put you off now that you know more about the job, the team, the organization and so on? Remember that you are not obliged to accept a job offered to you if it is not right for you. You may feel duty bound to respond positively to an offer of a job, and you may feel that it is being a bit cheeky to apply for a job, be offered it, and then turn it down but, if the job is not right for you, then it is not right for you. It would therefore be a significant mistake to bow to such pressure and accept the job that could turn out to be a big mistake. If you are not sure whether to accept the post or not, you may want to check things out with your potential employers or, indeed, with other people. You may want to ask about particular issues that remain unclear or seek reassurance about certain issues. This is perfectly legitimate as long as you are quite sensible and reasonable about how you go about it and do not make unreasonable demands.

There are also issues about confirmation of the post. Some employers take up references before interview, others leave it until afterwards, so it may well be the case that any offer of a post is subject to satisfactory references being received. If your referees have been tardy in responding, you may want to give them a gentle, friendly nudge, but you will need to be careful and sensitive in doing this. If you alienate such people, this may backfire on you in terms of the reference given but, of course, it is perfectly reasonable to give a gentle reminder if you are anxiously waiting for confirmation of your post. There may also be need for medical clearance, either through a form being completed or an actual medical, so do bear in mind that you may not receive your offer in writing of a post until these matters have been dealt with and this may take some length of time to come through. It is very unusual for complications to arise between a post being offered verbally and the confirmation in writing being received, but such complications are not unheard of. It is therefore very unwise, for example, to give notice from an existing job until you have received that job offer in writing.

It is also important to consider whether there is any scope for negotiation. Realistically, this is likely to be very limited, but you may wish to explore issues around salary levels, terms and conditions, and so on. You will need to be sensible and constructive about this and, again, not make unreasonable demands, but some people who have been appointed to positions have managed to negotiate significant improvements to the post simply by exercising their negotiation skills.

You will also need to consider what you can do to get maximum benefit from the job itself by undertaking any preparatory work. Are there any issues you can sort out before taking up the new post that will make things easier and smoother on your arrival? Are there people you can talk to? Are there documents you can read? Are there any issues you can resolve in your own mind that will make it easier for you to settle into a new post and get the maximum amount of job satisfaction from it? However, in doing this, be careful not to lose focus on your existing job or, if you are a student on a social work course, you need to be careful that you do not allow your academic work or any work on a practice learning opportunity to suffer as a result of being distracted by an emphasis on your new job. You will need to get the balance right.

conclusion

Job hunting is a nerve-racking, but necessary, evil. It is something that has to be done in order to first of all start a career and, at various points in the future, perhaps, to take your career forward. As with so many other things, the process can be enhanced by knowledge and skills. It is to be hoped that this chapter will help to give you a platform from which you will be able to develop your knowledge and skills in these issues. Going through the process of applying for a job can take a lot out of you but it can also give you a lot as well, not only in terms of actual employment opportunities and career outcomes, but also in terms of the learning that can be gained from it. Through this process, we can learn a lot not only about employment practices, not only about organizations and the social work practices that go on within them, but also about ourselves, how we react under pressure, how we can learn to deal with those pressures more effectively. This last point is a particularly important one because social work is necessarily a pressurized activity. The longer we stay in social work, the better we should be at dealing with those pressures, the more skilled and knowledgeable we should be. Applying for jobs can therefore be a useful part of our learning repertoire in its own right as well as a means to an end.

points to ponder

> Where are the jobs you might be interested in likely to be advertised?
> What preparatory work would you need to do before applying for a job?
> What preparatory work would you need to do before attending an interview?
> What can you do to keep your nerves under control before and during an interview?
> Whether or not you are successful in your application, how can you learn from the experience you have been through?

6.4 **conclusion**

Social work is not a static entity. Like everything else around us, it changes over time. If we are to keep up with such changes and make sure that we are not out of touch with developments, we will need to make sure that we keep learning. And, of course, we should be aiming for more than just staying abreast of developments. We should be thinking in terms of a career – that is, a pathway of development that allows us to grow and improve over time, a platform for progress in terms of continuous professional development.

NOS Key Role 6

Demonstrate professional competence in social work practice

Part 6 has sought to help with this by outlining a range of career opportunities and opportunities for learning; emphasized the importance of learning and provided guidance on applying for jobs.

Basically, social work is important. Given this importance, it is essential that we devote time and effort to making the best contribution we can. This involves finding the job and setting that enables us to achieve our potential and to continue to learn once we are in that post. As we grow and change, no doubt new opportunities will arise, and again it becomes a matter of working out where and how we can make the best contribution. It is not simply a matter of applying for a job and, in due course, applying for promotion. There is far more involved than this and we hope that Part 6 will help you in making sense of the complexities.

suggestions for further reading

career pathways

The *Community Care* website has a section called 'Care for your Career' and also offers discussion around post-registration training and learning.

www.communitycare.co.uk; see also www.socialworkandcare.co.uk

Compass is a careers guide for employees and employers in the fields of social work and social care. You may receive a copy without ordering it as it is currently distributed free of charge to final-year students, but the providers can also be reached via the link on the British Association of Social Workers' website.

www.basw.co.uk

You may also want to visit their website for careers advice and details of jobs fairs around the UK.

www.compassjobsfair.com

The websites of the various Social Care Councils (see 'Organizations' in Part 7) are worth a visit, although they vary a little in terms of the type of career information supplied. There may be links to information such as social work vacancies, training opportunities, employment issues in general, and information about professional organizations. organizations, see p. 341

See also:

Moss, B. (1999) *Careers in Social Care*, 7th edn, London, Kogan Page.

guide to further learning

7

introduction

This final part of the book is intended as a 'gateway' to other learning opportunities in the form of suggestions for further reading; relevant organizations and websites. Of course, you are not expected to read all of it – it is a menu to choose from, rather than a list of required reading. We would, however, strongly advise you to read as widely as possible. The more you read, the broader and deeper your understanding will be. It is also a good idea to get into the habit of doing a lot of reading so that you can maintain this throughout your career as part of a commitment to continuous professional development (see Part 6).

The sources we mention here are quite wide ranging. They include materials that have been written specifically for social work or social care readers, but also materials from other disciplines that are none the less relevant. Some materials can be very difficult to engage with but can repay the effort sometimes.

The fact that we list an item here should not be interpreted to mean that we necessarily agree with it or endorse what it has to say. Our choice of material is bound to be influenced by our own interests and approach, but it is not simply a matter of providing 'recommended reading'. What we find helpful and interesting may not appeal to you at all, while something that stimulates your interest may not be our cup of tea at all. We are providing potential pathways to follow rather than trying to impose a fixed curriculum, and it is up to you to decide which approaches you favour and wish to know more about, and which not to pursue.

We begin with suggestions for further reading, comprising various books and journals. We then move on to indicate some of the very many organizations and websites that you may wish to access to source further information. In all three cases (reading materials; organizations and websites), what we provide is far from comprehensive or exhaustive. What we offer should none the less provide a good platform for you to develop your own approach to continuing to develop your knowledge and understanding. It should be borne in mind that the suggestions we make here are general ones about social work and are in addition to those specific pointers provided at the end of each of the preceding six parts, although there may be some degree of overlap in places.

recommended reading

books

Brechin, A., Brown, H. and Eby, M. A. (eds) (2000) *Critical Practice in Health and Social Care*, London, Sage.

Cottrell, S. (2003) *The Study Skills Handbook*, 2nd edn, Basingstoke, Palgrave Macmillan.

Cottrell, S. (2005) *Critical Thinking Skills: Developing Effective Analysis and Argument*, Basingstoke, Palgrave Macmillan.

Davies, M. (ed.) (2000) *The Blackwell Encyclopaedia of Social Work*, Oxford, Blackwell.

Davies, M. (ed.) (2002) *The Blackwell Companion to Social Work*, 2nd edn, Oxford, Blackwell.

Doel, M. and Shardlow, S. M. (2005) *Modern Social Work Practice: Teaching and Learning in Practice Settings*, Aldershot, Ashgate.

Fook, J., Ryan, M. and Hawkins, L. (2000) *Professional Expertise: Practice, Theory and Education for Working in Uncertainty*, London, Whiting & Birch.

Gould, N. and Baldwin, M. (eds) (2004) *Social Work, Critical Reflection and the Learning Organization*, Aldershot, Ashgate.

Healy, K. (2005) *Social Work Theories in Context: Creating Frameworks for Practice*, Basingstoke, Palgrave Macmillan.

Healy, K. and Macdonald, J. (2007) *Writing Skills for Social Workers*, London, Sage.

Hek, G. and Moule, P. (2006) *Making Sense of Research: An Introduction for Health and Social Care Practitioners*, 3rd edn, London, Sage.

Jordan, B. (2006) *Social Policy for the Twenty-First Century: New Perspectives, Big Issues*, Cambridge, Polity.

Moss, B. (2007) *Values*, Lyme Regis, Russell House Publishing.

Office for National Statistics (2004) *Focus on Social Inequalities*, Basingstoke, Palgrave Macmillan.

Payne, G. (2006) *Social Divisions*, 2nd edn, Basingstoke, Palgrave Macmillan.

Payne, M. (2005) *The Origins of Social Work: Continuity and Change*, Basingstoke, Palgrave Macmillan.

Saraga, E. (ed.) (1998) *Embodying the Social: Constructions of Difference*, London, Routledge.

Thompson, N. (2002) *People Skills*, 2nd edn, Basingstoke, Palgrave Macmillan.

Thompson, N. (2003) *Communication and Language: A Handbook of Theory and Practice*, Basingstoke, Palgrave Macmillan.

Thompson, N. (2005) *Understanding Social Work: Preparing for Practice*, 2nd edn, Basingstoke, Palgrave Macmillan.

Thompson, N. (2006) *People Problems*, Basingstoke, Palgrave Macmillan.

Thompson, N. (2007) *Power and Empowerment*, Lyme Regis, Russell House Publishing.

Thompson, N. and Thompson, S. (2007) *Understanding Social Care*, 2nd edn, Lyme Regis, Russell House Publishing.

journals

There are numerous journals published by a variety of publishing houses, and many of these can inform social work education and practice. Some have a social work focus but are general in their coverage, while others are more directly linked to specific disciplines. In addition, there are journals which relate to human services issues more generally, and these can broaden your understanding of the wider context in which people live out their lives. Journals add an extra dimension to the list of resources you can call upon to inform your work, and we would urge you to take time to explore what is out there. The range of journals available is too big for us to even try to provide a comprehensive list of those which might meet your need or interest, but the list below should be a useful start:

Journal of Social Work — www.sagepub.co.uk/journals

British Journal of Social Work — http://bjsw/oxfordjournals.org

European Journal of Social Work — www.blackwellpublishing.com/

International Social Work — www.sagepub.co.uk/journals

Australian Social Work — www.tandf.co.uk/journals

Social Work (US-based) — www.naswpress.org

Canadian Social Work — www.casw-acts.ca/

Social Work Education — www.tandf.co.uk/journals

Journal of Social Work Practice — http://journalsonline.tandf.co.uk

Critical Social Policy — www.sagepub.co.uk/journals

Social Policy and Society — http://journals.cambridge.org

Learning in Health and Social Care — www. blackwellpublishing.com

Childcare in Practice — www.childcareinpractice.org

British Journal of Psychology — www.bps.org.uk/publications/journals

British Journal of Social Psychology — www.bps.org.uk/publications/journals

British Journal of Sociology — www.tandf.co.uk/journals/routledge

Youth Justice Journal — www.nayj.org.uk/

Illness, Crisis and Loss — www.baywood.com/journals

Ageing and Society — www.cambridge.org/journals

Ethics and Social Welfare — www.tandf.co.uk/journals/titles/17496535.asp

7.2 organizations and websites

organizations

Age Concern	www.ageconcern.org.uk
The Alzheimer's Disease Society	www.alzheimers.org.uk
Barnardo's	www.barnardos.org.uk
British Association of Social Workers	www.basw.org.uk
for regional contacts, email	info@basw.co.uk
British Association of Counselling and Psychotherapy	www.bacp.co.uk
The UK Disabled People's Council	www.bcodp.org.uk
The British Dyslexia Association	www.bdadyslexia.org.uk
The British Psychological Society	www.bps.org.uk
The Care Councils:	
The General Social Care Council	www.gscc.org.uk
The Care Council for Wales	www.ccwales.org.uk
The Northern Ireland Social Care Council	www.niscc.info
The Scottish Social Services Council	www.sssc.uk.com
Centre for Spirituality and Health Prof B.R. Moss, Director	b.r.moss@staffs.ac.uk
The Child Bereavement Trust	www.childbereavement.org.uk
The Centre for Policy on Ageing	www.cpa.org.uk
Department of Constitutional Affairs (Human Rights)	general.enquiries@dca.gsi.gov.uk
The Disabled Living Foundation	www.dlf.org.uk
The Joseph Rowntree Foundation	www.jrf.org.uk
Liberty	www.liberty-human-rights.org.uk
Mind	www.mind.org.uk
Nacro (resettlement of offenders)	www.nacro.org.uk
The National Autistic Society	www.nas.org.uk
The National Children's Bureau	www.ncb.org.uk
NSPCC	www.nspcc.org.uk
The National Youth Advocacy Service	www.nyas.net
People First (Learning Disabilities)	www.peoplefirst.org.uk

The Princess Royal Trust for Carers	www.carers.org
Royal National Institute of the Blind	www.rnib.org.uk
Royal National Institute of Deaf People	www.rnid.org.uk
SKILL (National Bureaux for Students with Disabilities)	www.skill.org.uk
The Social Care Association	www.socialcaring.co.uk
The Social Policy Research Unit	www.york.ac.uk/inst.spru
Stonewall (Gay and Lesbian Rights)	www.stonewall.org.uk
The Work Foundation	www.theworkfoundation.com

websites

student focused

www.vts.rdn.ac.uk (INTUTE) This virtual training suite has been constructed by staff at the Institute for Learning and Research Technology at the University of Bristol and offers help with internet literacy. Contributors to the site include experts from colleges, universities, research institutes and so on, and a tutorial can be tailored to its application in the social work field in particular.

www.support4learning.org.uk This useful site provides many links to other sites relevant to social work, including youth work, community work, welfare benefits, advocacy and carers' networks, and adult education in general. It also links into opportunities for acquiring publications offered by some of the organizations represented, such as the Child Poverty Action Group and the National Bureau for Students with Disabilities.

www.socialworkstudents.com This online student community has a number of opportunities for linking with other students for support and information sharing.

www.socialwork.ndo.co.uk Describes itself as a site for social work students and 'qualified social work technophobes'. With its links, discussion forums and directions for adding your details to mailing lists, it is worth a look.

www.bda-dyslexia.org.uk The aim of the BDA is to promote a dyslexia-friendly society. It seeks to educate and advise but also campaigns for changes that will promote inclusivity. This is a useful site both for students with dyslexia and those wanting to know more about the subject.

www.skill.org.uk This organization has been advising disabled students on matters relating to further and higher education for several decades now. This website reflects that role and also highlights campaigns seminars and publications about disability rights and other relevant issues.

general

www.communitycare.co.uk This complements the weekly publication of the same name and provides access to up to date information on relevant news items and legal and policy developments. There is a facility for accessing articles published in *Community Care* over the last 10 years and also a directory of practice-focused discussion. For those seeking employment it also highlights job vacancies across the whole of the UK.

www.gscc.org.uk The General Social Care Council site will keep you updated on social work training and registration matters in England. It provides information on what you need to do in order to become a registered social worker and how to maintain that registration. It has links to equivalent bodies in Northern Ireland (Northern Ireland Social Care Council), Wales (The Care Council for Wales) and Scotland (Scottish Social Services Council).

www.scie.org.uk As its name suggests, the main aim of The Social Care Institute for Excellence is to promote the highest possible standards in the social care field. It does so by disseminating knowledge about good practice. As such, then, this site is an excellent source of information on many topics in many forms - research papers, skills tutorials, government papers and so on – accessible via its free online search facility. See www.scie-socialcareonline.org.uk

www.sosig.ac.uk (INTUTE) This resource, the Social Science Information Gateway is well worth visiting as it comprises an extensive database of articles and information of use to students, practitioners and academics alike. It provides links to information sites across many subject areas, such as ethnicity, palliative care, social work research, human rights, child and family law to name but a few.

www.socialworkers.org The National Association of Social Workers is a US-based organization and some of the content of this site may not be relevant to a UK student audience. Nevertheless, it gives a sense of a broader perspective and discusses relevant themes such as professional growth and maintaining standards. It also makes available abstracts of international journal articles.

www.swap.ac.uk SWAP is the social work and social policy subject centre of the Higher Education Academy, which promotes good practice and research in assessment, teaching and learning. This site charts the organization's presence at events linked with education and learning in social work and also describes SWAP's collaboration in projects such as service user participation in social work education, and problem-based learning.

www.society.guardian.co.uk This is the online version of *The Guardian* newspaper's weekly supplement, which can be useful for keeping up to date with news stories in fields such as health and social care, local government and community regeneration.

www.basw.co.uk Website for the largest association in the UK supporting professional social workers. Offers advice, support and information. While much of the latter is restricted to BASW subscribers, there is a facility for obtaining copies of some articles on a 'pay per item' basis, which some readers may find useful.

www.direct.gov.uk This is an information site about public services in general and, as such, gives a useful overview. However, it has many sections that have particular relevance to social work including, for example, crime and justice, health and well-being and children and young people's rights. Within these subdivisions there are also links to relevant organizations such as charities and government departments.

www.york.ac.uk/inst/spru The Social Policy Research Unit, based at the University of York, is involved in research into social policy and service delivery to vulnerable people. It is an excellent source for acquiring information on current research in a wide range of fields. Some research papers are downloadable and others available for purchase.

www.ifsw.org The International Federation of Social Workers fosters international collaboration across a range of themes, particularly around issues of rights and social justice. In terms of exploring the wider context of social work this is an interesting site to visit.

www.statistics.gov.uk This site opens up access to statistics across a very wide spectrum and is therefore useful for setting the context in which individuals live out their lives. It allows for selecting a particular theme and included in those databases on offer are social/welfare, health and crime/justice.

www.dh.gov.uk Again, this Department of Health site is one with a very broad scope. Particularly helpful for social work students is its section on current law, which allows access to crucial legislation such as the Children Act 1989, The Care Standards Act 2000, The Data Protection Act 1998 and The Mental Capacity Act 2005.

www.socialpolicy.net The official website of The Social Policy Association. Those looking for links to the media and online journals should find this very helpful, especially given the range of academic publishers featured. The link to voluntary sector organizations is also a useful feature.

www.socialcaring.co.uk This is the official website of an organization which describes itself as the major professional association operating in the social care field. It aims to promote good practice across all specialisms. The links section is a useful one and there is a catalogue of books and monographs available for purchase.

www.jrf.org.uk The Joseph Rowntree Foundation operates to better understand and overcome social difficulties through its extensive research programme. Short summaries of the research undertaken are presented as *Findings* and these can be accessed through the search facility. Social work students should find the links pages very useful.

www.poverty.org.uk Sponsored by the New Policy Institute and the Joseph Rowntree Foundation, this site monitors social inclusion and poverty across the UK. Up to date statistics are available here and there are links to numerous relevant organizations and resources such as government departments, charities and research and policy bodies.

children and young people

www.nspcc.org.uk This explores the aims and activities of this organization which has a high profile in terms of campaigning around child abuse issues. Amongst other things, it details community-based projects, research, and the dissemination of information. There is a catalogue of up to date publications and also access to media briefings and updates on campaigns and policy debates.

www.cpag.org.uk The Child Poverty Action Group's website is a useful one to visit because it both highlights the extent of poverty amongst children and young people and explores strategies for combating it, including lobbying government and addressing welfare rights issues. The CPAG also has a range of publications, mostly around social policy and welfare rights matters.

www.nya.org.uk This is the website of the National Youth Agency which supports those involved in youth work. NYA publications can be accessed here and there is material about citizenship, inclusion and equality.

www.everychildmatters.gov.uk There is a good deal of useful information here about initiatives around the well-being of children and young people. Topics include social deprivation and exclusion, multi-agency collaboration, user involvement, Children's Fund, youth justice, inspection processes, Children Act guidance, early years support and many other areas of interest and relevance to social work with this client group.

www.byc.org.uk As an umbrella organization, The British Youth Council is a coalition of many youth organizations whose common goal is to promote the rights of young people and to give them a voice. This site's search facility points to relevant links.

www.childrenwebmag.com This is an internet-based childcare magazine which provides news updates, articles relating to a wide range of issues, regular features and also book reviews. As such, it can be a useful resource for students and practitioners operating in all aspects of childcare.

diversity/anti-discriminatory practice

www.cehr.org.uk The Commission for Equality and Human Rights is a non-departmental public body, covering England, Wales and Scotland, which brings under one body the work of the Commission for Racial Equality, the Equal Opportunities Commission and the Disability Rights Commission. Its purpose is to protect human rights, particularly by challenging inequality and discrimination (on the grounds of gender, disability, age, race, sexual orientation and religious belief) and to promote good relationships within a multicultural society. As such, it is well worth a visit in its own right and for its links to other sites.

www.mind.org.uk Mind works to challenge discrimination against and promote the inclusion of people experiencing mental health difficulties. This site informs of progress in terms of policy change and rights issues and highlights effective partnerships such as that with The Healthcare Commission, projects such as those particularly concerned with mental health in rural communities, and links to other sites.

www.ageconcern.org.uk A wide-ranging site which provides up to date news about developments that might be of interest to older people and those who support them. For example there are updates on health initiatives, policy change, welfare benefits and so on.

www.stonewall.org.uk This organization supports research into and lobbies against discrimination on the grounds of sexual orientation, promoting the rights of gay and bisexual men and women to equal opportunities. Details of research and campaigns around, for example, discrimination in the workplace, within the media, police and education systems are made available on this site.

www.nas.org.uk The National Autistic Society has been in existence in one form or another for over 40 years and uses its high profile to lobby on behalf of people with autism, raise public awareness and promote independence. This site contains a lot of information about autistic spectrum disorder and how it affects individuals and those who support them.

www.nimhe.org.uk This, the official site of The National Institute for Mental Health in England, is sponsored by the Department of Health, as part of its aim to promote better services for people with mental health problems and to challenge discrimination in this field. Of particular interest is the space it creates for the development of a 'knowledge community' where anyone with an interest in mental health issues can share news and views or search for relevant people, organizations and resources.

www.bild.org.uk The British Institute for Learning Disabilities advocates on behalf of and works towards empowering people with learning disabilities by influencing policymakers and highlighting good practice. This site has a large reference section, some of which is restricted to members, and also a bookshop featuring literature around this subject.

www.peoplefirst.org.uk This site is organized by people with learning disabilities and highlights the organization's aims, which include promoting independence and challenging negative stereotyping. The online bookshop stocks books covering a range of topics, including disability politics and disability and sexuality.

www.therowan.org This organization of disabled people promotes the social model of disability and, by promoting access to information and challenging discriminatory attitudes and practices, works to challenge some of the many barriers to inclusion that disabled people face. Its link section is well worth a look as it has a wide scope.

www.bda.org.uk The British Deaf Association website represents the Sign Language community and explains how the organization works to promote the rights of this linguistic minority to equality of opportunity in all aspects of life, particularly in terms of education and work.

www.together-uk.org A national charity, this organization supports people with mental health needs in a variety of ways, including outreach and day services, advocacy, work-related and personal skills development, and carer support. This site gives further information on these aspects and also highlights its campaigning, research, education and publication elements.

www.bcodp.org.uk The UK Council of Disabled People supports a large number of groups run by disabled people throughout the UK. The organization promotes the message that it is social arrangements, rather than impairments, that disable people and uses this premise to lobby for changes in law and policy. As such, this site is a useful focus for debates and developments in this field.

www.beliefnet.com This site provides an overview of the core beliefs of some of the main religious groups as well as commentary on their particular views about current issues.

probation/youth justice

www.nacro.org.uk NACRO works with individuals and communities towards crime reduction. This site has information relating to a range of issues, such as community safety and youth inclusion As well as detailing how to access reports and guides, there are many discussion forums on topics such as substance misuse, women and offending, and race and the criminal justice system.

www.everychildmatters.gov.uk/youthjustice This short section of a much broader website provides an overview and links which you may find useful.

loss and grief

www.growthhouse.org This site offers a gateway into a whole host of resources around the important topic of loss. In addition to its search facility it hosts discussion forums and has information on a huge range of associated topics and current debates at an international level.

www.compassionbooks.com This excellent resource is well worth a visit. A US-based company, it has an extensive list of books which relate to supporting children, young people and adults through a range of losses. The books they stock are carefully reviewed by professionals in this field to ensure that they are up to date and relevant.

references

Abercrombie, N. (2004) *Sociology*, Cambridge, Polity Press.

Adams, R., Dominelli, L. and Payne, M. (eds) (2002a) *Social Work: Themes, Issues and Critical Debates*, 2nd edn, Basingstoke, Palgrave Macmillan.

Adams, R., Dominelli, L. and Payne, M. (eds) (2002b) *Critical Practice in Social Work*, Basingstoke, Palgrave Macmillan.

Alderson, P., Brill, S., Chalmers, I. et al., (eds) (1996) *What Works? Effective Social Interventions in Child Welfare*, Barkingside, Barnardo's.

Aldridge, M. (1994) *Making Social Work News*, London, Routledge.

Amiel, S. and Heath, I. (eds) (2003) *Family Violence in Primary Care*, Oxford, Oxford University Press.

Banks, S. (2001) *Ethics and Values in Social Work*, 2nd edn, Basingstoke, Palgrave Macmillan.

Barry, M. and Hallett, C. (eds) (1998) *Social Exclusion and Social Work: Issues of Theory, Policy and Practice*, Lyme Regis, Russell House Publishing.

Bateman, N. (2000) *Advocacy Skills for Health and Social Care Professionals*, London, Jessica Kingsley.

Baxter, C. (ed.) (2001) *Managing Diversity and Inequality in Health Care*, London, Bailliere Tindall.

Beauvoir, S. de (1972) *The Second Sex*, Harmondsworth, Penguin.

Becker, S. and Bryman, A. (eds) (2004) *Understanding Research for Social Policy and Practice: Themes, Methods and Approaches*, Bristol, The Policy Press.

Bentall, R. P. (2003) *Madness Explained: Psychosis and Human Nature*, Harmondsworth, Penguin.

Beresford, P. (2003) *It's Our Lives: A Short Theory of Knowledge, Distance and Experience*, London, Citizen Press in association with Shaping Our Lives.

Beresford, P. and Croft, S. (1993) *Citizen Involvement*, Basingstoke, Macmillan – now Palgrave Macmillan.

Berger, P. and Luckmann, T. (1967) *The Social Construction of Reality*, Harmondsworth, Penguin.

Berne, E. (1970) *Games People Play: The Psychology of Interpersonal Relationships*, Harmondsworth, Penguin.

Berne, E. (1975) *What Do You Say After You Say Hello?*, London, Corgi Books.

Best, S. and Kellner, D. (1991) *Postmodern Theory: Critical Interrogations*, New York, Guilford Press.

Bevan, D, (1998) 'Death, Dying and Inequality', *Care: The Journal of Practice and Development*, **7**(1).

Bevan, D. (2002) 'Poverty and Deprivation', in Thompson (2002c).

Bevan, D. and Thompson, N. (2003) 'The Social Basis of Loss and Grief: Age, Disability and Sexuality', *Journal of Social Work*, **3**(2).

Beveridge, W. (1942) *Social Insurance and Allied Services (The Beveridge Report)*, London, HMSO.

Bono, E. de (2000) *Six Thinking Hats*, 2nd edn, Harmondsworth, Penguin.

Bornat, J., Johnson, J., Pereira, C., Pilgrim, D. and Williams, F. (eds) (1997) *Community Care: A Reader*, 2nd edn, Basingstoke, Macmillan – now Palgrave Macmillan.

Bowen, M. (1978) *Family Therapy in Clinical Practice*, New York, Jason Aronson.

Bowlby, J. (1944) 'Fourty-Four Juvenile Thieves: Their Characters and Home Life', *The International Journal of Psychoanalysis* (25).

Bowlby, J. (1951) *Maternal Care and Mental Health*, Geneva, World Health Organisation.

Bowlby, J. (1979) *The Making and Breaking of Affectional Bonds*, London, Tavistock.

Bracken, P. and Thomas, P. (2005) *Postpsychiatry: Mental Health in a Postmodern World*, Oxford, Oxford University Press.

Braye, S. and Preston-Shoot, M. (1997) *Practising Social Work Law*, 2nd edn, Basingstoke, Macmillan – now Palgrave Macmillan.

Brayne, H., Martin, G. and Carr, H (2005) *Law for Social Workers*, 9th edn, Oxford, Oxford University Press.

Brearley, P. (1982) *Risk and Social Work*, London, Routledge & Kegan Paul.

Brechin, A. and Walmsley, J. (eds) (1989) *Making Connections*, Sevenoaks, Hodder and Stoughton.

Bullock, A. and Trombley, S. (eds) (2000) *The New Fontana Dictionary of Modern Thought*, London, HarperCollins.

Burford, B. (2001) 'The Cultural Competence Model', in Baxter (2001).

Burr, V. (1995) *An Introduction to Social Constructionism*, London, Routledge.

Buzan, T. and Buzan, B. (2003) *The MindMap Book*, 2nd edn, London, BBC Worldwide.

Bytheway, B., Bacigalupo, V., Bornat, J., Johnson, J. and Spurr, S. (eds) (2002) *Understanding Care, Welfare and Community: A Reader*, London, Routledge, Open University.

Canavan, J., Dolan, P. and Pinkerton, J. (eds) (2000) *Family Support: Directions from Diversity*, London, Jessica Kingsley.

Canda, E. and Furman, L. (1999) *Spiritual Diversity in Social Work Practice: The Heart of Helping*, New York, The Free Press.

Carabine, J. (2004a) 'Sexualities, Personal Lives and Social Policy', in Carabine (2004b).

Carabine, J. (ed.) (2004b) *Sexualities: Personal Lives and Social Policy*, Bristol, The Policy Press.

Carnwell, R. and Buchanan, J. (eds) (2005) *Effective Practice in Health and Social Care: A Partnership Approach*, Maidenhead, Open University Press.

Carter, and Beresford, P. (2000) *Age and Change: Models of Involvement of Older People*, York, Joseph Rowntree Foundation.

Cashmore, E. (1996) *Dictionary of Race and Ethnic Relations*, 4th edn, London, Routledge.

Cavadino, P. (2000) 'Sex Offenders', in Davies (2000).

Chesler, (2000) 'Women and Madness: The Mental Asylum', in Heller et al. (2000).

Christie, A. (ed.) (2001) *Men and Social Work: Theories and Practices*, Basingstoke, Palgrave Macmillan.

Clarke, A. (2004) *e-Learning Skills*, Basingstoke, Palgrave Macmillan.

Clarke, J. (ed.) (1993) *A Crisis in Care: Challenges to Social Work*, London, Sage.

Connell, R. W. (2002) *Gender*, Cambridge, Polity Press.

Coulshed, V., Mullender, A., with Jones, D. and Thompson, N. (2006) *Management in Social Work*, 3rd edn, Basingstoke, Palgrave Macmillan.

Cranny-Francis, A., Waring, W., Stavropoulos, P. and Kirkby, J. (2003) *Gender Studies: Terms and Debates*, Basingstoke, Palgrave Macmillan.

D'Cruz, H. and Jones, M. (2004) *Social Work Research: Ethical and Political Contexts*, London, Sage.

Davies, D. (1996) 'Towards a Model of Gay Affirmative Therapy', in Davies and Neal (1996).

Davies, D. and Neale, C. (eds) (1996) *Pink Therapy: A Guide for Counsellors and Therapists Working with Gay, Lesbian and Bisexual Clients*, Buckingham, Open University Press.

Davies, H., Nutley, S. and Smith, P. (eds) (2000) *What Works? Evidence-Based Policy and Practice in Public Services*, Bristol, The Policy Press.

Davies, M. (1994) *The Essential Social Worker: A Guide to Positive Practice*, 3rd edn, Aldershot, Arena.

Davies, M. (ed.) (2000) *The Blackwell Encyclopaedia of Social Work*, Oxford, Blackwell.

Davies, M. (ed.) (2002) *The Blackwell Companion to Social Work*, 2nd edn, Oxford, Blackwell.

Desai, S. and Bevan, D. (2002) 'Race and Culture', in Thompson (2002c).

Doel, M. and Sawdon, C. (1999) *The Essential Groupworker: Teaching and Learning Creative Groupwork*, London, Jessica Kingsley.

Doel, M. and Shardlow, S. M. (2005) *Modern Social Work Practice: Teaching and Learning in Practice Settings*, Aldershot, Ashgate.

Doka, K. (2001) *Disenfranchised Grief: Recognising Hidden Sorrow*, 3rd edn, New York, Lexington.

Durkheim, E. (1912) *The Elementary Forms of the Religious Life*, London, George Allen & Unwin.

Durkin, K. (1995) *Developmental Social Psychology: From Infancy to Old Age*, Oxford, Blackwell.

Dwivedi, K. N. and Varma, V. P. (eds) (2002) *Meeting the Needs of Ethnic Minority Children, Including Refugee, Black and Mixed Parentage Children: A Handbook for Professionals*, 2nd edn, London, Jessica Kingsley.

Dwyer, P. (2004) *Understanding Social Citizenship: Themes and Perspectives for Policy and Practice*, Bristol, The Policy Press.

EDF (1999) 'How Article 13 Disability Directives Can Combat Disability Discrimination', *European Disability Forum* 99/13 (www.edf-feph.org).

EOC (2006) *Sex and Power: Who Runs Britain?* Manchester, Equal Opportunities Commission.

Erikson, E. (1977) *Childhood and Society*, London, Fontana.

Evans, R and Banton, M (2001) *Learning From Experience; Involving Black Disabled People in Shaping Services*, Warwickshire, Council of Disabled People.

Everitt, A. and Hardiker, P. (1996) *Evaluating for Good Practice*, Basingstoke, Macmillan – now Palgrave Macmillan.

Everitt, A., Hardiker, P., Littlewood, J. and Mullender, A. (1992) *Applied Research for Better Practice*, Basingstoke, Macmillan – now Palgrave Macmillan.

Farrell, F. and Watt, P (eds) (2001) *Responding to Racism in Ireland*, Dublin, Veritas.

Farrington, D. (2002) 'Understanding and Preventing Youth Crime', in Muncie et al. (2002).

Faubion, J.D. (ed.) (2002) *Michel Foucault – Power: Essential Works of Foucault 1954–1984*, Vol. 3, Harmondsworth, Penguin.

Fawcett, B. and Karban, K. (2005) *Contemporary Mental Health: Theory, Policy and Practice*, London, Routledge.

Fischer, C. S., Hout, M., Jankowski, M. S., Lucas, S. R., Swidler, A. and Voss, K. (1996) *Inequality by Design: Cracking the Bell Curve Myth*, Princeton, Princeton University Press.

Flaskas, C. (2002) *Family Therapy Beyond Postmodernism: Practice Challenges Theory*, London, The Psychology Press.

Fleet, F. (2000) 'Counselling and Contemporary Social Work', in Stepney and Ford (2000).

Flynn, R. J. and Nitsch, K. E. (eds) (1980) *Normalization, Social Integration, and Community Services*, Baltimore, University Park Press.

Fook, J. (2002) *Social Work: Critical Theory and Practice*, London, Sage.

Forte, J. A. (2001) *Theories for Practice: Symbolic Interactionist Translations*, New York, University Press of America.

Foucault, M. (1967) *Madness and Civilisation*, London, Tavistock.

Freire, P. (1972) *Pedagogy of the Oppressed*, Harmondsworth, Penguin.

Fröschl, E. (2002) 'Trafficking in Women', in Gruber and Stefanov (2002).

Frost, N. (2004) 'Evaluating Practice', in Adams et al. (2004).

Furman, B. and Ahola, T. (1992) *Solution Talk*, New York, Norton.

General Social Care Council (2002) *Code of Practice for Social Care Workers and Employers of Social Care Workers*, London, GSCC.

Gergen, K. J. (1999) *An Invitation to Social Construction*, London, Sage.

Giddens, A. (2006) *Sociology*, 5th edn, Cambridge, Policy Press.

Goldson, B. (2002) 'New Punitiveness: The Politics of Child Incarceration', in Muncie et al. (2002).

Greenan, L (2004) *Violence Against Women: A Literature Review*, Edinburgh, Scottish Executive Publications.

Grollman, E. A. (1988) *Suicide: Prevention, Intervention, Postvention*, Boston, MA, Beacon Press.

Gruber, C. and Stefanov, H. (eds) (2002) *Gender in Social Work: Promoting Equality*, Lyme Regis, Russell House Publishing.

Habermas, J. (1972) *Knowledge and Human Interests*, London, Heinemann.

Habermas, J. (1984) *Theory of Communicative Action*, Boston, MA, Beacon Press.

Habermas, J. (1987) *The Theory of Communicative Action Vol 2: Lifeworld and the Rationalization of Society*, Boston, MA, Beacon Press.

Hall, C., Juhila, K., Parton, N. and Pösö, T. (eds) (2003) *Constructing Clienthood in Social Work and Human Services: Interaction, Identities and Practices*, London, Jessica Kingsley.

Harris, P. (2005) *Drug Induced,* Lyme Regis, Russell House Publishing.

Harris, R. and Webb, D. (1987) *Welfare, Power and Juvenile Justice: The Social Control of Delinquent Youth*, London, Tavistock.

Harris, T. (1995) *I'm OK, You're OK*, London, Arrow.

Harrison, R., Mann, G., Murphy, M., Taylor, A. and Thompson, N. (2003) *Partnership Made Painless,* Lyme Regis, Russell House Publishing.

Hek, G., Judd, M. and Moule, P. (2002) *Making Sense of Research: An Introduction for Health and Social Care Practitioners*, 2nd edn, London, Continuum.

Heller, T., Reynolds, J., Gomm, R., Muston, R. and Pattison, S. (eds) (2000) *Mental Health Matters: A Reader*, Basingstoke, Macmillan – now Palgrave Macmillan.

Henderson, J. and Atkinson, D (eds) (2003) *Managing Care in Context*, London, Routledge.

Hernstein, R. and Murray, C. (1994) *The Bell-Curve: Intelligence and Class Structure in American Life*, New York The Free Press.

Heron, J. (2001) *Helping the Client: A Creative Practical Guide*, London, Sage.

Hickey, G. (1994) 'Towards a Responsive Service', *Community Care*, 20 May.

Hopkins, J. (1986) *Caseworker*, Birmingham, Pepar Publications.

Horwarth. J. and Shardlow, S. M. (eds) (2003) *Making Links Across Specialisms: Understanding Modern Social Work Practice* , Lyme Regis, Russell House Publishing.

Howe, D. (1995) *Attachment Theory for Social Work Practice*, Basingstoke, Macmillan – now Palgrave Macmillan.

Hughes, G. (ed.) (1998) *Imagining Welfare Futures*, London, Routledge.

Humphries, B. (ed.) (2000) *Research in Social Care and Social Welfare: Issues and Debates for Practice*, London, Jessica Kingsley.

Hunt, S. (2005) *The Life Course: A Sociological Introduction*, Basingstoke, Palgrave Macmillan.

Ixer, G. (1999) 'There's No Such Thing as Reflection', *British Journal of Social Work*, **29**(4).

Jack, G. (2000) 'Social Support Networks', in Davies (2000).

Jack, G. and Jack, D. (2000) 'Ecological Social Work: The Application of a Systems Model of Development in Context', in Stepney and Ford (2000).

Joas, H. (1996) *The Creativity of Action*, Chicago, University of Chicago Press.

Jones, C. and Novak, T. (1999) *Poverty, Welfare and the Disciplinary State*, London, Routledge.

Jones, D. and Mayo, M. (1974) *Community Work One*, London, Routledge.

Jordan, B. (1990) *Social Work in an Unjust Society*, London, Harvester Wheatsheaf.

Juhila, K., Pösö, T., Hall, C. and Parton, N. (2003) 'Introduction: Beyond a Universal Client', in Hall et al. (2003).

Kroll, B. (2002) 'Children and Divorce', in Thompson (2002c).

Kübler-Ross, E. (1969) *On Death and Dying*, New York, Macmillan.

Lacan, J. (1989) *Ecrits: A Selection*, London, Tavistock.

Laing, R. D. (1965) *The Divided Self*, Harmondsworth, Penguin.

Laing, R. D. and Cooper, G. (1971) *Reason and Violence: A Decade of Sartre's Philosophy 1950–1960*, London, Tavistock.

Laurance, J. (2003) *Pure Madness: How Fear Drives the Mental Health System*, London, Routledge.

Leathard, A. (ed.) (2003) *Interprofessional Collaboration: From Policy to Practice in Health and Social Care*, Hove and New York, Brunner-Routledge.

LEFÖ (1996) *Frauenhandel. Frauenpolitische Perspektiven nach der Weltfrauenkonferenz 95*, Bundesmininsterin für Fraueangelegenheiten, Vienna.

Levy, A. (2001) 'Foreword', in Brayne et al. (2001).

Lewis, G. (1998) 'Citizenship', in Hughes (1998).

Ligon, J. (2002) 'Fundamentals of Brief Treatment', in Roberts and Greene (2002).

Lloyd, M. (2002) 'Care Management' in Adams et al. (2002b).

Lorenz, W. (2004) 'Research as an Element in Social Work's Ongoing Search for Identity', in Lovelock et al. (2004).

Lovelock, R. and Lyons, K. and Powell, J. (eds) (2004) *Reflecting on Social Work: Discipline and Profession*, Aldershot, Aldgate.

Lustbader, W. (1991) *Counting on Kindness: The Dilemmas of Dependency*, New York, The Free Press.

Lymbery, M. and Butler, S. (eds) (2004) *Social Work Ideals and Practice Realities*, Basingstoke, Palgrave Macmillan.

Macdonald, G. (1996) 'Ice Therapy: Why We Need Randomised Controlled Trials', in Alderson et al. (1996).

Macdonald, G. (2002) 'The Evidence-Based Perspective', in Davies (2002).

Malone, C., Forbat, L., Robb, M. and Seden, J. (eds) (2005) *Relating Experience: Stories from Health and Social Care*, London, Routledge.

Marx, K. (1962) 'The Eighteenth Brumaire of Louis Bonaparte', in Marx and Engels (1962).

Marx, K. and Engels, F. (1962) *Marx and Engels: Selected Works*, London, Watts.

Maslow, A. (1970) *New Knowledge, Human Values*, Maidenhead. McGraw Hill.

May, M., Page, R. and Brundson, E. (eds) (2001) *Understanding Social Problems: Issues in Social Policy*, Oxford, Blackwell.

McLaughlin, E. and Muncie, J. (eds)(2001) *The Sage Dictionary of Criminology*, London, Sage.

Miller, A. (1983) *For Your Own Good,* London, Faber & Faber.

Mills, C. W. (1959) *The Sociological Imagination*, New York, Oxford University Press.

Minuchin, S. (1974) *Families and Family Therapy*, Cambridge, MA, Harvard University Press.

Mitchell, J. (2000) *Psychoanalysis and Feminism*, 3rd edn, Harmondsworth, Penguin.

Moss, B. (1999) *Values in Social Work*, Wrexham, Prospects Publications.

Moss, B. (2005) *Religion and Spirituality*, Lyme Regis, Russell House Publishing.

Moss, B. (2006) *Values*, Lyme Regis, Russell House Publishing.

Muncie, J. (2001) 'Individual Positivism', in McLaughlin and Muncie (2001).

Muncie, J. (2002) 'Failure Never Matters: Detention Centres and the Politics of Deterrence', in Muncie et al. (2002).

Muncie, J., Hughes, G. and McLaughlin, E. (eds) (2002) *Youth Justice: Critical Readings*, London, Sage.

Munford, R. and Walsh-Tapiata, W. (2000) *Strategies for Change: Community Development in Aotaeroa/ New Zealand*, Palmerston North, Massey University.

Munford, R. and Walsh-Tapiata, W. (2005) 'Community Development: Principles into Practice', in Nash et al. (2005).

Nash, M., Munford, R. and O'Donoghue, K. (eds) (2005) *Social Work Theories in Action*, London, Jessica Kingsley.

National Assembly for Wales (ed.) (2000) *'Moving On': A Report on the Lost in Care Conference*, Bangor, University of Wales, Bangor.

Neimeyer, R. A. (ed.) (2001) *Meaning Reconstruction and the Experience of Loss*, Washington, DC, American Psychological Association.

Neimeyer, R. A. and Anderson, A. (2002) 'Meaning Reconstruction Theory', in Thompson (2002c).

Nelson-Jones, R. (2005) *Introduction to Counselling Skills*, 2nd edn, London, Sage.

O'Brien, J. and Lyle, C. (1987) *Framework for Accomplishments: A Workshop for People Developing Better Services*, Dectaur, Georgia, Responsive Systems Associates.

Oliver, M. (2004) 'If I had a Hammer: The Social Model in Action', in Swain et al. (2004).

Oliver, M. and Sapey, B. (2006) *Social Work with Disabled People*, 3rd edn, Basingstoke, Palgrave Macmillan.

Panning, W. P. (2002) 'Gestalt Therapy', in Roberts and Greene (2002).

Parsons, T. (1967) *Sociological Theory and Modern Society*, New York, The Free Press

Parton, N. and O'Byrne, P. (2000) *Constructive Social Work: Towards A New Practice*, Basingstoke, Macmillan – now Palgrave Macmillan.

Payne, M. (1995) *What is Professional Social Work?*, Birmingham, Venture Press.

Payne, M. (2000) *Anti-Bureaucratic Social Work,* Birmingham, Venture Press.

Payne, M. (2005) *Modern Social Work Theory*, 3rd edn, Basingstoke, Palgrave Macmillan.

Pease, B. and Fook, J. (1999a) 'Postmodern Critical Theory and Emancipatory Social Work Practice', in Pease and Fook (1999b).

Pease, B. and Fook, J. (eds) (1999b) *Transforming Social Work Practice: Postmodern Critical Perspectives*, London, Routledge.

Petersen, A., Barns, I., Dudley, J. and Harris, P. (1999) *Poststructuralism, Citizenship and Social Policy*, London, Routledge.

Phillips, J. (1996) 'Reviewing the Literature on Care Management', in Phillips and Penhale (1996).

Phillips, J. and Penhale, B. (eds) (1996) *Reviewing Care Management for Older People,* London, Jessica Kingsley.

Piaget, J. (1955) *The Child's Construction of Reality*, London, Routledge.

Pilgrim, D. and Rogers, A. (2005) *A Sociology of Health and Illness,* 3rd edn, Maidenhead, Open University Press.

Powell, F. (2001) *The Politics of Social Work*, London, Sage.

Read, J. (2005) 'The Bio-bio-bio Model of Madness', *The Psychologist*, October.

Redmond, B. (2004) *Reflection in Action: Developing Reflective Practice in Health and Social Services,* Aldershot, Ashgate.

Reynolds, J., Henderson, J., Seden. J., Charlesworth, J. and Bullman, A. (2003) *The Managing Care Reader*, London, Routledge.

Riches, G. (2002) 'Gender and Sexism', in Thompson (2002c).

Roberts, A. R. and Greene, G. J. (eds) (2002) *Social Workers' Desk Reference*, Oxford, Oxford University Press.

Roberts, A. R. and Rock, M. (2002) 'An Overview of Forensic Social Work and Risk Assessments with the Dually Diagnosed', in Roberts and Greene (2002).

Rogers, C. (1951) *Client-Centred Therapy*, Boston, MA, Houghton Mifflin.

Rogers, C. (1961) *On Becoming a Person: A Therapist's View of Psychotherapy*, London, Constable.

Ryan, W. (1971) *Blaming the Victim, Ideology Serves the Establishment*, London, Pantheon.

Sapey, B. (2002) 'Physical disability', in Adams et al. (2002b).

Sartre, J.-P. (1955) *No Exit and Three Other Plays* – trans. Gilbert, S. and Abel, L., New York, Vintage.

Sartre, J.-P. (1958) *Being and Nothingness*, London, Methuen.

Sartre, J.-P. (1976) *Critique of Dialectical Reason*, London, Verso.

Saunders, C. (2002) 'The Philosophy of Hospice', in Thompson (2002c).

Schneider, J. (1994) *Finding My Way*, Colfax, WI, Seasons Press.

Schneider, J. (2000) *The Overdiagnosis of Depression: Recognizing Grief and its Transformative Potential*, Traverse City, MI, Seasons Press.

Schön, D. F. (1983) *The Reflective Practitioner*, New York, Basic Books.

Segal, L. (1999) *Why Feminism? Gender, Psychology, Politics*, Cambridge, Polity Press.

Shardlow, S. (2002) 'Values, Ethics and Social Work', in Adams et al. (2002a).

Shazer, S. de (1982) *Patterns of Brief Family Therapy*, New York, Guilford.

Shazer, S. de (1985) *Keys to Solutions in Brief Therapy*, New York, Norton.

Shazer, S. de (1991) *Putting Difference to Work*, New York, Norton.

Sheldon, B. (2001) 'Research Note. The Validity of Evidence-Based Practice in Social Work: A Reply to Stephen Webb', *British Journal of Social Work*, **31**(5).

Sheldon, B. and Chilvers, R. (2000) *Evidence-Based Social Care: A Study of Prospects and Problems*, Lyme Regis, Russell House Publishing.

Sibeon, R. (1996) *Contemporary Sociology and Policy Analysis*, Eastham, Tudor.

Sibeon, R. (2004) *Rethinking Social Theory*, London, Sage.

Smale, G. and The Practice Development Exchange, (1988) *Community Social Work: A Paradigm for Change*, London, NISW.

Smale, G., Tuson, G., with Biehal, N. and Marsh, P. (1993) *Empowerment, Assessment, Care Management and the Skilled Worker*, London, HMSO.

Smith, M. J. (1998) *Social Science in Question*, London, Sage.

Social Trends website – www.statistics.gov.uk

Stainton, T., Welshman, J. and Walmsley, J. (2005) *Pressures for Change*, 2nd edn, Unit 14 of The Open University Course: K202 *Care, Welfare and Community*, Milton Keynes, the Open University.

Stanworth, M. (1997) 'Just Three Quiet Girls', in Ungerson and Kember (1997).

Stepney, P. and Evans, D. (2000) 'Community Social Work: Towards an Integrative Model of Practice', in Stepney and Ford (2000).

Stepney, P. and Ford, D. (eds) (2000) *Social Work Models, Methods and Theories*, Lyme Regis, Russell House Publishing.

Stroebe, M. and Schut, H. (1999) 'The Dual Process Model of Coping with Bereavement: Rationale and Description', *Death Studies*, **23**(3).

Swain, J., French. S., Barnes, C. and Thomas, C. (eds) (2004) *Disabling Barriers – Enabling Environments*, 2nd edn, London, Sage.

Szasz, T. (1961) *The Myth of Mental Illness*, New York, Hoeber-Harper.

Tew, J. (2002) *Social Theory, Power and Practice*, Basingstoke, Palgrave Macmillan.

Thompson, N. (1992) *Existentialism and Social Work*, Aldershot, Avebury.

Thompson, N. (1995) *Age and Dignity: Working with Older People*, Aldershot, Arena.

Thompson, N. (2000a) 'Towards a New Professionalism', in National Assembly for Wales (2000).

Thompson, N. (2000b) *Theory and Practice in Human Services*, 2nd edn, Buckingham, Open University Press.

Thompson, N. (2000c) 'Existentialist Practice', in Stepney and Ford (2000).

Thompson, N. (2002a) *Social Work with Children, Young People and Their Families*, Lyme Regis, Russell House Publishing.

Thompson, N. (2002b) *People Skills*, 2nd edn, Basingstoke, Palgrave Macmillan.

Thompson, N. (ed.) (2002c) *Loss and Grief: A Guide for Human Services Practitioners*, Basingstoke, Palgrave Macmillan.

Thompson, N. (2003a) *Promoting Equality: Tackling Discrimination and Oppression*, 2nd edn, Basingstoke, Palgrave Macmillan

Thompson, N. (2003b) *Communication and Language: A Handbook of Theory and Practice*, Basingstoke, Palgrave Macmillan.

Thompson, N. (2004) 'All Stressed Out', *Community Care*, 25 November.

Thompson, N. (2005a) *Understanding Social Work: Preparing for Practice*, 2nd edn, Basingstoke, Palgrave Macmillan.

Thompson, N. (2005b) 'Equality and Diversity: Making Training and Development Count', *British Journal of Occupational Learning*, **3**(2).

Thompson, N. (2006a) *Anti-Discriminatory Practice*, 4th edn, Basingstoke, Palgrave Macmillan

Thompson, N. (2006b) *People Problems*, Basingstoke, Palgrave Macmillan

Thompson, N. (2006c) *Promoting Workplace Learning*, Bristol, The Policy Press.

Thompson, N. (2007) *Power and Empowerment*, Lyme Regis, Russell House Publishing.

Thompson, N. and Thompson, S. (2005) *Community Care*, Lyme Regis, Russell House Publishing.

Thompson, N. Murphy, M. and Stradling, S. (1994) *Dealing with Stress*, Basingstoke, Macmillan – now Palgrave Macmillan.

Thompson, S. (2002a) 'Older People', in Thompson (2002c).

Thompson, S. (2002b) *From Where I'm Sitting: A Manual for Those Working with Older People in the Social Care Sector*, Lyme Regis, Russell House Publishing.

Thompson, S. (2005) *Age Discrimination*, Lyme Regis, Russell House Publishing.

Thornton, P. and Tozer, R. (1994) *Involving Older People in Planning Community Care: A Review of Initiatives,* York, University of York Social Policy Research Unit.

Townsend, P., Davidson, N. and Whitehead, M. (1988) *Inequalities in Health*, Harmondsworth, Penguin.

Trinder, L. (2000) 'A Critical Appraisal of Evidence-based Practice', in Trinder with Reynolds (2000).

Trinder, L. with Reynolds, S. (eds) (2000) *Evidence-Based Practice: A Critical Appraisal*, Oxford, Blackwell.

Truman, C. and Humphries, B. (eds) (1999) *Research and Inequality*, London, Routledge.

Twelvetrees, A. (2001) *Community Work*, 3rd edn, Basingstoke, Palgrave Macmillan.

Ungerson, C. and Kember, M. (eds) (1997) *Women and Social Policy: A Reader*, 2nd edn, Basingstoke, Macmillan – now Palgrave Macmillan.

Ussher, J. (1991) *Women's Madness: Misogyny or Mental Illness*, Hemel Hempstead, Harvester Wheatsheaf.

Walker, R. (2000) 'Welfare Policy: Tendering for Evidence', in Davies et al. (2000)

Walker, S. and Beckett, C. (2003) *Social Work Assessment and Intervention*, Lyme Regis, Russell House Publishing.

Walmsely, J., Bornat, J. and Goodley, D. (2005) *Advocacy and Campaigning* in Workbook 7, of Open University Course K202 (Care, Welfare and Community) 2nd edn, Milton Keynes, Open University.

Waterhouse, R. (2000) *Lost in Care*, London, The Stationery Office.

Watson, S (2005) 'Attachment Theory and Social Work', in Nash et al. (2005).

Webb, S. (2001) 'Some Considerations on the Validity of Evidence-Based Practice in Social Work, *British Journal of Social Work*, **31**(1).

Weber, M. (1968) *Economy and Society Vol. 1*, New York, Bedminster Press,

Weinstein, J., Whittington, C. and Leiba, T. (eds) (2003) *Collaboration in Social Work Practice*, London, Jessica Kingsley.

Whitehead, M. (1988) 'The Health Divide', in Townsend et al. (1988).

Williams, C,. Soydan, H., and Johnson, M. R. D. (eds) (1998) *Social Work and Minorities: European Perspectives*, London, Routledge.

Williams, D. (1996) *Autism: An Inside-Out Approach*, London, Jessica Kingsley.

Williams, F. (1998) 'Agency and Structure Revisited: Rethinking Poverty and Social Exclusion', in Barry and Hallett (1998).

Winnicott, D. (1965) *The Maturational Processes and the Facilitative Environment*, New York, International Universities Press.

Wolfe, A. (1992) 'Sociological Theory in the Absence of People: The Limits of Luhmann's Systems Theory', *Cardoza Law Review,* 13, pp. 1729–43.

index